Strategic Studies Institute
and
U.S. Army War College Press

STRATEGIC STABILITY:
CONTENDING INTERPRETATIONS

Elbridge A. Colby
Michael S. Gerson
Editors

February 2013

The views expressed in this report are those of the authors and do not necessarily reflect the official policy or position of the Department of the Army, the Department of Defense, or the U.S. Government. Authors of Strategic Studies Institute (SSI) and U.S. Army War College (USAWC) Press publications enjoy full academic freedom, provided they do not disclose classified information, jeopardize operations security, or misrepresent official U.S. policy. Such academic freedom empowers them to offer new and sometimes controversial perspectives in the interest of furthering debate on key issues.

*****

*****

Comments pertaining to this report are invited and should be forwarded to: Director, Strategic Studies Institute and U.S. Army War College Press, U.S. Army War College, 47 Ashburn Drive, Carlisle, PA 17013-5010.

*****

CONTENTS

FOREWORD

My first question on approaching this volume was, "What is strategic stability," or "What are the different meanings of strategic stability?" My second was, "Is strategic stability always, usually, or seldom, a good thing?" My third was, "When strategic stability is a good thing, how do we arrange to bring it about? Is it a weapons result, a diplomatic result, or a result of a common understanding?"

I was brought up on the "stability of mutual deterrence," half a century ago, and it was not all that difficult to understand. The Gaither Committee of 1957 had, after 12 years of the nuclear era, finally identified that deterrence via threat of retaliation depended on the recognized ability of a retaliatory force to survive an attack intended to destroy it, and that the U.S. retaliatory force was not able to promise its own survival.

The international conference on "measures to safeguard against surprise attack" brought five western nations to Washington in 1958, before moving to Geneva to meet the five eastern nations. It became clear that the problem of surprise attack was not merely that it was dastardly, or worse than an anticipated attack, but that it might be attractive to a nuclear enemy if the enemy thought it might catch unlaunched response forces and destroy them, especially if the nuclear enemy feared an imminent attack by those very forces.

Albert Wohlstetter's not yet published paper, "Delicate Balance of Terror," circulated among the Washington conferees and had an immediate impact. Later published in *Foreign Affairs* (January 1959), it became the decisive document contrasting "delicate" with "stable." The "stable" terminology came from an elementary physics term, in which an "equilibrium" could be stable or unstable. A stable equilibrium was one that, if disturbed, could recover; an unstable one, when disturbed, decomposed quickly. "Balance" was a synonym for "equilibrium"; and "delicate" was a synonym for "unstable." Wohlstetter's document was convincing.

Morton Halperin and I participated in a "summer study program" of arms control, oganized by the Massachusetts Institute of Technology (MIT) with a score of regulars and a dozen visitors, and published a small book in early 1961, *Strategy and Arms Control*, which reflected most of the conclusions reached by the study group. The Harvard-MIT faculty seminar on arms control critiqued the book's hypotheses through the fall of that year. The first sentence of the first chapter was, "The most mischievous character of today's strategic weapons is that they may provide an enormous advantage, in the event that war occurs, to the side that starts it." This was simply Wohlstetter's point, and it was the basis for most cold-war arms control analysis.

It also became the basis for unilateral efforts to stabilize deterrence, first with "airborne alert" of a fraction of the bomber force always safely in the air on the way to Soviet targets; second, with abandonment of the Atlas and Titan missiles that depended on fueling procedures that could take longer than the missile flight time from the Union of Soviet Socialist Republics (USSR); and third, with focus on the solid fuel "Minuteman" quick-launching ground-based missile in dispersed hardened silos and the underwater Polaris system then believed to be immune to detection and targeting.

Further, the "delicate" argument became the basis for the treaty banning active defenses against ballistic missiles. Secretary Robert McNamara persuaded the

Soviets that ballistic missile defenses were complementary to pre-emptive attack and contrary to the stability of mutual deterrence.

All of that, despite its having taken more than a decade to become obvious, was sensible, simple, and effective. We all knew what we meant by "stability." We usually called it stability of deterrence, not "strategic stability," but we knew we did not want deterrence to be too "delicate," and we knew that stability was a mutual goal.

When Secretary McNamara testified to the Senate that we were developing invulnerable systems of retaliation and that he was pleased that the Soviets were doing the same, some questioned why he did not prefer the enemy be susceptible to our attack. He answered that the Soviets could not possibly entertain any idea of attacking the United States unless they thought they were vulnerable to a preventive or pre-emptive attack. It made sense to the senators. "Too much stability" was recognized by some analysts as possibly immunizing a Soviet attack on Western Europe from a U.S. nuclear response, but after the 1962 Cuban escapade, that issue seemed to disappear.

Now we are in a different world, a world so much more complex than the world of the East-West Cold War. It took 12 years to begin to comprehend the "stability" issue after 1945, but once we got it we thought we understood it. Now the world is so much changed, so much more complicated, so multivariate, so unpredictable, involving so many nations and cultures and languages in nuclear relationships, many of them asymmetric, that it is even difficult to know how many meanings there are for "strategic stability," or how many different kinds of such stability there may be among so many different international relationships, or what "stable deterrence" is supposed to deter in a world of proliferated weapons.

That is where this book, organized by Elbridge Colby and Michael Gerson, comes to our aid. It does not give us THE definition of strategic stability. It gives us a variety of perspectives from a varied group of authors who deal with different strategic relationships around the world and offer different perspectives. It is not a treatise but a collection of essays on different dimensions of strategy and stability as they arise around the world. It cannot be the last word on the subject since the subject will not stand still. But for now it provides as thorough an understanding of this subtle and complex subject as possible.

The editors and authors have produced an insightful set of chapters on some of the most difficult issues of strategy in an era of such uncertainty.

THOMAS C. SCHELLING
Professor of Economics
University of Maryland

CHAPTER 1

THE ORIGINS OF STRATEGIC STABILITY: THE UNITED STATES AND THE THREAT OF SURPRISE ATTACK

Michael S. Gerson

The Barack Obama administration's April 2010 *Nuclear Posture Review* (NPR) *Report* advances an ambitious and wide-ranging agenda for the future of U.S. nuclear weapons policy. While the United States will maintain a safe, secure, and effective nuclear arsenal as long as nuclear weapons exist, the NPR also placed significant emphasis on reducing the role of nuclear weapons in U.S. national security strategy, further reducing nuclear weapons, and setting the conditions for the eventual global abolition of nuclear weapons. For the Obama administration, the NPR and the New Strategic Arms Reduction Treaty (New START) are just the first steps in a long, perhaps generational, effort to transform the international nuclear environment.

As part of these efforts, the Obama administration has placed high priority on maintaining and strengthening strategic stability with Russia and China. According to the NPR, the United States will pursue "high-level, bilateral dialogues . . . aimed at promoting more stable, resilient, and transparent strategic relationships." This emphasis on the importance of strategic stability reflects the recognition that changes in nuclear policies and force postures must be done carefully, as movement too far, fast, or without appropriate consideration could generate instabilities that adversely affect international security. Reductions in the number and salience of nuclear weapons; the increased role of U.S. conventional forces in deterrence, especially the introduction of Conventional Prompt Global Strike (CPGS); sea- and land-based missile defense; follow-on arms control agreements covering tactical nuclear weapons and deeper cuts in strategic forces; nuclear proliferation; nuclear modernization programs in Russia and China; and broader political relations all affect the strategic stability equation.

Yet, while the concept of strategic stability features prominently in current discussions and debates about nuclear policy and force posture, strategic stability is—and has always been—a widely used concept without a common understanding. There is no single, universally accepted definition of stability, which factors contribute to and detract from it, or agreed upon metrics for how to measure it. Consequently, there are significant gaps in understanding in the United States and around the world about how nuclear-armed countries view and define the requirements of stability.

This chapter seeks to contribute to the ongoing debates about strategic stability by examining the development of the concept during the Cold War. An historical approach to understanding strategic stability emphasizes how changes in military technology and strategy encouraged a new way of thinking about the causes of war and the requirements of peace and security. As contemporary scholars and policymakers continue to grapple with the unique challenges of an increasingly multipolar nuclear world, an examination of the history of strategic stability will provide an important perspective on how their predecessors thought about and dealt with the nuclear revolution. By studying the development of the concept of stability, this chapter attempts to combine interpretations of the past with the realities of the present, in order to develop insights for the future.

THE NUCLEAR REVOLUTION

The core ideas that underpin the concept of strategic stability date as far back as the early 1950s, as both the United States and the Soviet Union began to build an arsenal of atomic bombs. A precise date or particular work that first introduced the concept is difficult, if not impossible, to pinpoint, as many scholars and military and civilian officials were circling around the same basic set of ideas at the time. Indeed, in looking back at the history of the concept, no one can be credited with its whole-cloth creation. Rather, the fundamentals of the concept developed incrementally over the course of the 1950s, both within and outside of government, as scholars, defense analysts, and civilian and military officials built upon and expanded the insights of their colleagues. The concept grew out of a logical progression in thinking about the consequences of the nuclear revolution, the challenge of surprise attack, the kinds of targets upon which nuclear weapons might be used, how a nuclear war might be fought, and the requirements of credible deterrence.

In many instances, especially in the 1950s, analysts and defense officials wrote about and spoke of the core idea of strategic stability before the concept had been given an official name and without identifying it as a discrete strategic concept. When the word "stability" first entered the nuclear lexicon in the later 1950s and early 1960s, it was not preceded by the word "strategic," "crisis," "arms race," or "first strike." In the heyday of the concept's development, "stability" was the only word used to describe the idea. Nevertheless, given the interest on decisionmaking in a crisis, these early discussions focused almost exclusively on what today would be termed "crisis stability."

The progression in thinking that led to the concept of stability began with the earliest appraisals of the consequences of the nuclear revolution. In 1946, two books were published that ultimately laid the foundations for both deterrence and strategic stability theory. The first was Bernard Brodie's edited volume, *The Absolute Weapon*. The second, published just weeks after Brodie's and considerably less well-known among contemporary nuclear analysts, was William Borden's *There Will Be No Time*.

Drawing on the recent history of the conventional bombing of Germany and Japan and the way in which atomic bombs were used on Hiroshima and Nagasaki, Brodie argued that nuclear weapons were principally a threat to the enemy's cities, and famously emphasized the importance of averting war in the atomic age through the ability to retaliate in kind. Borden, however, had a very different view. He believed that atomic weapons would soon spread to U.S. adversaries, and in such a world a nuclear war was almost inevitable. In such a war, Borden believed, the principal role and purpose of atomic weapons would be to disarm the opponent by attacking its nuclear forces. A nuclear war would thus be an "aerial duel," a "war-between-the-bases," in which victory "will not be won [by] pulverizing cities and industry, but by destroying the enemy's military power of retaliation." Whereas Brodie saw little utility in a surprise attack, arguing that "if retaliation is accepted no victory is worth it,"[1] Borden believed a carefully orchestrated surprise attack on the enemy's atomic forces could be decisive. In making the case both for attacking the other's nuclear forces in a war and for doing so at the outset utilizing the element of surprise, Borden asked rhetorically, "Why squander the previous assets of surprise and the initiative by attacking cities, a mission which can so easily be carried out later, when the main obstacle to a lightning victory is air forces-in-being?"[2]

Taken together, Brodie's and Borden's early work highlighted both the central challenge of strategic stability — the vulnerability of nuclear forces to surprise attack — and one of the essential solutions — the assured ability to retaliate in kind. As the nuclear component of the Cold War unfolded over the next 45 years, these issues would dominate the strategic discourse.

Perhaps more than any other issue, the threat of surprise attack was the catalyst to the line of thinking that ultimately led to the concept of strategic stability. With the relatively recent — and still stinging — physical and psychological wound from Japan's surprise attack on Pearl Harbor ever on their minds, U.S. officials were determined to prevent an atomic redux. Even before the Soviet Union acquired an atomic bomb of its own, the issue of surprise attack was already beginning to play a leading role in U.S. thinking about the Soviet threat. In 1947 the Joint Chiefs of Staff Evaluation Board wrote a top secret report entitled, "The Evaluation of the Atomic Bomb as a Military Weapon," which concluded:

> The value of surprise attack has increased with every increase in the potency of weapons. With the advent of the atomic bomb, surprise has achieved supreme value so that an aggressor, striking suddenly and unexpectedly with a number of atomic bombs might, in the first assault upon his vital targets, achieve such an order of advantage as would insure [sic] the ultimate defeat of an initially stronger adversary.[3]

By the early 1950s, as both the United States and the Soviet Union were building up their nuclear arsenals, the threat of surprise attack was at the forefront of U.S. concerns. Despite the fact that the United States enjoyed a significant margin of nuclear superiority over the Soviet Union—in 1951, for example, the United States had 428 atomic weapons while the Soviet Union possessed only 25, and by 1953 the United States has 1,169 and the Soviets had 120[4]—there was a growing fear that the Soviet acquisition of the bomb would shift the balance of military power toward the Soviet Union due to its already superior conventional might, and that such a shift would give Moscow strong incentives for aggression. Many official U.S. assessments at the time argued that a "window of opportunity" was opening up for the Soviet Union.[5]

According to the National Security Council Report 68 (NSC-68), perhaps the most influential policy document of the early Cold War, there was "great advantage" in "initiative and surprise" in the event of an atomic war, and the Soviet Union, by virtue of its tightly controlled political structure, had an "enormous advantage in maintaining the necessary security and centralization of decision required to capitalize on this advantage." Consequently:

> when [the Soviet Union] calculates that it has a sufficient atomic capability to make a surprise attack on us, nullifying our atomic superiority and creating a military situation decisively in its favor, the Kremlin might be tempted to strike swiftly and with stealth. The existence of two large atomic capabilities in such a relationship might well act, therefore, not as a deterrent, but as an incitement to war.[6]

A 1950 study for the Joint Chiefs of Staff concluded, "were war to break out . . . a tremendous military advantage would be gained by the power that struck first and succeeded in carrying through an effective first strike."[7] U.S. intelligence officials believed that Soviet leaders might make these kinds of calculations sooner rather than later. A Central Intelligence Agency (CIA) *National Intelligence Estimate* in November 1950 posited that the Soviets "may deliberately provoke a war at the time when, in their opinion, the relative strength of the USSR is at its maximum." This period of strength, the CIA believed, would exist from "now through 1954, with the peak of Soviet strength relative to the Western Powers being reached about 1952."[8]

These concerns about surprise attack extended up to the highest levels of government. The Dwight Eisenhower administration's *Basic National Security Policy*, enshrined in the National Security Council Report 162/2 (NSC-162/2) of October 30, 1953, noted that the Soviet Union "has sufficient bombs and aircraft, using one-way missions, to inflict serious damage on the United States, especially by surprise attack." Foreshadowing the coming discourse on strategic stability and Mutually Assured Destruction, the document proclaimed:

> When both the USSR and the United States reach a stage of atomic plenty and ample means of delivery, each will have the probable capacity to inflict critical damage on the other, but is not likely to be able to prevent major atomic retaliations. This could create a stalemate, with both sides reluctant to initiate general warfare; although if the Soviets believed that initial surprise held the prospect of destroying the capacity for retaliation, they might be tempted into attacking.[9]

It was within the context of these concerns that Albert Wohlstetter, then a researcher at the RAND Corporation, led a study for the U.S. Air Force on strategic air bases. At that point in time, the only available means of delivering atomic weapons was by aircraft, so the Strategic Air Command's (SAC) array of strategic bomber bases in the United States and its network of bases in Europe were lynchpins of the U.S. nuclear deterrent. Wohlstetter and his team found that SAC had essentially planned for atomic war in the same way the Army Air Force, the precursor to the U.S. Air Force, had in World War II: in the event of a crisis or war, the nuclear-capable bombers would go from the United States to bases in Europe where they would be re-fueled, loaded with bombs, and sent on their strike missions.

The problem, however, was that many of these overseas bases were within striking distance of the Soviet Union. To make matters worse, for the purposes of economizing space on the airfields, the bombers were parked close together and near fuel tanks, repair facilities, and other critical support infrastructure, thereby providing a "force multiplier" for the attacker.[10] Wohlstetter calculated that 120 atomic bombs of 40 kilotons each could destroy 75 to 85 percent of the U.S. B-47 bombers moved to overseas bases in preparation for war. The end result, he concluded, was that the U.S. nuclear force was highly vulnerable to a Soviet pre-emptive strike. According to historian Fred Kaplan:

> The Strategic Air Command ... was appearing so vulnerable in so many ways that merely putting it into action—moving it overseas in accordance with the Mobility plan—created a target so concentrated that it invited a pre-emptive attack from the Soviet Union.[11]

If deterrence rested on the threat of retaliation in kind, then the fact that U.S. bombers at bases in Europe—as well as those at bases in the United States—could be destroyed on the ground by the Soviet Union meant that the deterrent power of the U.S. nuclear arsenal was in serious jeopardy.

Wohlstetter was not alone in recognizing the vulnerability of U.S. nuclear forces. As early as 1952, in a classified lecture at the Air War College, Brodie stressed the importance of "reducing the almost comic opera vulnerability of our military structure." It was extremely unwise that U.S. atomic weapons were stored "in only three or four sites, the locations of those being very well-known to the enemy and each individually being very slightly guarded."[12] Yet, while Brodie was certainly correct in highlighting these vulnerabilities, at the time he did not place much emphasis on these issues in his published work. As such, this vulnerability issue did not reach a level of prominence in the strategic debate until Wohlstetter published his work on the subject.

Regardless of which defense analyst first recognized the problem of vulnerability, two important and consequential implications followed from this analysis. First, as Wohlstetter later argued in his seminal article, "The Delicate Balance of Terror," in the January 1959 issue of *Foreign Affairs*, deterrence was not automatic.[13] Whereas many had seemingly assumed that simply matching or surpassing the size of the Soviet Union's nuclear arsenal was sufficient for deterrence, the real issue, Wohlstetter argued, was the ability to survive a nuclear attack and strike back. In fact, the whole reason why he argued that the nuclear balance was so "delicate" was because of the vulnerability of nuclear forces to a surprise attack. Having identified the problem, the solution was logical and obvious: if deterrence depended on the ability to retaliate after an attack, and if U.S. nuclear forces deployed in such way that they could be destroyed in a Soviet first strike, then deterrence required making the U.S. nuclear arsenal more survivable.

The second implication, which proved especially important for the early development of the concept of strategic stability, had to do with how the United States should deal with the problem of vulnerability during the period in which it was in the process of making its forces more survivable. Wohlstetter had successfully convinced high-ranking Air Force and civilian officials in Washington that U.S. nuclear forces were vulnerable to a Soviet pre-emptive attack and that this vulnerability severely weakened deterrence, but making U.S. forces more survivable was going to take a lot of time and money.[14] Moreover, the advent of the Soviet hydrogen bomb and the coming age of long-range ballistic missiles — and especially the prospect of a hydrogen bomb-equipped ballistic missile — added new challenges to developing a survivable force.[15] Thus, while senior decisionmakers were committed to solving the vulnerability problem, rectifying it was not going to be easy, quick, or inexpensive, and consequently many officials believed that U.S. nuclear forces were going to be susceptible to a Soviet pre-emptive attack for a period of time. Given this reality, the near-term solution to the vulnerability problem was to pay extremely close attention to the Soviet Union's growing nuclear capability and, upon indication that the Soviets were preparing to attack, to launch its nuclear forces first. If U.S. nuclear forces could not yet survive an attack, then the answer was to get them off the ground before the Soviet bombs fell on their targets.

Pre-emption, therefore, temporarily solved the vulnerability problem. Since there was no sufficiently effective defense against nuclear weapons, and since the majority of U.S. weapons would not survive a surprise nuclear attack, the United States must launch its nuclear-loaded airplanes upon sufficient warning of an impending Soviet attack. Such a strategy would contribute to deterrence by convincing the Soviet leaders that they could not escape retaliation, since U.S. nuclear weapons would already be on their way to the Soviet Union (and its Warsaw Pact allies) by the time Soviet weapons arrived on their targets. If deterrence appeared likely to fail, a pre-emptive strategy would attempt to protect the United States by destroying as much of the Soviet atomic arsenal as possible before their bombs could launch.

These implications met a receptive audience among senior U.S. political and military officials. In fact, in some important ways the U.S. Government was ahead of the burgeoning community of nuclear strategists on these issues. This was especially true regarding pre-emption. Even though NSC-68 had ruled out preventive war as "generally unacceptable to Americans,"[16] pre-emption was an important part of some of the earliest thinking about atomic war. Given the tremendous advantages of surprise attack, the aforementioned 1947 report by the Joint Chiefs of Staff (JCS) recommended a "revision of our traditional attitudes toward what constitute acts of aggression." Given the "realities of atomic warfare," the report continued, "offensive measures will be the only generally effective means of defense, and the United States must be prepared to employ them before a potential enemy can inflict significant damage on us." Whereas in the past the President "has been restricted to action only after the loss of American lives and treasure, it must be made his duty in the future to defend the country against imminent or incipient atomic weapon attack."[17]

By the early 1950s, pre-emption was a key feature of U.S. nuclear war plans. For senior political and military officials at the time — and especially for President Eisenhower — pre-emption not only made good strategic sense, it was also necessary. The requirement for a nuclear strategy of pre-emption stemmed from two factors. First, the early use of nuclear weapons was an essential component of the Eisenhower administration's plans for defending the North Atlantic Treaty Organization (NATO). President Eisenhower believed that a major war with the Soviet Union would inevitably be a nuclear war, and he had little faith in the prospect of controlling escalation and fighting a limited nuclear conflict.[18] In his view, it was "fatuous to think that the U.S. and USSR would be locked into a life and death struggle without using atomic weapons."[19] This core view, combined with his strong desire to avoid the substantial costs of a massive conventional build-up by instead relying on nuclear weapons to balance the Warsaw Pact's numerical advantage in conventional forces, underpinned the President's thinking about nuclear weapons and thus the administration's military strategy.

President Eisenhower believed that despite the West's numerical disadvantage, the United States and NATO could still defeat the Soviet Union in a major war in Europe by using forward-deployed tactical nuclear weapons to forestall an initial Soviet conventional assault, and at the same time launching the SAC for a full nuclear assault on the Soviet Union and many of its Warsaw Pact allies. Eisenhower told the JCS in December 1954 that in the event of a major war in Europe, the immediate use of tactical nuclear weapons would provide strategic time for the "first priority" of launching SAC to "blunt the enemy's initial threat—by massive retaliatory power and the ability to deliver it." Despite his use of the term "retaliatory power," Eisenhower's strategy was clearly preemptive in nature, since the only way to "blunt" the Soviet threat—meaning to destroy the Soviet Union's nuclear forces—was to launch U.S. nuclear weapons first.[20] The President was actually quite clear on this point, telling the JCS of his "firm intention to launch a strategic attack in case of alert of actual attack,[21] and arguing that in the event of impending conflict the United States should "knock out their SAC first."[22]

In Eisenhower's view, the "only chance of victory in a third world war against the Soviet Union would be to paralyze the enemy at the outset of the war . . . we have got to be in a position to use that weapon if we are to preserve our institutions in peace and win the victory in war."[23] In more colorful terms, the essence of this strategy, popularly known as "massive retaliation," was, as the President told a congressional delegation in 1954, to "blow the hell out of them in a hurry if they start anything."[24] In fact, Eisenhower believed he had a duty to strike pre-emptively if given sufficient warning of a Soviet attack. The President once told a group of congressmen, "if you were away and I waited on you [before taking action], you'd start impeachment proceedings against me."[25]

The second factor contributing to the necessity of a pre-emptive strategy was the then well-known vulnerability of SAC to a surprise Soviet first strike. The Air Force acknowledged that SAC bases were "jammed with as many as 130 aircraft" and thus presented "a highly profitable target" for the Soviet Union. Moreover, the atomic stockpile itself was vulnerable to a

Soviet strike, since all of SAC's allocated weapons were stored at just a handful of locations. Out of 45 total atomic weapons storage sites, 38 were located on SAC bases—the "primary aiming points" for a Soviet strike. By 1957, "over 50 percent [of U.S. nuclear warheads] will be located at only 13 sites."[26]

President Eisenhower was firmly convinced that if the Soviets decided to start a major war, "the pressure on [the Soviets] to use atomic weapons in a sudden blow would be extremely great." The Soviet Union, he argued, would "use these weapons at once, and in full force."[27] The vulnerability problem thus reinforced the critical importance of pre-emption in Eisenhower's defense strategy, for if the defense of NATO required a pre-emptive strike to blunt the Soviet Union's atomic power, and if U.S. nuclear forces were susceptible to a Soviet strike, then any chance of victory hinged upon launching SAC bombers as soon as conflict appeared likely. "Prudence would demand," the President told his senior military advisors, "that we get our striking force into the air immediately upon notice of hostile action by the Soviets."[28] Reflecting his keen awareness of SAC's susceptibility to a Soviet strike, Eisenhower said, "The [U.S.] attack once in the air could be recalled . . . if it stayed on the ground it might never get off."[29]

Coping with the Threat of Surprise Attack.

By the mid-1950s, there was a lively debate both inside and outside of the U.S. Government over how to make nuclear forces less vulnerable to surprise attack. In an effort to better understand how the United States should deal with the vulnerability problem, President Eisenhower requested on March 27, 1954, that the Technological Capabilities Panel of the Science Advisory Committee undertake a study to examine how the United States could use technological capabilities to reduce the threat of surprise attack. Dr. James Killian, the president of the Massachusetts Institute of Technology (MIT) and a chief science advisor to Eisenhower, chaired the study. On February 14, 1955, the study group presented its report to the President. Formally titled "Meeting the Threat of Surprise Attack" but more commonly referred to as the "Killian Report" or the "Killian Committee," the report argued that SAC vulnerability "tempted [the Soviets] to try a surprise attack," and that Moscow might be especially willing to strike "before we achieve a large multimegaton capability."[30]

The study examined the current state and future trajectory of U.S. and Soviet technological development, and analyzed the risks to and opportunities for the United States given likely advancements in weapons capabilities. The current period, the report argued, was characterized by an offensive advantage for the United States, but one that was tempered by SAC's continued vulnerability to surprise attack. The second period, perhaps beginning around 1956-57 and lasting until 1958-60, would be one in which the United States alone possessed a large number of multimegaton weapons. At that time, "our military power relative to that of Russia [is] at its maximum. The United States can mount a decisive air strike; the USSR cannot." While the United States would face severe damage in a conflict with the Soviets, the United States would still emerge as a "battered victor even if the USSR mounted a surprise attack on the U.S." Given that "our military superiority may never be as great again," the report recommended that an additional study determine how to use this period to "our best advantage and to the advantage of the free world."[31]

This U.S. advantage, however, might be short-lived. In Period III, the Soviets would have multi-megaton weapons and possess a large number of nuclear-capable aircraft able to reach targets in the United States. On the other hand, the United States would have strengthened its continental air defenses, reduced the vulnerability of SAC, and improved its own nuclear delivery systems. In assessing the consequences of these developments for U.S. security, the key variable was timing. The report argued that if the United States strengthened its defense before the Soviets attained multimegaton weapons, "the deterrent power of the U.S. is increased." However, if the Soviets developed high-yield weapons and improved and expanded their delivery capabilities before the United States improved its warning and defense systems, "the deterrent effect of U.S. power [would be] dangerously lessened."[32] In this situation, which the study suggested might occur as early as 1958, the United States "would be in a poor position to ward off Russian political and diplomatic moves or to make such moves of our own."[33]

Period IV, which was expected to occur in the mid-1960s and last indefinitely, would be a period of strategic stalemate characterized by what would later be termed Mutually Assured Destruction (MAD). In this period, both countries "will be in a position from which neither country can derive a winning advantage, because each country will possess enough multi-megaton weapons and adequate means of delivering them." Consequently, "the ability to achieve surprise will not affect the outcome because each country will have the residual offensive power to break through the defenses of the other country and destroy it regardless of whether the other country strikes first."

Interestingly, whereas this condition would later be regarded as the hallmark of strategic stability and thus U.S. security, the committee did not view this as a welcome situation. Rather, the report argued that this would be a period of "instability" that was "fraught with danger," and strongly encouraged the United States to "push all promising technological development so that we may stay in Periods II and III as long as possible, and, if we pass into Period IV, may escape from it into another period resembling II or III."[34]

The Killian Report made a large number of recommendations for reducing the threat of surprise attack, including extending the Distant Early Warning Line, installing a radar line 500 to 700 nautical miles from U.S. continental boundaries to provide "unmistakable signal of an actual attack," providing SAC with additional bases "to permit its bombers to be airborne towards target within the warning interval," and using nuclear warheads as the "major armament for our air defense forces."[35] One of the most important and consequential recommendations was to accord the Air Force's program to develop an intercontinental ballistic missile (ICBM) as "a nationally supported effort of the highest priority." The National Security Council spent several subsequent meetings discussing this particular recommendation. Eisenhower believed that the United States needed some ballistic missiles "as a threat and a deterrent," but he did not want to build more than a thousand because "we can't fight that kind of a war." If "the Russians can fire 1000 [ballistic missiles] at us and we can fire 1000 a day at them," the President quipped, he "personally would want to take off for the Argentine."[36]

The President ultimately accepted many of the report's recommendations, though he remained cautious about over-reacting to and overspending on the threat. In early December, at another meeting to discuss some of the Killian Report's recommendations, Eisenhower noted that no one from the Killian Commission had provided the "Russian side of the story." He believed that the Soviets also had "major problems to be met in this whole area," and cautioned that there was a "limit to the amount of money that the United States can spend on such improvements." The United States must, he argued, "keep within budget levels in thinking of such problems over the next 60 years or so."[37]

Eisenhower's concerns about the amount of money required to reduce SAC's vulnerability and mitigate the threat of surprise attack reflected one of the key limitations of the Killian Report—virtually all of its recommendations discussed only one side, focusing exclusively on things that the United States alone should do. Nowhere, for example, did the report suggest that the United States might be able to cope with this threat by engaging with the Soviet Union in arms control or other kinds of mutually beneficial and security-enhancing agreements. The U.S.-focused recommendations contained in the Killian Report thus provided only half of the solution to the problem of surprise attack. Going forward, Eisenhower would attempt to combine unilateral technological solutions, such as enhanced surveillance and early warning capabilities and continued funding for the development of the less vulnerable Polaris submarine launched ballistic missile, with a concerted effort to reach an agreement with the Soviet Union that would help to lessen the fear of surprise attack.

Eisenhower did not wait long to make his first attempt at proposing an agreement with the Soviet Union on the issue of surprise attack. In a speech at the Geneva Summit on July 21, 1955, President Eisenhower argued that the possession of large numbers of nuclear weapons by the United States and the Soviet Union would "give rise in other parts of the world, or reciprocally, to the fears and dangers of surprise attack."[38] Given these risks, the President proposed that the superpowers undertake an "arrangement" whereby both countries would provide "a complete blueprint of our military establishments, from beginning to end," and:

> provide within our own countries facilities for aerial photography to the other country — we to provide you with facilities within our country, ample facilities for aerial reconnaissance, where you can make all the pictures you choose and take them to your own country to study, and you to provide exactly the same facilities for us.[39]

Such an arrangement, Eisenhower concluded, would "convince the world that we are providing as between ourselves against the possibility of great surprise attack, thus lessening danger and relaxing tension."[40]

This initiative, dubbed the "Open Skies" proposal, marked an important step toward the development of the concept of strategic stability. Whereas previous U.S. efforts to cope with the threat of surprise attack focused on reducing SAC's vulnerability and adopting a pre-emptive nuclear strategy, the Open Skies proposal sought to reduce this threat by making both sides more confident that the other was not preparing for a surprise attack. Thus the logic of Open Skies contained an early seed of an idea that would eventually grow into one of the essential underpinnings of strategic stability — that security in the nuclear age is interdependent, and therefore the United States was more secure not only when it was assured that the Soviet Union was not preparing to attack, but also when the Soviets were assured that the United States was not preparing to strike. Some senior U.S. officials recognized this new—and, at the time, seemingly counterintuitive—reality, though the idea had yet to be placed under the label of strategic stability. According to a special study prepared for President Eisenhower on U.S. disarmament policy, the United States should "forego the opportunity to launch a surprise attack upon the USSR in exchange for substantial assurance against a surprise attack upon the United States."[41]

The Soviet Union ultimately rejected the Open Skies proposal, claiming that it had no relation to the real problem of curbing the arms race and, in any case, it did not really reduce the danger of war because it did not include U.S. allies. Moreover, the Soviets argued that the level of transparency created by Open Skies might actually increase, rather than decrease, the possibility of surprise attack because such a scheme would put both states "under a constant threat that the other party which has the proper information at its disposal may utilize it for a surprise attack and for aggression." This kind of arrangement would only "intensify" the "fear and mutual suspicion" between the countries.[42] The Soviets later argued that Eisenhower's proposal "can only be regarded as a trick designed to distract attention from the pressing problems of disarmament and to win complete freedom of aerial reconnaissance in order to prepare aggression."[43]

The failure to reach an agreement on any kind of inspections regime or an arms limitation agreement, coupled with advances in ballistic missile systems capable of delivering thermonuclear warheads with increasing accuracy at intercontinental distances, preceded a growing chorus of advocates both within and outside of the U.S. Government for significant increases in defense spending. In response to these demands, especially the call for a multibillion dollar nationwide blast and radioactive fallout shelter program, the National Security Council decided to form a blue-ribbon commission tasked with examining "the relative value of various active and passive measures to protect the civil population in case of nuclear attack."[44]

The commission, headed by H. Rowen Gaither and thus known as the "Gaither Committee," produced a final report that went far beyond the group's limited tasking. Formally titled, "Deterrence and Survival in the Nuclear Age," the report provided a wide-ranging assessment of the requirements of deterrence and defense in an age of expanding nuclear arsenals. On many issues, especially those regarding surprise attack, the Gaither Committee echoed many of the sentiments of the Killian Report from 2 years prior. The Gaither Report argued that the "current vulnerability of SAC to surprise attack" requires "prompt remedial action." Such actions included reducing SAC's reaction time so that "an adequate number (possibly 500) of SAC planes can get off, weapons aboard, on way to target, within the tactical warning time," dispersing SAC aircraft to a wider number of bases, deploying missiles defense systems around SAC bases, and building hardened shelters to protect SAC aircraft.[45] Yet, the Gaither Report also contained at least one important difference from its predecessor—whereas the Killian Report did not advocate for or even mention the possibility of arms control negotiations with the Soviets, this report made a strong case for "the great importance of a continuing attempt to arrive at a dependable agreement on the limitation of armaments."

In fact, the Gaither Committee argued that the United States should attempt to negotiate an arms control agreement within the next 2 to 3 years because, once SAC acquired an effective alert status and could thus mount an effective retaliation even after a surprise attack, it would be "the best time to negotiate from strength, since the U.S. military positions vis-à-vis [the] Russians might never be as strong again."[46]

Less than a year after the Gaither Committee presented its report to President Eisenhower, the United States and the Soviet Union would again attempt to work together to ease the mutual fear of surprise attack. The origins of this new effort grew out of a series of letters and statements exchanged between Washington and Moscow in the first half of 1958.[47] These documents reflect an evolution in thinking on both sides that would eventually lead to the codification of the concept of strategic stability. One particular statement, given by Soviet Foreign Minister Andrei Gromyko on April 18, 1958, epitomized the growing appreciation on the Soviet side for how the fear of surprise attack—and the reactions and counter-reactions these fears can produce—could lead to a conflict that neither country intended. In the context of protesting the U.S. practice of flying nuclear weapons-loaded aircraft over the Arctic, Gromyko said:

> And what would happen if the military air forces of the USSR began to act in the same way as the United States air forces are now acting? Naturally, meteors and electronic disturbances cause images on Soviet radars, too. And if in such instances Soviet aircraft loaded with atomic and hydrogen bombs were to take off in the direction of the United States and its bases in other States, then the air formations of the two sides, seeing each other somewhere over the Arctic wastes,

would come to the conclusion—very natural in the circumstances—that there was justification for an outright attack on the enemy and mankind would be plunged into the maelstrom of an atomic war.[48]

By the end of July 1958, after several letters had been exchanged between the U.S. and Soviet leadership, the superpowers agreed to hold a joint conference of experts to examine how to reduce the danger of surprise attack.[49] Formally titled, "The Conference of Experts for the Study of Possible Measures Which Might Be Helpful in Preventing Surprise Attack and for the Preparation of a Report thereon to Governments," but more commonly called the Surprise Attack Conference, the group met in Geneva from November 10 through December 18.

From the start, however, Washington and Moscow had divergent expectations and objectives for the meeting, and these differences ultimately doomed the Surprise Attack Conference to failure.[50] Whereas the United States argued the objective was strictly to produce a "technical report which could be recommended for consideration by governments," the Soviets contended that the conference should focus on "working out practical recommendations on measures for prevention of surprise attack in conjunction with definite steps in the field of disarmament."[51] The United States wanted to have a highly technical discussion that would narrowly focus on inspections of weapons systems and other military capabilities.[52] The Soviet Union, on the other hand, sought a broader and less technical discussion that focused on the range of factors that increased the risk of surprise attack, and that linked surprise attack to the reduction or elimination of certain capabilities. The Soviets went so far as to propose a one-third reduction in the number of foreign troops stationed in Europe and a ban on deploying nuclear weapons in Germany, since these issues, in their view, created substantial tensions between the superpowers and thereby increased the risk of surprise attack.[53] According to the Soviets, a sole focus on technical solutions:

> would not prevent a surprise attack but would, in the best circumstances, give warning of the fact that such an attack was imminent. We, on the other hand, are trying to obtain an agreement, the aim of which would be . . . the elimination of the threat of surprise attack at its sources by the creation of conditions which would make such an attack impossible.[54]

This core issue could not be reconciled, and the conference adjourned on December 18 without having even scratched the surface on reducing the risk of surprise attack.

It is important to note that thinking about how to reduce the threat of surprise attack did not occur only among the civilians inside and outside of the U.S. Government. Within the U.S. military, the competition for funding between the Air Force and the Navy spurred some important insights that would eventually form some of the essential underpinnings of the concept of strategic stability. This was especially true for the Navy, which used SAC's vulnerability to argue for a greater role in the nuclear mission and thus for more resources.

In making the case for a new U.S. nuclear strategy that came to be called "finite deterrence," the U.S. Navy, led by Chief of Naval Operations Admiral Arleigh Burke, developed arguments that utilized the core logic encapsulated by strategic stability. At its core, finite deterrence held that only a small number of highly survivable nuclear weapons capable of destroying a limited set of targets were necessary for effective deterrence. Rather than building a large land-based arsenal that was vulnerable to surprise attack, the Navy argued that "deterrence is more effectively achieved by a small retaliatory capability secure against surprise attack than a much larger force calculated to provide the same 'residual' capability."[55] The Navy, conveniently enough, had just the right capability for this purpose, namely its fleet of submarines equipped with Polaris ballistic missiles.

The survivability of Navy systems not only obviated the need for the expense of a large arsenal but, equally important, it provided unique benefits in a crisis. In making this case, the Navy helped make great strides in developing the logic of crisis stability. "When jumping the gun confers a clear advantage," an internal Navy document on nuclear policy noted, "a hasty decision to initiate war in periods of tension is greatly encouraged."[56] In a memo on nuclear strategy to all flag officers, Admiral Burke noted that "there may be periods of tension in which there are some indications that missiles might be launched by the enemy but these indications are not positive." In this situation, "our political leaders will then be in a quandary as to whether or not to launch missiles before they are sure the enemy has launched its attack. If they wait, our ballistic missiles in known locations may be destroyed. If they launch on false information, we will have started a devastating war."[57]

A Navy-centric nuclear strategy, however, would alleviate this dilemma, since the invulnerability of Polaris-equipped submarines would "not lead to the build-up of psychological 'pressures' to push the button first in fear that our reprisal capability might be knocked out by surprise."[58] Indeed, "perhaps the most important pay-off from making our future strategic forces proof against surprise attack," Admiral Burke argued, was that it would "gain time to think in periods of tension." With survivable forces, "retaliation will lose this nightmarish, semi-automatic, 'hair-trigger' quality. The constant pressure to strike first in order to avoid being disarmed, the most dangerous feature of vulnerable striking systems, will be eliminated."[59]

The Concept of Strategic Stability Takes Shape.

The research and analysis on the surprise attack problem in the early and mid-1950s helped bring some of the basic tenets of strategic stability into focus. Given U.S. vulnerability to surprise attack, the immediate solution was to keep U.S. nuclear forces on high alert and launch them as soon as there was sufficient evidence of an impending Soviet attack. At the same time, the United States would also devote significant resources to improving its early warning capabilities and increasing the survivability of its forces.

In terms of the development of the concept of strategic stability, however, this early thinking was only half of the equation. Strategic stability is a dynamic phenomenon, focusing on the interactions and incentives of two (or more) parties. Consequently, the concept did not take full shape until strategists began to consider not only how the United States should deal with the vulnerability of its forces, but also how the Soviet Union would deal with the same problem. The essential idea of strategic stability came to fruition when defense strategists deliberately imparted what the United States deemed the logical response to vulnerability — to launch nuclear forces upon warning of an enemy's attack — on to the Soviet Union. If the United States would be under great pressure to launch its vulnerable forces, the argument ran, then so, too, might the Soviet Union.

Thus, the key element of the line of reasoning that ultimately formed the logic of strategic stability involved a logical leap — a mirror-imaging of sorts — that assumed the Soviets would think the same way and have the same incentives as the United States in a similar situation. This leap was based on little, if any, evidence, since the nuclear age was still too young to have any clear and well-informed evidence about how the Soviets thought about or behaved with nuclear weapons. In the late 1950s, American defense strategists privy to classified information could know how the United States would likely react to indications of an impending Soviet attack, but any assessment of how the Soviets would react if they feared a U.S. attack was based more on inference than on evidence, given the paucity of U.S. information about Soviet thinking on these issues. To be sure, this inference may have in fact been correct. The relevant Soviet archives remain closed, so historians do not yet have sufficient access to primary source documents and other materials that would shed light on if and how the Soviets thought about vulnerability and surprise attack. Nevertheless, it is still interesting to note that for all of the discussion throughout the 1950s about the Soviet Union's supposedly aggressive and expansionist aims, and for all of the rhetoric about Soviet ideology, many defense analysts were quite willing to assume that Soviet leaders thought about the "absolute weapon" in the same way that American leaders did.

While this leap in reasoning seems to have taken hold in the late 1950s and early 1960s, after analysts had a number of years to think about how the United States should deal with the problem of vulnerability, there were some earlier works that touched on the stability issue. As early as 1954, Bernard Brodie wrote:

> If, for example, we are living in a world where either side can make a surprise attack upon the other which destroys the latter's capability to make a meaningful retaliation, then it makes sense to be trigger-happy with one's strategic air power. How could one afford under those circumstances to withhold one's SAC from its critical blunting mission while waiting to test other pressures and strategies? This would be the situation of the American gunfighter duel, Western frontier style. The one who leads on the draw and the aim achieves a good clean win. The other is dead. But if, on the other hand, the situation is such that neither side can hope to eliminate the retaliatory power of the other, that restraint which was suicidal in one situation becomes prudence, and it is trigger-happiness that is suicidal.[60]

Similarly, in February 1954 Albert Wohlstetter and Fred Hoffman wrote in an internal RAND publication:

> If the [ICBM] is a probable threat, and we cannot protect our strategic force against it, then our advertised capability for retaliation will be fictitious. We could not expect to hurt the Russians very much, unless we could be sure to strike first blows. This should make us rather trigger happy, particularly if we were to couple this fragile strategic capability with an announced policy of relying mainly on a threat of major strategic atomic attack to deter even minor war. It would appear also to make the Russians equally trigger-happy. Because in this case striking the first blow is the only

means of defense, any delay in striking the first blow by either side risks the chance that the enemy will be the only one to have this prerogative. . . . Then it is clear not only that an invulnerable SAC is a deterrent but also that a vulnerable SAC is an urgent invitation.[61]

These statements demonstrate that at least two of the most original and influential analysts were thinking ahead, pushing the logical consequences and implications of vulnerability beyond the present state of thinking. Yet, because almost everyone else involved in the vulnerability and surprise attack issues at the time were fixated on reducing U.S. exposure—and because Brodie's article was not printed in a widely circulated publication and the RAND document was for internal use only[62]—these early flirtations with the notion of strategic stability largely went unnoticed or, at least, underappreciated.

By the end of the decade, as U.S. nuclear capabilities grew in size and accuracy, civilian and military nuclear specialists began to move beyond the narrow confines of how the United States should deal with the issue of vulnerability and surprise attack and considered how the Soviet Union might deal with the same problems. One stimulus to this expansion in thinking was the significant increase in the size and accuracy of U.S. nuclear capabilities. After living through the supposed "window of vulnerability" and the then-discredited bomber and missile gaps of the 1950s, the United States had emerged the superior nuclear power. Consequently, while concerns about U.S. vulnerabilities remained, there now was more discussion about the Soviet Union's vulnerabilities.

Another particularly important stimulus was the preparation for the 1958 Surprise Attack Conference.

Despite the conference's failure to produce any kind of agreement between the superpowers, the run-up to the conference was a watershed moment in the development of the concept of strategic stability because it served as a forcing function for several influential nuclear experts to consider these issues from a more dynamic and bilateral perspective. In preparation for the conference, Secretary of State John Foster Dulles, Secretary of Defense Neil McElroy, and presidential science advisor James Killian appointed an Interagency Working Group on Surprise Attack to "study the problem of reducing the danger of surprise attack, with the objective of presenting an analysis which would facilitate further studies in preparation for discussion between U.S. and Soviet experts."[63]

In what was probably one of the earliest explicit uses of the term in official government documentation, the working group argued:

> the stability, i.e., freedom from the threat of surprise attack . . . depends not only on an inspection of one's potential enemy and limitations on his forces, but also very heavily on the vulnerability of one's own retaliatory forces. . . . [It] remains a matter of extreme importance that the vulnerability of such forces be reduced to acceptable levels in order to safeguard their effectiveness as retaliatory forces.[64]

While the importance of survivability had been highlighted many times before, what is important about this statement is that it did not focus solely on the inspection of Soviet forces and the survivability of U.S. nuclear forces. This was a general statement about the requirements of stability, meaning that it applied to the Soviet Union as well as to the United States.

As part of the preparations for the Surprise Attack Conference, Albert Wohlstetter circulated a draft of his "Delicate Balance of Terror" article, which was at that time an unpublished RAND paper.[65] Wohlstetter's paper was a longer version of the article he would publish just a few months later in the January 1959 issue of *Foreign Affairs*. While this article is widely regarded as a seminal text on the requirements of deterrence—specifically the ability to survive an attack and inflict unacceptable damage in retaliation—it also broke ground on strategic stability. Although the bulk of the article is dedicated to an assessment of the vulnerability of U.S. nuclear capabilities to a Soviet strike, near the end of the paper, in a single paragraph, Wohlstetter considered the consequences of a situation in which both sides were vulnerable. He wrote:

> Suppose both the United States and the Soviet Union had the power to destroy each others' retaliatory forces and society, given the opportunity to administer the opening blow. The situation would then be like the old-fashioned Western gun duel. It would be extraordinarily risky for one side not to attempt to destroy the other, or to delay so doing, since it not only can emerge unscathed by striking first but this is the sole way it can reasonably hope to emerge at all. Evidently such a situation is extremely unstable. On the other hand, if it is clear that the aggressor too will suffer catastrophic damage in the vent of his aggression, he then has strong reason not to attack, even though he can administer great damage. A protected retaliatory capability has a stabilizing influence not only in deterring rational attack, but also in offering every inducement to both powers to reduce the chance of accidental war.[66]

Wohlstetter's article — and especially the paragraph above — had a tremendous influence on the development of the concept of strategic stability. While Wohlstetter and Brodie had made similar observations as early as 1954, the publication of the "Delicate Balance of Terror" in an esteemed and widely circulated journal such as *Foreign Affairs* ensured that these ideas reached a wide audience.

The article had particular influence on Thomas Schelling, then a Harvard professor also affiliated with RAND, who still regards it as "one of the two or three most important articles on the subject [of strategic stability] that I ever read."[67] Around the same time that Wohlstetter was working on his "Delicate Balance" article, Schelling was also working on a paper for RAND entitled "Surprise Attack and Disarmament."[68] Whereas Wohlstetter's article only briefly touched on the issue of stability, this was the focal point of Schelling's paper.

Schelling took a basic idea about the consequences of the mutual vulnerability of strategic forces and developed a rich and complex theory of nuclear war causation. Indeed, one of Schelling's many unique contributions to the development of strategic stability was that he clearly explained how a primary incentive for starting a nuclear war could be the fear that the enemy was about to start one. "We live in an era," Schelling wrote in his RAND paper, "in which a potent incentive on either side — perhaps the main incentive — to initiate total war with a surprise attack is the fear of being a poor second for not going first."[69] The fear of surprise attack could lead to a kind of mental gymnastics that could ultimately lead to nuclear war, since "we have to worry about his striking us to keep us from striking him to keep him from striking us . . ."[70]

Given these dynamics, simplistic assessments of the U.S.-Soviet nuclear relationship based only on the size of their respective nuclear arsenals missed a key point:

> It is not the 'balance' — the sheer equality or symmetry in the situation — that constitutes 'mutual deterrence'; it is the stability of the balance. The situation is symmetrical but not stable when either side, by striking first, can destroy the other's power to strike back; the situation is stable when either side can destroy the other whether it strikes first or second — that is, when neither in striking first can destroy the other's ability to strike back.[71]

More than anyone else, Schelling developed and popularized the idea that the key to preventing a nuclear war was not only having secure and survivable forces for retaliation, but also ensuring that the opponent was equally confident in his ability to retaliate. Harkening back to the core idea behind President Eisenhower's Open Skies proposal, Schelling argued that in the nuclear age, the United States must not only be interested in "assuring ourselves with our own eyes that he is not preparing an attack against us; we are interested as well in assuring him through his own eyes that we are preparing no deliberate attack against him."[72]

Schelling provided in this paper another major innovation, one that would highlight the unique and often paradoxical logic of the nuclear age, by categorizing certain types of nuclear weapons as "good" and "bad." A "good" weapon, Schelling argued, is one "that can only hurt people and cannot possibly damage the other side's strategic striking force." A "bad" weapon, by contrast, is one that "can exploit the advantage of striking first and consequently provide a temptation to do so."[73] Thus mutual vulnerability was a central ingredient to strategic stability—but it was the vulnerability of one's society, not of one's weapons. This core insight would later form the logical underpinning of the concept of MAD, and would be used as one of the primary arguments against an explicit counterforce targeting policy.

Schelling's "Surprise Attack and Disarmament" paper was originally slated to be published in the same issue as, or in the issue after, Wohlstetter's "Delicate Balance" article, but for reasons that remain unclear a senior editor at *Foreign Affairs* decided not to publish it.[74] The article nevertheless received widespread circulation when a shortened version was published in the December 1959 issue of the *Bulletin of the Atomic Scientists* (which was subsequently reprinted in the journal, *Survival*), and when a revised version of the original, lengthier RAND paper was printed in an edited volume published by Princeton University Press in 1959. Between Wohlstetter's "Delicate Balance" article in *Foreign Affairs* and three versions of Schelling's piece, all of which were published in the span of a year, no serious student of nuclear weapons and deterrence could have been unaware of the stability issue.

Schelling's subsequent work continued to explore the logic of stability. His 1960 book, *Strategy of Conflict*, devoted an entire chapter to the "reciprocal fear of surprise attack," and also included a chapter with a revised version of his "Surprise Attack and Disarmament" paper.[75] In *Arms and Influence*, published in 1966, Schelling probed further into the factors that influence incentives to strike first. Not only were both sides faced with extremely difficult dilemmas about whether to launch nuclear forces, but these decisions would have to be made very quickly, lest one wait too long and risk being on the receiving end of a first strike:

> The premium on haste — the advantage, in case of war, in being the one to launch it or in being a quick second in retaliation if the other side gets off the first blow — is undoubtedly the greatest piece of mischief that can be introduced into military forces, and the greatest source of danger that peace will explode into all out war.[76]

Schelling's work on stability had a tremendous effect on the strategic studies community because it added a new, more rich and complex set of issues to the nuclear debate. The concept of stability provided an over-arching theoretical framework for thinking about security in the nuclear age. Stability became an essential metric for evaluating nuclear forces, particularly regarding the wisdom of new nuclear capabilities and deployment options. Equally important, stability became the new rationale for U.S.-Soviet nuclear arms control. Whereas in the past arms control was often viewed as synonymous with disarmament, in the early 1960s a group of scholars and defense analysts, led by Schelling and Morton Halperin, began arguing that the goal of arms control in the nuclear age should be to reduce the risk of nuclear war by enacting restrictions on both sides' nuclear arsenals that helped minimize the fear of surprise attack and ensure that both sides possessed a second strike capability.[77] This view of arms control quickly took hold, further elevating the importance of strategic stability and entrenching it into virtually every serious discussion about security in the nuclear age.

By the end of the 1960s, the concept of strategic stability was firmly established in the strategic lexicon. Nuclear experts would continue to debate the importance of and metrics for stability in the U.S.-Soviet nuclear relationship, but no one could deny that the concept of strategic stability was now an essential element of the nuclear debate.

CONCLUSION

The early insights about strategic stability raised more questions than they answered, thereby opening up new areas for research within the nuclear community. It encouraged scholars, analysts, and civilian and military officials to move beyond thinking only about how to deter a deliberate and premeditated nuclear attack, and to also consider how nuclear war might occur through miscalculation or accident. The emphasis on stability in a crisis brought psychology, stress, and strategic culture into the equation, as well as provided fertile ground for game theorists. By the early 1960s, there was a growing cadre of analysts from a variety of academic disciplines who were incorporating stability issues into their work.[78]

Within the U.S. Government, however, it took slightly longer for the concept to gain formal acceptance. It was not until 1969 that the concept of stability formally appeared in the *Draft Presidential Memorandum on Strategic Offensive and Defensive Forces*, an annual document written to the President by the Secretary of Defense outlining the planned nuclear force posture and procurement decisions. Reflecting the growing role of stability in arms control, the document argued, "adequately safeguarded arms control agreements . . . could help us meet our basic strategic objectives and increase the stability of our deterrent."[79]

Over time, stability became a central component of the nuclear debate within and outside of government, especially regarding arms control. Stability issues played an important role in the debates over SALT I and especially SALT II, and by the early 1980s it was so established that even President Ronald Reagan told his arms control negotiators that the goal of the Strategic Arms Reduction Treaty (START) was to "enhance deterrence and to achieve stability through significant reductions in the most destabilizing nuclear systems."[80] While there was significant debate about the requirements of stability and the role it should be accorded in U.S. nuclear policy, there was also some important consensus. According to the President's Commission on Strategic Forces, a commission formed by President Reagan and chaired by Brent Scowcroft, "stability should be the primary objective of both the modernization of our strategic forces and of our arms control proposals."[81] As President George H. W. Bush described in his 1991 submittal letter of START to the Senate, "The fundamental premise of START is that, despite significant political differences, the United States and the Soviet Union have a common interest in . . . enhancing strategic stability."[82]

The history of strategic stability demonstrates how thoughtful and creative thinking can have an enormous effect on U.S. policy. Perhaps more than any other concept in the nuclear arena, stability epitomized how the nuclear revolution required some fundamental rethinking about the nature of security and the characteristics of military forces. As policymakers, defense officials, and scholars continue to debate the requirements of security in today's nuclear world, they should remember and carefully consider the lessons and insights about strategic stability from the Cold War.

ENDNOTES - CHAPTER 1

1. Bernard Brodie, ed., *The Absolute Weapon: Atomic Power and World Order*, San Diego, CA: Harcourt, 1946.

2. William L. Borden, *There will be no Time: The Revolution in Strategy*, New York: Macmillan Co., 1946.

3. "The Evaluation of the Atomic Bomb as a Military Weapon," Report by the Joint Chiefs of Staff Evaluation Board on Operation CROSSROADS, Washington, DC: Joint Chiefs of Staff, June 30, 1947, p. 10, available from *www.trumanlibrary.org/whistlestop/study_collections/bomb/large/documents/pdfs/81.pdf*.

4. These figures are from Robert S. Norris and Hans M. Kristensen, "Global Nuclear Inventories, 1945-2000," *Bulletin of the Atomic Scientists*, July/August 2010, p. 81. Moreover, in the early 1950s, the United States also enjoyed a significant numerical advantage in delivery vehicles.

5. For an excellent analysis of this line of thinking in the U.S. Government during this period utilizing a significant amount of primary sources, see Marc Trachtenberg, "A 'Wasting Asset:' American Strategy and the Shifting Nuclear Balance, 1949-1954," in Marc Trachtenberg, *History and Strategy*, Princeton, NJ: Princeton University Press, 1991, pp. 112-113.

6. "A Report to the National Security Council by the Executive Secretary on United States Objectives and Programs for National Security," April 12, 1950, pp. 37-38, available from *www.trumanlibrary.org/whistlestop/study_collections/coldwar/documents/pdf/10-1.pdf*.

7. Quoted in Scott Sagan, *Moving Targets: Nuclear Strategy and National Security*, Princeton, NJ: Princeton University Press, 1989, p. 19.

8. "Soviet Capabilities and Intentions," National Intelligence Estimate, NIE−3, April 15, 1950, Washington, DC: Central Intelligence Agency, available from *www.foia.cia.gov/docs/DOC_0000269240/DOC_0000269240.pdf*. Also quoted in Trachtenberg, "A 'Wasting Asset,'" p. 113.

9. "A Report to the National Security Council by the Executive Secretary on Basic National Security Policy," October 30, 1953, available from *www.fas.org/irp/offdocs/nsc-hst/nsc-162-2.pdf*.

10. On the basing study, see Fred Kaplan, *The Wizards of Armageddon*, Stanford, CA: Stanford University Press, 1991, pp. 98-101; and Gregg Herken, *Counsels of War*, Oxford, UK: Oxford University Press, 1987, pp. 89-94.

11. Kaplan, *The Wizards of Armageddon*, p. 99.

12. The Brodie quotes are from his lecture at the Air War College on April 12, 1952, and are found in Marc Trachtenberg, "Strategic Thought in America," in Trachtenberg, ed., *History and Strategy*, p. 19.

13. Albert Wohlstetter, "The Delicate Balance of Terror," *Foreign Affairs*, Vol. 37, No. 2, January 1959, pp. 211-212.

14. In addition, there was significant pushback from the Strategic Air Command (SAC), especially from SAC Commander General Curtis Lemay. Lemay believed the answer to bomber vulnerability was not to spend vast sums of money to protect them, but rather to simply buy more bombers. There were bureaucratic reasons for the SAC's resistance, too. The Air Staff in the Pentagon funded the basing study, and Lemay was loathe to accept the recommendations of a Pentagon-funded study because it might open the door for further intrusions of SAC by the Air Staff. On these points, see Kaplan, *The Wizards of Armageddon*, p. 104.

15. Herken, *Counsels of War*, p. 92.

16. NSC-68, pp. 52-53. The idea of preventive war resurfaced many more times in the 1950s. In 1954, for example, the Joint Chiefs of Staff (JCS) President Eisenhower on a study that recommended the United States consider "deliberately precipitating a war with the U.S.S.R in the near future." Eisenhower ultimately rejected this view, approving language in an updated *Basic National Security Policy* document that stated, "[T]he United States and its allies must reject the concept of preventive war or acts intended to provoke war." See David A. Rosenberg, "The Origins of Overkill: Nuclear Weapons and American Strategy, 1945-1960," *International Security*, Vol. 7, No. 4, Spring 1983, p. 34. For

a comprehensive analysis of preventive war thinking during the Cold War, see Marc Trachtenberg, "Preventive War and U.S. Foreign Policy," *Security Studies*, Vol. 16, No.1, January-March 2007, pp. 1-31.

17. "The Evaluation of the Atomic Bomb as a Military Weapon," pp. 10-11.

18. For a thorough, and somewhat controversial, assessment of Eisenhower's views on nuclear weapons, see Campbell Craig, *Destroying the Village: Eisenhower and Thermonuclear War*, New York: Columbia University Press, 1998.

19. Colonel A. J. Goodpaster, "Memorandum of Conference with the President," May 24, 1956, p. 2, *Declassified Documents Reference System* [hereafter cited as DDRS].

20. By 1950, the JCS had identified three objectives for U.S. nuclear war plans: the blunting of Soviet capability to deliver an atomic offensive against the United States and its allies; the disruption of vital elements of the Soviet warmaking capacity; the retardation of Soviet advances in Western Eurasia. The missions were codenamed Bravo, Delta, and Romeo, respectively. See David Rosenberg, "Smoking Radiating Ruin at the End of Two Hours: Documents of American Plans for Nuclear War with the Soviet Union, 1954-1955," *International Security*, Vol. 6, No. 3, Winter 1981-82, p. 9.

21. See, for example, Rosenberg, "The Origins of Overkill," p. 34; Trachtenberg, "A 'Wasting Asset,'" p. 162; and Sagan, *Moving Targets*, p. 22.

22. "Memorandum of Discussion at the 257th Meeting of the National Security Council," August 4, 1955, *Foreign Relations of the United States* [hereafter cited as FRUS], 1955-57, Vol. 19, p. 98.

23. "Memorandum of Discussion at the 227th Meeting of the National Security Council," December 3, 1954, FRUS, 1952-54, Vol. 2, part 1, p. 805.

24. Quoted in Sagan, *Moving Targets*, p. 23. It is important to note that while many at the time believed the strategy of "massive retaliation" meant that the United States was threatening

to launch a large-scale, countervalue attack against the Soviet Union for virtually any kind of aggression, large or small; in reality this was not the case. Not long after Dulles gave his speech at the Council on Foreign Relations announcing the administration's nuclear policy, he and other members of the administration wanted to clarify what the policy actually meant and clear up some misconceptions. Rather than threatening a massive nuclear strike for any kind of Soviet aggression, Dulles and others argued that the objective was to have a range of nuclear options, from an all-out nuclear response to more limited strikes. "Massive retaliation" was thus just one possibility along a continuum of nuclear options. While the primary mechanism of deterrence would be principally based nuclear weapons, the scope and scale of the nuclear response if deterrence failed would depend on the situation. See John Foster Dulles, "Policy for Security and Peace," *Foreign Affairs*, Vol. 32, No. 3, April 1954, pp. 358-359. For insightful analysis on the strategy of massive retaliation, see David N. Schwartz, *NATO's Nuclear Dilemmas*, Washington, DC: Brookings Institution Press, 1983, pp. 24-25; and Lawrence Freedman, *The Evolution of Nuclear Strategy*, New York, NY: St. Martin's Press, 1981, pp. 76-88.

25. This paragraph draws heavily from Rosenberg, "The Origins of Overkill," p. 34-35; and Sagan, *Moving Targets*, pp. 22-24.

26. "Memorandum of Discussion at the 292nd Meeting of the National Security Council," p. 340.

27. Goodpaster, "Memorandum of Conference with the President," p. 2.

28. *Ibid.*, p. 3.

29. Quoted in Rosenberg, "The Origins of Overkill," p. 42.

30. "Report by the Technological Capabilities Panel of the Science Advisory Committee: Meeting the Threat of Surprise Attack," FRUS, 1955-57, Vol. 19, p. 42.

31. *Ibid.*, p. 43.

32. *Ibid.*

33. *Ibid.*

34. *Ibid.*, p. 44.

35. The Report's list of recommendations are at *Ibid.*, pp. 46-53.

36. "Memorandum of Discussion at the 257th Meeting of the National Security Council," p. 101.

37. "Memorandum of Discussion at the 270th Meeting of the National Security Council," pp. 170-171.

38. "Statement by President Eisenhower at the Geneva Conference of Heads of Government," July 21, 1955, reprinted in *Documents on Disarmament, 1945-1959*, Washington, DC: U.S. Government Printing Office, 1960.

39. *Ibid.*

40. *Ibid.*, pp. 487-488.

41. "A Progress Report on a Proposed Policy of the United States on the Question of Disarmament," Special Staff Study for the President, NSC Action No. 1328, May 26, 1955, FRUS, 1955-57, Vol. 20, p. 103.

42. See "Statement by the Soviet Foreign Minister, Molotov, at the Geneva Meeting of Foreign Ministers," November 10, 1955, *Documents on Disarmament*, pp. 538-545; and "Letter from the Soviet Premier, Bulganin, to President Eisenhower," February 1, 1956, *Documents on Disarmament*, p. 590.

43. "Soviet Statement on the Disarmament Talks," August 27, 1957, in *Ibid.*, p. 863.

44. "Memorandum of Discussion at the 318th Meeting of the National Security Council," April 4, 1957, FRUS, 1955-57, Vol. 19, p. 463.

45. "Report to the President by the Security Resources Panel of the ODM Science Advisory Committee on Deterrence and Survival in the Nuclear Age," November 7, 1957, FRUS, 1955-57, Vol. 19, pp. 638-643.

46. *Ibid.*, pp. 651-653.

47. For excellent histories of the Surprise Attack Conference, see Jeremi Suri, "America's Search for a Technological Solution to the Arms Race: The Surprise Attack Conference of 1958 and a Challenge for 'Eisenhower Revisionists,'" *Diplomatic History*, Vol. 21, No. 3, Summer 1997, pp. 417-451; and Johan J. Holst, "Strategic Arms Control and Stability: A Retrospective Look," in Johan J. Holst and William Schneider, Jr., ed., *Why ABM? Policy Issues in the Missile Defense Controversy*, New York: Pergamon Press, 1969, pp. 245-284.

48. "Statement by the Soviet Foreign Minister, Gromyko, Regarding Arctic Flights by the United States Military Aircraft," April 18, 1958, *Documents on Disarmament*, p. 986.

49. President Eisenhower initially proposed a joint meeting in a letter to Soviet Premier Bulganin on January 12, 1958. In a letter to Eisenhower dated July 2, 1958, Khrushchev proposed that the governments meet for a joint study of the surprise attack problem, and on July 31, the United States accepted the offer.

50. For analysis on the different positions, and how these positions impeded a successful outcome, see Suri, "America's Search for a Technological Solution to the Arms Race," and Holst, "Strategic Arms Control and Stability."

51. See "Note from the American Embassy to the Soviet Foreign Ministry Regarding Surprise Attack Negotiations," October 10, 1958; and "Note from the Soviet Foreign Ministry to the American Embassy Regarding Surprise Attack Negotiations," November 1, 1958, both in *Documents on Disarmament*, pp. 1145, 1214.

52. See "Proposed Plan of Work Submitted by the Western Experts at the Geneva Surprise Attack Conference," November 11, 1958, *Documents on Disarmament*, p. 1223.

53. "Declaration Submitted by the Soviet Government at the Geneva Surprise Attack Conference: Measures for Preventing Surprise Attack," November 28, 1958, *Documents on Disarmament*, pp. 1269-1271.

54. Quoted in Holst, "Strategic Arms Control and Stability," p. 269.

55. "Adaptation of the National Military Posture to the Era of Nuclear Parity; A Suggested Navy Position," December 3, 1957, p. 3, available from *www.gwu.edu/~nsarchiv/nukevault/ebb275/02.pdf*.

56. *Ibid.*

57. Admiral Arleigh Burke, "Memorandum for All Flag Officers," March 4, 1959, p. 11, available from *www.gwu.edu/~nsarchiv/nukevault/ebb275/07.pdf*.

58. Admiral Arleigh Burke to Flag and General Officers, CNO Personal No. 35, March 5, 1958, p. 15, available from *www.gwu.edu/~nsarchiv/nukevault/ebb275/03.PDF*.

59. Admiral Arleigh Burke, "Summary of Major Strategic Considerations for the 1960-1970 Era," July 30, 1958, p. 2, available from *www.gwu.edu/~nsarchiv/nukevault/ebb275/05.pdf*.

60. Bernard Brodie quoted in Freedman, *The Evolution of Nuclear Strategy*, pp. 131-132.

61. A. Wohlstetter and F. Hoffman, *Defending a Strategic Force After 1960*, Santa Monica, CA: RAND, 1954, pp. 3-4.

62. The RAND document was stamped, "For RAND Use Only: Do Not Quote or Cite in External RAND Publications or Correspondence."

63. "Report of the Interagency Working Group on Surprise Attack," August 15, 1958, p. 1, DDRS.

64. *Ibid.*, p. 5.

65. Albert Wohlstetter, *The Delicate Balance of Terror*, Santa Monica, CA: RAND, 1958. The paper is dated November 6, 1958, and marked "Revised December 1958." On his circulation of the draft during preparations for the Surprise Attack Conference, see Trachtenberg, *History and Strategy*, p. 23.

66. Albert Wohlstetter, "The Delicate Balance of Terror," *Foreign Affairs*, Vol. 37, No. 2, January 1959, p. 230. In the draft RAND paper of the article, this quote—save for a few minor differences in word choice—is found at pp. 37-38.

67. Personal correspondence with Thomas Schelling, April 29, 2012.

68. T. C. Schelling, *Surprise Attack and Disarmament*, Santa Monica, CA: RAND, December 10, 1958.

69. *Ibid.*, p. 2.

70. *Ibid.*

71. *Ibid.*, p. 4.

72. *Ibid.*

73. *Ibid.*, p. 6.

74. Personal correspondence with Thomas Schelling, April 29, 2012.

75. See Thomas Schelling, *The Strategy of Conflict*, Cambridge, MA: Harvard University Press, 1960, chaps. 9-10.

76. Thomas Schelling, *Arms and Influence*, New Haven, CT: Yale University Press, 1966, p. 227.

77. The classic text is Thomas C. Schelling and Morton H. Halperin, *Strategy and Arms Control*, New York: The Twentieth Century Fund, 1961. See also Schelling, "Reciprocal Measures for Arms Stabilization," *Daedalus*, Vol. 89, No. 4, Fall 1960, pp. 892-914.

78. See, for example, Henry A. Kissinger, "Arms Control, Inspection and Surprise Attack," *Foreign Affairs*, Vol. 38, No. 4, July 1960, pp. 557-575; Glenn H. Snyder, *Deterrence and Defense: Toward a Theory of National Security*, Princeton, NJ: Princeton University Press, 1961, pp. 107-108; and Herman Kahn, *On Escalation: Metaphors and Scenarios*, New York: Praeger Publishers, 1965.

79. "Draft Presidential Memorandum on Strategic Offensive and Defensive Forces," January 9, 1969, p. 2, available from *www.dod.mil/pubs/foi/homeland_defense/strategic_offensive_defensive_forces/324.pdf*.

80. "U.S. Approach to START Negotiations," *National Security Directive No. 33*, May 14, 1982, p. 1, DDRS.

81. *Report of the President's Commission on Strategic Forces*, April 1983, p. 3.

82. Quoted in *Beyond New START: Advancing U.S. National Security Through Arms Control with Russia*, Washington, DC: Center for Strategic and International Studies, 2011, pp. 3-4.

CHAPTER 2

DEFINING STRATEGIC STABILITY: RECONCILING STABILITY AND DETERRENCE

Elbridge Colby

The author would like to thank Paul Davis, Michael Gerson, Robert Jervis, Richard Brody, George Quester, the participants in the November 2, 2011, workshop on strategic stability, and especially Linton Brooks for their helpful and constructive comments on and critiques of this chapter. The views herein as well as any errors and omissions remain the author's own and do not necessarily reflect the positions of any institution with which he is affiliated.

Strategic stability has been a stock in trade of discussions about nuclear issues for over half a century. Yet there has been little success in developing a consensus understanding of the concept that provides a meaningful framework for evaluating nations' force postures and plans. This chapter seeks to draw from the long debate on the meaning and nature of the term to propose a concept of strategic stability that is concrete and narrow enough to provide analytical clarity in judging nations' nuclear forces while sufficiently comprehensive to be politically meaningful. In light of the proposed definition, the chapter will analyze in particular detail the strategic posture of the United States and provide recommendations for how to modify it to conform more completely to this conception.

The Debate over Strategic Stability.

Strategic stability emerged as a concept during the Cold War as part of an effort to find a *modus vivendi* for the two hostile superpowers.[1] Its basic logic was to stabilize the bipolar confrontation by ensuring that each side had the ability to strike back effectively even after an attempted disarming first strike by its opponent. This would give each party the confidence to wait even in the event of attack by the other party, while removing the obverse temptation to strike first to gain fundamental advantage. Thus the chances of war through the fear of disarmament or through the temptation to gain an advantage by attacking first would lessen.[2]

The core of the concept was "first-strike stability," defined at the end of the Cold War by Glenn Kent and David Thaler as a situation in an adversarial context in which, "after considering the vulnerability of strategic forces on both sides, neither leader perceives the other as pressured by the posture of forces to strike first in a crisis [and n]either leader sees an advantage in striking first to avoid the potentially worse outcome of incurring a first strike if he waits."[3] In simpler terms, a situation would be stable when both parties would see that massively launching first — whether to avoid being neutered or to try to disarm one's opponent — would be either unnecessary or foolish.[4] The search for first strike stability therefore led to a focus on increasing the survivability of *both* U.S. and Soviet forces and command and control systems.[5] To this end, both sides poured tremendous resources into ensuring the survivability of their systems and, more broadly, into ensuring their ability to retaliate.

A related idea was "crisis stability," which was in the same genus as first-strike stability but focused on mitigating any pressures, including psychological ones, that would push a crisis towards spinning out of control. Supplementary to these concepts was the notion of arms race stability, the proposition that the costly and possibly deadly spiral of the arms race could be averted if each side's arms developments were manifestly designed to conform to the enduring reality of mutual vulnerability rather than as plausible attempts to gain strategic superiority.[6]

Few disputed that minimizing first-strike instability was a worthy and important goal, but differences arose as to whether first-strike stability alone would suffice to guarantee a genuinely and meaningfully stable strategic situation. Many argued that it would, seeing the prospect of nuclear retaliation and escalation, however improbable, as sufficient to deter the West's opponents, and worrying more that once the nuclear "firebreak" was breached, Armageddon would too plausibly follow.[7] They thus focused on eliminating any incentive to first nuclear use.[8] Others, however, recognized that the obviation of *any* rational purpose for using nuclear weapons first could well undermine deterrence of old fashioned non-nuclear aggression, especially since it was the West that relied on the threat to escalate to nuclear use to compensate for the Soviet and Warsaw Pact superiority in non-nuclear arms.[9] Those in this camp feared that an ambitious Moscow might doubt the West's resolve and saw the limited use of nuclear weapons as both plausibly sensible and its threat as an important deterrent. They thus concentrated on reconciling the effort to minimize pre-emptive or accidental nuclear war with a posture of discriminate nuclear use.[10] Still others rejected the notion of strategic stability entirely, seeing it as a dangerous delusion that would weaken deterrence.[11] Skeptics of the concept and the proponents of the equation of stability with eliminating incentives for first nuclear use did share one view, however — the United States could pursue strategic stability or it could pursue the capability and affirm its resolve to use nuclear weapons first, but not both.[12] Proponents of discriminate use, on the other hand, believed they could reconcile strategic stability and first use.

These debates about whether strategic stability was a useful concept and, if so, what its definition should be were, unsurprisingly, never resolved, for they turned on differential assessments of risk, the salience of rationality in crises, the aggressiveness and decisionmaking calculus of the Soviet foe, and other judgments not susceptible to definitive calculation.[13] But the Cold War experience did appear to make some important things clear, most pertinently that the U.S. role as security guarantor of key regions of the world, a guarantee underwritten by its nuclear force, stood in serious tension with the objective of removing *any* reason to resort to nuclear force, the objective implicit in a sole focus on reducing incentives for nuclear use. Indeed, the observation was not lost on threatened allies that a too perfect stability at the strategic level could and perhaps did undermine U.S. nuclear umbrella guarantees, a point made with special force by those sheltering under that umbrella, such as German Chancellor Helmut Schmidt in the late 1970s.[14] Consequently, while the U.S. Government came to embrace the pursuit of strategic stability, it consistently concluded after the late 1960s that a focus only on minimizing incentives to nuclear use would not suffice for the United States.[15] The mere prospect of a large-scale strategic attack, that in a situation of mutual assured destruction would be of only the most dubious rationality, was seen as inadequate to deter the Soviets and assure U.S. allies. Rather, the United States needed to be able to retain not only the ability but also the resolve to use nuclear weapons first in a manner that was at least minimally rational and thus discriminate.[16]

These debates, while less salient than they were in the Cold War, have not ended, and are taking on renewed importance as the U.S. margin of conventional military strength narrows in the face of the rise of China as a great power and the proliferation of nuclear arms and advanced conventional weapons.[17] More to the point, major war among the major powers remains possible. Because of this enduring possibility, one that gives no evidence of disappearing, it is important that the United States develop and adopt a conceptual framework that enables it to pursue policies to protect it and its allies' vital interests while minimizing the reasons for and chances of nuclear use. Given that the United States continues to shelter dozens of nations under its nuclear umbrella, including a number of states that have been quite insistent that Washington be prepared to use nuclear weapons on their behalf, these questions remain of the gravest import.[18]

A Definition of Strategic Stability: No Incentives for Nuclear Use Save For Vindication of Vital Interests.

In light of these developments, it is important to develop a conception of strategic stability that can both minimize the chances of major war, including nuclear war, among the great powers while also ensuring that the United States is able to fulfill its extended deterrence objectives. Such a conception should be able to provide an analytical basis for determining, in the context of relations with those states with which the United States has accepted a relationship of strategic stability, whether each nation's force posture conduces to stability.[19] Logically, nations with which the United States must accept a stability relationship are those that, even in the wake of an attempted U.S. disarming first strike, can deliver a devastating nuclear blow against the United States itself. Today and for the foreseeable future the nations that fall into this category are Russia and China.[20] That said, such a conception should also be flexible and adaptable enough to extend to additional states should the United States come to accept such a relationship with additional powers, though such an extension seems neither likely nor necessary for the time being. Moreover, substantial elements of the conception's logic should be able to apply to states with which Washington emphatically does not accept a stability relationship. For instance, even with states that Washington seeks to overpower, there should be no reason to go to nuclear war accidentally.[21]

To begin with, a worthy conception of strategic stability must incorporate the basic goods contained in the notion of first-strike stability. But first-strike stability cannot alone suffice to create genuine stability.[22] There are two reasons why first-strike stability alone is inadequate.

A thoroughgoing elimination of incentives to use nuclear weapons first would undermine the goal of deterring major war in general, since a unitary focus on ensuring that nuclear weapons are not used would, to the extent it was successful, perforce lead to a correlatively lesser degree of risk in the initiation of sub-nuclear war. If a situation were to be deemed "strategically stable" because no one would ever dream of using nuclear weapons first, then no one would need to worry about conventional conflict—especially relatively limited conventional conflict—leading to nuclear escalation. In effect, to reach a situation of strategic stability would be to undo the "nuclear revolution" and thus destabilize the sub-strategic level, since it would cordon off the deterrent effects of nuclear weapons.[23]

Second and more realistically, however, such a cordoning off could never truly succeed. But it could be perilously deceptive, actually increasing the chances not only that war would start, but also that such a war would involve the use of nuclear weapons. This is because, while a pursuit of this conception of strategic stability could never guarantee that an opponent would not use nuclear weapons first, the pretense that it could or had might well dull the potential attacker's sensitivity to the tremendous risks of crossing an adversary's red lines with non-nuclear forces.[24] A nation possessed of a too complacent view that first-strike stability had marginalized nuclear weapons could well believe that it could press an advantage and cross an opponent's red lines with non-nuclear forces, brazenly relying on the alleged stability at the strategic level to obviate the threat from the adversary's nuclear forces. This could trigger the defending party's use of nuclear weapons. For, even in a situation of first-strike stability, the threatened party could sensibly use nuclear weapons, especially if the asymmetry of stakes favored the defense, gambling—potentially reasonably because of the favorable balance of resolve for the defense and the existence of a situation of mutual vulnerability—that the other side would not reply with a total strike.

In other words, just because one nation believes in marginalizing nuclear weapons does not mean others do—in the blunter terminology of Leon Trotsky, you may not be interested in nuclear weapons, but they may be interested in you. This reality is evident in the fact that at different times both Americans and Russians have emphasized nuclear forces for deterrence of conventional aggression over the past 60 years. Nonetheless, this temptation to believe nuclear weapons can be marginalized is especially potent for Washington, which today enjoys an impressive, albeit probably declining, margin in conventional military force and has trumpeted the virtues of the tradition of nuclear nonuse.[25]

Thus, as crucial as concerns about minimizing the pressures towards pre-emption and accidental war based on an incorrect belief that an attack is in progress are, strategic stability cannot be solely about minimizing incentives to use nuclear weapons. Rather, if the concept of strategic stability is actually to contribute to a *genuine* stability between potential adversaries, it must incorporate rather than implicitly exclude the ways in which nuclear weapons deter not only massive nuclear attack, but also other forms of aggression against a nation's core interests. A useful conception of strategic stability must, then, seek to minimize or eliminate *fundamentally immaterial* or *peripheral* incentives to using nuclear weapons first, while *preserving* and even *validating* those incentives to use nuclear weapons that are essential for effective deterrence, and thus genuine stability. Such a framework must indicate not only the ways in which nuclear weapons should not be used, but also those ways in which their use would be legitimate.

In this light, strategic stability should be understood to mean a situation in which no party has an incentive to use nuclear weapons *save for vindication of its vital interests in extreme circumstances.* While one cannot define the precise nature of "vindicate,", the essence of the concept is that the only reason a nation should see sufficient reason to use nuclear weapons is in response to major aggression against its established, well-understood, and reasonably conceived vital interests.[26] Terms like "major aggression," "reasonably conceived," and "extreme circumstances" cannot be neatly defined and delineated, given the inherently shifting and contingent nature of politics, but the essence of the phrase is that nuclear weapons should only be used in dire scenarios in which a party finds itself under grave pressure from significant attacks that do not offer reasonable alternative means of redress.[27] From this standpoint, the U.S. 2010 *Nuclear Posture Review*'s confining of threatened first use to "extreme circumstances" involving itself or its allies satisfies this criterion.[28] So, too, would Russia's stated policy of narrowing its threat of first use of nuclear weapons to contingencies in which the survival of the Russian state is in jeopardy.[29]

In a strategically stable situation, then, a nation would see neither need nor incentive to use nuclear weapons *except* to make clear to an opponent that he had crossed a most vital red line with the probability that he would suffer further—and perhaps catastrophic—loss if he continued his aggression. Incorporating the important traditional conception of first strike stability and predicated on the assessment that vulnerability to some degree of nuclear retaliation is a given, fears of disarmament or decapitation on the one hand and ambitions for military advantage through a disarming strike on the other would have little to no place. Rather, in the beau ideal of this conception nuclear weapons would become essentially purely political weapons, instruments of violent signaling and a terrible indicator of the willingness to escalate to levels of gross destruction.[30] Naturally, no sharp distinction can be drawn between the domains of the "political" and the "military," but the point would be to narrow the purposes of employment of nuclear weapons down to its deterrent essence by subordinating military objectives to broader political aims.[31] The use of nuclear weapons in this fashion could—and generally speaking should—involve a military purpose, but this military purpose would be embedded in, oriented towards, and limited by broader political objectives. Such nuclear strikes would demonstrate a party's willingness to inflict grievous cost on an opponent, to threaten more such strikes, and to run the risk of general war in order to persuade him of the folly of his aggression and the necessity of terminating the conflict on grounds acceptable to the defending party.[32]

By stripping away the essentially accidental aspects of a nuclear deterrent relationship to its core of bargaining through the infliction of pain and the manipulation of fear, this conception of strategic stability would be a crystallization, a refinement to its essence, of nuclear deterrence. Nuclear weapons would, like Samuel Johnson's gallows, concentrate the minds of an opponent's leadership, ensuring that there could be no misunderstanding of the strength of one's resolve to escalate and to risk general war. Such an understanding of strategic stability would encompass the essential concerns of first-strike stability in minimizing the reasons for nuclear use, while recognizing that *some* uses of nuclear weapons must be valid for real stability to endure. *In a stable situation, then, major war would only come about because one party truly sought it, not because of miscalculation.* Given the nature of the nuclear revolution, this should make major war exceedingly unlikely.[33]

If nuclear use would only be acceptable for vindication of vital interests, though, what types of use would be appropriate? Because the point of strategically stable nuclear use would be to de-escalate a spiraling conflict on satisfactory terms, such uses would need to be limited, discriminate, and evidently restrained, designed to demonstrate both resolve and the willingness to escalate further as well as the readiness to restrain further use. The point of nuclear use under this conception of strategic stability would definitively *not* be to attempt to break out of a situation of mutual vulnerability, given such an effort's toxic combination of futility and dramatic escalatory impetus, but rather to signal to an opponent that he had transgressed a most vital interest, to demonstrate one's resolve about climbing the imperfectly controllable ladder of escalation, and to inflict pain on the opponent to attempt to dissuade him from pursuing his course of action.

Discriminate options would play a particularly important role in this conception of stability, essentially as mechanisms for insisting upon war termination. Since the effectiveness of nuclear deterrence rests ultimately on the prospect of tremendous damage that outweighs any meaningful political end, the most effective nuclear threats must connect to the credible possibility of such devastation resulting from triggering them. The essence of stabilizing nuclear use, then, is the demonstration of the willingness to begin mounting the inherently uncertain ladder of nuclear escalation towards large-scale war while also offering the opponent the chance to agree to terminate the conflict. But, since escalation to large-scale nuclear war would in almost any plausible contingency be *in se* irrational, given the yawning disjuncture between the devastation that such a war would cause and almost any cognizable political objective, the threat to resort to a large-scale nuclear strike would need to rely on the explicit or implicit threat that matters might get truly out of control and so, even despite the best intentions of the actors, escalate to a level of intolerable destruction.

In this light, discriminate and controlled nuclear capabilities would play an important role. The point of these specifically discriminate options would be to give each side the ability to impose limited but very real harm, while also increasing the number and type of discrete steps one could take between supine inaction and total nuclear attack. The availability of such intermediate steps would fortify the potency of the overall threat to escalate to total war by providing visceral, punctuated notifications that the parties were descending to catastrophe. If two adversaries are tied together next to a cliff, one's threat to take both over the precipice is almost certainly more compelling if he has pulled them perceptibly closer to the edge. Stabilizing nuclear strikes would serve as sharp demands that the adversary cease and desist—but, vitally, leave him the opportunity to back away with at least some dignity intact.

This is not to imply that such capability for discriminate attacks would need to be *equal*—quite the contrary, one side could (and, in the case of the United States, should)—profit in strategic terms from having greater flexibility in its ability to use nuclear weapons. Any limited nuclear contest would be resolved not only by the fear of escalation to general war but also by calculations as to how a more limited iterative exchange would proceed. The side with a greater variety of and more tailored options for limited nuclear use would be in a strong position in such a struggle, since his threats to strike would be both more credible and his strikes more damaging. Possessing a limited nuclear war advantage would not change the basic dynamic of bargaining with an opponent to whom one is vulnerable, but it would improve one's coercive negotiating position, which could be vital especially if the balance of resolve favored one's adversary.

Stabilizing limited nuclear strikes could, then, focus on targets linked directly to the nature of the aggression while minimizing collateral damage—for instance striking at bases clearly and directly associated with the opponent's initial attack on one's vital interests.[34] Other criteria could include: selecting targets away from national and strategic command and control and warning facilities, population centers, and strategic force bases or supporting facilities; selecting targets within a clearly defined theater of conflict or some other recognizably limited physical space; using lower-yield weapons, especially in the single kiloton range; and using a small number of nuclear weapons all delivered in a relatively short period of time.[35] While strategically stable nuclear uses would not necessarily need to inflict grievous harm, at least in the initial stages, purely demonstrative strikes would risk displaying more indecision and fear than resolve.[36] If multiple nuclear exchanges ensued, progressively more and more valuable targets could be targeted or more targets could be attacked in successive iterations. Such escalation would both inflict more harm on the adversary and also raise the risk of uncontrolled escalation, intensifying pressures for war termination.

Effective communication mechanisms would be essential to a strategically stable posture because of their essential role in ensuring the survivability of each side's forces and in enabling de-escalation of a nuclear conflict. Needless to say, it is of supreme importance that nations maintain effective command, control, and communications (C3) of and with their forces to ensure the ability to operate them deliberately and discriminately. Indeed, to the extent that each side's forces could survive and still discriminately strike back even after an enemy first strike, even though escalation would inevitably be a real and increasing possibility, limited nuclear strikes would become less likely to lead to escalation because of each side's confidence in the resilience of its forces and their command and control.[37] Of comparable importance, however, a stabilizing force posture would need to focus on communication with an opponent, both explicitly and implicitly, in order to make one's terms and actions clear and to facilitate de-escalation. In such circumstances, perceptions would be just as, if not more, important than material facts. It is therefore as important that discriminate strikes *appear* restrained to the targeted party as that they actually are limited. This could be accomplished both demonstrably through the nature of the attacks and through direct communications with the adversary. Coupling evidently limited strikes with clear and credible statements of one's restraint as well as one's terms and purposes could raise the probability that one's intent is correctly understood by an opponent and thus would aid in de-escalation.[38]

But of course such evidences of restraint would always be conditional and uncertain, for limited nuclear options would not undo the basic logic of the nuclear standoff—that escalation to a level of cataclysmic destruction would always be possible. This possibility would intensify as nuclear weapons began to be used, even in discriminate fashion, as the tradition of nuclear nonuse was breached, command and control systems came under greater strain, mobile forces reached the point at which they required replenishment and so became more vulnerable, and the effect of psychological strain upon leadership compounded. In such circumstances, no one could be confident that discriminate exchanges could go on indefinitely. But this is precisely the point of limited options. Their value lies not in any attempted deviation from the possibility of mutual devastation but rather as a terrifyingly concrete reminder of one's willingness to risk it in order to vindicate one's core interests—playing with fire would not be worth paying attention to if the fire could not get out of control. The party willing to begin to walk down such a path would, by showing the willingness to escalate further, demonstrate tremendous resolve.[39]

The distinctive essence of this understanding of strategic stability is the combination of the importance placed on restraint *and* the validation of discriminate use on behalf of a nation's vital interests, and that it sketches out the *only* circumstances in which nuclear weapons can be acceptably used rather than merely designating those situations in which they should not be. Thus, as in the classic understanding of first-strike stability, a stabilizing force posture should both be demonstrably survivable and exhibit restraint such that an opponent does not fear excessively for the effectiveness of his retaliatory capability.[40] But this conception also endorses discriminate options, options that can communicate, even in the crude language of violence, both the willingness to inflict pain, including further

61

and greater pain, and to exercise restraint if one's terms are met. Moreover, *all* parties in a stable situation must have both the assured capability to retaliate massively and the ability to conduct at least some limited strikes—thus not just the United States but also Russia and China—though by no means the *equal* ability. Not only does one want one's opponent to have confidence in the survivability of his forces, but also in his capacity for discriminate attack. One does not want his opponent to resort to a massive attack out of frustration at having no limited options as much as because he fears for the survival of his retaliatory capability. But it bears emphasizing that it is clearly in the interests of the United States to have *better* options for discriminate attack.

In all this discussion of nuclear strikes, it is essential to bear in mind the fundamental point of applying this conception of strategic stability, which would be to move all involved parties towards a stable equilibrium that protects their vital interests while reducing the chances of major war.[41] In such a situation, all sides' nuclear forces would have the potential to satisfy Hans Morgenthau's wise criterion for the purposes of arms in international politics, that adversaries can see "that their legitimate interests have nothing to fear from a restrictive and rational foreign policy and that their illegitimate interests have nothing to gain in the face of armed might rationally employed."[42]

Implications for the Future of the U.S. Strategic Posture.

Concrete and distinct implications flow from this conception of strategic stability for the U.S. strategic posture. The conception's prime dictate is that the basic capability of the U.S. strategic force as a whole to weather a first blow and to respond deliberately and devastatingly is assured—or, as nuclear submarine godfather Admiral Arleigh Burke once put it, that the United States should have "the ability, right now, to destroy any enemy that wants to attack us or does attack us, regardless of what it [the enemy] does, or when it does it, or how it does it, or anything else."[43] This capability provides the ultimate groundwork for deterrence as it gives the option to wreak destruction clearly incompatible with any gains from aggression. Needless to say, this objective has long enjoyed pride of place in U.S. force planning considerations and, as long as the United States maintains and appropriately modernizes the Triad of delivery systems with its interlocking attributes, this criterion will continue to be satisfied.[44]

Equally important is that the U.S. national command and control system (NCCS) be effective, reliable, resilient, enduring, and redundant.[45] Given a lack of attention to nuclear matters since the end of the Cold War, however, the NCCS requires considerable investment to ensure it meets these exacting standards.[46] Moreover, because of the importance of conveying one's restraint to an adversary even during conflict, the ability to communicate with the opponent, even during a conflict, is also essential to a fully stabilizing posture. National leaders initiating an avowedly limited strike must be able to make that restraint abundantly clear to an enemy through both public and private channels. Hotlines are one well-understood mechanism for this purpose.[47]

Also important, and also long the subject of concentrated focus, is the importance of minimizing the destabilizing aspects of the U.S. force, commensurate with the requirements of deterrence. The George W.

Bush administration's decision to retire the Peacekeeper intercontinental ballistic missile (ICBM) and the Barack Obama administration's decision to "de-MIRV" (multiple independently-targetable re-entry vehicles) the entire ICBM force both represent steps in this direction.[48] One factor that is not, absent perceptual considerations, relevant to strategic stability is numerical parity. So long as the two sides deploy forces sufficient in size to conduct devastating retaliatory strikes and a substantial set of limited options, it does not matter if they are equivalent in size.

Under this conception, any and all effective ballistic missile defenses would be appropriate against states falling outside of a strategic stability relationship with the United States, such as Iran and North Korea. Indeed, missile defenses would have the virtue of raising the barriers to entry for those nations seeking to compel the United States to accept such a relationship with them. With respect to those nations with which Washington does accept a stability relationship, on the other hand, missile defenses would be wholly appropriate in tactical contexts, such as for defense of conventional military bases necessary for the prosecution of military campaigns in the Western Pacific or Europe. Missile defenses' role at the strategic level with those nations, however, would be more complex. The basic reality is that, for the foreseeable future, mutual vulnerability with those states, such as Russia and China, which can develop and deploy significant numbers of the most sophisticated methods of delivery for nuclear weapons, is a fact rather than a choice. Such nations can far more easily and cost-efficiently overwhelm U.S. defenses than the United States can develop and deploy them.[49] Because of these factors and because the attempt to develop a complete missile shield against Russia or China could well impel these states to adopt less stable and thus more dangerous force postures to ensure penetration, it is inadvisable for the United States to seek to develop a comprehensive strategic missile shield against Russia or China. That said, more limited missile shields against the strategic-range forces of these states could in some circumstances be worthwhile. For instance, the United States could reasonably develop and deploy missile defenses to defend critical C3 nodes and forces important for retaliation, including limited and controlled retaliation, or, if certain technologies are favorable, to impose developmental or deployment costs on Russia and China in the interests of diverting them from spending resources on capabilities in ways less advantageous to the United States.[50]

Less characteristic of existing or planned U.S. forces, but essential for this conception of strategic stability, however, is the ability to conduct nuclear strikes that are both discriminate and manifestly so to the adversary. Today the U.S. strategic force as a whole has the capability to craft discriminate, well-planned strikes and to deliver lower-yield weapons accurately against targets selected in accordance with such a plan. This itself is a signal improvement from earlier years, as well into the 1980s the U.S. ability to plan and execute discriminate strikes was woefully limited. But the U.S. force is less capable of conducting strikes that are *both* discriminate *and* evidently limited and restrained. This is because, while the United States possesses a number of options for limited strikes, each offers some positive attributes but lacks others. The resulting effect is that any limited strike the United States could initiate today would pose risks that would be reduced if the United States enjoyed an option or options that combined more of these positive attributes.

Today, for instance, the United States can launch discriminate strikes from its *Ohio* class submarines using the very reliable and accurate Trident II D5 submarine-launched ballistic missile (SLBM) or from its ICBM fields using the comparably reliable and accurate Minuteman III ICBM. But, in light of the current force, such attacks would compel the United States to use a warhead on the order of a 100 kiloton yield (in the case of an SLBM attack) or much higher in the case of a Minuteman III strike.[51] Thus, while options using an SLBM or ICBM would boast reliability and accuracy, they would lack limitation in yield.

Alternatively, the United States could use its bomber force for discriminate attacks. According to unofficial sources, the B-2A bomber can carry the several variants of the B-61 and the B-83 gravity bombs, which together offer considerable selectivity in the yield of the weapon's detonation.[52] Moreover, because these are gravity bombs, they offer a high degree of accuracy so long as the bomber is able to penetrate air defenses to its target area. Meanwhile, the B-52H bomber does not have to penetrate enemy air defenses to launch the AGM-86B air-launched cruise missile (ALCM), which is reported to have lower yield options. Finally, the United States could use its dual-capable F-16, F-15E, or, in the future, F-35 attack aircraft to deliver gravity bombs.

Each of these elements of the bomber force poses problems, however. The increasing sophistication of air defenses, the aging of the ALCM, B-2A, F-15, and F-16 systems, and the diminishing promise of stealth technology for both veteran and new systems mean that a U.S. President could not be highly confident that he could carefully tailor a strike package and have it be delivered precisely as he ordered.[53] Yet such discrimination is precisely what is required in such a dangerously delicate endeavor. Moreover, dual-capable attack aircraft, which today and in future plans are all land-based, would in any plausible contingency have to be launched from allied territory, inevitably complicating and perhaps entirely obviating such an option.

Thus the United States today can rely on the Trident II D5 and the Minuteman III to penetrate defenses, but the higher yield of these weapons makes them less readily discernible as limited. Conversely, the United States fields bombers that can deliver lower-yield weapons, but the ability of these aircraft to penetrate defended environments is increasingly questionable. What the United States lacks is the *assured* ability to deliver a discernibly limited strike against an opponent possessed of next-generation air defense capabilities—precisely those nations against whom a limited strike would be most needed.

This lacuna could be rectified in ways that would give the United States better discriminate options, while also telegraphing restraint to those nations with which the United States recognizes a strategic stability relationship—primarily Russia and China.[54] Such a capability should give U.S. leadership the assured ability to penetrate even sophisticated air defenses and accurately and reliably deliver a lower-yield weapon to target. The assured ability to penetrate and the accuracy and reliability of the system would all contribute to the ability to control escalation by precisely tailoring the strike; the lower yield of the weapon, meanwhile, would hold the promise of communicating limitation and restraint to the adversary.

This logic points in the direction of the U.S. fielding a highly accurate method of delivery able reliably to penetrate air defense networks that can carry a low-yield nuclear warhead. The simplest, most reliable, least technically risky, and cheapest solution to this problem is to deploy a certain number of Trident II D5s on each nuclear-powered ballistic missile submarine (SSBN) with the missiles loaded with several W76 warheads, each with only the primary retained and with some additional appropriate modifications. These W76 warheads, without secondary warheads, would cause a detonation in the lower rather than the much higher yield range that would result from their employment with their secondary warheads installed, which is how they are deployed today. This would satisfy the criterion of low yield. Mounted on the extraordinarily reliable and accurate Trident II D5 SLBM, these warheads could be precisely and independently targeted across a wide distance with a high confidence of the warheads arriving at their targets, meeting the criterion of accuracy. Further, because the U.S. nuclear weapons establishment understands this technique of modifying the warheads well, the President could have high confidence that the warheads would detonate as planned, meeting the criterion of assured precision. Moreover, the President would have a variety of options in terms of the number of warheads delivered, ranging from the maximum number on a proximate SSBN or SSBNs to just a very few or one. Extraneous warheads on launched missiles could be rendered inoperative by technical means. Such steps would satisfy the criteria of discrimination and control.

Deploying W76s in this fashion would also have the advantage of being a relatively cheap option and would cause minimal disruption to the force, unlike alternatives such as deploying a new nuclear-armed sea-launched cruise missile. A nonexplosive test facility could be constructed at the Y-12 National Security Complex and the warheads themselves could be modified at the Pantex Plant. These steps would not be inexpensive or without difficulty, but they would be far cheaper and less technically risky than other possibilities involving construction of new warheads, for instance. That said, the ideal course would be to deploy warheads with a dial-a-yield function, giving the maximum degree of flexibility. If it could be done to the W76 at a reasonable cost and with minimal technical risk, this would be preferable.

In terms of operational deployment, one workable posture would be to dedicate two Trident II D5 SLBMs on each SSBN to this limited nuclear use function and to mount four modified W76s on each dedicated missile, for a total of eight warheads on each boat. This would provide an ample number of warheads for limited employment while not drawing too many SLBMs away from those assigned to general war scenarios, thus preserving the essential link to the threat of massive attack. Warheads removed from the dedicated SLBMs and still under the ceiling imposed by the New Strategic Arms Reduction Treaty (New START) meanwhile, could be loaded onto SLBMs assigned to general war missions.[55]

Needless to say, a modified W76 option would not be a perfect solution. Ideally, for instance, the United States would be able to field a limited nuclear option on a platform entirely dedicated to such use which would both be survivable and would give off distinctive signatures to an opponent that would convey that any launch from it would be a limited strike. In reality, however, such an option would be prohibitively expensive, likely operationally disruptive, and, most importantly, largely academic given the imperfect warning and ascertainment capabilities of Russia and China. Moreover, it is not at all clear that either Moscow or Beijing would care to any significant degree about the launching point and characteristics of a limited strike when weighed against the strike's target and destructiveness.

Other methods for making the U.S. nuclear force more compatible with this conception of strategic stability are possible. Similar steps could be taken with the W78 on a selection of Minuteman IIIs. Modifying Trident II D5s would be preferable, however, as the Minuteman III has a much less elastic range of flight trajectories, many of which would cause significant overflight problems under a variety of contingencies. A better option is to develop and procure a follow-on penetrating ALCM with a lower-yield capability. This would allow the air-breathing leg of the Triad to continue to contribute to the limited and discriminate strike mission. Fortunately, a follow-on ALCM is already programmed in the defense budget and is, separate from considerations of limited options, important for the long-term viability of the Triad and thus should be procured anyway.[56]

Conclusion.

Does all this matter, though? Many would argue that perhaps in the old world of the bipolar nuclear standoff such "theological" disquisitions had their proper role, but that in today's world they have become anachronistic. The great nuclear nations—the United States, Russia, and China—hardly seem primed to go to war and, in any case, they are all led by reasonably sensible leadership sensitive to the terrible risks of large-scale conflict among them. Perhaps, then, it would be enough to stick with a conception of strategic stability aimed simply at avoiding war, especially nuclear war, or one focused solely on eliminating incentives to nuclear use. In such a world, discriminate options would be not only unnecessary, but might be positively harmful in exhibiting an imperfect commitment to a more peaceful order.

Such sanguinity would be ill-advised, however. It is true that today, fortunately, great power war seems exceedingly unlikely. But this could well change in the future, especially as the global power structure of the last 20 years, founded on a U.S. military and economic ascendancy, comes under increasing strain, and as the memories of the terrors of the world wars and the nuclear fears of the Cold War fade. More concretely, the rise of China will place considerable pressure on the security environment of East and Southeast Asia. Unless Beijing's ascendance proves to be extraordinarily pacific, the United States and its allies in the region must expect China to seek increasing influence over this most vital part of the globe. Even if such a dynamic is managed skillfully and peacefully, it will almost certainly result in a strategic rivalry between Washington and Beijing, one in which war will be possible. Moreover, as China's economy grows and its military power continues to expand and improve in quality, so too will the dominance of the U.S. military over the waters of the Pacific Ocean come under increasing challenge, making it more plausible that the United States could face a contingency in which it believed it needed to use nuclear weapons first to defend its interests. Indeed, in key respects we may already be beginning to find ourselves in such a situation.[57] The dangers associated with a weakened and resentful but revanchist Russia that has increasingly relied on its nuclear forces in its security posture also loom over an increasingly fractured and discontented Europe. It is therefore essential that the United States adopt an understanding of strategic stability that can both support the defense of American interests and minimize the chances of war and especially of nuclear war between the great powers, and that Washington develop and deploy strategic forces that comport with such an understanding. This is the only prudent course in a world in which major war remains ever-possible.

ENDNOTES - CHAPTER 2

1. See Michael Gerson's chapter in this volume for a history of the concept. See also David S. Yost, *Strategic Stability in the Cold War: Lessons for Continuing Challenges*, Paris, France: French Institute of International Relations (IFRI) Security Studies Center, Winter 2011.

2. For an analysis of the concept, see Thomas C. Schelling, *Arms and Influence*, New Haven, CT: Yale University Press, 1966, Chap. 6, p. 246. As Schelling described it, "If both sides have weapons that need not go first to avoid their own destruction, so that neither side can gain great advantage in jumping the gun and each is aware that the other cannot, it will be a good deal harder to get a war started. Both sides can afford the rule: When in doubt, wait."

3. Glenn A. Kent, and David E. Thaler, *First-Strike Stability: A Methodology for Evaluating Strategic Forces*, R-3765-AF, Santa Monica, CA: RAND Corporation, 1989, p. v.

4. As Schelling put it, "[t]he balance is stable only when neither, in striking first, can destroy the other's ability to strike back." Thomas C. Schelling, *The Strategy of Conflict*, Cambridge, MA: Harvard University Press, 1960, p. 232. See also Schelling, *Arms and Influence*, p. 229.

5. Disturbingly, it has emerged that the Soviets feared a decapitating strike from this suite of systems sufficiently to deploy a so-called "Dead Hand" system, a semi-automated message sys-

tem to launch a nuclear counterattack in the event of a loss of contact with designated leadership, to ensure that no American attack would go unanswered. David E. Hoffman, *The Dead Hand: The Untold Story of the Cold War Arms Race and its Dangerous Legacy.* New York: Doubleday, 2009, pp. 23-24, 60 *et seq.*

6. See, for instance, Thomas C. Schelling and Morton H. Halperin, *Strategy and Arms Control*, New York: The Twentieth Century Fund, 1961, esp. Chap. 3.

7. For arguments for a no first use of nuclear weapons policy from the 1980s, see John D. Steinbrunner and Leon V. Sigal, eds., *Alliance Security: NATO and the No-First-Use Question*, Washington, DC: The Brookings Institution, 1983; Robert S. McNamara, "The Military Role of Nuclear Weapons: Perceptions and Misperceptions," *Foreign Affairs*, Vol. 62, No. 1, Fall 1983, pp. 59-80; and "No First Use: A Report by the Union of Concerned Scientists," Cambridge, MA, 1983. For the strongest recent argument for a no first use policy for the United States, see Michael S. Gerson, "No First Use: The Next Step for U.S. Nuclear Policy," *International Security*, Vol. 35, No. 2, Fall 2010, pp. 7-47.

8. See, for instance, McGeorge Bundy, George F. Kennan, Robert S. McNamara, and Gerard Smith, "Nuclear Weapons and the Atlantic Alliance," *Foreign Affairs*, Vol. 60, No. 4, Spring 1982, pp. 753-768.

9. This quandary, that too much safety at the nuclear level could make war more "calculable" at the sub-nuclear level, was termed the "stability-instability paradox." The concept is usually cited to Glenn Snyder, "The Balance of Power and the Balance of Terror," in Paul Seabury, ed., *The Balance of Power*, San Francisco, CA: Chandler, 1965. Robert Jervis gave it further analysis in Robert Jervis, *The Illogic of American Nuclear Strategy.* Ithaca, NY: Cornell University Press, 1984, pp. 31-33.

10. See, for instance, Secretary of Defense James R. Schlesinger, *Annual Defense Department Report for FY1975*, Washington, DC: Government Printing Office, 1974.

11. See Colin Gray and C. Dale Walton's essay in this volume, as well as Gray's classic statement in "Nuclear Strategy: The Case

for a Theory of Victory," *International Security*, Vol. 4, No. 1, Summer 1979, pp. 58-61, 82-87. For a more recent detailed elaboration, see Payne's *The Great American Gamble: Deterrence Theory and Practice From the Cold War to the Twenty-First Century*, Fairfax, VA: National Institute Press, 2008, esp. Chap. 3.

12. See, on one side, Herbert Scoville, "Flexible Madness," *Foreign Policy*, Vol. 14, Spring 1974. For the other side, see Gray, "Nuclear Strategy," p. 86; and Payne, *The Great American Gamble*, Chaps. 8-9, esp. p. 425.

13. A particular point of contention during the Cold War was between those who argued for the essentially cautious decision-making calculus of the Soviet Union as against those who argued that the Union of Soviet Socialist Republics (USSR) was inherently aggressive and dedicated to a warfighting nuclear posture. See, for instance, Robert Osgood *et al.*, eds., *Containment, Soviet Behavior, and Grand Strategy*, Berkeley, CA: University of California: Institute of International Studies, 1982.

14. Chancellor Helmut Schmidt, 1977 Alastair Buchan Memorial Lecture, October 28, 1977, available in *Survival*, Vol. 20, No. 1, January/February 1978, pp. 2-10. See also Henry Kissinger, "The Future of NATO," in Kenneth A. Myers, ed., *NATO — The Next Thirty Years: The Changing Political, Economic, and Military Setting*, Boulder, CO: Westview Press, 1980, pp. 3-14.

15. Although the actual strategic balance during these years only approximated these qualities, the objective did receive official imprimatur from both superpowers in the START Treaty of 1991. See Message of President George H. W. Bush to the Senate, transmitting the START Treaty for the advice and consent of the Senate to ratification, July 31, 1991. Unsurprisingly, given the differences between U.S. and Soviet views as well as within the United States on the nature of "strategic stability," the term was not defined in the otherwise exhaustive START proceedings. But the Treaty did privilege so-called "stabilizing" — that is, survivable — systems and penalized those that were "destabilizing" — that is, vulnerable and especially those that were both vulnerable and ill-suited for any mission other than holding at risk the strategic forces of the opponent. For a discussion of these issues, see Kerry M. Kartchner, *Negotiating START: Strategic Arms Reduc-*

tion Talks and the Quest for Strategic Stability New Brunswick, NJ: Transaction Publishers, 1992. See also the influential Report of the President's Commission on Strategic Forces, April 1983, p. 3. This latter document helped set the course for the U.S. land-based strategic force and the Ronald Reagan administration's arms control negotiating positions.

16. For more on this topic, see Elbridge A. Colby, "The United States and Discriminate Nuclear Options in the Cold War," in Jeffrey A. Larsen and Kerry M. Kartcher, eds., *Limited Nuclear War in the 21st Century*, forthcoming.

17. The thorough analysis of the Center for Strategic Budgetary Assessments provides abundant support for the proposition that the margin of U.S. conventional advantage is narrowing. See, for instance, Andrew F. Krepinevich, Jr. *et al., Strategy for the Long Haul: The Challenges to U.S. National Security.* Washington, DC: Center for Strategic and Budgetary Assessments, 2008; and Andrew F. Krepinevich, Jr., "The Pentagon's Wasting Assets: The Eroding Foundations of American Power," *Foreign Affairs*, Vol. 88, No. 4, July/August 2009, pp. 18-33. As Krepinevich put it in the *Foreign Affairs* article:

> The military foundations of the United States' global dominance are eroding. . . . The diffusion of advanced military technologies, combined with the rise of new powers, such as China, and hostile states, such as Iran, will make it progressively more expensive in blood and treasure—perhaps prohibitively expensive—for U.S. forces to carry out their missions in areas of vital interest.

See also Paul K. Davis and Peter A. Wilson, *Looming Discontinuities in U.S. Military Strategy and Defense Planning: Colliding RMAs Necessitate a New Defense Strategy*, Santa Monica, CA: RAND Corporation, 2011.

18. See, for instance, Richard Halloran, "Nuclear Umbrella," *Realclearpolitics.com*, June 21, 2009, available from *www.realclearpolitics.com/articles/2009/06/21/nuclear_umbrella_97104.html*; Richard Halloran, "Doubts Grow in Japan Over U.S. Nuclear Umbrella," *Taipei Times*, May 27, 2009, p. 9; and Indira A. R. Lakshmanan, "Iran Might Be Deterred by U.S. Nuclear Umbrella, Gulf

Ally Says," *Bloomberg News*, April 9, 2009, available from *www.bloomberg.com/apps/news?pid=newsarchive&sid=aOSbraDk5bvI*.

19. U.S. Department of Defense, *Nuclear Posture Review Report*, Washington, DC: U.S. Department of Defense, April 2010, pp. x-xi. While Washington has accepted a relationship of strategic stability with Moscow and Beijing, it has definitively not accepted such a relationship, implying an acceptance of vulnerability, with any other states.

20. U.S. Department of Defense, *Nuclear Posture Review Report*, Washington, DC: U.S. Department of Defense, April 2010, pp. x-xi. While some dispute that the United States finds itself in a situation of mutual vulnerability with China, the Council on Foreign Relations Task Force on U.S. nuclear weapons policy spoke for the majority of observers in "conclud[ing] that mutual vulnerability with China — like mutual vulnerability with Russia — is not a policy choice to be embraced or rejected, but rather a fact to be managed with priority on strategic stability." Council on Foreign Relations Independent Task Force Report, *U.S. Nuclear Weapons Policy*, William J. Perry and Brent J. Scowcroft, co-chairs, New York: Council on Foreign Relations, 2009, p. 45.

21. The question of which elements of this concept of strategic stability should apply to states with which the United States does not accept a relationship of strategic stability, such as Iran and North Korea, is an important and highly complex issue which is beyond the parameters of this chapter. The fact that this conception of stability applies only to the great powers should not, however, be seen as a major defect. Maintaining both deterrence against and peace with the other great powers must be the primary objective of U.S. foreign policy, in light of the persisting possibility of great war, as only these nations can wreak truly cataclysmic damage on the United States.

22. For a recent defense of a more narrow conception of strategic stability, see James M. Acton's chapter in this volume as well as his *Deterrence During Disarmament: Deep Nuclear Reductions and International Security*, London, UK: International Institute of Strategic Studies, 2011, pp. 15-21.

23. Some argue that this is to the benefit of the United States because of current U.S. conventional force advantages. As U.S. conventional superiority diminishes, however, this argument will lose its appeal. For the classic discussion of the "nuclear revolution," see Robert Jervis, *The Meaning of the Nuclear Revolution: Statecraft and the Prospect of Armageddon*, Ithaca, NY: Cornell University Press, 1989.

24. The enormous focus on a nuclear "taboo" could be a species of this.

25. *Nuclear Posture Review Report*, p. v.

26. The word "vindicate" has a particular suitability in this context, for it has multiple meanings each of which is an object or method of nuclear deterrence: to punish or avenge; to see free or deliver (as from bondage); to assert one's interest by means of action; and to defend against encroachment or interference. See "vindicate," *The Compact Oxford English Dictionary*, 2nd Ed., Oxford, UK: Clarendon Press, 1998, p. 2237.

27. Ambiguity is useful in such contexts because it allows the establishment of principles by which to judge in circumstances that can rarely be precisely anticipated in advance.

28. *Nuclear Posture Review Report*, p. ix. "Extreme circumstances" is preferable to "last resort" because the former does not connote that nuclear weapons would only be used after all other options had been exhausted. This temporal requirement could give an opponent the impression that he could climb the ladder of escalation but get off before all other options had been exhausted. The point is that nuclear weapons would only be used in the gravest situations. Additionally, any conception of vital interests must encompass those of a nation's established allies in order to meet legitimate U.S. criteria for its extended deterrence obligations as well as broader nonproliferation objectives linked to the maintenance of those obligations.

29. See "The Military Doctrine of the Russian Federation, available from *carnegieendowment.org/files/2010russia_military_ doctrine.pdf*, and specifically: "The Russian Federation reserves the right to utilize nuclear weapons . . . in the event of aggression

against the Russian Federation involving the use of conventional weapons when the very existence of the state is under threat."

30. For the classic description of this conception of nuclear deterrence, see Schelling, *Arms and Influence*, especially pp. 201-204.

31. Lawrence Freedman provided a pithy summation of this point of view: "The essence of the strategy that emerged was that any use or threat of use of nuclear weapons should be seen as a supremely political act, reducing the potential relevance of purely military considerations." Lawrence Freedman, *The Evolution of Nuclear Strategy*. New York: St. Martin's Press, 1983, p. 176. For the classic statement on the impossibility of severing the political from the military, see Carl von Clausewitz, *On War*, Michael Howard and Peter Paret, eds. and trans., New York: New Everyman's Library, 1993, pp. 98-100.

32. Schelling, *The Strategy of Conflict*, Chap. 8.

33. This was the conception of the eminent nuclear theorist and policymaker Michael Quinlan, who argued that the purpose of nuclear use would be "to defend us not by disarming the foe, as in past times, but by persuading him that he has miscalculated the risk and our resolve." Tanya Ogilvie-White, *On Nuclear Deterrence: The Correspondence of Sir Michael Quinlan*, London, UK: International Institute of Strategic Studies, 2011. I am indebted to Walter Slocombe for this reference.

34. Limited nuclear strikes could also be used to affect the conventional balance during a conflict. During the Cold War, U.S. limited nuclear strikes were planned to delay or retard Soviet and Warsaw Pact aggression against Western Europe. This is a conceptually distinct objective the pursuit of which could add to escalatory pressures. In certain circumstances, however, such risks may be worthwhile or even necessary, as for the United States and the North Atlantic Treaty Organization (NATO) during the Cold War. This question, however, is inherently context-specific. For more on this point, see Colby, "The United States and Discriminate Nuclear Options in the Cold War."

35. Other but lesser possibilities include launching weapons from delivery systems known to the adversary not to be associ-

ated with the mission of large-scale nuclear attack and launching weapons from delivery systems within or near to a theater of conflict rather than the United States itself. Needless to say, the nature of the target and the scale of destructiveness are orders of magnitude more important than the characteristics of the launch.

36. Whether to inflict harm should be a purely instrumental consideration under this conception. If it were possible to achieve one's purposes without inflicting damage but simply by making a harmless demonstrative detonation, this would surely be the best course for both moral and prudential reasons. Unfortunately, such a course might not work and, some argue, might actually convey a lack of resolve or even weakness in certain contingencies. During the Richard Nixon administration, Henry Kissinger, for instance, dismissed a Joint Chiefs of Staff contingency plan for a nuclear response to a Soviet attack on Iran that called for using three nuclear weapons, remarking that Moscow would think the U.S. President was "chicken" if he used so few weapons. Fred Kaplan, *The Wizards of Armageddon*, New York: Simon and Schuster, 1983, p. 371. In today's context, this concern seems grossly overstated; any use of nuclear weapons would convey a tremendous message.

37. "[If] there is never any incentive to do quickly what might be done slowly, or to jump to conclusions, limited nuclear reprisals become a good deal less immediately dangerous." Thomas C. Schelling, "Comment," in K. Knorr and T. Read, eds., *Limited Strategic War*, New York: Frederick A. Praeger, 1962, p. 251. The collection as a whole offers a very useful selection of reflections on the nature of limited strategic war by some of nuclear strategy's most eminent analysts, such as Schelling, Herman Kahn, and Klaus Knorr. For a skeptical view of the prospects of controlling escalation, see Desmond Ball, *Can Nuclear War Be Controlled?* London, UK: International Institute for Strategic Studies, 1981.

38. This chapter does not discuss the fraught political implications of this approach. In summary, however, this approach implies the forbearance of absolute victory as an objective, since an opponent would need to find a dignified way out of his predicament. Just as violence would need to be kept limited, so war objectives would also necessarily need to be kept limited. For a similar view, see U.S. Department of Defense, *Deterrence Joint Operating Concept*, Version 2.0, December 2006, p. 24.

39. For like-minded discussions of the problems of nuclear war termination, see George H. Quester, "War Termination and Nuclear Targeting Strategy," Desmond Ball and Jeffrey Richelson, eds., *Strategic Nuclear Targeting*, Ithaca, NY: Cornell University Press, 1986, pp. 285-306; George H. Quester, "The Difficult Logic of Terminating a Nuclear War" and Leon Sloss and Paolo Stoppa-Liebl, "Objectives and Problems of War Termination," in Stephen Cimbala, ed., *Strategic War Termination*, Washington, DC: Praeger, 1986, pp. 53-74, 99-119; and Leon Sloss, "Flexible Targeting, Escalation Control, and U.S. Options," in Stephen J. Cimbala and Joseph D. Douglass, Jr., eds., *Ending a Nuclear War: Are the Superpowers Prepared?* Washington, DC: Pergamon-Brassey's, 1988, pp. 1-9.

40. It is important to note that some degree of fear on the part of an opponent is fully compatible with, if not indeed necessary, under this conception of strategic stability. For deterrence to be effective, an opposing leadership must ultimately fear for its own lives or the existence of whatever else it values. Without such fear, deterrence would be greatly weakened. That said, there is no advantage, under this conception, of making that deterrent threat *quick* rather than simply *sure*. Allowing an opponent the time to decide on his course but assuring him that he definitively will suffer if he chooses against one's interests would be the ideal course of action, but of course the factors of certainty and time cannot be so neatly separated in practice.

41. It is also worth noting that, while a multipolar relationship would surely complicate strategic stability, there is no logical reason why it should not be capable of being stable. As long as a state's nuclear forces are sufficiently developed, properly deployed and controlled, and adequately numerous, their effectiveness as deterrents should not diminish because it is applied to more than one potential opponent. The United States adequately deters both Russia and China, for instance. For a somewhat extreme version of the argument that nuclear multipolarity is not necessarily unstable, see Kenneth W. Waltz, *The Spread of Nuclear Weapons: More May Be Better*, Adelphi Paper 171, London, UK: International Institute of Strategic Studies, 1981.

42. Hans J. Morgenthau, "Another 'Great Debate': The National Interest of the United States," *American Political Science Review*, Vol. 46, 1952, p. 978.

43. Quoted in Desmond Ball, *Politics and Force Levels: The Strategic Missile Program of the Kennedy Administration*, Berkeley, CA: University of California Press, 1980, p. 12.

44. Unfortunately, in light of fiscal and disarmament pressures, the maintenance and modernization of the Triad cannot now be taken for granted. Although President Obama affirmed his commitment to modernizing all three legs of the Triad in connection with gaining the Senate's advice and consent to ratification of the New Strategic Arms Reduction Treaty (New START), there are consistent reports that influential members of the Obama administration and in Congress have pushed for a dyad. For President Obama's commitment to modernizing the Triad, see Message of President Barack H. Obama to the U.S. Senate on the New START Treaty, February 2, 2011, available from *www.whitehouse.gov/the-press-office/2011/02/02/message-president-new-start-treaty-0*. For suggestions that the administration might consider a dyad of delivery platforms, see "Pursuing the Prague Agenda: An Interview with White House Coordinator Gary Samore," Arms Control Association, April 2011, available from *www.armscontrol.org/print/4898*.

45. See, for instance, A.B. Carter *et al.*, eds., *Managing Nuclear Operations*, Washington, DC: Brookings Institution, 1987, including the chapter "Continuing Control as a Requirement for Deterring" by Albert Wohlstetter and Richard Brody, pp. 142-196.

46. For a warning of deficiencies in this field, see Defense Science Board Task Force on the Survivability of Systems and Assets to Electromagnetic Pulse and other Nuclear Weapons Effects, Summary Report No. 1, Interim Report, August 5, 2011. Some efforts are being taken in this direction. See *Nuclear Posture Review Report*, p. 26.

47. See, for instance, the "Hot Line" agreement between the United States and the USSR (subsequently expanded and modernized) in U.S. Arms Control and Disarmament Agency, *Arms Control and Disarmament Agreements: Texts and Histories of the Negotiations*. Washington, DC: Government Printing Office, 1996, p. 21.

48. For the Bush administration's decision to eliminate the Peacekeeper intercontinental ballistic missile (ICBM), see "Special Briefing on the Nuclear Posture Review" by Assistant Secretary of Defense J. D. Crouch, January 9, 2002, available from *www.defense. gov/transcripts/transcript.aspx?transcriptid=1108*. For the Obama administration's decision, see *Nuclear Posture Review Report*, p. 23.

49. As former Secretary of Defense James Schlesinger pointed out in connection with the ratification of the New START Treaty in 2010, "And so, in dealing with the major powers, China and Russia, we must be careful, I think, not to convey to them that we are threatening their retaliatory capability. . . . It's not because we would not like to have an impenetrable defense, as President Reagan had hoped for. It's just beyond our capability. They can always beat us with the offensive capabilities." United States Senate, *The New START Treaty: Hearings before the Committee on Foreign Relations*. S. HRG. 111-738, April 29, 2010, p. 25.

50. Thus, in a similar vein, formidable U.S. anti-submarine warfare capabilities compel other nations to invest far greater resources to ensure the effectiveness of their ballistic missile submarine programs, potentially taking funds away from investment in, for instance, conventional ballistic missile or cyber programs.

51. For the 100 kiloton (kt) yield figure, see Amy F. Woolf, *U.S. Strategic Nuclear Forces: Background, Developments, and Issues*, Washington, DC: Congressional Research Service, July 14, 2009, p. 17. Unless otherwise specified, all information on warhead types is by necessity drawn from unofficial sources and so of imperfect reliability.

52. For official acknowledgment of the varying yields offered by the B-61 variants, see *Nuclear Weapons: DOD and NNSA Need to Better Manage Scope of Future Refurbishments and Risks to Maintaining U.S. Commitments to NATO*, Washington, DC: Government Accountability Office, May 2011, p. 11.

53. For a measured discussion of the diminishing promise of stealth, see Barry Watts, *The Maturing Revolution in Military Affairs*. Washington, DC: Center for Strategic and Budgetary Assessments, 2011, Chapter 7. For a discussion of "tailoring" deterrence, see M. Elaine Bunn, *Can Deterrence Be Tailored?* Washington, DC: Institute for National Strategic Studies, 2007.

54. *Nuclear Posture Review Report,* p. x.

55. The author is indebted to the ever generous Ambassador Linton Brooks for the suggestion to use a modified W76.

56. See *comptroller.defense.gov/execution/reprogramming/fy2011/ prior1415s/11-11_PA_February_2011_Request.pdf.* For the author's argument for the Triad, see Elbridge A. Colby and Thomas C. Moore, "Maintaining the Triad," *Armed Forces Journal,* December 2010, pp. 28-29.

57. See, for instance, Admiral Dennis C. Blair, USN (Ret.), "Nuclear Deterrence and War Plans," in Taylor Bolz, ed., *In the Eyes of the Experts: Analysis and Comments on America's Strategic Posture: Selected Contributions by the Experts of the Congressional Commission on the Strategic Posture of the United States,* Washington, DC: U.S. Institute of Peace Press, 2009, p. 55.

CHAPTER 3

THE GEOPOLITICS OF STRATEGIC STABILITY: LOOKING BEYOND COLD WARRIORS AND NUCLEAR WEAPONS

C. Dale Walton
Colin S. Gray

"Strategic stability" is a much-used, but under-analyzed, term. Before launching into any discussion of strategic stability in this century, it is necessary first to ask what we actually *mean* by strategic stability. Game theorists endeavor to define the phrase in very precise mathematical terms, but even among these specialists there is no settled agreement on its proper definition.[1] In policy debates, meanwhile, the term is used very loosely to describe anything from rough parity in the sizes of nuclear arsenals to the perceived unlikelihood of an acute political crisis.

The argument herein will hinge on the distinction between what will be called "weapons-oriented" and "holistic" conceptions of strategic stability. The former is flawed because of its narrowness, but the latter may play a useful role in policy debate. While the material military balance may be an important — sometimes even the most important — factor in keeping the peace between two particular states, *context is sovereign.* It is only when one considers weaponry in its broader political context that one can assess its role in maintaining stability accurately.

WEAPONS AND STRATEGIC STABILITY

Weapons-oriented analyses of strategic stability focus on how fluctuations in the balance of military power may impact the likelihood of war. In particular, issues such as the increase or decrease in the number of nuclear weapons and their delivery systems, the potential vulnerability of nuclear forces, appropriate basing modes and doctrine, and the deployment (or nondeployment) and character of anti-ballistic missile (ABM) systems, have tended to be at the center of debate. This was particularly characteristic of the Cold War era, when most of the strategic literature concentrated obsessively on U.S.-Soviet competition in the nuclear realm.[2] Given the Cold War political context, one of the authors of this chapter noted over 30 years ago that "discussion of stability and its possible requirements is, in fact, a discussion of deterrence theory, which in reality is a debate about the operational merits of different postures and doctrines. No useful, objective, doctrine-neutral exploration of the idea of stability is possible."[3] The U.S. debate over stability — regardless of whether "arms-race," "crisis," or "strategic" was the chosen modifying adjective — was, at its core, an argument about how to "do" nuclear deterrence successfully.

The then-prevailing focus on nuclear armament was understandable, but overly restricted. To be sure, both superpowers focused acutely on the quality and quantity of their arsenals. However, it should be remembered that the Soviet-American relationship never was *defined* by nuclear weapons — the latter were merely tools that each superpower, profoundly mistrustful of its peer, accumulated in great quantity. The deeper reasons for the mistrust were ideological, historical, and geopolitical in character: nuclear weapons did not cause the Cold War any more than tanks and aircraft carriers caused World War II. Each of the superpowers simply put together what it considered a sensible military toolkit for the deterrence, and if necessary fighting, of a world war. Given the destructive power of nuclear weapons, it was entirely understandable that they would stand out from supposedly "normal" conventional weapons. However, the concept of deterrence itself was not new — to modify and adapt Clausewitz, nuclear weapons changed the grammar of deterrence, not its character.[4]

Discussions of arsenal survivability, equality/parity of arsenals, and strategic stability were inherently entangled during the Cold War. However, as the struggle unfolded there was a subtle shift in how the United States discussed strategic stability. After the brief period of U.S. nuclear monopoly ended and as it became increasingly clear that the Soviet Union was intent on producing a sizable nuclear arsenal of its own, particular emphasis was placed on arsenal survivability, with the possibility of a Soviet surprise attack being a paramount concern.[5] However, as time passed, the U.S. arsenal became both larger and more technologically sophisticated (including, notably, ongoing improvements in command, control, and communications systems and in the accuracy of submarine-launched ballistic missiles), and concern that the United States would be unable to respond effectively to a first strike receded. At the same time, the increasing size and sophistication of the Soviet arsenal made it ever-clearer to Washington that a nuclear first strike on the Union of Soviet Socialist Republics (USSR) would be risky in the most extreme sense of the word.

The dynamic that dampened fears about survivability — the increase in the size and sophistication of nuclear arsenals — also had the effect of heightening concern that the purported nuclear arms race itself lessened strategic stability,[6] undermining efforts to build trust between the superpowers and encouraging a confrontational mindset on the part of U.S. and Soviet leaders. Interest in bilateral arms control increased: if uncontrolled nuclear competition seemed to be dangerous, it seemed to follow logically that limitations on the number and quality of nuclear arms would enhance strategic stability.

When the Strategic Arms Limitation Talks (SALT) negotiations opened in 1969, the United States still maintained a clear advantage in the number of warheads deliverable at intercontinental range; Moscow, however, clearly was not willing to accept ongoing perceived inferiority in nuclear armaments. In this regard, the political-strategic logic of the process SALT negotiations was quite different from, say, the multilateral naval arms control process of the 1920s. The surrender of existing superiority might appear to make bilateral negotiations unattractive from an American perspective, and some hawkish policymakers resisted the realization of the SALT process. However, arms control proponents could argue, not unreasonably, that Moscow had a massive ongoing missile-building program and that, unless Washington either negotiated arms limits or greatly increased its own spending in this area, a Soviet Union, unencumbered by treaty, eventually might overtake the United States and establish nuclear superiority. Moreover, equality could be framed as an essential component of stability: if, despite efforts to build U.S.-Soviet trust through negotiation, a major crisis did occur, rough parity in overall nuclear capabilities might encourage restraint on both sides, as neither party would enjoy a significant advantage. This would underline the apparent inescapability of mutual assured destruction (MAD), and thus discourage the outbreak of war.

The association of nuclear equality with stability in the U.S.-Russian relationship did not dissolve with the end of the Cold War. Indeed, two Strategic Arms Reduction Treaties (START I and II) were signed in the early 1990s, and both were predicated on the assumption that the United States and Russia would endeavor to maintain approximate parity in their strategic arsenals. In the 2000s, the George W. Bush administration came into office intending to sever the "numerical equality-strategic stability" link, but it soon signed the Strategic Offensive Reductions Treaty (SORT) — and, overall , SORT was not radically dissimilar from earlier nuclear arms control treaties.[7] In the Barack Obama years, the previous administration's modest deviation from arms control orthodoxy essentially was abandoned, as demonstrated by the text of the 2010 New Strategic Arms Reduction Treaty (New START).[8]

When considering the development U.S.-Soviet/Russian arms control over the years from circa 1969 to the present, its most striking quality is its continuity. This is despite the fact that in the middle portion of this history, the fundamental character of the Washington-Moscow relationship changed as the Soviet empire in East-Central Europe, and then the USSR itself, collapsed. What had previously been an ideologically-driven competition between (at least seeming) peers had transformed into something entirely different. The cutthroat competition for global mastery had ended definitively.

These epic events allowed for an ironic reversal in the logic of Cold War arms control: now that American and Russian leaders both considered a central nuclear war very unlikely, agreement on truly drastic cuts in arsenals became possible. Rather than arms control shoring up a seemingly fragile peace, a peace that was seemed robust enabled more arms control. This underscores the limitations inherent in a militarily-focused,and, in the Cold War case, even more narrowly strategic nuclear-focused, vision of strategic stability. In some circumstances, the military balance may be a critical factor in specific decisions regarding war and peace, a theme explored below in greater detail. However, strategic stability is not only, or usually even primarily, a function of potential foes balancing the military component of national power. Rather, strategic stability reflects the overall condition of the international system — *and it can be very difficult to judge systemic stability accurately*. In 1988, the overwhelming majority of observers did not anticipate massive political instability in East-Central Europe in the following year; however, in autumn 1989 the fact that the strategic environment was profoundly unstable was obvious, given that momentous political changes were ongoing and the Soviet reaction to those changes was not safely predictable. Yet, of course, the U.S.-Soviet nuclear balance had not changed to any significant degree between 1988 and 1989.

This does not mean that decisions about the size and composition of nuclear arsenals, and the doctrine for nuclear use, inherently are trivial. Indeed, in certain political circumstances, the lives of tens, even hundreds, of millions may be placed at great risk if nuclear strategy is designed poorly. The Cold War era U.S. policymaking establishment's careful attention to issues about nuclear weapons was entirely warranted, regardless of whether the prevailing judgment of the efficacy of bilateral arms control as an instrument for the maintenance of peace was flawed. However, in shaping the future discussion of strategic stability, one should keep in mind the deficiencies in a weapons-oriented vision of strategic stability. It is possible for the international system to be reasonably stable even when the military power of the leading polities is not particularly well-balanced; conversely, it is possible for the international system to be deeply unstable even when great powers (or alliances of great powers) appear closely matched militarily. The factors that determine whether war or peace will prevail are myriad, and an undue focus on weaponry sometimes may distract attention from more critical considerations.

In the 2 decades between 1969 and 1989, precise calculation of the minutia of nuclear arms control was the focus of obsessive attention. In retrospect, though, it appears unlikely that the throw-weight of SS-19 missiles or even the number of *Ohio*-class submarines deployed determined whether a Third World War occurred. Instead, whether peace prevailed probably was more an issue of the personality and values of individual leaders (most critically, Mikhail Gorbachev),[9] caution and generally sound judgment on the part of the George H. W. Bush administration, and simple good fortune. That combination worked well enough, but it is disconcerting to consider how, in contrast to massive effort devoted to arms control, relatively little intellectual energy occurred before 1989 to considering how best to ensure that the Soviet Union would not lash out militarily if its satellite empire began to collapse. Hopefully, in the years preceding the next great crisis in the international system, the United

States will have a clearer vision of likely forthcoming events, and already have developed a sophisticated, well-considered strategy for how to cope with them; after all, good luck is an occasional occurrence, not the foundation stone of grand strategy.

The United States is in need of a holistic conception of strategic stability in which calculations of relative military power are *only one component* in the overall strategic picture, and not necessarily the most important one. Military power is only one of the many factors that comprise a state's overall power, but which of those factors are key to strategic stability will vary according to political circumstances. Furthermore, when considering calculations of stability in the future, it is vital that we consider the strategic complications that accompany multipolarity.

A HOLISTIC VIEW OF STRATEGIC STABILITY AND INSTABILITY

If a narrow focus on military power does not provide a satisfactory lens for addressing strategic stability, and constricted attention to nuclear arsenals in particular is excessively narrow, one is left with two general possibilities. The first is that strategic stability is so fundamentally flawed an idea that it should be discarded altogether. Given the difficulty in defining and assessing stability, it is tempting to do so. However, this chapter argues for a second possibility: that strategic stability is a concept that can be rescued, if it is used with an awareness of its problems and limitations.

Indeed, whatever its flaws, strategic stability is a necessary phrase insofar as it expresses something that is vital to the study of strategy: the notion that relationships among particular states vary over time, and there may be points in their relationship when war is a very real prospect. Moreover, there are periods when the international system as a whole is highly unstable. At such times great power war is unusually likely, particularly if the system is a dynamic multipolar one in which powers cannot feel secure in their position. *Strategic instability is a genuine circumstance, but a relative one* – there is, in practice, never a perfect strategic equilibrium, just as there is never perfect economic, environmental, or social stability. True strategic stability is a Platonic ideal, useful as a yardstick for judging real world conditions, but inherently unattainable as a policy goal. One can, however, seek to create a more stable bilateral relationship with a given country, or even a more stable overall international security environment, than the one that exists at present.

Rescuing strategic stability requires that we broaden the concept to reflect the myriad factors that impact political stability. There most assuredly have been historical periods in which relationships between polities have been particularly unstable, and this has implications for the likelihood of war. The conditions that might contribute to such instability are myriad – *social, economic, technological and other factors can create the conditions for international instability*, either brief or prolonged. If they are to reflect complex political reality, discussions of strategic stability must include such considerations.

The Europe of the early 16th century illustrates this point in a striking manner. The application of a mixture of seafaring technologies had allowed Columbus' voyages to the New World and Spain's establishment of colonies that offered a continuing income to the Spanish Crown, and, somewhat later, the expropriation of the awesome wealth of the Aztec and Incan Empires. In 1517, 2 years before the conquest of the Aztec Empire commenced, a theretofore minor German theologian composed, in Latin, a document challenging the sale of indulgences. The printing press already was widespread in Western and Central Europe by this point, and the subsequent translation of the *Ninety-Five Theses on the Power and Efficacy of Indulgences* into German permitted what began as a theological controversy among clergy to become the catalyst for a mass movement.[10] This, of course, generally is treated as the beginning of what was to become known as the Protestant Reformation. Slightly over a decade later, both dynastic considerations (the desire to divorce an aging Queen Catherine, so as to permit marriage to a woman who might bear him a male heir) and, apparently, straightforward infatuation with the fetching Anne Boleyn, convinced Henry VIII—the one-time author of a book criticizing Martin Luther and Protestantism—to begin the process of separation from Rome.[11]

These factors, along with others too numerous to mention, created the conditions necessary for over a century of politico-religious warfare in which the House of Habsburg, particularly its Spanish line (the House effectively split into two branches in 1521), would bid unsuccessfully for European hegemony—an endeavor which France vehemently resisted;[12] France would suffer intermittent, sometimes crippling, religious civil war;[13] the Dutch Republic would both fight for independence from Habsburg control and establish itself as a leading economic power;[14] and the Thirty Years' War would devastate Central Europe, leaving much of Germany in ruin and millions dead.[15] The 1648 Peace of Westphalia represented a more-or-less successful effort by an exhausted Europe to establish strategic stability and bring an end to a cycle of violence that was enormously costly to all the powers involved.

No single variable caused the 16th and early 17th centuries to unfold as they did; many factors converged to cause cataclysmic upheaval. Coincidence played a role, as it often does in history: Catholic Spain happened to begin receiving a massive influx of revenue during the same period in which the Protestant Reformation was taking hold, and that revenue would allow Spain to fight a seemingly endless series of wars against both Catholic and Protestant foes. Moreover, the Reformation itself was, at least to some degree, technology-dependent: in a Europe without large numbers of printing presses, and the resulting encouragement both of middle-class literacy and the free flow of ideas, the various religious strands that together comprised the Reformation might never have gained momentum. After all, over the centuries there had been numerous major heretical sects in Catholic Europe (and untold hundreds of minor ones) that ultimately were quashed, even though some managed to survive for decades or even centuries.

The Peace of Westphalia did not resolve many of the social issues that encouraged political violence in Europe—for instance, it was *after* Westphalia that the religion-fueled English Civil War entered perhaps its ugliest period, which included the execution of Charles I and Parliament's re-conquest of Ireland.[16] Moreover, it certainly did not solve the "problem" of interstate warfare—indeed, the Franco-Spanish War, which started in 1635 as a component of the Thirty Years' War, continued until 1659. Nevertheless, the Peace did reflect the fact that European politics and society had shifted decisively—it represented an implicit acknowledgement that Protestantism would endure permanently—and that the Habsburg bid for European hegemony had failed. Although it was not obvious in 1648, Spain had begun a permanent political decline from which it would never recover, while the eastern branch of the Habsburgs was compelled to accept that the position of Holy Roman Emperor would be much weakened, as power in the Empire would be even more decentralized than had previously been the case.

A *prerequisite* to the Peace of Westphalia, in short, was that certain conditions first had to improve; most critically, the intellectual "fever" driving the wars of religion on the Continent had to break, and Spanish power had to become less disproportionate to that of the other great powers. The rise of England, Sweden, and the Dutch Republic, France's brutal settling of its internal religious discord, and Portugal's decision in 1640 to sever itself from the Spanish crown—and the resulting war between Lisbon and Madrid—all aided in creating the latter. The meeting of these prerequisites, in turn, allowed the crafting of a Peace that would further encourage strategic stability.

The example of the Europe of the 16th and early 17th centuries starkly illustrates how varied and complex the factors are that determine international stability and how costly and enduring highly unstable conditions can be. Moreover, although the events in question are rather distant chronologically, religious discord and the use of new media to mobilize popular passions are themes that have more than a little resonance today. One key difference between the 16th century and more recent times, however, would appear to be the time which it takes for destabilizing factors to converge, creating the conditions for major volatility. The stability of the 16th century multipolar European system degraded at, by today's standards, a leisurely pace. In the last couple of centuries, however, history has moved at a rapid clip—an understandable result of the interrelated trends of sharply increasing economic prosperity, speedy social change (and resulting instability), and the momentous increase in scientific knowledge and application of that knowledge to create new technologies or improve existing ones.[17] In considering the meaning of strategic stability for this century, it perhaps is useful also to consider an example drawn from an international system that already had been altered profoundly by the Industrial Revolution and all that attended it.

ASSESSING STRATEGIC STABILITY: THE CASE OF WORLD WAR I

Strategic stability is an appealing notion in large part because it contains an underlying assumption that intelligent and well-meaning policymakers can *determine* when a relationship is becoming unstable and then act to correct that instability. This can be hazardous, as it may obscure how dangerous the international environment actually may be—and the illusion easily may incline policymakers to pursue a course of action that is overly bold, or even outright reckless.

The outbreak of World War I provides an excellent illustration of how difficult it is for contemporaries to judge systemic instability. Given that nearly a century has passed since mid-1914, we might reasonably claim to have enough historical distance from the event to enjoy at least some perspective on it. After all, we know how the rest of the 20th century turned out, for both good and ill. Yet, we also have a staggering quantity of government documents, memoirs, and other materials produced by the participants themselves, as well as a huge secondary literature created by thousands of scholars. This is a rare combination: the world is far enough away from the war that it can be treated as "distant" history, as opposed to "contemporary" history, but the main combatants were recognizably modern states which left massive paper trails that in large part survived the conflict.

The most basic elements of the drama are well-known.[18] The two states anchoring the Central Powers at the time appeared to be in very different stages of their "imperial life cycles." Austria-Hungary was a dignified but rather feeble multinational empire suffering from intense centrifugal forces fed by nationalism; somewhat paradoxically, Vienna believed that the solution to its problems might be found in further expansion into the Balkans.[19] The German Empire was youthful, vigorous, and dissatisfied with its global status, militarily confident but nonetheless concerned that the rapid growth of Russia's population and economy soon would make it impossible to win a two-front war against a Franco-Russian alliance.

The Triple Entente states also each faced unique problems. France had an impressive colonial empire and desired revenge for the Franco-Prussian War, but its relatively stagnant population and economic limitations created justifiable pessimism as to the likelihood of victory against Germany. Britain's empire truly was awesome, but its government worried about Germany's long-term intentions, particularly its seafaring ambitions; however, London was unsure as to whether to engage in a potentially costly continental war for which it was ill-prepared. The Russian

Empire was poor, backward, and under continuing threat of domestic insurrection; yet, it also was experiencing rapid economic growth, beginning to turn its great mass of peasants into an educated industrial work force, and undertaking a serious program of political reform. Moscow was ambitious in the Balkans and elsewhere, but very much aware that the troubled Russian state might be unable to bear the weight of a long war.[20]

With retrospect, almost every scholar would agree that in 1914 the European great power system did not enjoy strategic stability, and that this made the war possible. Yet, at what point did the great power system become critically unstable? Had it been precariously unstable for a decade or more, but merely lacked a catalyst that would touch off a war? Perhaps the latter is the case, but there were events before 1914 that presumably could have served as "good enough" catalysts for a European war—the First and Second Moroccan Crises of 1904 and 1911, for instance, were treated quite seriously by contemporaries. The European balance of military power did not change significantly from 1911 to 1914, but in the first case diplomacy defused the crisis , while, in the second, war was the outcome.

One of course could argue that tensions built up over time, with goodwill and trust slowly disintegrating because of progressive crises. This is not an unreasonable supposition, but it does not necessarily bolster the notion that strategic stability is readily calculated—indeed, it perhaps undermines this notion. In 1904 and 1911 crises were resolved through negotiation, but in 1914 the system was not stable enough to prevent war. In the immediate aftermath of the assassination of Franz Ferdinand, most thoughtful observers did not expect war. Quite the opposite, in fact: they trusted that any crisis resulting from the murder would end peaceably, in keeping with the pattern of the recent past.

What, then, would have given the international system the stability necessary to prevent war? Although Germany very much *hoped* that it would be able to crush France in a matter of weeks, no major power could be certain that it would be able to strike a quick, fatal blow to its enemies—all the participants knew that they were risking participation in a disastrous bloodletting. Of course, that is precisely what then occurred; the two sides were balanced closely enough that a long war, from which either side could have emerged victorious, resulted. Indeed, in 1917 the Central Powers were dictating peace terms to the former Russian Empire, and it appeared likely that France and Italy soon would be in a similar position.

Given the attitudes and fears of great power policymakers of the day, it is plausible that crisis stability would have been enhanced if there had been a greater *inequality* in military power—although in mid-1914 no great power could be sure of victory, all of them believed that, if they fought cunningly, meaningful victory could be attainable at a nonruinous price. Yet, even if it is true that a starker imbalance between the two sides would have prevented war, we cannot know definitively how much deeper military inequality would need to have been to prevent war in 1914. It is possible to develop all manner of counterfactual scenarios in which war would not have occurred in 1914, but we cannot test them (e.g., perhaps the existence of an additional ten active German army divisions would have convinced Russia and France to abandon Serbia to its fate—or, perhaps, it would have made no political difference whatsoever).

These historical questions and problems underscore the disconcerting fact that strategic stability is inherently flawed insofar as human events have a chaotic component: given that individuals interact with each other in unpredictable, and sometimes surprising, ways, seemingly rock-solid strategic stability can be illusory.[21] Efforts to foster strategic stability may fail not because of some miscalculation of the balance of military forces or similar flaw, but simply because actual human beings are not perfect rational actors — pride, arrogance, fear, and other attitudes and emotions can lead to disaster.

The implications of this simple observation potentially are significant: if strategic stability can fail at unpredictable times for unpredictable reasons, efforts to assess stability not only are inherently unreliable but sometimes may be dangerous, as a leader who assumes that a relationship with another state is stable unwittingly may tempt fate. Indeed, if a potential opponent apparently much desires continued peace, an actor has a particularly strong incentive to exploit that agreeableness by acting aggressively, as war seems unlikely. In this way, apparent stability can indirectly encourage reckless behavior. However, the aggressive state may well miscalculate how tolerant its peer will be of provocative behavior. For example, having calculated that strategic stability will ensure that any political crisis will not result in warfare with another state, a leader may choose to play to domestic jingoism, saber-rattling and making intentionally hollow threats. Most likely, the results will be what he or she expects — a domestic political gain and the ultimately peaceful resolution of the crisis. Sometimes, however, the outcome will be a catastrophic 1914 result.

The balance of military forces certainly is a component in the maintenance of peace, but it is only one in an overall context that encompasses all the major factors shaping the relationship between two security communities—and, that relationship, in turn, influences and is influenced by the overall international system. Moreover, one also must keep in mind the "deep" factors that shape relationships between and among states—such as physical geography and strategic history—and which themselves are inextricably intertwined. Physical geography does not straightforwardly determine strategic history, but it does shape the advantages and disadvantages that a security community enjoys, and remains meaningful throughout that community's existence, disciplining the options available to it. In turn, the interaction of that community with other strategic actors will craft a strategic history that is unique to it. That security community will have a "folk memory" that, while not necessarily accurate in its historical details, will shape its attitudes and behavior toward its peers.

GETTING PAST THE COLD WAR: STRATEGIC STABILITY IN THE 21ST CENTURY

Any useful discussion of future strategic stability must be grounded firmly in an understanding of how the international system has changed in the past 2 decades. In the 20th century, the international system experienced two tectonic shifts.[22] First, a multipolar great power system whose center of gravity was in Western and Central Europe—one which already had been gravely stressed by World War I—collapsed altogether in the mid-1940s. In its place, a bipolar system took shape. However, by historical standards it did not last for long; in well less than half a century bipolarity collapsed—happily, though surprisingly, with relatively little violence. For the purposes herein, the Post-Cold War period that followed lasted for approximately 1 decade, from December 26, 1991 (the date of the USSR's dissolution), to September 11, 2001 (9/11). This era was marked by U.S. unipolarity and limited global hegemony.

Although it was common at the time for observers to refer to Washington as the global hegemon, this rather overstated the power of the United States: the rest of the world was not reduced to satellite status, and Washington encountered frustrating limits to its power. Among other things, it attempted and failed to: mediate an end to Israeli-Palestinian hostilities; convince Russia to remain on the path to development of a healthy democratic system; and end warlordism in Somalia to create a stable government in that country. Nevertheless, during this time the United States was by far the greatest individual power, with clear conventional superiority over any other military power, the world's largest economy in both absolute or purchasing power parity terms (unless one treats the European Union [EU] as a single unit), and the diplomatic sway that one would expect such a mighty polity to enjoy.

The 9/11 attacks did not bring an abrupt end to U.S. quasi-hegemony. However, they did mark the beginning of a new emphasis in U.S. foreign policy. During the Post-Cold War years, U.S. grand strategy was decidedly fuzzy. Washington put forward broad policy goals, such as furthering democratization and economic liberalization globally, but pursued them in an unfocused manner—the result was a jumble of regional (e.g., North Atlantic Treaty Organization [NATO] expansion) and country-specific (e.g., containment of Iraq) strategies that did not form a coherent global whole. The Bush administration's declaration of a Global War on Terrorism solved this problem, but created a potentially larger one: a near-obsessive focus on the threat presented by Islamist terrorist movements and a related impatience for the final resolution of the "Saddam Hussein Question."[23]

While the Obama administration dropped the use of the phrase "Global War on Terrorism," it did not radically shift the grand strategic focus of the United States: it de-emphasized Iraq, but shifted attention to Afghanistan and Pakistan. More recently, the Arab Spring created circumstances in which the United States found itself attempting to cope with rapid political change in several North African and Southwest Asian countries. The Arab Spring itself was a good demonstration of the reality that apparent strategic stability can be an illusion that dissipates in an eye blink. Although the particular circumstances leading to the Afghanistan, Iraq, and Libya Wars were very different, if one steps back they all form a somewhat coherent but deeply flawed grand strategy: the United States continues to focus its military power on certain countries in the Muslim world and attempts to use that power to stabilize them and, in turn, build a long-term partnership. In other Islamic countries, it does not use kinetic military action, but attempts to accomplish similar goals through diplomacy and economic incentives.[24]

The reason for this focus on specific Islamic countries is partly due to the simple pressure of events: the wars in Afghanistan and Libya were "random" insofar as they resulted, respectively, from the Taliban's unwillingness to hand over individuals responsible for a surprise attack on U.S. soil and Muammar Qaddafi's obstinate refusal to slip gently into prosperous retirement — and the resulting Franco-British conviction that he therefore must be removed militarily by NATO. For a cocktail of reasons, there has been a good deal of "action" — both violent and nonviolent — in Islamic countries in recent years, and the attention of U.S. policymakers often follows television cameras. However, U.S. policymakers also tend, by their behavior, to drive those television cameras to particular places. If the American government were as inclined to intervene in, say, the Democratic Republic of Congo, as it has been in certain other parts of the world, Kinshasa's hotels today would be overflowing with journalists and camera crews.

This does not imply that there is a clear, multistage U.S. strategy to change the Islamic world into something new — indeed, the opposite is more nearly the case: American actions often have been ad hoc; insofar as there has been a panoramic vision (as in the Bush administration's quasi-plan for counterterrorism through the spread of democracy), it has been unrealistic. There is, however, a clear pattern to U.S. behavior, with counterterrorism and a related concern for the political health of Islamic countries having become the central focus of U.S. grand strategy. By all appearances, Washington's attitude essentially is that strategic stability in the Islamic world is the most fundamental challenge to global strategic stability.

This is, however, not necessarily an accurate perception. It is becoming increasingly clear that unipolarity is, at best, very deeply corroded — and, given the spectacular rise of China, it would not be unreasonable to declare it dead. China's rise, however, has not resulted in the recreation of bipolarity, but, rather, is part of the re-emergence of multipolarity: Russia, troubled though it is, remains a great power; Japan has the economic resources necessary for great power status, even if it remains reticent politically; India is rapidly emerging both economically and politically; and Brazil clearly is bidding for acknowledgement as a top-tier power, though it thus far has failed to demonstrate global influence commensurate with such a status. At this point, we cannot confidently predict precisely what states will be on the list of great powers 2 decades from now—for instance, by then the EU might have welded itself into a great power, acrimoniously collapsed, or remained somewhere between these two extremes. It is clear, however, that a multipolar global system is taking shape. Moreover, because we are in a period of, historically speaking, quite rapid transformation in the global system, strategic instability is endemic.

In addition, just as in the 16th century, technological, economic, and social factors are conspiring to encourage instability in the international system. Even absent war, the fortunes of individual states can rise or fall with surprising speed; the best illustration of this is the contrast between the impoverished China of the Cultural Revolution—an ideologically bizarre near-failed state in which a scientist was more likely to be sent to the countryside to do stoop labor than to receive a research grant—and today's near-superpower. There is no sign that this is slowing down; indeed, we should expect further acceleration in the pace of socio-political change.

It is notable that, just as in the 16th century, social and religious change menaces stability both within and among countries. Religious awakenings are occurring not only in the Muslim world, but also in Christian countries in Africa—and, in an obvious formula for trouble, in mixed Christian-Muslim states such as Nigeria.[25] China may also be in the early stages of a mass religious awakening, with unpredictable effects. India remains religiously tense, and not only because of the always strained Hindu-Muslim relationship; rapid economic and social change appears to be intensifying the political struggle between those who would define India as a nonsectarian democracy (the traditional preference of the Indian political elite) and those who wish India to have a more assertively Hindu identity. At the same time, in many countries there are non-religiously-driven calls for political change—or, as in Libya, cases in which democratic secularists, sincere proponents of both electoral democracy *and* greater religiosity in government, and would-be totalitarian theocrats find themselves temporarily thrown together, with an unpredictable ultimate outcome. One might hope that in the 21st century religious sentiment will not cause as much violence as it did in the 16th and 17th centuries, but the record of the last decade does not inspire confidence.

This "perfect storm of instability" has serious implications for the security of the United States, though it should not be the cause of undue panic. Washington remains, by a long stretch, the greatest military power, and its economy is the world's largest, unless the EU is counted as a single whole (a practice with obvious shortcomings, given the ongoing European debt crisis). The gap between the power of the United States and its nearest peer, China, remains enormous—and, if it is prudent, the United States can take advantage of this fact to act as a force for global peace. Washington cannot artificially *create* strategic stability—the global strategic environment is inherently unstable. It can, however, exert much influence over how the multipolar system develops in coming years.

Unfortunately, this is no simple matter of being hawkish or dovish, but requires a sophisticated grand strategy that is constantly being re-evaluated and rebalanced to account for changing circumstances. In such a grand strategy, U.S. goals would include: maintaining its position as the greatest individual power; seeking to discourage the creation of great power alliances that would threaten U.S. interests (such as a Sino-Russian axis); preventing great power war, if possible; preparing to win a great power war militarily and craft a postwar global security environment friendly to U.S. interests, should it prove impossible to prevent a conflict; and attempting to craft institutions, whether formal or informal, that will serve to diffuse enmity between great powers and allow the powers to work together to cope with global strategic instability.[26]

This is a very tall order, but it is the most sensible blueprint for the reorientation of U.S. grand strategy. The continuing U.S. focus on the Islamic world is myopic. Certainly, events in some Islamic countries are very important, but—especially as the large-scale production of fossil fuels is becoming far more evenly distributed globally, with new technologies promising a massive increase in output in many countries, including Brazil, Canada, and the United States[27]—there is little reason to believe that they offer some sort of key that will solve the puzzle of global strategic stability. Washington would benefit from a broader perspective that considers the international system as a whole and focuses particular attention on competition and cooperation among the great powers.

CONCLUSION: STRATEGIC STABILITY IN A CHANGING WORLD

Cold War-era conceptions of strategic stability have little salience in the 21st century security environment. At this point, a focus on nuclear arsenals—particularly on just the Russian and American nuclear arsenals—is archaic. There is good reason to question, for instance, whether MAD can carry the weight of ensuring that there is no naval clash between China and the United States over the issue of Taiwanese independence. Even the consideration of military power more broadly is only partially illuminating. We now are in a multipolar environment in which many factors, including alliance relationships among the various great and medium powers, will impact the character of the security environment.

As discussed above, the entire global system is a period of epochal change; this transformation cannot be prevented or controlled, only guided to a limited degree. With that in mind, the following general points concerning strategic stability are offered:

1. Social, economic, technogical, religious/ideological, and other broad trends impact global strategic stability deeply. Military power is only part of the enormously complex strategic stability equation.

2. Strategic stability is fluid to the degree that the term itself is problematic. Events do not invariably follow a clear timeline in which one event builds on another to create a stable environment. International circumstances can change quickly—for example, the French Revolution radically altered a seemingly stable (if competitive) European security environment. Similarly, the "Velvet Revolutions" in East-Central Europe and the collapse of the Soviet Union demolished a bi-

polar system that appeared stable to the point of being nearly inert.

3. Problematic though the term might be, strategic stability does express an important truth: at some points the international system is far more prone to extreme political violence than it is at other times.

4. Strategic stability and strategic instability are not absolute conditions, especially in a vibrant multipolar system. It is more helpful to think of a "stability continuum" that, in practice, ranges from extremely stable to extremely unstable. However, *precisely where the global system is on that continuum at a given time cannot be measured reliably*—at best, one can make an educated guess.

5. Leaders who are excessively confident in the stability of the international system are apt to make decisions that increase the likelihood of war.

6. As the second example cited in #2 above illustrates, strategic stability is not inherently good—sometimes instability can allow for positive change. However, generally speaking, great power warfare is more likely when the security environment is highly unstable.

7. Strategic stability cannot *reliably* be increased through arms control or similar measures. It is true that arms control agreements may assuage the fears of particular states and thus might have a positive impact on the overall security environment. However, the historical evidence would seem to indicate that this is a minor effect that is easily overwhelmed by negative events: the golden age for arms control was the 1920s, but the Great Depression created conditions ripe for hyper-nationalist militarism and eventual war.

The United States would do well to engage in a so-phisticated discussion of strategic stability that places the term solidly in the political context of this century. Two decades now have passed since the collapse of the Soviet Union, and it is well past the point where it is possible to have any confidence that the prevention of warfare is a matter of balancing nuclear arsenals. Rather, Washington must be intellectually prepared to grapple with the enormously more complicated task of working to guide a rapidly emerging multipolar international system that will be confronted by the crushing pressures of technological, social, and economic change.

ENDNOTES - CHAPTER 3

1. See John Hillas, Mathijus Jansen, Jos Potters, and Dries Vermeulen, "On the Relation Among Some Definitions of Strategic Stability," *Mathematics of Operations Research*, Vol. 26, No. 3, August 2001, pp. 611-635.

2. In regard to varied and problematic uses of the term "stability" during the Cold War era, see Colin S. Gray, "The Urge to Compete: Rationales for Arms Racing," *World Politics*, Vol. 26, No. 2, January 1974, pp. 229, f. 57.

3. Colin S. Gray, "Strategic Stability Reconsidered," *Daedalus*, Vol. 109, No. 4, Fall 1980, pp. 135.

4. See Carl von Clausewitz, *On War*, Michael Howard and Peter Paret, eds. and trans., indexed ed., Princeton, NJ: Princeton University Press, 1984, p. 605.

5. See Albert Wohlstetter's highly influential 1958 RAND report *The Delicate Balance of Terror*, reprinted in Robert Zarate and Henry Sokolski, *Nuclear Heuristics: Selected Writings of Albert and Roberta Wohlstetter*, Carlisle, PA: Strategic Studies Institute, U.S. Army War College, 2009, pp. 177-212.

6. Like "strategic stability," the notion that arms race is contestable. See Colin S. Gray, *Weapons Don't Make War: Policy, Strategy, and Military Technology,* Lawrence, KS: University Press of Kansas, 1993; and *Idem*, "Arms Races and Other Pathetic Fallacies: A Case for Deconstruction," review essay on *Plowshares into Swords: Arms Races in International Politics, 1840-1991,* by Grant T. Hammond, *Review of International Studies,* Vol. 22, No. 3, July 1996, pp. 323-336.

7. See C. Dale Walton, "Nuclear Questions: Bush Administration WMD Security Strategy and the Second Nuclear Age," in Stephen J. Cimbala, ed., *The George W. Bush Defense Program: Policy, Strategy and War,* Herndon, VA: Potomac Books, 2010, pp. 185-202.

8. Recently, the State Department has indicated an interest in moving toward an international environment in which "mutual assured stability" (MAS) would underpin strategic stability, but at this point MAS is little more than a vague concept. See Ellen O. Tauscher, "Strategic Deterrence and the Path to a World of Mutually Assured Stability," July 5, 2011, available from *www.state. gov/t/avc/rls/170575.htm*.

9. The degree to which the Soviet leadership was confused and disoriented by the events of the 1989-91 is vividly recorded in Stephen Kotkin, *Armageddon Averted: Soviet Collapse, 1970-2000,* updated ed., New York: Oxford University Press, 2008.

10. As Diarmond MacCulloch notes:

It was not the first time that the new medium of print had provoked a general debate, way beyond those who could actually read the pamphlets and books involved: that had happened over the previous decade, when European authorities launched an ambitious publicity campaign to raise a new continent-wide crusade against the Turks. However, what the Luther furor now demonstrated was that there was an independent public opinion, and the printing presses that fuelled it could not be controlled by the existing hierarchies in Church and Commonwealth.

The Reformation: A History, New York: Penguin Books, 2005; originally published 2003, pp. 124.

11. On King Henry's decision to seize political control of the Church in England, see G. W. Bernard, *The King's Reformation: Henry VIII and the Making of the English Church*, New Haven, CT: Yale University Press, 2007; and Richard Rex, *Henry VIII and the English Reformation*, 2nd Ed., London, UK: Palgrave Macmillan, 2006.

12. On Spain's hegemonic ambitions, see Geoffrey Parker, *The Grand Strategy of Philip II*, New Haven, CT: Yale University Press, 1998; and *Idem, Success is Never Final: Empire, War, and Faith in Early Modern Europe*, New York: Basic, 2002.

13. See Mack P. Holt, *The French Wars of Religion, 1562-1629*, 2nd Ed., Cambridge, UK: Cambridge University Press, 2005; and Robert Knect, *The French Religious Wars, 1562-1598*, Oxford, UK: Osprey, 2002.

14. See Jonathan I. Israel, *The Dutch Republic: Its Rise, Greatness, and Fall, 1477-1806*, Oxford, UK: Oxford University Press, 1996.

15. On the origins and course of the war, see Ronald G. Asch, *The Thirty Years War: The Holy Roman Empire and Europe, 1618-48*, Basingstoke, UK: Palgrave, 1997; and Peter H. Wilson, *The Thirty Years War: Europe's Tragedy*, Cambridge, MA: Belknap Press of Harvard University Press, 2011, originally published 2009.

16. On the latter, see Micheál Ó Siochrú, *God's Executioner: Oliver Cromwell and the Conquest of Ireland*, London, UK: Faber and Faber, 2008.

17. A deep appreciation of how such trends can interweave to power political change undergirds Daniel Walker Howe's magisterial history of the United States in the decades immediately following the War of 1812. See his *What God Hath Wrought: The Transformation of the United States, 1815-1848*, New York: Oxford University Press, 2009.

18. For an especially detailed exploration of the period before the outbreak of the conflict and the months following its outbreak, see Hew Strachan, *The First World War, Volume I: To Arms*, New York: Oxford University Press, 2003.

19. Austria-Hungary's political atmosphere in this period is vividly portrayed in the classic Edward Crankshaw, *The Fall of the House of Habsburg*, New York: Penguin Books, 1983, originally published 1963.

20. An intriguing challenge to the conventional interpretation of which state bears the greatest responsibility for the outbreak of the war is offered by Sean McMeekin, who argues for Russian culpability. See his *The Russian Origins of the First World War*, Cambridge, MA: Belknap Press of Harvard University Press, 2011. A more traditional view, that Germany was chiefly at fault for the conflict, is argued vigorously in Donald Kagan, *On the Origins of War and the Preservation of Peace*, New York: Doubleday, 1994.

21. On the question of how chaos shapes strategy, see Colin S. Gray, *Strategy for Chaos: Revolutions in Military Affairs and the Evidence of History*, London, UK: Frank Cass/Routledge, 2002; and Barry D. Watts, *Clausewitzian Friction and Future War*, McNair Paper #52, Washington, DC: Institute for National Strategic Studies, National Defense University, 1996.

22. On this theme, see C. Dale Walton, *Geopolitics and the Great Powers in the 21st Century: Multipolarity and the Revolution in Strategic Perspective*, London, UK: Routledge, 2007.

23. This is not to claim that the Iraqi government had any significant operational relationship with al-Qaeda. Rather, the point is that if one views the globe through a "counterterrorism lens," the creation of a Middle East anchored by a stable, democratic, and U.S.-friendly Iraq truly would appear to be a triumph. Whether that goal was *realistic* is another question entirely. See C. Dale Walton, *Grand Strategy and the Presidency: Foreign Policy, War, and the American Role in the World*, London, UK: Routledge, 2012.

24. During the Bush years, democratization was seen as a key aspect of this process of stabilization and partnership; however, the Obama administration appears (prudently) to be somewhat less centered on this area. For instance, it ultimately acquiesced to President Hamid Karzai remaining in office despite the voter intimidation and massive fraud that marked the 2009 Afghan presidential election. By doing so, it tacitly admitted that the democratization project in Afghanistan had collapsed. More

recently, the administration took noticeably little action, even rhetorically, when protesters calling for democracy were quite publicly crushed in Bahrain.

25. See Philip Jenkins, *The Next Christendom*, 3rd Ed., New York: Oxford University Press, 2011, p. 208.

26. How the United States might best attain these strategic goals is discussed in detail in Walton, *Grand Strategy and the Presidency*.

27. See Daniel Yergin, "Oil's New World Order," *Washington Post* online ed., October 28, 2011, available from *www. washingtonpost.com/opinions/daniel-yergin-for-the-future-of-oil-look-to-the-americas-not-the-middle-east/2011/10/18/gIQAxdDw7L_story.html*.

CHAPTER 4

RECLAIMING STRATEGIC STABILITY

James M. Acton

The author of this chapter is grateful to Jaclyn Tandler for research assistance.

From almost as soon as the term "strategic stability" first entered the nuclear lexicon, there have been calls to redefine it. During the Cold War, critics often advocated for a redefinition on the grounds that the quest for stability led to a nuclear policy that was at variance with effective deterrence.[1] More recent arguments for reconceptualization—and even abandonment—tend to be based on the assertion that strategic stability premised on Cold War logic is about as relevant today as the challenge of defending the Fulda Gap from advancing Soviet armor.[2]

Yet, for all the talk of redefining strategic stability, the reality is that its proponents have never actually been able to coalesce around a single definition (where, that is, they have chosen to define it at all). Edward Warner, who served as the U.S. Secretary of Defense's representative to the New Strategic Arms Treaty (New START) talks, has observed that the term "strategic stability" is used in three broad ways:[3]

- Most narrowly, strategic stability describes the absence of incentives to use nuclear weapons first (crisis stability) and the absence of incentives to build up a nuclear force (arms race stability);
- More broadly, it describes the absence of armed conflict between nuclear-armed states;

117

- Most broadly, it describes a regional or global security environment in which states enjoy peaceful and harmonious relations.

Governments, in particular, are guilty of using the term "strategic stability" without definition or clear meaning. Of those that regularly invoke the phrase, the United States is the most consistent in usage, frequently employing "strategic stability" in the narrowest of the three senses listed above. The 2010 *U.S. Nuclear Posture Review* (NPR) *Report*, for instance, uses the terms "stable," "stability," and "instability" 49 times in the main text. Although these terms are not defined, most of these usages are associated with policies such as "deMIRVing" (multiple independently-targetable re-entry vehicles) the U.S. intercontinental ballistic missile (ICBM) force, which is advocated in order to increase "the stability of the nuclear balance by reducing the incentives for either side to strike first."[4]

Yet, occasionally the NPR report appears to impute broader meaning to stability.[5] For instance, the Barack Obama administration supports ratification of the Comprehensive Test Ban Treaty partly because it "would enable us to encourage non-NPT [Nuclear Non-Proliferation Treaty] Parties to follow the lead of the NPT-recognized Nuclear Weapon States in formalizing a heretofore voluntary testing moratorium, and thus strengthen strategic stability by reducing the salience of nuclear weapons in those states' national defense strategies."[6] Meanwhile, nuclear weapons are seen as playing a role in "promoting stability globally and in key regions."[7]

The Russian government has a tendency to use the term "strategic stability" like some form of diplomatic spackling paste, and what it means by the phrase is less than clear. Russian Foreign Minister Sergei Lavrov, for instance, has stated that Russia will not agree to further nuclear arms reductions unless all factors affecting strategic stability are addressed.[8] Some of his concerns—such as ballistic missile defense and "non-nuclear strategic" weapons, which he fears could undermine the survivability of Russia's nuclear forces—are consistent with a narrow understanding of strategic stability in terms of minimizing first use incentives. Yes, his invocation of imbalances in "conventional armaments and armed forces"[9]—a reference to the North Atlantic Treaty Organization's (NATO) conventional superiority and possibly China's too— implies a broader understanding.[10] Along apparently similar (if somewhat opaque) lines, the 2010 *Russian Military Doctrine* identifies "the attempts to destabilize the situation in individual states and regions and to undermine strategic stability" as the second most significant military threat facing Russia.[11] If anything, this usage appears to be consistent with the second of the three definitions listed above.

In an interesting twist, there is a debate in China over whether the concept of strategic stability is even applicable to the Sino-U.S. relationship. Much of the Chinese literature argues that "'Balance' (*pingheng*) and 'symmetry' (*duicheng*) are integral to the concept of strategic stability"[12] and that, because of the current asymmetry in American and Chinese power, "the concept of strategic stability in classic arms control theory cannot be applied directly to the framework of Sino-U.S. relations."[13] Yet, this theoretical concern does not stop Chinese officials from regularly urging that "all disarmament measures should follow the guidelines of 'promoting international strategic stability' and 'undiminished security for all',"[14] although exactly what is meant by "strategic stability" here is not entirely clear.

The absence of an agreed definition for a term as widely used as "strategic stability" seriously detracts from the quality of debate on nuclear policy. Without an agreed definition of such a common term, arguments about the pros and cons of, say, ballistic missile defense or high-precision conventional weapons tend to be at cross purposes, creating much heat and little illumination. Indeed, critics tend to capitalize on this confusion, arguing that the term is ill-defined or setting up a weak definition as a straw man.[15] Accordingly, it is useful to ask — as this chapter does — how the term should be defined. Definitions are, of course, to some extent arbitrary; strategic stability *could* be defined in all the ways Warner identifies above and more. But the principal criterion for how it should be defined ought to be conceptual clarity. A good definition for strategic stability might conceivably lead to more agreement on policy prescriptions, and, even if not, it might enable a better understanding of why we disagree.

DEFINING CRISIS AND ARMS RACE STABILITY

The theory of crisis stability was first expounded at length in Thomas Schelling's 1960 masterpiece, *Strategy of Conflict* (although, as discussed elsewhere in this volume, others had explored some of the ideas previously).[16] Schelling observed that, in a crisis, the fear of being pre-empted could itself create pressure to pre-empt. Specifically, because one side's nuclear weapons could destroy an opponent's, there might be real advantages to landing the first nuclear blow. In consequence, two states could be pushed over the brink of war because one state decided the risks of striking first outweighed the risks of waiting to be struck. It bears emphasizing from the outset that Schelling never argued that such dynamics were the only — or even perhaps the main — reason why states would go to nuclear war. Rather, his point was that if international relations were already severely strained — for whatever reason — the "reciprocal fear of surprise attack" might cause them to rupture entirely. Or, as he put it, "[a]rms and military organizations can hardly be considered the exclusively determining factors in international conflict, but neither can they be considered neutral."[17]

Within Schelling's conception of stability — the "traditional" conception, if you will — a crisis can be defined as stable *if neither side has or perceives an incentive to use nuclear weapons first out of the fear that the other side is about to do so*. This definition — the one I advocate in this chapter — is, in fact, even narrower than the first of Warner's three definitions (under his definition any first use of a nuclear weapon — whatever the motivation — would be categorized as an instability). By analogy with crisis stability, my preferred definition of arms race stability is *the absence of perceived or actual incentives to augment a nuclear force — qualitatively or quantitatively — out of the fear that in a crisis an opponent would gain a meaningful advantage by using nuclear weapons first.*[18]

The Cold War discourse on stability — crisis stability in particular — was overly narrow in two important ways. First, concern generally focused on the possibility of a state launching a large-scale damage-limiting first strike if it believed nuclear war had become imminent. However, such a strike is not the only — or even the most likely — response of a state fearful of an adversary's using nuclear weapons first. An alternative would be the limited use of nuclear weapons in an attempt to scare the opponent into backing down.[19] This form of crisis instability seems much more likely than a large-scale damage-limiting first strike. Indeed, in a conflict against the United States, only Russia has anything approaching the capability to execute such a strike.

Second, the Cold War literature tended to focus on instabilities arising from the technical characteristics of each side's strategic forces, that is, on *first strike stability*. These characteristics (the hardness of silos, the accuracy of missiles, the effect of missile interceptors, and so on) are only some of the factors that would play into a decision to pre-empt. First strike stability is, therefore, a necessary — but not sufficient — condition for crisis stability.[20] The sometimes exclusive focus on the technical characteristics of strategic forces arose at least in part because these factors could be easily quantified, whereas other factors relevant to crisis stability — emotion, pressure, bad advice, miscalculation, misperception or poor communication — could not. During the Cold War, tremendous efforts were put into developing mathematical models for first strike stability. The aim was to quantify the incentives to strike first by modelling a nuclear exchange and using the results to determine whether either side was best served by waiting or attacking.[21] These efforts certainly had some value; ensuring that vulnerable nuclear forces did not encourage pre-emption was important, and, for that matter, it still is. But, because the models narrowly focused on only some of the potential causes of nuclear war they were, as their developers sometimes acknowledged, limited and they attracted considerable and reasonable criticism. However, a number of contemporary analysts have gone further and used the inadequacies of such models to attack the entire concept of strategic stability.[22] Such an attack is unreasonable; there is a clear difference between the concept of stability and specific, contingent mathematical models that try to quantify it. Using the inadequacies of such models to reject the former is like dismissing the concept of nuclear deterrence out of distaste for the game theoretic analysis that is beloved by a small number of formal deterrence strategists.

This is certainly not to argue that the technical characteristics of weapon systems are irrelevant to strategic stability. Indeed, the range of relevant systems has broadened as a result of technological change. Early in the Cold War, when stability concerns first emerged, the only plausible "defense" to a nuclear attack was a pre-emptive nuclear first strike. Today, however, there are concerns—particularly among potential U.S. adversaries—that high-precision conventional weapons, including cruise missiles as well as developmental weapons such as "boost-glide" systems, could be used to attack their nuclear forces before launch, while ballistic missile defenses could "mop up" any that survived and were launched. These fears—whether or not they are technically justified—could lead to anxieties about the possibility of a pre-emptive strike during a crisis. A full description of strategic stability in today's world must, therefore, include conventional capabilities that could be used to destroy an opponent's nuclear forces (or its ability to operate them).

DEFINING STRATEGIC STABILITY

Strategic stability is usually defined as the combination of crisis stability and arms race stability. This definition suffers from the disadvantage of making crisis stability and arms race stability appear to be fundamentally different phenomena. In reality, they are actually two manifestations of the same phenomenon on very different timescales. To demonstrate this it is helpful to lay out the range of actions that could be taken by a state worried about being on the receiving end of a nuclear attack in a crisis, classified by the time required to implement them.

Seconds, Minutes, Hours, or Days: Use of Nuclear Weapons.

While nuclear weapons have never been used out of the fear of an impending nuclear attack, war planning—especially in the United States and the Soviet Union—has certainly included pre-emptive options:

- Soviet war planning during the 1960s was based exclusively on pre-empting an American attack—not least because the Union of Soviet Socialist Republics (USSR) was convinced that the United States was also planning to preempt. From the early 1970s, launch-on-warning and delayed retaliation options were developed, although pre-emption appears to have remained a possibility.[23]
- As in the Soviet case, early U.S. war planning was heavily based on pre-emption.[24] Retaliatory options began to enter war planning in the late 1950s with the development of submarine-launched ballistic missiles (SLBMs).[25] However, it seems unlikely that the United States has ever abandoned the option of pre-emption.

Hours or Days: Increasing the Alert Levels of Nuclear Forces.

On a day-to-day basis, states generally keep substantial portions of their nuclear forces off alert. In the event of a crisis, they can—in hours or days—raise the alert level of some or all of their forces to enhance their survivability and ready them for possible use. Increasing alert levels might involve dispersing mobile forces—bombers, mobile missiles, and ballistic missile submarines (SSBNs)—or mating warheads with delivery systems, if the former are not emplaced on the latter as a matter of routine. While doing so may make forces more survivable, it can also send escalatory signals—which could be problematic if a decisionmaker does not want to send them. Moreover, the dispersal of mobile forces can increase the probability of an accidental or unauthorized launch, especially if dispersal is accompanied by a pre-delegation of launch authority, which may be seen to be necessary if technology or the military balance seems to require it.[26]

There are a number of historical examples of states' increasing their alert level in response to a perceived increase in the threat to their nuclear forces:

- While it is widely assumed that Soviet nuclear forces were not alerted during the Cuban Missile Crisis, Pentagon documents suggest otherwise. Declassified documents from 1962 and 1963 indicate Soviet nuclear forces were alerted on October 24, 1962.[27] Separately, an originally classified 1981 study of the Cold War arms race mentions an alert of Soviet submarines during the crisis.[28]
- On October 18, 1969, at the height of the Sino-Soviet border crisis, Chinese Defense Minister

Lin Biao ordered an alert of Chinese nuclear forces, fearing that a Soviet nuclear attack was imminent.[29]

- In August 1978, the United States raised the alert level at five Strategic Air Command bases—and then dispersed planes from those bases—after two Soviet SSBNs moved "dangerously close to the East Coast of the United States," thus "significantly rais[ing] the threat" to those bases.[30]
- In November 1983, during NATO exercise Able Archer-83, the Soviet Union may have alerted some of its nuclear forces.[31]

Months or Years: Deploying or Redeploying Existing Weapons.

Outside of a crisis, a state concerned about the survivability of its forces—and hence its ability to use them in the event of a sudden crisis—could try to augment its forces relatively rapidly by deploying or redeploying existing weapons. There is at least one extremely notable example of such an action, which also demonstrates how this kind of instability can damage international relations:

- Prior to 1962, Soviet Premier Nikita Khrushchev had been content with a "second-best strategic posture" consisting of a limited force of long-range nuclear weapons.[32] In early 1962, he learned that the United States had examined a first strike plan during the previous summer when the Berlin Crisis was at its height. This appears to have "stirred fears that the Americans were eager to capitalize on their strategic advantage" and partly catalysed his decision to deploy two existing types of missile, SS-4 and SS-5, to Cuba.[33]

Years: Building More Weapons and Developing New Systems.

Over the course of a few years, a state that is afraid its forces could be vulnerable in a crisis can augment its arsenal by building more warheads and delivery systems (to new or existing designs). Such build-ups can be interpreted (rightly or wrongly) by an adversary as an aggressive action—that is, they can create a security dilemma—and thus carry the risk of exacerbating international tensions. These long-time scale dynamics—arms race instabilities—have plenty of historical precedents:

- As noted above, survivability concerns appear to have been important in catalyzing Khrushchev's decision to authorize a major build-up in long-range Soviet forces in 1962.[34]
- Every state with nuclear weapons has road-mobile ballistic missiles or SSBNs (or both). Most, if not all, of the programs to develop these systems were presumably motivated—in whole or in part—by the survivability advantages of mobile weapons, in light of their generally reduced accuracy and throw-weight.
- Survivability concerns *may* be an important factor motivating China's current build-up (although making definitive statements on the relative balance of strategic to bureaucratic considerations in Beijing's decisionmaking is impossible in light of the information available).

This entire range of phenomena—stretching from the shortest timescales (crisis instabilities) to the longest (arms race instabilities)—can be captured within the following definition of strategic stability: *A deterrence relationship is stable if neither party has or perceives an incentive to change its force posture out of concern that an adversary might use nuclear weapons first in a crisis.* The focus on force posture (which includes but is not limited to use) emphasizes that responding to vulnerability lies at the root of instability.

It cannot be emphasized enough that this definition does *not* imply that the only reason why a state might change its force posture is fear of an adversary's using nuclear weapons first. Obviously, there are plenty of other reasons why a state might do so. Nonetheless, changes in force posture in response to the perceived threat of nuclear attack constitute a theoretically and historically significant class. The remainder of this chapter explores why it is conceptually helpful to reserve the term "strategic stability" for this particular class of phenomena.

WHY NOT ADOPT A MUCH BROADER DEFINITION OF STRATEGIC STABILITY?

One of the most enduring criticisms of strategic stability is that the concept is too simplistic to account for conflict (or the absence thereof). In 1988, Stephen Prowse and Albert Wohlstetter—reflecting the views of many strategists—rejected the concept of strategic stability on the grounds that it is based on the misplaced belief that "the primary motive for one country to attack another springs simply from a misunderstanding that the other side might attack."[35] Looking back at the Cold War more than 2 decades later, David

Yost, in a similar vein, has argued that "[t]he mutual vulnerability model that was supposed to simultaneously provide 'crisis stability,' 'first strike stability,' and 'arms race stability' was alluring and elegant, but based on false premises . . . about how decisions are made to go to war—as if force posture characteristics were the decisive factor."[36]

Looking at a "contemporary global security context [that] no longer bears any resemblance to the Cold War context,"[37] contemporary critics have argued that any utility strategic stability offered then has now evaporated entirely. Frank Harvey, for instance, has written that:

> Expanding levels of economic co-operation, interdependence, and, in Russia's case, vulnerability have created an environment in which large-scale conflict involving those major powers is increasingly remote and, for many reasons, obsolete. Economic and trade relationships are far more useful than military competition in predicting interactions between the United States and Russia, and there is no compelling reason to expect this to change. Indeed, Russian officials are now more inclined to define strategic stability in terms of assured economic viability, not assured destruction. Survival of the Russian state depends less on the balance of nuclear forces and more on the Russian economy and foreign investment from the U.S., Europe, and Asia.[38]

All these arguments are—on their own terms— true. It is *obviously* the case that the primary drivers of conflict are political (or cultural or economic or historical or ideological) and that, to the extent deterrence is immediately relevant in preventing conflict, it is probably conventional forces—rather than nuclear weapons—that act as a day-to-day restraint. But, advocates of strategic stability never said otherwise. Their—or rather our argument is that if international relations become severely strained for any reason and the use of nuclear weapons becomes a realistic proposition, it would be highly desirable that none of the protagonists feels pressured into using weapons out of the fear that another might do so first. In other words, as Robert Jervis succinctly noted, "[c]risis instability can interact with political conflict; arms controllers never suggested that the former in the absence of the latter would yield war."[39]

If one accepts that crisis instability is only one potential pathway by which the nuclear threshold might be crossed and, accordingly, that it is only one criterion for assessing force posture (albeit an important one), then it can stand on its own as a useful strategic concept. Defined narrowly, it provides specific insight into an important, if only partial, aspect of nuclear deterrence. Needless to say, other concepts, not least the effectiveness of deterrence, are required to capture the totality of international strategic dynamics. Recognizing this, there is no need to attempt to broaden the concept of strategic stability, as some critics have called for, to try and embrace all factors relevant to the outbreak of war.[40]

WHY NOT ADOPT A SLIGHTLY BROADER DEFINITION?

Under the definition of strategic stability proposed here, the use of nuclear weapons for a reason other than fear of an impending nuclear attack would not be classed as a type of crisis instability. This definition, however, is controversial. The doctrines of conventionally weaker but nuclear-armed states or blocs generally call for the use of nuclear weapons in the event of a non-nuclear attack by a stronger neighbor (Russia's defense doctrine vis-à-vis NATO and China is a case in point). This raises the question of whether the definition of stability should expand to classify *any* first use of a nuclear weapon—whatever the motivation—as an example of strategic instability (as in the first of Warner's three definitions discussed in the introduction to this chapter).

It should, of course, be a goal of policy to create the political and security conditions that would minimize all incentives for the first use of nuclear weapons.[41] However, that does not mean that it is conceptually helpful to include all possible incentives for first use within the definition of strategic stability. As explored in this section, mitigating different pathways to first use requires different approaches. Moreover, there may even be trade-offs—reducing the probability of first use for one reason could simultaneously increase the probability of first use for another. These distinctions and trade-offs would be obscured by a broader definition.

Effectively reducing the likelihood of nuclear first use depends on identifying why it might occur. If such use is most likely to result from fear of an adversary's striking first, then the most effective methods to minimize the incentives to use would include increasing the survivability of nuclear forces, hardening command and control systems, enhancing early warning, and improving crisis communication channels. By contrast, reducing a weak state's reliance on nuclear threats to deter non-nuclear aggression might require narrowing a conventional imbalance (whether through a conventional build-up or arms control), eliminating—or finding non-nuclear means to counter—chemical and biological weapons, or eschewing policies such as regime change that might lead weak states to proliferate.[42] These differences in the tools required to mitigate the different pathways to first use are one reason not to broaden the concept of crisis instability to include all reasons for nuclear first use.

More theoretically, there is no a priori reason why reducing one motivation for using nuclear weapons first will simultaneously reduce another. Indeed, some strategists, particularly in the United States, argue—for a variety of different reasons—that, in order to enhance deterrence, it is actually desirable for U.S. adversaries to worry that Washington might attempt a disarming first strike. They argue that the risks of this strategy—including increased pre-emptive pressures on the adversary—are outweighed by the benefits of enhanced deterrence, which include the reduced likelihood of an adversary's using nuclear weapons first to try to coerce the United States or of the United States being forced into using nuclear weapons to respond to non-nuclear aggression.

For instance, some contemporary strategists observe that, fearing regime change, the leader of a state facing conventional defeat by the United States might use nuclear weapons in a last desperate attempt to make Washington back down. They argue that in order to deter the use of nuclear weapons in this scenario, Washington needs to be able to eliminate—completely or almost completely—the adversary's nuclear forces.[43] Advocates acknowledge that such a strategy might "exacerbate the problem of controlling escalation if an adversary feels so threatened that it adopts a hair-trigger nuclear doctrine" but argue that, on balance, "the benefits . . . trump the costs."[44] In other words, they posit that their strategy will have the net effect of reducing the probability of nuclear use by reducing the likelihood of a U.S. adversary's using nuclear weapons for coercive purposes, even if there is an increased chance it will employ them because of pre-emptive pressures.

Similar issues were debated during the Cold War. A fundamental strategy debate—perhaps *the* fundamental debate—of that era centered on the question of whether deterrence would be enhanced if the United States had the ability to launch a damage-limiting strike against the Soviet Union. Proponents of damage limitation argued that if the Soviet Union believed the United States could emerge relatively unscathed from a nuclear war, Moscow would be less inclined to undertake conventional aggression in Europe.[45] These strategists were willing to accept what they believed would be a small increase in the probability that Moscow would use nuclear weapons to pre-empt a U.S. first strike in return for a more substantial decrease in the probability that the United States would have to resort to the use of nuclear weapons to counter Soviet conventional aggression in Europe, because war would be less likely to break out in the first place.

Even strategists who oppose "warfighting" doctrines sometimes see similar—if much less severe—potential trade-offs. Many such strategists view the credibility of nuclear threats as resting on the "threat that leaves something to chance," that is, the possibility of unintended escalation from lower levels of violence to nuclear use.[46] In a crisis, the steps that a U.S. adversary might take—such as dispersing mobile missiles or sending submarines out to sea—may be stabilizing on balance (since they significantly enhance force survivability), but they can simultaneously increase the chance of unintended escalation through miscalculation, accident or unauthorized launch. Thus, Jervis has argued that "if security is linked in part to the danger of inadvertent war, then too much stability could make the world safe for coercion and violence" (although he does go on to add that, in practice, "it is doubtful that arms control could succeed too well and produce arrangements that would drive the danger of undesired escalation close to zero.")[47] For present purposes, it is unnecessary to critique these arguments and reach a conclusion about whether inducing fear in an opponent that the United States might use nuclear weapons first does, in fact, enhance deterrence and hence lessen the net probability of nuclear use; it is enough to note the existence of important arguments for this proposition. It is precisely because such arguments are made that it is most advantageous to define crisis stability (and, by extension, strategic stability) in the narrow way advocated above. This definition enables a clearly delineated debate about whether there is, in fact, a trade-off between crisis stability and the effectiveness of deterrence and, if there is, what the optimal balance should be. By contrast, using "strategic stability" as a catch-all term that tries to capture every possible motive for using nuclear weapons first tends to obscure the reasons why strategists disagree and thus confuses the debate.

DOES IT MATTER IF AN ADVERSARY DOES NOT SHARE THE U.S. CONCEPT OF STRATEGIC STABILITY?

Yet another criticism of the narrower understanding of strategic stability is that it is only a useful tool for policymakers if other states share the U.S. conception. In practice, they rarely do. This argument has recently been advanced by David Yost with regard to the U.S.-Soviet relationship during the Cold War. Central to Yost's argument is a considerable body of evidence that "the Soviet political-military leadership appears to have rejected the 'mutual assured destruction' reasoning advanced by Robert McNamara and his followers as the desirable foundation of strategic stability, including 'crisis stability' and 'arms race stability'."[48] The salient question here is whether this rejection actually nullified the utility of U.S. policies designed to promote stability.

In an attack on the concept of arms race stability, Yost observes that the Soviet nuclear arms build-up of the 1970s "did not conform to U.S. 'arms race stability' theories" and "gave many American observers the impression that the USSR was seeking superiority."[49] Soviet behavior was indeed confounding to some in the United States. A number of American analysts originally assumed that the primary — if not the sole — reason for the Soviet build-up was enhancing the survivability of its nuclear forces. Given that the drivers for Soviet procurement were actually more complex, it was inevitable that these analysts would be disappointed when the Soviet Union did not terminate its build-up upon acquiring a survivable second strike capability.[50] However, Yost's observation says much more about a lack of imagination on the part of American analysts than it does about any deficiencies with strategic stability. As noted above, there are plenty of reasons why a state might build up its forces besides fear of an adversary's first strike and nothing in strategic stability "theory" says otherwise (a point that some over-enthusiastic advocates may have forgotten). Achieving an assured second-strike capability was a *necessary* condition for the Soviet Union to cease its arms build-up but certainly not a *sufficient* one. Accordingly, Soviet behavior in the 1970s is not a valid reason for rejecting the concept of arms race stability.

Ultimately, whether states stop an arms build-up after achieving an assured second-strike capability is not really a fair test of the usefulness of arms race stability. A better test is to examine whether states that fear for the survivability of their forces *start* an arms build-up. The U.S.-Soviet experience from the Cold War certainly meets this criterion. As noted above, a major factor in precipitating the Soviet long-range arms build-up appears to have been concern in Moscow that, at the height of the Berlin Crisis in 1961 and during the Cuban Missile Crisis in 1962, the vulnerability of its forces had proved a significant disadvantage.[51]

The motivation of the Soviet Union in continuing to augment its nuclear forces long after it had achieved a credible second-strike capability forms the basis for Yost's critique of crisis stability. Yost points to considerable evidence that the Soviet Union adopted a warfighting doctrine, which, he argues, led it to seek superiority in order to limit the damage it would suffer in a nuclear war.[52] By contrast, he claims that the United States "at times exercised restraint" in developing equivalent counterforce capabilities, although, strangely, he gives just a single minor example of such restraint and glosses over continual and relentless improvements in U.S. missile accuracy that far outstripped the Soviet Union.[53] In light of this disparity, Yost argues that a "shared commitment to a theory of 'crisis stability'" cannot explain the absence of conflict.[54] Instead, he attributes it to the bipolar structure of the Cold War international order and the "profound fear of nuclear war" that the superpowers shared.[55]

Contrary to Yost's explanation, however, it is precisely because the Soviet Union *had* a warfighting doctrine that it was important to ensure crisis stability during the Cold War.[56] As Yost himself observes, the Soviet Union was prone, rightly or wrongly, to project its own dedication to nuclear warfighting onto the United States.[57] Had the Soviet Union come to believe that the United States was about to strike then — according to Yost's own interpretation of Soviet doctrine — it may have tried to pre-empt such an attack. In a crisis, therefore, it was critically important for Moscow to believe that Washington thought it could not meaningfully lessen the horror of a nuclear war by striking first. Thus, crisis stability is not inconsistent with Yost's explanation that the Cold War did not turn hot because each side had a profound fear of nuclear war. On the contrary, it is precisely *because* there generally was a sufficient degree of crisis stability that this fear was able to play a restraining role.

Of course, to the extent that the Soviet Union did not accept mutual vulnerability as a policy goal and sought to attain superiority, it was, as a practical matter, harder for Moscow and Washington to agree upon bilateral measures to enhance stability. However, such measures were negotiated — most notably the Anti-Ballistic Missile Treaty and START I — and they played a positive if modest role in enhancing strategic stability, even if the Soviet Union was motivated to agree to them for other reasons. Moreover, the Soviet Union's failure to accept mutual vulnerability certainly did not stop the United States from taking unilateral steps to enhance strategic stability, such as developing SSBNs (which, until the final years of the Cold War, were particularly stabilizing because they were too inaccurate to threaten an adversary's strategic forces).

In fact, the development and procurement of survivable nuclear forces — unilateral decisions originally taken outside of an arms control framework — did more than anything else to ensure mutual vulnerability and hence crisis stability during the Cold War.

CONCLUSIONS

It might have been better if strategic stability had an alternative, less grandiose name ("deterrence stability" springs to mind as one alternative). The very words "strategic stability" give the impression of a broad concept that pretends to predict whether and how states can enjoy stable relations. In reality, however, strategic stability is most useful if it is narrowly defined — in terms of whether fear of an adversary's using nuclear weapons motivates a state to change its force posture — and modestly applied, that is, with the recognition that it is one — and not the only — criterion against which to assess nuclear policy.

While fear of an adversary's first strike has never led to nuclear use, it has led states to change their force postures in sometimes dangerous ways, whether by dispersing mobile forces, redeploying existing systems or developing entirely new ones. None of these actions have been cost free, not least because they have sometimes exacerbated international tensions and created new risks of further escalation. Reducing similar pressures on states in the future — that is, ensuring and enhancing strategic stability — remains a worthwhile, and in fact a vital policy goal.

That said, it is not the only relevant goal. Nuclear strategy must also be assessed along other axes — deterrence effectiveness, cost effectiveness, bureaucratic feasibility, domestic politics, and alliance politics to name but five—and we should certainly not assume a priori that the policy that maximizes strategic stability will simultaneously maximize all—or even any— of the other variables. Crafting the optimal nuclear strategy almost certainly involves trade-offs and it is by defining strategic stability most narrowly that we are most likely to set up a sensible debate about what those trade-offs should be.

ENDNOTES - CHAPTER 4

1. See, for example, Colin S. Gray, "Strategic Stability Reconsidered," *Daedalus*, Vol. 109, No. 4, Fall 1980, pp. 135-54.

2. See, for example, Colin Powell, prepared statement to the hearings before the Committee on Foreign Relations of the United States Senate on "Treaty on Strategic Offensive Reduction," S. HRG. 107-622, July 9, 2002, available from *www.access.gpo.gov/congress/senate/senate11sh107.html*; Camille Grand, "Ballistic Missile Threats, Missile Defenses, Deterrence, and Strategic Stability," *International Perspectives on Missile Proliferation and Defenses*, Occasional Paper 5, Monterey, CA: Monterey Institute for International Studies, 2001, pp. 5-11, available from *cns.miis.edu/opapers/op5/op5.pdf*; Thérèse Delpeche, "Nuclear Weapons—Less Central, More Dangerous?" in Burkard Schmitt, ed., *Nuclear Weapons: A New Great Debate*, Challiot Papers 48, Paris, France: Institute for Security Studies, Western European Union, 2001, pp. 14-22, available from *www.iss.europa.eu/uploads/media/cp048e.pdf*; Thomas Scheber, "Strategic Stability: Time for a Reality Check," *International Journal*, Vol. 63, No. 4, Autumn 2008, pp. 893-915.

3. Edward L. Warner, remarks on "How is Deterrence and Stability Enhanced/Diminished by Arms Control Beyond New Start?" 2011 United States Strategic Command Deterrence Symposium, Omaha, NE, August 3-4, 2011, available from *www.stratcom.mil/video/deterrence/67/Panel_2_-_How_is_deterrence_and_stability_enhanceddiminished_by_arms_control_bey/*.

4. U.S. Department of Defense, *Nuclear Posture Review Report*, April 2010, p. 23, available from *www.defense.gov/npr/docs/2010%20*

nuclear%20posture%20review%20report.pdf. Similarly, in a nod towards the concept of arms race stability, the *Nuclear Posture Review Report* argues that "a carefully crafted and verifiable [Fissile Material Cutoff Treaty] will . . . contribute to nuclear stability worldwide"(p. 13), although it is unclear why "stability" here is qualified by "nuclear" instead of "strategic" as elsewhere.

5. Other statements by U.S. officials also imply a broader meaning. Assistant Secretary of State Rose Gottemoeller has, for instance, stated that the end of the Cold War:

> doesn't mean we've been able to disentangle our nuclear relationship. In fact, that's something we're working on very seriously now to try to work with the Russians to have a relationship of assured stability, rather than this mutual deterrence, this standoff of nuclear weapons. Because although that prevented a shooting war during all the years of the Cold War, nevertheless we feel that nuclear terror is not the kind of environment we want to continue with.

Rose Gottemoeller, interview on 'Washington Journal,' C-SPAN, December 23, 2011, available from *www.c-span.org/Events/Washington-Journal-Friday-December-23/10737426583/*.

6. *Nuclear Posture Review*, p. 13.

7. *Ibid*, p. 6.

8. Sergei Lavrov, Remarks to the State Duma, Moscow, Russia, January 14, 2011, in Russian, available from *www.mid.ru/brp_4.nsf/0/B4B970B7D9B7FAD9C3257818005CDBD2*.

9. *Ibid*.

10. For an insightful analysis of Russian views of strategic stability, see Alexei G. Arbatov, Vladimir Z. Dvorkin, Alexander A. Pikaev and Sergey K. Oznobishchev, *Strategic Stability after the Cold War*, Moscow, Russia: IMEMO, 2010, pp. 27-9, available from *www.nuclearsecurityproject.org/uploads/publications/STRATEGIC-STABILITYAFTERTHECOLDWAR_020211.pdf*.

11. *The Military Doctrine of the Russian Federation*, February 5, 2010, para. 8b (unofficial translation).

12. Lora Saalman, *China & the U.S. Nuclear Posture Review*, Carnegie Paper, Beijing, China: Carnegie-Tsinghua Center for Global Policy, 2011, p. 5, available from *carnegieendowment.org/files/china_posture_review.pdf*.

13. Li Bin and Nie Hongyi, "Zhongmei zhanlue wendingxing de kaocha" ("A Study of Sino-U.S. Strategic Stability"), *Shijie jingji yu zhengzhi (World Economics and Politics)*, No. 2, 2008, p. 13, quoted in Saalman, *China & The U.S. Nuclear Posture Review*, p. 5.

14. This specific phrase is regularly employed by Chinese officials. See, for example, Cheng Jingye, Statement to the Third Session of the Preparatory Committee for the 2010 Review Conference of the Parties to the Treaty on the Non-Proliferation of Nuclear Weapons, New York, May 4, 2009, p. 3, available from *www.chinesemission-vienna.at/eng/fyywj/t562218.htm*.

15. See note 2.

16. Thomas C. Schelling, *The Strategy of Conflict*, Cambridge, MA: Harvard University, 1960, ch. 9. For the development of the concept, see Lawrence Freedman, *The Evolution of Nuclear Strategy*, 3rd Ed., Basingstoke, UK: Palgrave Macmillan, 2003, pp. 180-184.

17. Thomas C. Schelling, *Arms and Influence*, New Haven, CT: Yale University Press, 1966, p. 234.

18. In a previous work on deterrence at low numbers, I defined arms race stability as the absence of *any* incentive to augment a nuclear force. While it is clearly important to examine all possible incentives for rearmament in assessing whether deep reductions are desirable, I have come to the conclusion that it is helpful to reserve the term "arms race stability" for a build-up motivated by concern about an opponent's using nuclear weapons first in a crisis. James M. Acton, *Deterrence During Disarmament: Deep Nuclear Reductions and International Security*, Adelphi 417, Abingdon, UK: Routledge for the International Institute of Strategic Studies, 2011, p. 17.

19. Michael S. Gerson, "No First Use: The Next Step for U.S. Nuclear Policy," *International Security*, Vol. 35, No. 2, Fall 2010, pp. 38-39; Acton, *Deterrence During Disarmament*, p. 38.

20. Equally, crisis stability does not guarantee first-strike stability because a bolt-out-of-the-blue first strike during peacetime could be categorized (depending on the motive) as a first strike instability but not a crisis instability.

21. For a classic example see Glenn A. Kent and David E. Thaler, *First-Strike Stability: A Methodology for Evaluating Strategic Forces*, R-3765-AF, Santa Monica, CA: RAND, 1989.

22. Scheber, "Strategic Stability," pp. 895-897; David S. Yost, *Strategic Stability in the Cold War: Lessons for Continuing Challenges*, Proliferation Papers 36, Paris, France: Ifri, 2011, pp. 16-19, available from *www.ifri.org/downloads/pp36yost.pdf*.

23. John G. Hines, Ellis M. Mishulovich, and John F. Shull, *Soviet Intentions 1965-1985*, Vol. I, *An Analytical Comparison of U.S.-Soviet Assessments During the Cold War*, McLean, VA: BDM Federal, 1995, pp. 27-45, available from *www.gwu.edu/~nsarchiv/ nukevault/ebb285/*.

24. David Alan Rosenberg, "The Origins of Overkill: Nuclear Weapons and American Strategy, 1945-1960," *International Security*, Vol. 7, No. 4, Spring 1983, pp. 33-5.

25. *Ibid*, pp. 50-54.

26. Gerson, "No First Use," p. 37.

27. Scott D. Sagan, *The Limits of Safety: Organization, Accidents and Nuclear Weapons*, Princeton, NJ: Princeton University Press, 1993, p. 144.

28. Ernest R. May, John D. Steinbruner and Thomas W. Wolfe, *History of the Strategic Arms Competition 1945-1972*, Part I, Washington, DC: Office of the Secretary of Defense, Historical Office, 1981, p. 475, available from *www.dod.gov/pubs/foi/homeland_ defense/missile_defense_agency/226.pdf*.

29. Michael S. Gerson, "The Sino-Soviet Border Conflict: Deterrence, Escalation, and the Threat of Nuclear War in 1969," Alexandria, VA: Center for Naval Analyses, 2010.

30. David M. Alpern with David C. Martin, "A Soviet War of Nerves," *Newsweek*, January 5, 1981, p. 21.

31. Director of Central Intelligence, "Implications of Recent Soviet Military-Political Activities," Special National Intelligence Estimate 11-10-84/JX, May 18, 1984, para. 2, available from *www. foia.cia.gov/docs/DOC_0000278546/DOC_0000278546.pdf*. See also Peter Vincent Pry, *War Scare: Russia and America on the Nuclear Brink*, Westport, CT: Praeger, 1999, pp. 41-42; David E. Hoffman, *The Dead Hand: The Untold Story of the Cold War Arms Race and its Dangerous Legacy*, New York: Doubleday, 2000, pp. 94-95.

32. The term "second-best strategic posture" was coined by May, Steinbruner, and Wolfe, *History of the Strategic Arms Competition 1945-1972*, Part I, p. 341. Modern historians with access to the Soviet archives have reached a similar conclusion. See, for instance, Aleksandr Fursenko and Timothy Naftali, *Khrushchev's Cold War: The Inside Story of an American Adversary*, New York: W. W. Norton and Company, 2006, pp. 243-244.

33. Fursenko and Naftali, *Khrushchev's Cold War*, p. 424.

34. May, Steinbruner, and Wolfe, *History of the Strategic Arms Competition 1945-1972*, Part I, ch. X. The Berlin Crisis may have been a more significant factor in Khrushchev's decision than May, Steinbruner, and Wolfe recognize. See Aleksandr Fursenko and Timothy Naftali, *"One Hell of a Gamble:" Khrushchev, Castro, and Kennedy 1958-1964*, New York: W. W. Norton & Company, 1997, p. 171.

35. Stephen Prowse and Albert Wohlstetter, "Stability in a World With More Than Two Countries," in Sanford Lakoff, ed., *Beyond START?* IGCC Policy Paper 7, La Jolla, CA: University of California at San Diego, Institute on Global Conflict and Cooperation, 1988, p. 46, available from *igcc.ucsd.edu/assets/001/501173.pdf*.

36. Yost, *Strategic Stability in the Cold War*, pp. 27-28.

37. Scheber, "Strategic Stability," p. 898.

38. Frank P. Harvey, "The Future of Strategic Stability and Nuclear Deterrence," *International Journal*, Vol. 58, No. 2, Spring 2003, p. 327. See also Scheber, "Strategic Stability."

39. Robert Jervis, "Arms Control, Stability, and Causes of War," *Daedalus*, Vol. 120, No. 1, Winter 1991, p. 249.

40. Scheber, "Strategic Stability," pp. 903-904.

41. For clarity, this section focuses on crisis stability, but the argument applies to longer timescale instabilities too.

42. Of course, some measures might address both problems. Most obviously, improving political relations would clearly help reduce all incentives for using nuclear weapons first. However, at the level of practical policy — the kind of arms control steps that adversaries might agree to as part of a confidence-building pro-cess — the measures needed to address the different drivers for first use are largely distinct.

43. Keir A. Lieber and Daryl G. Press, "The Nukes We Need: Preserving the American Deterrent," *Foreign Affairs*, Vol. 88, No. 6, November/December 2009, pp. 39-51.

44. *Ibid*, p. 50.

45. See, for example, Gray, "Strategic Stability Reconsidered."

46. Schelling, *The Strategy of Conflict*, ch. 8.

47. Jervis, "Arms Control, Stability, and Causes of War," p. 177.

48. Yost, *Strategic Stability in the Cold War*, p. 22. One problem with Yost's analysis is his comparison of U.S. declaratory policy to (what we know about) Soviet war plans. Many analysts who have examined U.S. force posture and what is known about its nuclear war planning have reached the conclusion that, in spite of its declaratory policy, the United States also rejected mutual vul-nerability and pursued a war-winning strategy. See, for example,

Robert Jervis, *The Illogic of American Nuclear Strategy*, Ithaca, NY: Cornell University Press, 1984, ch. 3; Scott D. Sagan, *Moving Targets: Nuclear Strategy and National Security*, Princeton, NJ: Princeton University Press, 1989, ch. 1; Austin Long, *Deterrence from Cold War to Long War: Lessons from Six Decades of RAND Research*, Santa Monica, CA: RAND Corporation, 2008, pp. 25-43, available from *www.rand.org/pubs/monographs/2008/RAND_MG636.pdf*.

49. Yost, *Strategic Stability in the Cold War*, p. 23.

50. The most authoritative account of the Soviet build-up is Hines, Mishulovich, and Shull, *Soviet Intentions 1965-1985*, Vol. I, ch. IV. They argue that much of this build-up was supply driven. Specifically, the defense-industrial sector "used its political clout to deliver more weapons than the armed services asked for and even to build new weapon systems that the operational military did not want" (p. 61). Unlike the U.S. Cold War assessments on which Yost bases most of his analysis, *Soviet Intentions* (which Yost does occasionally cite) is based on interviews with senior Soviet officials.

51. See note 34.

52. Yost, *Strategic Stability in the Cold War*, pp. 19-23. See also note 50.

53. Yost, *Strategic Stability in the Cold War*, p. 17. The most complete account of the evolution of missile accuracy during the Cold War is Donald MacKenzie, *Inventing Accuracy: A Historical Sociology of Nuclear Missile Guidance*, Cambridge, MA: The MIT Press, 1990. See, in particular, Appendix A. For the impact this trend had on the "lethality" of the U.S. arsenal, see Lynn Eden, "The U.S. Nuclear Arsenal and Zero: Sizing and Planning for Use—Past, Present and Future" in Catherine McArdle Kelleher and Judith Reppy, eds., *Getting to Zero: The Path to Nuclear Disarmament*, Stanford, CA: Stanford University Press, 2011, pp. 71-73.

54. Yost, *Strategic Stability in the Cold War*, p. 28.

55. *Ibid*, p. 9.

56. In fact, crisis stability is *only* relevant where states have a propensity towards warfighting. If two states reject pre-emption — and can somehow do so credibly — then neither would have to worry about the consequences of the other side's striking first, thus making the entire issue of crisis stability moot.

57. Yost, *Strategic Stability in the Cold War*, p. 38.

CHAPTER 5

FUTURE TECHNOLOGY AND STRATEGIC STABILITY

Ronald F. Lehman II

THE DYNAMICS OF STABILITY AND THE ROLES OF TECHNOLOGY

Strategic stability is often associated with enduring relations among powerful nations, particularly those with nuclear forces or the potential to acquire them. This inevitably spotlights the role of technology as an equalizer or counterweight. Strategic stability, however, is ultimately the product of a broader political, economic, and military dynamic among many players in which technology performs multiple roles including that of being an agent of change.

The greatest dangers, such as war, arise mainly out of the escalation of complex interactions at lower levels of competition or conflict. More than technology is involved. Successful approaches to strategic stability therefore must emphasize creating a wider set of conditions in an effort to avoid the feared outcomes.

These conditions for promoting strategic stability can vary from case to case. Change is inevitable, and change generates many stresses. When managed successfully, strategic stability is enhanced while advancing opportunities and avoiding dangers. When the stress of uncertainty and surprise creates dysfunctional behavior or undermines the effectiveness of planned responses, dangerous instabilities can result.

The key to preventing disasters is nearly always found in the successful management of lesser events that might otherwise encourage or enable dangerous outcomes we wish to avoid. Thus, the human factor is more important to maintaining strategic stability than is the technological factor. Nevertheless, technology influences both the context for human behavior and decisionmaking itself. Of course, technology also provides tools to create strategic change or respond to it.

Individuals and organizations never have all the information and resources necessary to guarantee the avoidance of dire outcomes, but technology can help us do better at coping with uncertainty and establishing priorities. Given the greater complexity anticipated in the 21st century, a diversity of options will be needed at all levels of cooperation, competition, and conflict. This diversity must be analyzed and exercised intensely by the most modern means to produce synergism rather than disruption and to ensure the wise investment of scarce resources.

CONTINUITY AND UNCERTAINTY

Technological advancement and social change have been dramatic during the nuclear age. Nevertheless, most analysis of strategic stability, as the name implies, emphasizes continuity. Certainly, players, interests, strategies, and weapon systems can exist for long periods. Antagonistic forces can co-exist and counterbalance for decades. Thus, stability studies often seem "set piece" and familiar. Indeed, strategic change usually is gradual—but not always.

The history of the last 67 years is punctuated by momentous changes—the atomic bomb; the end of World War II; the "Iron Curtain"; the dismantlement of colonial empires; the hydrogen bomb; the intercontinental ballistic missile; the nuclear submarine; the moon landing; the transformation of Maoist China by Den Xiaoping; ubiquitous precision-guided munitions; the breakup of the Soviet Union; large reductions in superpower nuclear arsenals; the emergence of additional nuclear weapons-capable states; the rise of new economic powers; a resurgence of ethnic and sectarian violence; the beginning of high technology-empowered terrorism; and the globalization of information, innovation, technology, capital, markets, and people. Demographics, economics, politics, and science suggest that more profound strategic shifts are possible in the decades ahead.

Whether we use the word "stability" to describe actual strategic relationships or to refer to a policy goal, stability in our world should ultimately be seen as "dynamic," not "static." Stability needs to be associated with concepts such as robustness, persistence, and durability. Over time, however, sustaining stability should be seen less as avoiding or ignoring change and more as shaping change or responding to it. In particular, managing stability requires sufficient awareness of what is going on including relevant technological developments. Even in anticipating human behavior, we should expect some outliers. Combining new inventions with human volatility will confound our vision of the future even more. Thus, in projecting the stability implications of science and technology (S&T), we need to expect surprise.

If strategic technologies are those that most influence change and our responses to it, then the fundamental strategic inventions concern what we know and how we think—languages, alphabets, the printing press, radio, television, the internet, smart phones, data fusion, interactive multimedia. Even in the age of nuclear deterrence, when weapons are powerful symbols and their deployments are exclamation marks, critical strategic technologies involve gathering or signaling information. Strategic stability calculations are therefore less about the power and number of weapons than they are about anticipating human responses to new, different, and possibly inaccurate information about the circumstances, capabilities, and intent of others and ourselves. Strategic policies and programs therefore must focus on the management of uncertainty and the promotion of change that may mitigate dangers that might accompany human reactions to surprise.

Given the specter of nuclear devastation, modifications to strategic policies and forces have been especially cautious and evolutionary during and after the Cold War. This morphing process makes adjustments difficult to see unless one looks back over larger periods of time.[1] Nevertheless, one can argue that the strategy of the United States, however incrementally it changes, has always mandated flexibility and diverse capabilities to shape and then respond to momentous changes that could threaten the United States or its allies. When big changes did occur, the strategy was successful, managing both certainty and uncertainty to keep the "Big Peace." Developing or responding to new technology was an important part of that strategy and remains so.

How will technology contribute or detract in the decades ahead? The right answers are not obvious. While seeking to optimize our efforts in the face of trends that may change or predictions that may prove wrong, we can navigate dangerous waters more safely by keeping some agility. Both optimization and flexibility require a better understanding of the manifold interactions of man and machine.

In strategic relationships, shaping the context in which decisions are made is a major means for influencing behavior. Technology can be a powerful tool for altering a context or changing those perceptions that increase or decrease stability. The sword, crossbow, gunpowder, fortifications, railroads, the telegraph, machine gun, battleship, submarine, airplane, tank, nerve gas, radio, radar, and cruise and ballistic missiles — these and other technologies affected stability even before the nuclear age. Thus, understanding the vagaries of technological trends is vital to managing strategic stability. Furthermore, an examination of science and technology can provide insights into the dynamics of stability, analytically and cautiously by analogy.[2]

The history of invention proves that uncertainty about the technical feasibility of an emerging technology is compounded many times over by uncertainty about its real world viability and competitiveness. The up and down economics of venture capital reinforces that caution. The many failed or disappointing technology outcomes and the resulting high risk of prediction failure, however, cannot erase three fundamental realities that the 21st century has inherited from the 20th; namely, that (1) technology is advancing rapidly, (2) many predictions ultimately do come true, and (3) inept response to surprise is common, even if someone had already predicted what ultimately happened.[3]

Making irremediable decisions about the impact of future technology on strategic stability is neither easy nor safe. We may deeply regret locking in decisions early if we subsequently find the path taken was based upon erroneous predictions. This is particularly true when the plans and programs we create under routine conditions must provide sound options for future decisions that may be made in time of crisis. A crisis is almost defined by unclear, tense, and emotional circumstances in which someone is experiencing the unexpected and is not at their rational best. Individuals and organizations can easily falter in these circumstances.

Debates related to strategic stability become intense every dozen years or so when they get caught up in enduring policy and partisan conflicts within and among nations. Technological options such as nuclear modernization or missile defense are often the catalyst of these debates. Despite considerable background polarization, however, the literature on technology and strategy remains staid. Even the basic technologies and some of the actual aircraft associated with central nuclear stability have been around for over half a century. Most nuclear weapons and their delivery and support systems were acquired decades ago. Revisiting these issues today runs the risk of ". . . déjà vu all over again."

Nevertheless, we are entering a period of significant geopolitical and economic change, in part the product of the global advance and spread of technology. Now may be an excellent time to take a fresh look at issues of strategic stability through the lens of technological change.[4] Evidence of rapid change around the world suggests we have steep "learning curves," but a survey of the current discussion suggests that we also have deep "forgetting curves." Looking at classic issues from the perspective of new technology and geo-strategic transformations could provide some fresh perspectives while testing older thinking against changed circumstances as well.

Confidence that one can predict the future with any precision is never well placed. We have been surprised before and will be surprised again. Studying the source of surprise may help minimize the magnitude of it, mitigate any downsides, maximize possible benefits of change, and manage the process of creative technological advance and obsolescence. Sources of surprise include difficulties in (1) detecting change, (2) identifying possibilities, (3) calculating probabilities, (4) evaluating trends, (5) clarifying consequences, (6) anticipating reactions, (7) foreseeing counter-reactions, (8) computing complex dynamics, and (9) compensating for emergent behavior.[5] Surprise is a process. Big surprises tend to be the cumulative result of smaller, earlier changes being missed, misunderstood, or ignored or of responses to the initial surprises escalating unexpectedly.

Consider "Sputnik," which presents a classic illustration of surprise and the complexity of strategic stability. The U.S. Government was not very surprised that the Soviet Union launched Sputnik, the world's first artificial satellite. Of course, Washington was surprised that, after two successful Soviet launches and two failed American launches, the United States had to restart a competitive program in order to launch its own satellite.

Perhaps the greatest surprise, however, was the resulting, widely held conclusion at home and abroad that the unending "Sputnik Crisis" reflected a declining United States and a rising Union of Soviet Socialist Republics (USSR).[6] In response, within a few months the Department of Defense (DoD) had created the Advanced Research Projects Agency (now Defense Advanced Research Projects Agency [DARPA])[7] and Congress had passed the National Defense Education

Act (NDEA). Occurring just 1 month after the establishment of the North American Air Defense Command (NORAD), Sputnik fueled debates over the intercontinental ballistic missile (ICBM) implications of space launch vehicles and reopened the debate over "surprise attack," "crisis stability," and the "weaponization of space." Sputnik had a powerful and lasting effect on elections, the Cold War, the "missile gap," the Cuban missile crisis, the space race, arms control, missile defense, and President John Kennedy's decision to put a man on the moon.

This reference to the well-known Sputnik story is only to note that relatively simple acts of technology demonstration can have strategic stability implications that go far beyond their immediate, often minimal military impact. Moreover, the manner and context of response can amplify effects and promulgate influence long after the event. In the future, nation-states and perhaps even terrorists may display new capabilities that could have Sputnik-like strategic impact involving space activities, weapons of mass destruction (WMD), cyber crime, unmanned vehicles, advanced conventional weapons, or even economic disruption through dominant new civilian applications of technology. The longer our time horizon, the more likely this will happen. Technological change is normally incremental, but can be very rapid. The time frame for response is important to stability calculations.

Gauging the future simply by weighing the past is dangerous in periods of rapid change. Still, history gives various examples of how far into the future we must anticipate in order to make portentous decisions prudently. Twenty to 40 years may seem too distant when we consider that the United States, from decision to deployment, put new ballistic missiles on new submarines including novel, lightweight warhead designs in 4 years (1957-60). The delivery of the first atomic bomb by a B-29 bomber was just 42 years after the Wright brothers' first primitive, powered flight at Kitty Hawk, North Carolina, and only 3 years after Enrico Fermi first produced a self-sustaining critical nuclear reaction in Chicago Pile-1. The first test launch of an operational nuclear warhead from a submerged ballistic missile submarine was 5 years after Sputnik, only 17 years after the Trinity test in New Mexico. In just 1 year, 1958, the United States increased the number of nuclear warheads in its official stockpile by over 5,000.[8] Likewise, in 1 year, 1992, the United States reduced its nuclear weapons stockpile by that much.[9] Thus, by 2009, the entire U.S. official stockpile was 5,113, roughly the amount by which the United States had previously increased or decreased its stockpile number in single years.[10] At the mathematical average rate that the official stockpile number was reduced between 1967 and 2009, in theory, the official stockpile would reach zero about the time the New Strategic Arms Reduction Treaty (New START) ceilings take effect, some 5 years from now.[11] Reductions are continuing, but at some point the rate of reduction is likely to slow down well before zero because of uncertainty and fear of instabilities at low numbers.

On the other hand, nearly all of the weapons and delivery systems in the U.S. nuclear arsenal now date back 20 to 40 years or more. Of course, strategic systems procured may be upgraded many times in order to serve for decades. That is the dilemma of thinking about the future. The time horizon changes on us, and we cannot completely control developments. What we think might happen in 20 years may actually happen in 10 years, or 5 years, or 1 year. Or it may take more than 40 years, or not happen at all. The decisions we make must permit us to sustain or change as needed.[12]

ELABORATING TECHNOLOGY AS PRODUCT OR PROCESS

What technologies are likely to have the greatest impact on strategic stability in the decades ahead? Multidisciplinary teaming in diverse research fields is resulting in an explosion of technologies. Cross-fertilization among materials science, sensors, diagnostics, robotics, nanotechnology, synthetic biology, genetics, information technology, neuropsychology and the cognitive sciences, micro-electronics, quantum effects, photonics, energetic materials, propulsion, space vehicles, agile manufacturing, automated laboratories, and other fields, including big physics, has opened doors that even the greatest minds recently did not expect. Accelerated engineering techniques and advanced industrial practices are rushing through some of those doors. Not only have basic and applied sciences grown closer together in many fields, but theoretical and experimental sciences have expanded to include what may be a third arm of science — high performance simulations[13] and a fourth arm, data-intensive scientific discovery.[14] These four arms now overlap and are synergistic, further accelerating successful S&T and reducing costs.

A rapid and diverse compounding of technologies can make forecasting problematic, but historically not all paths are explored and even fewer persist over time. We may pursue basic science for its own sake, but sustained investment in applied S&T requires a demonstration of utility. For strategic players, that utility is predominantly calculated relative to the technology and strategy of others. Stimulus-response and measure-countermeasure are not the only dynamics of strategic innovation, but they provide a gravita-

156

tional pull or common attractor that brings different technologies into a relationship with each other.

Consider the basic nuclear delivery systems. Replacing reciprocating engines with jets, the manned bomber flew ever higher and faster to overcome defenses. To escape new high altitude air defense missiles, bombers returned to low altitude using terrain-following radars, electronic countermeasures, and chaff to escape the technological response, the lookdown/shoot-down interceptor. With stealth technology, bombers returned to high altitude, but have kept the option to go low again as concerns about bi-static radars and networked sensors complicate their future. Large, inaccurate, liquid-fueled, surface-launched missiles, initially of medium range, were replaced with solid rocket ICBMs, quickly launched out of hardened underground silos. These were supplemented by the development of ballistic missiles, carried on nuclear-powered submarines, that were launchable underwater.

To reduce costs per warhead, improve military effectiveness, overwhelm defenses, and limit damage around the intended target, all means of delivery took advantage of increases in accuracy and reduction in the size of warheads. Bomber loads were increased with standoff ballistic and air launched cruise missiles (ALCMs). Stealth was even applied to cruise missiles. The single large warheads on ballistic missiles were replaced with multiple independently-targetable re-entry vehicles (MIRVs) accompanied by "penetration aids (PENAIDS)" such as dummy decoy warheads. Small, fast, maneuverable re-entry vehicles replaced large, slow, blunt body ballistic re-entry vehicles that could be intercepted by advanced air defense systems.

To find targets, provide early warning of attack, communicate with forces and even with the enemy, new generations of sensors, communications, and data processing pushed the electronics revolution to provide accuracy, reliability, and survivability in the nuclear environment. Though this intense bilateral competition in both offensive and defensive military technology at the height of the Cold War seems alien to our world today, in reality intense global technology development continues to fuel many dual-use applications that have significant implications for the future of strategic stability.

Over the next 20 to 40 years, what technologies could be the counterpart of the World War II and Cold War developments? Will weapons of concern be more or less powerful? Nuclear or non-nuclear? Will they be explosive or even kinetic? Will their delivery be faster or slower, more or less discriminate? Will they involve physical or functional "kill mechanisms?" Will their delivery systems be manned or unmanned? Will situational awareness be more complete or much dimmer? These issues will be extremely important for considerations of strategic stability. Examining specific technology paths in light of such questions makes possible alternatives seem more concrete, but caution is warranted. Given that much more technology will emerge in the years ahead and many paths will be dead-ends, the strategy of "learning to fish" rather than "receiving a fish" is likely more valuable. More than picking winners, we must try to understand the game.

We often misjudge how steep the classic learning or performance curves for a given technology will be. Early enthusiasts may overestimate progress only to be silent when progress takes off. This cycle of exaggeration followed by underestimation is as common among experts as it is among the "talking heads" and is an important amplifier of technological surprise. Other amplifiers include the growing portfolios of technologies near application that are then packaged by others differently than we might anticipate. These "latent" technologies are often open to many players. Thus, the short lead times to implementation and diverse packaging almost guarantee that multiple players will surprise each other.

In a sense, we are looking at how science fiction today, often speculating from basic science facts, becomes applied technology in the future. Science fiction books and films frequently go beyond the possible, but science fiction sometimes points toward what becomes real. Consider the atomic bomb images of Robert Cromie (1895) and H. G. Wells (1914).[15] Or science fiction may become approximately true by analogy or function. Consider Sir Arthur C. Clarke's wormhole camera that could look back in time.[16] Consider also that expensive, exclusive, limited capabilities available only to a few large governments today eventually may become cheap, ubiquitous, multifunction capabilities for millions of individuals in the future. For example, modern, mobile smart phones with digital cameras, computers, sensors, global positioning system (GPS), packet switching, and Internet access look back not just to science fiction but to technologies funded not that many years ago through DARPA for the DoD.

A look at categories one might find in any taxonomy of technology maturity might be useful. Even *"impossible science"* bounds problems and provides insights. From the perspective of even the most theoretical science, the wormhole camera postulated by Sir

Arthur C. Clarke is emphatically fiction.[17] No one can be certain his wormholes really exist, and the idea of a consumer camera that could exploit such a cosmological speculation to look into the past seems out of this millennium. Nevertheless, the use of staring sensors far more advanced than the security cameras found at automatic teller machines (ATMs) and in parking lots to document and revisit past events and patterns is now commonplace. New networked, highly sensitive, multispectral, mobile, and often miniature sensors and surveillance systems will acquire immense data that must be processed by high performance computers whose capabilities are currently growing faster than Moore's law.[18] This has important implications in the decades ahead for delivery platforms such as aircraft, submarines, and mobile missiles that rely on location uncertainty or stealth for their survival and/or effectiveness.

Categories overlap and technologies move between categories. Science fiction's canonical "death rays" were once, at best, *theoretical science*. They are now *breakthrough science* as, for example, high-energy lasers for industrial purposes approach power levels necessary for effective weapons. High-energy lasers passed through a phase in which they were *extrapolated S&T* as militaries speculated about the future after seeing so many low-powered lasers on the battlefield. Light Emitting Diodes (LEDs) are an *enabling industry* rapidly becoming a *ubiquitous technology* in the quest to reduce demand for electricity, much of which is provided by carbon fuels linked to other strategic issues such as overseas energy dependence and climate change. At the same time, LEDs are increasingly components of military systems and may provide another path to highly efficient weapons. Cutting edge enabling industries include rapid prototyping, agile and additive manufacturing, and, in the chemical industry, flow-process micro-reactors, all potentially dual-use technology that is becoming globally accessible.

Strategic stability can also be influenced by technologies far short of the cutting edge. Nuclear reactors became status symbols for a number of emerging nation-states and remained so even after new technologies stalled and the economics of nuclear power turned dim. In some cases, the nuclear technologists recruited for what turned out to be disappointing domestic nuclear power programs emigrated to the West or turned to other fields. Some, however, became involved in nuclear weapons work of proliferation concern.

Biotech is a new *status technology*, all the more worrisome because, as with the chemical industry, controversial activities often migrate out of the rule of law democracies to avoid regulation or "NIMBY (Not in my back yard.)." Like the boy who cried "Wolf!" the bio-security community warns again and again that biological weapons are becoming WMD that could be available to small groups or individuals and certainly to most nations of concern. A few attempts to use biological weapons have taken place, but the WMD biological "wolf" has not yet struck. It could. What if it does? Similarly, a blurring between cyber crime and cyber warfare is taking place as information technology hubs grow in troubled regions. Does our interdependent networking give us greater redundancy and robustness or more common modes of failure?

The geostrategic impact of *status technologies* is uneven. Nuclear energy provided political top cover for covert weapons programs in India, North Korea, and Iran, but the tragedy of Chernobyl, Ukraine, may have been a catalyst that accelerated the end of the Soviet

Union. Failed chemical and biological terrorism by the cult Aum Shinrikyo brought about its suppression and the successful prosecution of its leadership and has mobilized governments, industry, and science organizations to revisit rules of responsible science.

Students of strategic stability often focus on *monopoly technologies* such as stealthy aircraft like the F-117A fighter bomber and the B2 strategic bomber or the hypersonic boost-glide vehicle, looking to see when they will become *oligopolistic technologies*, available to a number of the great and rising powers. In time, these may become *new baseline technologies* in the same way that unmanned aerial vehicles (UAVs) are spreading even to nonstate actors. When a technology spreads, however, it may not be of the same value to different players. Whatever their military value, difficult to detect explosives are an *asymmetric technology* of particular value to terrorists. Nonlethal weapons are often criticized as asymmetric advantages for intervention or suppression. Advances and constraints on technology do not affect all players equally, and this too can create instabilities.

Most technology that may ultimately influence strategic stability contributes incrementally and as components of systems, not as dramatic "silver bullets." *Accretion technologies* where use builds up over time, such as the vacuum tube, the transistor, and the solid state micro-chip, have radically transformed weapons and war, yet they are seldom seen to alter stability calculations, except perhaps to the degree that they may become massively vulnerable to cyber attack or to nuclear weapons effects such as electromagnetic pulse (EMP).[19]

Some of these embedded technologies, however, might have a more direct impact on strategic stability due to *"highly leveraging effects,"* such as:

- *"Butterfly effects,"* wherein small changes in initial conditions result in radically different outcomes,[20]
- *Horseshoe Nail effects,"* wherein a small loss under the wrong conditions yields a large undesirable outcome,[21] and
- *"Transmutation effects,"* wherein accumulation of small improvements in quality may morph into a major new level of performance.[22]

The "Y2K millennium bug" provides some insight into the implications of such highly leveraging effects.[23] Y2K glitches proved far less serious than some had predicted, but reports spotlighted problems in embedded microchips in older military systems and in government procured equipment that was not from the larger civilian marketplace. The Y2K experience accelerated interest within the Pentagon in the advantages of using "commercial off-the-shelf" (COTS) procurement to obtain economy of scale price advantages and also the quality advantages of dynamic competition among ever more mature technologies. High volume sales can also permit more quality evaluation in a greater variety of environments. Low volume procurements and deployments can complicate both quality control and risk assessment.

On the other hand, the very civilian electronics being used by the military to modernize more cheaply and quickly through COTS may have vulnerabilities in a hostile military environment. In the nuclear context, civilian electronics, even those ruggedized for rough consumer use, are seldom hardened against EMP and thus may be vulnerable to high altitude nuclear detonations whose blast, heat, and other radiation effects otherwise may not reach close to the earth. Also, cyber hacking that can be expensive to financial institutions in peacetime could be devastating in command and control systems in time of war. In short, technology developments, ranging from weapons themselves to components of nonweapons can advance strategic stability or militate against it, depending on scenarios.

STRESS, STRATEGY, AND INFORMATION

If we must keep an eye on what we mean by "future technology," we must also keep an eye on what we mean by "strategic stability," a policy backdrop against which one can assess technological change. Most discussion of strategic stability deals with concepts such as "geo-strategic stability," "political-military stability," "arms race stability," "crisis stability," and "first strike stability." In the last half-century, these subsets of stability were associated largely with comparative nuclear weapons postures. A comprehensive and effective analysis of strategic stability, however, cannot be confined to nuclear, or military, or geopolitical considerations, and certainly not only to technology. Rather, it must encompass a far broader array of considerations to be meaningful and provide useful guidance for both for policy and technology. As we shall see, information is a vital common factor.

Strategic stability is traditionally described as a balance of "capability and intent" among competitors. "Capability" is primarily physical—applied technology and organizations to use it. "Intent" is mental, individual or collective—the goals driving decision-makers. Perhaps a more functional focus would be on "options and behavior" given certain scenarios and players. Changes in technology influence options and behavior as well as the background information and circumstances and the number and style of the players. Whether the new technology increases or decreases stability is the question.

Technology can produce surprise, an information problem, because we do not see the change coming or do not understand its implications. Surprise can produce stress. Stress can drive individuals or groups to mobilize their minds and resources effectively, but stress can also lead to unwise decisions and unsafe behavior. Stability in a sense exists when circumstances, options, and other players permit nations and their allies to manage stress productively while we cope with the physical, mental, and sociological consequences of change. Technology can produce stress or help us reduce and/or manage it.

Thus, stability is promoted by creating conditions in which undesirable effects of surprise are reduced because players can avoid unwanted outcomes better than with some other set of conditions. Whether or not players share the same goals or seek optimal outcomes only for themselves or collectively, in both cooperative and competitive scenarios, outcomes are possible that are worse for everyone. Stability is not about preventing all change or eliminating all conflict. Rather, stability is about avoiding conditions and discouraging behavior that increases the probability of unwanted outcomes, especially those unwanted by almost everyone. This observation about contemporary policy and behavior is similar to more precise concepts found in game theory such as Nash Equilibria.

In the real world, stability may not be precisely calculable, but its dynamic nature requires management nevertheless. Moreover, stability itself competes with other policy goals. In the "Cold War," the Soviet Union and the United States each exhibited revolutionary behavior and status quo behavior at the same time. Often engaging in indirect wars, they avoided society-destroying military conflict even as they presented to each other both acute, existential nuclear threats and chronic alternative political-economic challenges. Technology and information played an important role in all of this. Despite many chaotic events and surprises, including the rapid collapse of the Soviet Union, the classic, bipolar "Cold War" judgment was that the superpower balance was stable. This is attributed to a shared recognition of the horror of nuclear war. The perceived reality of that era was that instability and wars in the Third World should not be allowed to lead to World War III. That was considered a source of strategic stability on the largest scale.

In a sense, however, large-scale strategic stability is the product of many, smaller strategic stabilities that may not follow predictable or desirable paths. The ultimate fear is that a small change in initial conditions can unknowingly result in radically different outcomes from those expected. That is often what we mean by strategic instability. Technological change can cause that kind of strategic instability at both lower and higher levels of competition and conflict. Technological change may also help reduce that instability.

Rapid technological change is inevitable. Exploiting that change may be necessary to rebalance and provide stability, but rapid technological change can also be destabilizing. Consider again just the idea of "information," central not only to our digital electronic age, but also to modern neuroscience, game theory, behavioral economics, mathematics, and even cosmology. Information is a concept that unites two great components of strategic stability; namely, technology and psychology.

Imagine two alternative worlds. At one extreme, consider a world in which "situational awareness" is almost total. At the other extreme, consider situational awareness that is nearly zero. In the first of these worlds, the players have nearly complete knowledge of the capabilities, deployments, intentions, and behavior of others and themselves. In the second of these hypothetical worlds, that knowledge has disappeared. The real world is somewhere in between and has the added complication that some information may be false or misleading, a possibility magnified in our age by cyber intrusion and attack. In a stable world, significant changes in the quantity and quality of information that might alter calculations are slow and predictable relative to the required response time, permitting timely analysis and adjustments.

Many doomsday scenarios, particularly those invoking nuclear or cyber warfare, grow out of a change from a condition of much reliable information to one of insufficiently complete or unreliable information. This may be rapid or slow. One can see this in all of the classic realms of strategic stability from "first-strike stability" up to "geo-strategic stability." A brief review of the impact of technology on the gain or loss of information in each realm of strategic stability is useful given concerns that future technology may permit more rapid and radical swings in situational awareness.

In many discussions, strategic stability is defined solely as crisis stability, which in turn means "first strike stability" — a condition in which no player has an incentive to initiate an attack. In most rational decision models, first strike stability reflects calculations of "force exchange ratios" or of surviving warheads reaching some minimum required number of targets.

More sophisticated thinking looks at the dynamics. This ranges from the already complex psychology of sequential response through the more complicated worlds of simultaneous actions.

Information provided by advanced technology is a critical part of any first strike stability analysis. Classic strategic technologies such as digital satellite photography and early warning radars inform the comparison of forces and their deployment status. Is an adversary preparing an attack? What kind of attack? Are we under attack? Have we already lost our bomber and submarine bases? Are our land-based missiles under attack? Did any bombers escape their bases? Have we lost submarines at sea or communications with them? Is anybody in charge, and do they know what is happening? Confidence that our technology will give us instantly and accurately needed answers to these questions is the foundation of nuclear crisis stability. The more we lose confidence that these questions would be answerable, the more uncomfortable we feel.

Access to accurate information is also important to "mobilization stability," the ability of adversaries to adjust their forces or readiness short of hostilities, hopefully to increase stability. Inadequate preparedness may invite a first strike in a crisis. An overzealous rush to preparedness may provoke a pre-emptive strike in a crisis. Controlling escalation—important for damage limitation, war termination, and even prevention in the first place—presents further challenging demands for information.

Information is central to what is often called "arms race stability" or in some cases "proliferation stability." "National technical means" (NTM) of verification, often supplemented with cooperative and intrusive measures that may also use technology, assist in acquiring confidence that the parties respect the limitations of arms control agreements. With or without agreed limitations, however, these technologies are critical to assessing the military balance and anticipating measures for which countermeasures are required.

Inadequate information may result in a dangerous failure to respond or to a dangerous overreaction. "Qualitative" and "quantitative" arms races exist when a cycle of excessive responses are provoked. What is "excessive," of course, depends upon knowing what, in fact, is necessary. When the increases are among existing players, it is called "vertical proliferation." When other players enter the game, it is "horizontal proliferation." Whether quantitative or qualitative, proliferation is ultimately about the spread of information and technology. Whether transparency is good or not, depends very much on its ultimate impact on strategic stability.

Crisis stability and arms race stability pre-date the nuclear age and ultimately are linked to what one may call "military stability" — the balance of overall military forces. Much analysis of "crisis stability" in the nuclear age focused on the hypothetical "bolt out of the blue" nuclear first strike based upon a perceived nuclear imbalance. Few such scenarios seem realistic. Even at the height of the Cold War, both sides saw nuclear use as likely only in the context of a major war involving conventional forces. Through this continuum of deterrence, the "nuclear threshold" was linked in some way to the "conventional threshold." The high consequence/low probability event of nuclear use was linked to the lower consequence/higher probability of conventional war.

Some of the more contentious issues of nuclear policy such as "no first use" or a "flat" versus a "steep" escalatory ladder are fundamentally tied to questions involving information about the conventional balance and its impact on behavior. Here technology played a decisive role. Whether in the North Atlantic Treaty Organization (NATO) in the 1950s or in Russia and Pakistan today, we can see that nations have compensated for perceived conventional weakness with nuclear weapons. The trade-off, however, can go the other way. With advances in conventional technology, the United States has substituted conventional weapons for nuclear ones in air defense, missile defense, anti-submarine warfare, anti-tank warfare, area denial, and many other military missions.

The essential ingredient in substituting conventional munitions for nuclear weapons was the ability to acquire accurate, real-time information about many point targets and attack them individually. Consider, for example, the highly decentralized anti-tank mission for which the nuclear-armed Davy Crockett recoilless rifle was once deployed. Today, a non-nuclear U.S. Army relies on systems such as the conventional FGM-148 Javelin third generation man portable fire-and-forget precision guided anti-tank missile. The more centralized, longer-range anti-tank mission was once planned for the "Enhanced Radiation Warhead," the so-called "neutron bomb." Today, concentrations of tanks might be targeted with advanced conventional munitions such as the U.S. Air Force CBU-97 bomb or the Army MGM- 140 Army Tactical Missile System (ATacMS) launched from the Multiple Launch Rocket System (MLRS), each of which dispenses dozens of individual, sensor guided anti-tank munitions over an extensive area. Similar trade-offs exist between nuclear and conventional technologies for other missions, both offense or defense. Again, a major consideration is the availability of target information, particularly after hostilities have begun, when networked sensors, data processing, and decisionmaking may fail.

Concepts like crisis stability, arms race stability, and military stability exist within a larger framework that might be called "geostrategic stability." The scope of geostrategic stability is too large to deal with in this chapter, but it is important to recognize that classic issues of international relations such as democracy, the rule of law, economic development, natural resources, ideological differences, historic resentments, national prestige, and ethnic and religious divisions provide the powerful influences on human behavior that are the foundation of all calculations of strategic stability all the way down to crisis stability. A vast literature exists on the impact of technology and information in each of these areas.

TECHNOLOGY FOR READINESS, RESPONSE, AND RESTRAINT

How does technology serve strategic stability's three policy focal points; namely, "deterrence," "defense," and "disarmament?" Deterrence here is a focus on the destructive consequences of war to influence behavior. Defense is the capability to conduct both the offensive and defensive components of a military campaign. Disarmament is the total range of restraints on military hardware and activities undertaken multilaterally, bilaterally, or unilaterally to reduce by limitation the size, probability, costs, and consequences of conflict. This can include abolition or bans on weapons, limits on force structures and other arms control, transparency and confidence-measures, and a wide range of cooperative threat reduction and engagement measures.[24]

Deterrence, defense, and disarmament each have definitions that distinguish them from each other. Deterrence, defense, and disarmament, however, interrelate, as do the technologies associated with each. Defense and deterrence overlap in the concept of "deterrence by denial."[25] Deterrence and disarmament overlap in that both are meant to avoid war and are often invoked in order to avoid the costs of preparing for war, i.e., to de-emphasize defense spending. Both defense and disarmament are often cited as alternatives to deterrence. Perhaps, then, a Venn diagram of three overlapping circles would be better, indicating that all three may overlap. Best of all, however, might be to consider an analogy to a color wheel in which every possibility is some combination of three basic components in differing degrees of intensity (see Figure 5-1). Like the three horses of a "troika," they work together.

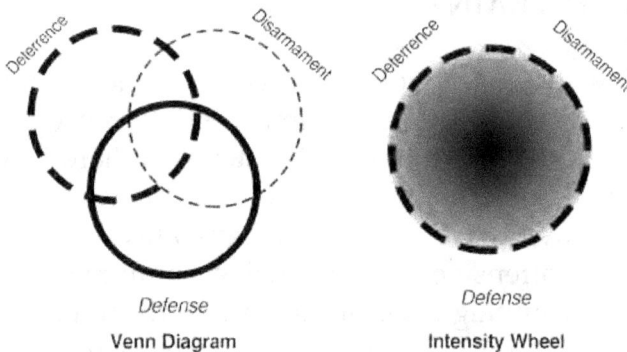

Defense — Venn Diagram

Defense — Intensity Wheel

Figure 5-1. Strategic Stability Troika: Defense, Deterrence, Disarmament.

At the highest policy level, one can see the overlap. Genghis Khan and Albert Nobel shared the view that the horror of war would end hostilities, each for a different purpose. H. G. Wells believed that the horror of war would, as described in his book *The Shape of Things to Come*, result in the engineers of the world uniting to build a new political order of peace and technological/sociological advancement.[26] Even Clausewitz, tailoring military force to serve clear policy objectives, invokes both escalation and proportionality, as does the "just war" tradition in international law and theology.

Technology aids in meeting these requirements, but it is not the only factor. More than explosive yield, accuracy, reliability, and numbers, targeting policy would determine the human consequences of an attack. In an age of mass urban concentrations, few weapons are necessary to cause the most unspeakable death and destruction. By law, policy, and strategy, U.S. weapons targeting must avoid as much as possible civilian populations. Against a given set of targets, discrimination militates toward striking each appropriate target separately and accurately only with the force necessary to destroy or disable the target itself based upon reliable, updated information.

This also applies to nuclear weapons. The destructiveness of even a few nuclear weapons detonating in cities requires both the attacker and the retaliator to focus on the potential societal consequences of their use, but the mere possibility of societal destruction, however much it promotes caution, may be ineffective in actually deterring low-level conflicts that could escalate to the nuclear level. U.S. nuclear policy, like other weapons policy, imposes restraints on targeting designed to keep any potential use within the realm of military credibility as well as the dictates of international law. Development of nuclear, conventional, and nonlethal weapons and command, control, and intelligence technology during the Cold War was greatly influenced by these policies demanding greater discrimination.

The overlap of defense, deterrence, and disarmament, or perhaps their avatars, military readiness, responsiveness, and restraint, can be seen in many nuclear policy and technology decisions. The evolving U.S. effort to de-MIRV its ICBM force provides a simple example. If the United States reduces the number of warheads on each missile from three to one, the consequences of the loss of any one missile to attack or maintenance are reduced. This may enhance stability. Greater targeting flexibility and efficiency is then provided because targets can be selected more on their true priority rather than some trade-off within the limited footprint of a MIRVed missile. This enhances military capability. At the same time, this de-MIRVing is also a form of restraint. The number of weapons is reduced. Also, greater flexibility in targeting may create opportunities to reduce collateral damage and to signal limited escalation more clearly, both complicated by extensive MIRVing. If some of the approximately 1,000 removed warheads remain as a nondeployed hedge so that they can redeploy in the future if needed, however, this is also a form of responsiveness. Because hedge warheads are "de-alerted" and would take a very long time to reload, they would not be available on tactical warning. In this case, de-MIRVing is again a form of restraint. If, perhaps after clear strategic warning, the warheads were deployed again, we would have returned to our original level of military readiness through an act of responsiveness.

Deterrence, military defense, and disarmament work together providing responsiveness, readiness, and restraint. This puts certain requirements on those military forces used to shape strategic stability. With these requirements come demands on technology to help in the (1) preparation of forces, support systems, and infrastructure, (2) prevention of war in the first instance, (3) provision of initial response to hostilities, (4) creation of options to de-escalate hostilities, (5) maintenance of options to escalate hostilities, (6) termination of hostilities, and (7) re-establishment of strategic stability after hostilities have ceased. The technological challenges imposed by these requirements are significant.

Consider demands created by common elements found in discussions of deterrence. Successful deterrence must create in the mind of a potential aggressor the uncertainty that his plan of attack can be successful, yet also, the certainty that the price would be too high, even if his attack were successful. Nuclear weapons are typically "weapons of last resort," but even then they must be more than sources of retribution. As with the entire spectrum of deterrent forces, they must be militarily effective, appropriate to the circumstances, manage escalation and help end conflict at the lowest level of destruction. Therefore, collateral damage must be limited both to meet the needs of strategy and law and to avoid self-deterrence. This requires a high degree of professionalism, sustained situational awareness, and an emphasis on safety, security, and reliability, as well as effectiveness.

Maintaining all of these capabilities requires forces, personnel, and infrastructure of sufficient quantity and quality to provide necessary options, responses, and hedges. All of this in turn must meet legal, moral, and budgetary constraints and the dictates of a balanced political-military strategy. Better technology can help, but the requirements are daunting even in the best of times and become even more challenging by the prospects of uncertainty in the years ahead.

DIVERSITY AS A POLICY AND TECHNOLOGY STRATEGY

Among the most effective strategies for dealing with uncertainty and surprise is diversification. The United States has historically sought variety in all its approaches to defense, deterrence, and disarmament in its efforts to shore up strategic stability. A look at nuclear delivery platforms and associated technology provides a classic example of this thinking.

Recalling the "air, earth, water, and fire" of antiquity, most discussion of technology and strategic stability involves the classical "Triad" of aircraft, ICBMs, submarine-launched ballistic missiles (SLBMs) and the weapons they carry. Often missed is the diversity within each category and the synergism among them. Also, weapons and delivery systems are part of a broader system shaped by technology supporting nuclear, conventional, and unconventional capabilities. This broader system, in turn, nests into a system of policies, process, and organizations that exploit technology and are influenced by it.

The manned bomber was the first nuclear delivery system and has been retained for the nuclear mission with and without standoff missiles for many reasons. Because they are already assigned conventional missions, manned bombers, including tactical aircraft, are readily available, dual-use assets. Placing bombers on alert and dispersing or deploying them in highly visible ways makes them the favored force for strategic signaling, and dual-use aircraft are important elements of extended deterrence for some allies. Upgrades such as stealth, standoff missiles, and electronic counter-measures increase the cost of air defense against them. Their slow flight times, "man-in-the-loop," and ability to be recalled are stabilizing characteristics even when they are involved in nuclear signaling. If deployed in combat for conventional or nuclear strikes, surviving bombers can in theory be reconstituted as a deterrent in efforts to re-establish stability. In general, bombers have been favored in arms control agreements over fast flying ballistic missiles. They were excluded from SALT I, favored under discounting rules in START I, and more heavily discounted in New START.

Bombers present some concerns as well. Maintaining high readiness and alert levels, highly trained personnel, and tankers for air-to-air refueling can be very expensive. Aircraft not on alert are vulnerable to surprise attack, and any on alert would still face demanding time requirements to escape ballistic missile attack, especially from depressed trajectory attacks from SLBMs. Uncertain bomber performance against improved air defenses can lead to uncertainty about survivability and the inability to reach all targets. Long flight times and uncertain penetration could complicate some escalation control and damage limitation missions, especially if other nuclear systems get diverted to thin out air defenses. Bomber bases are few, and the number of bombers is small. Deployments overseas can be difficult and controversial. As symbols of coercion or defiance, both nuclear and conventional bombers and their bases are also potentially prime targets.

The land-based missile, ultimately of intercontinental range, revolutionized nuclear deterrence. With relatively low operating costs, very high readiness rates, timely response, considerable targeting flexibility, and high confidence in reaching and destroying point targets, ICBMs became the centerpiece of force exchange analysis and the psychology and dynamics of deterrence. For the Soviet Union in the Cold War, they were the measure of merit among nuclear-armed missiles. Deployment of single-warhead ICBMs is widely seen as stabilizing because any attack on them would likely require more warheads than those destroyed, possibly many more. Attacking single warhead missiles deployed in hardened silos or on mobile launchers would require a major escalation of warfare across the sovereign heartland of a nuclear-armed nation. As a total force, they do not offer an attacker the prospect of a simple *fait accompli*. With secure and reliable communications to command centers capable of obtaining the most up to date information, launch orders could occur shortly before the required "time on target." This could give decisionmakers more time to consider options, including escalation restraint or damage limitation. Accurate attribution of who had attacked and from where is also a stabilizing feature of ICBMs.

ICBMs, too, present challenges. Some operational ICBM trajectories might overfly populated areas or might be misinterpreted by a country not under attack. More significantly, highly MIRVed ICBMs became the symbol of instability arithmetic because every missile with multiple warheads attacking multiple missiles with multiple warheads greatly leveraged the value of striking first. This also magnified their coercive symbolism. The low cost of such systems per warhead made such MIRVed systems attractive when deployed nuclear arsenals were very large, even if they constituted only a small percentage of the total force. Nevertheless, existence of MIRVed ICBMs drove much of the force exchange ratio calculations that still inhabit nuclear stability analysis. The subsequent search for more survivable basing modes also drove up costs and generated NIMBY backlashes against new deployments, particularly in democratic nations.

The SLBM carried on nuclear submarines overcame a number of concerns associated with ICBMs and bombers. Submarines were not on sovereign soil if attacked. They could be relocated so as not to overfly nonhostile countries. Nuclear submarines with ballistic missiles (SSBNs) could remain underwater on long voyages through large patrol areas, providing a high degree of survivability to the large number of nuclear warheads deployed on each submarine at sea. Modern SLBMs can be highly accurate. Although some SLBMs have intercontinental range, SLBMs could use depressed trajectories from launch points closer to their targets to reduce flight time. SLBM flight paths can be more variable, thus complicating defenses against them. America's nuclear allies have SLBMs, giving them somewhat more political acceptability.

The SSBN force also presents challenges. SSBNs are expensive to acquire and operate. As the number of warheads on each submarine is reduced, "sticker shock" in the form of cost per warhead on station goes up radically. The alternative, continued concentration of large numbers of warheads on just a few submarines means that at low force levels only a small percentage of the total warheads will actually be at sea. At very low numbers, attacks, accidents or human incidents could reduce or eliminate a sea-based component unexpectedly. Depending on the size of the submarine force and its deployment status, maintenance requirements can mean that many, most, or nearly all warheads on submarines will be vulnerable in port.

Submarine bases thus can be highly attractive iconic targets in attempts at "*fait accompli*" strikes, catalytic interventions by third parties, and conceivably symbolic attacks by terrorists.

At sea, SSBNs benefit from Navy-wide counter-antisubmarine warfare (ASW) advances. The oceans are huge. Still, advanced ASW capabilities are in great demand.[27] SSBNs could become vulnerable even during the conventional phase of a conflict. In any phase of conflict, a submarine launching any limited attack runs the risk of disclosing its position. All nuclear delivery platforms run the risk of loss of communications under attack, but securing extensive, reliable communications with a submarine underwater during hostilities can present additional challenges. Although missile submarines can add targeting flexibility, they are sometimes equated in public debate with all out nuclear use or pre-emptive and decapitating strikes. Generally, submarines have avoided NIMBY problems except around bases, although accidents at sea and the disposal of reactor cores have been issues for several countries. Those nuclear-weapons states that deploy SLBMs have made clear that they currently will not accept any nuclear-free zones that would ban nuclear weapons or nuclear reactors at sea or constrain transit. Entry of nuclear-powered ships is denied to some ports, but SSBNs do not normally have that requirement. Still, movement to global nuclear zero may increase pressure to ban nuclear weapons and even nuclear propulsion in international waters.

The diversity of the nuclear "Triad," or "Tetrad" if one counts dual-use fighter-bombers, is often described as a hedge with one or more backups for the failure of any one leg. That is only part of the story.

U.S. strategy has sought to exploit diversity to get greater synergism and flexibility at lower cost. Each component has its special strengths, but also its weaknesses. Diversity aims at having the total contribution be greater than the sum of the parts, but diversity is not always the lowest cost.

Many decisions about the employment of technology, including military technology, involve trades between the virtues and vices of simplicity with those of diversity. Simplification typically offers reductions in Research and Development (R&D) and support base costs, brings economy of scale to production and operations, and permits a narrower business focus. Diversity typically offers more flexibility and resiliency, but with that comes further complexity. Each has its advantages. Each tends toward a different form of optimization. Simplification often optimizes toward unit economic cost or inputs. Diversity tends to look at unit mission cost, largely an output. Simplification seeks harmony with expectations and trends. Diversity tends to hedge against uncertainty.

Diversity is a common strategy for dealing with uncertainty, surprise, and complexity, whether we are dealing with finance, sports, technology start-ups, or strategic stability. Investors are discouraged from concentrating their assets. Athletic teams pick players with different size, speed, and skills, hoping to find the winning mix at the right price. High tech entrepreneurs seek to leverage the undervalued.

Diversity makes available a number of tactics, for example:

- Complementation, the ability to assist or enable others;
- Supplementation, an ability to make up for deficiencies of others;
- Substitution, an ability to switch one for another to compensate for losses;
- Synergism, the ability for the total to be greater than the sum of the parts;
- Agility, the ability to move quickly or alter direction as scenarios change;
- Cost-effectiveness, the ability to reduce cost per unit benefit by re-optimizing a mix of assets;
- Competition, the ability to motivate alternative options to be better or discourage monopolies or oligopolies from extracting large rents;
- Specialization, an ability for each to concentrate on comparative advantage, reducing any need to compromise those advantages to compensate for its own disadvantages;
- Differentiation, the ability to signal different messages more clearly;
- Diffusion, an ability to force those who would threaten to divide their resources to solve multiple problems;
- Robustness, an ability to withstand pressure by spreading it around; and
- Resilience, the ability to cope with error by having alternative options.

Trades between simplification options and diversification options can be made, but ultimately the question becomes: "What is the determining measure of merit?" Is it "more bang for the buck?" Less "sticker shock" per warhead? More stability per resource expended? Or something else? Not surprisingly, every strategic power has begun with more simplicity because of limits on knowledge and resources. Bombs on aircraft are the classic first step. Nevertheless, the quest for diversity is sometimes seen very early — the Manhattan Project developed both a uranium gun assembly and a plutonium implosion device. Most nuclear powers move to greater diversity over time, but some have reduced diversity as security improves, numbers go down, or budgets become tight. This includes the United States.

Still, more than any other country, the United States has emphasized diversity in its approach to strategic stability, including technology. Why? A number of causes seem active. The first is capability. The United States is big. It has resources. It is a strategic leader and has extended responsibilities. The United States has a dynamic technology culture including numerous defense corporations. It has "think tanks," interest groups, and activists asking "What if?" It has democracy and debates that invite a "marketplace of ideas." All of these can create pressure for diversity. In the end, however, the primary drivers of diversity for the United States have been the strategic convictions that, in working to prevent nuclear war, (1) more options are necessary because one size does not fit all, (2) change is inevitable, as is surprise, and (3) the consequences of failure could be tragic.

A few words of caution are in order about strategies employing diversity. Investors who pay multiple fees for mutual funds that contain mostly the same securities are not as diversified as they think, and even very different assets may be subject to the same market forces. The same is true of technologies associated with strategic stability. Different strategies, forces, organizations, operations, and technologies can have common modes of failure. For example, aircraft and submarines have very few bases, all soft. ICBMs and SLBMs could someday face highly effective missile defenses. All components are dependent on communications ultimately from the National Command Authority (NCA).

TECHNOLOGY AND THE HUMAN FACTOR

The most common mode of failure in strategic stability could be the human factor, however. Good decisions require more than good people. We have already discussed the importance of relevant, accurate, and timely information. We have noted the value of options. Technology is vital to providing both. But what of the decisionmaking process and implementation? Here too technology can help, but its role is subservient.

In science, theorists and experimentalists challenge each other and try to reconcile their differences. Similarly, in examining strategic stability we tend to look at how policy and forces are harmonized. Because of vast advances in electronics, data processing, and graphic interfaces, simulations are becoming an essential tool to elaborate theory and focus research more effectively in science. Likewise, advanced simulations and gaming are being used for both training of military forces and analysis of military options.

Some of the most useful tactical innovations and analytical insights develop when training and analysis combine. Technology permits more options to be explored more realistically, quickly, at less expense and permits more free play. Strategies, forces, players, and scenarios can be altered and explored not only by the professionals responsible, but also by analysts seeking to understand how strategies, systems, organizations, and individuals function under stress.

Much of the literature on strategic stability is based upon game theory and related fields such as economics. Like Newtonian physics, these classics remain valuable, but are insufficient for some purposes. These fields have advanced along with other social, behavioral, and cognitive sciences in parallel with a geostrategic world that looks more like quantum mechanics, with its uncertainty principles, entanglement, and action at a distance. The largely bipolar Cold War was crudely analogous to the "Two-Body problem" in physics, easier to calculate especially when any other bodies are satellites. Multiple independent players may be more analogous to the "n-Body problem" in physics with its links to complexity theory and chaotic behavior wherein small changes translate into radically different outcomes. In other words, multipolarity might pose substantially more severe complexity problems than did bipolarity.

Moreover, human beings operate in given cultures. A common logic and language of strategic stability may eventually emerge across cultures, but we cannot yet make that assumption. Even within a single culture, individual differences in risk assessments and cost-benefit analysis can differ greatly and change in unexpected ways. If small numbers of nuclear weapons make the "unthinkable" more thinkable, understanding how people think under pressure becomes vital. Although smaller nuclear arsenals may make the incalculable more calculable, the greatest uncertainty remains understanding human behavior, which will be complex with more and different players.

Simulations of battlefield outcomes or weapons effects have become more sophisticated. As computations and networking enhance virtual reality and connectivity, extensive cross-cultural simulations and gaming may help us understand possible adversaries –and ourselves – better. It may also help us refine our strategies and programs. Nevertheless, gaming and simulations about WMD can be very controversial, and extensive excursions, no matter how heuristic or analytical, are likely to be more so. Ironically, concerns about terrorism, first responders, and consequence management are encouraging diverse professionals to work together to understand the interaction of technology and cultures in a more realistically simulated homeland security environment. Whether conducted together or separately, training, evaluation of policies and programs, and analysis of the human factor will advance with greater use of more realistic simulations. More rigorous analysis and greater realism undoubtedly would make clearer the horrors of war even as we learn better how to prevent war in the first place.

Technology is intimately linked to a related human issue, "the man in the loop." Tailoring a military response to meet rational objectives requires sound human judgment. Decisionmakers need time to evaluate a crisis and select the best option. Technology is exploited to provide more time, accurate information, meaningful visualization, relevant options, better decisions, and appropriate responses. Timely implementation is necessary so that changing circumstances do not make a good decision bad. On the tactical battlefield, Pilots and Soldiers employ direct fire weapons and forward observers guide indirect fire weapons based on immediate information. Strategic missions, whether nuclear or conventional, have similar concepts, but may have longer timelines.

The time between the authorization to respond and the arrival of the weapon on the target can vary greatly depending on communications and on the transit times of the platforms and weapons. Keeping "the man in the loop" is a fundamental part of U.S. policy and, in fact, plays a key role in the laws of warfare. Nevertheless, differences exist as to how long it is responsible to have a human out of the decision implementation sequence. This was a controversial issue, for instance, in the negotiation of the treaty banning anti-personnel landmines.

Where do we locate the "man in the loop?" The technology associated with UAVs and unmanned aerial systems (UAS) has advanced rapidly around the world to include use by nonstate actors. Interest is also growing in civilian applications.[28] The unmanned aircraft or drone evolved from an unguided vehicle to a remotely piloted vehicle. Now the drone is often a semi-autonomous vehicle that flies itself where it is told to go. A number of drones can carry out missions such as surveillance with little human intervention. Unmanned aircraft vary in size from those of a hummingbird[29] to those of real airplanes. A Congressional Research Service study, examining resupply, search and rescue, refueling and air combat, concluded: "In short, UAS are expected to take on every type of mission currently flown by manned aircraft."[30] The goal is to remove the operators from harm's way and simplify the workload to permit concentration on quality decisions and mission performance.

The percentage of attack or surveillance missions flown by unmanned aircraft is growing. Some believe that unmanned vehicles will inevitably become the dominant means of weapons delivery by air, land, and sea, not simply as an extension of the manned aircraft, vehicles, ships, or submarines, but as replacements. Manned platforms are unlikely to go away completely. From the bottom of the ocean to the Moon or Mars, humans are looking for transportation. Nevertheless, manned vehicles are no longer the dominant workhorses deep in the ocean or in outer space, and as warhorses, manned systems are given unmanned extensions like cruise missiles and long-range torpedoes and are augmented by unmanned ballistic missiles and armed drones. How far will this trend toward control from a distance evolve?

Unarmed unmanned platforms have some public acceptability problems. Because unmanned systems need not be as reliable as their manned counterparts, they may not be engineered to be as reliable. But they could be. We trust millions of cars with drivers on our freeways, but would we let robotic automobiles into our traffic jams and mixing bowls? DARPA has had Grand Challenges in which driverless vehicles compete in traffic,[31] and the States of Nevada and California have passed laws that would permit driverless automobiles.[32] We already accept driverless people movers on rails,[33] and, of course, the U.S. military de-conflicts aircraft and drones over Afghanistan routinely.

In time, driven by policy, technology, and budgets, unmanned weapons delivery systems may expand their contributions to a wider range of strategic and tactical military missions involving reconnaissance, conventional strike, electronic warfare, and nuclear deterrence. A key consideration will be the relationship between human decisionmaking and execution of the military mission. Technology will undoubtedly be examined for its contributions to advanced command and control, safety and security of on-board weapons, better situational awareness, real time status reports, and improved means to deny weapons, electronics, or information to an enemy if the vehicle is shot down or crashes. Interest in improved capabilities like these will be valuable no matter what the payload, but these capabilities would be greatest for highly classified missions and weapons.

TECHNOLOGY, SURPRISE, AND OPTIONS TO STRENGTHEN STABILITY

The discussion above is not comprehensive, but the themes explored do spotlight several key interactions, challenges, and opportunities technology may present for strategic stability in the next few decades. Clearly, strategic stability is the product of complex political, social, economic, military, and technological dynamics. Change is inevitable and can create instabilities. Technology is neither the source of all challenges to stability nor the sole source of solutions to problems that arise, but it has always been a major factor in both.

The history of strategic stability displays both continuity and surprise. Surprise is never total, but it can be decisive. Analysis of technology and strategic stability must inevitably focus on change and uncertainty. Issues 2, 3, or 4 decades from now may be very different from those that preoccupy us today. Wise use of technology can help reduce uncertainty and provide options for responding when surprise occurs.

Key policy and technology tools for managing strategic stability are found in nuclear, conventional, and unconventional capabilities, including cyber and space. All are being transformed by technology. Whatever the proportion of responsibility for stability carried by each, these tools are linked and can reinforce or undermine the contributions of others. The same is true in finding the proper mix of defense, deterrence, and disarmament. More functionally, how can technology best complement our day-to-day military posture with sound, technology-enabled options for escalation or restraint in such strategic realms as geo-strategic, political-military, mobilization, crisis, and first-strike stability?

Much public debate focuses on the top of the escalatory ladder where remaining nuclear arsenals still present existential threats even to the largest nations. Wars at those levels of destruction, however, are unlikely unless stability is lost at lower levels of conflict and escalation control fails. Unfortunately, the spread of WMD and advanced conventional technology is increasing the potential destruction associated with those smaller, but more likely conflicts. This in turn may increase the danger of escalation. For that reason, refining our understanding of escalation dynamics and control is every bit as vital in today's complex, multi-player world as it was during the Cold War.

Traditional notions of victory and defeat also must be revisited in light of cultural differences. For example, rather than seeking military advantage in an attack, terrorists or outlaw states may be more interested in inflicting iconic, catalytic, or demoralizing damage in attacks on cultural and economic centers, leadership, communications and transportation hubs, bomber or submarine bases, space assets, and the like. At the same time, we must avoid errors associated with cultural stereotyping or mirror imaging of potential adversaries. The connectivity made possible by information technology can help us better understand allies and adversaries and our own behavior as well.

The human factor may be the most common mode of failure if the stress of circumstances, inadequacy of information, mistaken analysis, confused processes, lack of time, or inappropriate options result in bad decisions. More realistic training has become possible by advances in simulations technology. Combining this with analysis of more extensive excursions in strategy and behavior may reduce the dangers associated with failures to understand how the human factor might play in more complex scenarios. Despite possible controversy, more "What if?" scenarios need to be gamed and analyzed. They can also provide testing grounds for alternative strategies and technologies for defense, deterrence, and disarmament.

Technology can help us gather more information and better understand the meaning of what we do obtain. It can help us communicate, consult, compare, and create. Technology offers scenarios in which awareness is extensive, but common mode vulnerabilities of information technology may also expose us to scenarios in which awareness is weak, information is inaccurate, and communications uncertain. We must train and game in scenarios in which situational awareness expands and contracts significantly.

The human being, a source of great strength in revising judgments as information changes, is so important that we look to technology to provide a "man in the loop" in key decisions at all levels of escalation, whether pre-conflict, against terrorists, on the conventional battlefield, or facing WMD. Technology such as UAVs permit us to remove the operator from the immediate danger of the battlefield and reduce his workload, hopefully enabling better decisionmaking.

Budgets are tight. The most attractive strategies involve maintaining options while seeking to better understand possible futures. One could focus on conserving existing policy and forces, adjusting slowly as the future becomes clearer. Alternatively, one could focus on seeing the future more clearly to build forces better suited to that future. Each has long-term and short-term advantages and disadvantages in performance and cost. Given the serious downsides associated with any failure of deterrence in this altered, but persistent nuclear age, caution is warranted.

Measuring the robustness of strategic stability has always required dynamic rather than static analysis of force exchanges, but at low numbers of weapons with additional, different players, this is more important. Technology complicates both offense and defense. The measure/countermeasure dynamic is most intense where leverage may be high as in air and missile defenses, anti-submarine warfare, or the use of conventional systems to attack high value, strategic assets.

Reductions in numbers of weapons without modernizing infrastructure or streamlining support processes can drive up unit costs, increasing pressure to reduce diversity to gain economies of scale. This may save dollars but reduce performance. Successful strategies for maintaining flexibility at lower numbers require more efficient, properly sized infrastructure and multi-use systems. The measure of merit should be cost effectiveness rather than just cost.

Diversity and competition provide resiliency in the face of uncertainty, not just as hedges, but also especially by providing more options. The total can be greater or less than the sum of the parts depending on the synergism achieved or denied. Alan C. Kay once said, "The best way to predict the future is to invent it."[34] Certainly, the United States must lead, but neither it nor the many other nations involved can completely control the future. By exploiting technology to improve both our tools and our decisionmaking, however, we can shape forces in play and be better prepared for surprise when it comes.

ENDNOTES - CHAPTER 5

1. Many declaratory policies have been announced over the years, but their core principles emphasized a form of flexible response long before that policy was named and has retained extensive flexibility long after new declarations were made. Consider:

1945 = World War Termination/Counter-Genocide
1947 = Sole Nuclear Power, Component-based
1954 = Massive Retaliation, New Look/Pentomic Army
1963 = Flexible Response, Escalation Dominance
1965 = Assured Destruction/Damage Limiting
1967 = Mutual Assured Destruction
1969 = Sufficiency, Escalation Control
1974 = Essential Equivalence
1976 = Rough Equivalence
1979 = PD-59/Countervailing Strategy
1981 = National Security Decision Directive (NSDD)-13/ Peace through Strength
1983 = Strategic Defense Initiative
1989 = Weapons of Last Resort
1994 = *Nuclear Posture Review Report* (NPR), de-targeting
1997 = Post Cold War Deterrent w/Hedge
2002 = NPR/Assure Dissuade, Deter, Defend/Defeat (ADDD)
2010 = NPR/Reduce Reliance on Nuclear
20xx = Capability Based? Discriminate Deterrence? Adaptive Planning? Transformation? Responsive Infrastructure? Non-nuclear strategic? Missile defense leveraged?
20xx = Minimal Deterrent? Recessed Deterrent? Virtual Deterrent? Undeterrent?
2xxx = "Held in Trust for Mankind?" "Latency?" "Reconstitution as a safeguard?"

2. By analogy, I mean the use of scientific thought to illustrate or illuminate policy concepts. For example, much strategic stability analysis uses the ideas and terminology of classical physics, mostly Newtonian but partly Relativistic. The language of satellites, equilibrium, and perspective, however, is increasingly be-

ing supplemented by the ideas of quantum mechanics with its uncertainty principles, action at a distance, and entanglement. Mathematics, computations, chemistry, and biology provide both subject matter and models for thinking about strategic stability. Indeed, the concepts and language of medicine and public health are also increasingly valuable. Any use of analogy, however, requires caution that we do not transfer something from the analogy that does not exist in what we are trying to understand.

3. Internal combustion engines seemed an ugly alternative to the electric motor as a source of transportation in the 19th century, yet each had advocates and critics, often based on uncertain extrapolations from basic science or the prospects for engineering improvements. Both the internal combustion engine and the electric motor are mature technologies, yet both have continued to improve and compete.

4. The authors of this book seek to update and enrich the literature on strategic stability. Applying a technology overlay to concepts of strategic stability that will be presented in depth by other authors in this volume runs some risk of disconnect, but I hope I present here a basic, *albeit* fairly dense matrix that captures most of the important structure of the various concepts.

5. Emergent behavior occurs when a combination results in behavior not characteristic of the components, or at least not immediately obvious. Table salt is a classic example. Sodium and chlorine are each toxic and sodium is explosive in water, but together as sodium chloride, they are stable and, in water, vital to life. Such emergence is described in mathematics, biological systems, the social sciences, and the arts and humanities. From the perspective of strategic stability, one of the most persistent ideas of emergence is the notion that greater explosive power in the hands of armies leads to peace; i.e., destructiveness leads to deterrence, then to disarmament. Consider the words of Alfred Nobel contrasting his expectations for the dynamite he invented with the expectations of Austrian peace campaigner Countess Bertha von Suttner: "Perhaps my factories will put an end to war sooner than your congresses: on the day that two army corps can mutually annihilate each other in a second, all civilised nations will surely recoil with horror and disband their troops." Available from *www.nobelprize.org/alfred_nobel/biographical/articles/tagil/*.

6. Available from *www.nytimes.com/partners/aol/special/sputnik/sput-10.html*.

7. Available from *www.darpa.mil/About/History/History.aspx*.

8. See U.S. Department of Energy, Office of Declassification, "Drawing Back the Curtain of Secrecy": Restricted Data Declassification Decisions, 1946 to the Present (RDD-3), January 1, 1996, Appendix D, Nuclear Weapons Stockpile Data Table, at *https://www.osti.gov/opennet/forms.jsp?formurl=document/rdd-3/rdd-3i.html#ZZ80*, which shows the official stockpile increased from 12,298 in 1959 to 18,638 in 1960, an increase of 6340.

9. Note, not all those weapons were dismantled in 1 year.

10. See Department of Defense Fact Sheet, *Increasing Transparency in the U.S. Nuclear Weapons Stockpile,* May 3, 2010 available from *www.defense.gov/npr/docs/10-05-03_Fact_Sheet_US_Nuclear_Transparency__FINAL_w_Date.pdf*, which reports a stockpile number of 19,008 in 1991 reduced to 13,708 in 1992, a difference of 5,300.

11. See Department of Defense Fact Sheet, *Increasing Transparency in the U.S. Nuclear Weapons Stockpile,* May 3, 2010 available from *www.defense.gov/npr/docs/10-05-03_Fact_Sheet_US_Nuclear_Transparency__FINAL_w_Date.pdf*, which shows the stockpile at 31,255 in 1967 and at 5113 in 2009, a reduction of 26,142 over 42 years, an average reduction of about 622 a year. Again, this is not the same as dismantlement, which usually takes a number of years.

12. Science and Technology (S&T) through Research, Development, Test, and Evaluation (RDT&E) is about how knowledge becomes things. Processes such as those in the Defense Department provide phases and decision points involving the application of more resources as the confident application of technology to requirements become clearer. In general, the process has grown slower, but numerous initiatives have been implemented to fast track special needs.

13. See DOI: 10.1126/science.256.5053.44, *The Third Branch of Science Debuts, Science* 3, Vol. 256, No. 5053, April 1992: pp. 44-47, available from *www.sciencemag.org/content/256/5053/44.extract*.

14. See Tony Hey, Stewart Tansley, and Kristin Tolle, eds., *The Fourth Paradigm: Data-Intensive Scientific Discovery*, available from *research.microsoft.com/en-us/collaboration/fourthparadigm/contents.aspx*.

15. See Robert Cromie, *The Crack of Doom*, London, UK: Digby, Long, & Co., 1895, available through the Gutenberg Project from *www.gutenberg.org/ebooks/26563*; and H. G. Wells, *The World Set Free – A Story of Mankind*, London, UK: MacMillan and Co., Limited, 1914.

16. Stephen Baxter and Sir Arthur C. Clarke, *The Light of Other Days – A Novel*, New York: A Tor Book, 2000, based upon Sir Arthur C. Clarke, *Profiles of the Future: An Inquiry into the Limits of the Possible*, New York: Millennium Edition, Indigo Paperbacks, 2000.

17. See Baxter and Clarke, *The Light of Other Days*.

18. Gordon Moore, one of the founders of Intel, postulated that the number of transistor equivalents on a chip doubled every 2 years, i.e., that its price halved. Moore acknowledged that this was not a law of nature, but rather a description he had to adjust several times to fit the data. Its persistence, however, may be driven in part because the law became prescriptive, that is, Intel did not want to fail to meet expectations created by the popularization of Moore's Law.

19. Electromagnetic pulse (EMP) can be generated by nuclear weapons but also by nonexplosive EMP generators. For an official discussion of EMP weapons effects, see *The Nuclear Matters Handbook*, Expanded Ed., Appendix F available from *www.acq.osd.mil/ncbdp/nm/nm_book_5_11/index.htm*.

20. Edward Lorentz, a meteorologist, discovered the chaotic effects of small changes at the beginning of computer simulations, a phenomenon labeled the "butterfly effect" after he gave a talk entitled "Does the flap of a butterfly's wings in Brazil set off a tornado in Texas?"

21. Often quoted from Benjamin Franklin, Poor Richard's Almanack:

> For want of a nail, the shoe was lost.
> For want of a shoe, the horse was lost.
> For want of a horse, the rider was lost.
> For want of a rider, the message was lost.
> For want of a message, the battle was lost.
> For want of a battle, the kingdom was lost.
> And all for the want of a horseshoe nail.

22. That many small improvements in quality throughout a system can have dramatic total effects is associated with the work of Dr. W. Edwards Deming, who is credited with providing the strategy for industrial success by Japan in the post-War automobile and consumer electronics industries.

23. Early computer programs, still being used as we approached the year 2000, recorded the year in two digits rather than four. Tests indicated that important financial, operational, and safety programs might fail when the year 2000 rolled over to "00." Of particular concern were embedded microchips that existed in many military, space, and safety systems. As New Year's Eve moved around the time zones of the earth, few problems were reported, and these were mostly from the United States, which, having advocated the most aggressive countermeasures seemed to have found the most problems. The Y2K panic seemed exaggerated in retrospect. Perhaps the original problem was overestimated. Steps taken in advance, however, may also have prevented extensive problems. Dynamic market economies purchased widespread upgrades. Precautionary steps involving operational and safety systems taken first in advanced countries quickly spread to the developing world, highlighting the globalization of the computer service industry.

24. For an attempt to integrate these concepts, one could look at Ronald F. Lehman II, "Chapter 12: International Arms Restraint by Treaty, Law, and Policy," in John Norton Moore and Robert F. Turner, eds., *National Security Law*, 2nd Ed., Durham, North Carolina: Carolina Academic Press, 2005, pp. 523-660.

25. If deterrence involves persuading a potential attacker that the cost is too high relative to the chance of success, then "deterrence by punishment" aims to increase the cost and "deterrence by denial" aims to reduce the chance of success. Although deterrence by denial is often associated with active and passive defenses, the two overlap in the concept of escalation control and damage limitation.

26. H. G. Wells, *The Shape of Things to Come*, 1933, at ebooks, Adelaide, 2006, available from *ebooks.adelaide.edu.au/w/wells/hg/w45th/index.html#contents*. In this book, Wells anticipates SLBMs and the use of nonlethal gas for peacekeeping.

27. The Defense Advanced Research Projects Agency (DARPA) posted an anti-submarine warfare (ASW) game on its website to encourage public competition to generate innovation in ASW technology and operations. See *archive.darpa.mil/actuv/*.

28. Jeremiah Gertler, Specialist in Military Aviation, U.S. Unmanned Aerial Systems CRS Report for Congress, *Prepared for Members and Committees of Congress*, January 3, 2012, Washington, DC: Congressional Research Service, 7-5700, available from *www.fas.org/sgp/crs/natsec/R42136.pdf*.

29. See DARPA, "Time Magazine Recognizes DARPA's Hummingbird Nano Air Vehicle," available from *www.darpa.mil/News Events/Releases/2011/11/24.aspx*.

30. Gertler, p. 6.

31. "The DARPA Urban Challenge was held on November 3, 2007, at the former George Air Forse Base in Victorville, CA. Building on the success of the 2004 and 2005 Grand Challenges, this event required teams to build an autonomous vehicle capable of driving in traffic, performing complex maneuvers such as merging, passing, parking, and negotiating intersections. This event was truly groundbreaking as the first time autonomous vehicles have interacted with both manned and unmanned vehicle traffic in an urban environment," available from *archive.darpa.mil/grandchallenge/*.

32. Available from *cyberlaw.stanford.edu/node/6688*.

33.   Available   from   *www.bombardier.com/en/transportation/ products-services/transportation-systems/driverless-systems/ automated-people-movers?docID=0901260d8000a53a*.

34. "Look, the best way to predict the future is to invent it," wrote Alan C. Kay in "Predicting The Future," address before the 20th annual meeting of the Stanford Computer Forum, *Stanford Engineering*, Vol. 1, No. 1, Autumn 1989, pp. 1-6, available from *www.ecotopia.com/webpress/futures.htm*. A similar thought was expressed by Dennis Gabor in *Inventing the Future* (1963), Gretna, LA: Pelican Books, 1964, p. 161, "The future cannot be predicted, but futures can be invented."

CHAPTER 6

ANYTHING BUT SIMPLE: ARMS CONTROL AND STRATEGIC STABILITY

Christopher A. Ford

"Strategic stability" does not appear to have any generally-agreed definition. Contributors to this volume, for instance, take a range of positions—from focusing very specifically upon the incentives nuclear-armed powers face to alter their nuclear force posture for fear of pre-emptive strike, to very broad understandings that sweep within their reach almost the entire spectrum of interstate violence. This chapter will outline one particular conception of strategic stability—a definition focusing upon the incentives for general war between great powers—before exploring the relationship between *this* idea of stability and arms control policy.

I will argue herein that despite the common assumption in the U.S. and global policy communities that arms control is essential to strategic stability, the reality is that the two concepts actually have an ambivalent relationship, and that arms control sometimes fosters stability and sometimes undermines it. Moreover, stability, per se, is of indeterminate value. In assessing whether to seek strategic stability and whether to use arms control in its pursuit, one cannot rely upon a priori assumptions but must instead carefully examine the circumstances involved and the interests served by various different policy options—including nontraditional forms of arms control, or perhaps none at all.

"STRATEGIC STABILITY" AND ITS IMPLICATIONS

A Working Definition.

This chapter conceives strategic stability in the geopolitical arena as being loosely analogous to a military "Nash Equilibrium" between the principal players in the international environment (i.e., the "great powers") as it pertains to the possibility of their using force against each other. It defines strategic stability as being a situation in which no power has any significant incentive to try to adjust its relative standing vis-à-vis any other power by unilateral means involving the direct application of armed force against it. General war, in other words, is precluded as a means of settling differences or advancing any particular power's substantive agenda. The environment is thus strategically stable if no player feels itself able to alter its position *by the direct use of military force against another player* without this resulting in a *less* optimal outcome than the alternative of a continued military stalemate and the pursuit of national objectives by at least somewhat less aggressive means.

This model, of course, is—like all social science models—only an imperfect description of any situation in the real world, and does not purport to incorporate every relevant component of, or possibility for, state behavior. It revolves, for instance, around a general assumption of rationality, presuming that decisions on matters of war and peace usually occur as the result of calculations about the costs and benefits of contending courses of action, and not simply randomly, accidentally, or as a matter of emotional reflex (e.g., visceral hatred or exuberance). This Nash-inspired approach does not well accommodate these latter possibilities. Accidental war, for instance, might yet occur between powers in a "stable" relationship — a question that has arisen with particular acuteness in the era of nuclear weaponry.

This model also tends to assume that players are generally at least passably knowledgeable about their adversaries' capabilities — that is, that they are not radically incorrect in the beliefs they hold and assumptions they make about other players. I do not assume *perfect* information, of course, and indeed, as we shall see, this model explicitly envisions that confidence-building measures may be able to lessen misperceptions and at least partly attenuate the security dilemma created as uncertainty about one's opponent drives behaviors that themselves elicit seemingly threatening countermoves by that opponent. Nevertheless, this model has some difficulty accommodating the possibility of *dramatic* misapprehension, for in extreme cases divergences of perspective may become the functional equivalent of eliminating my assumption of basic rationality, for neither side would *really* be responding to the actions and position of the other at all.

Despite its flaws, however, I believe this Nash-inspired conception of stability is useful in the way that good models are supposed to be. As a heuristic, it provides a way of describing important aspects of real world behavior, identifying characteristic trends or tendencies, and providing a valuable tool with which policy choices and outcomes can be evaluated. As we shall see, this model offers a valuable prism through which to think both about stability dynamics within the international system, and about the potential benefits and costs of arms control.

It is important, however, to be clear about what the model actually envisions. Its focus upon the preclusion of general war between the great powers, for instance, does not imply that *all* means of conflict are ruled out. Indeed, strategic stability may *create* incentives for other types of competition, or for more indirect military clashes, if basic political or systemic rivalries are displaced into other arenas that carefully stop short—or are at least *intended* to stop short, for statesmen do not always get their calculations right, of course—of direct military conflict. This is what tended to happen during the Cold War, when both the United States and the Soviet Union became in various ways ensnarled in proxy wars, either themselves fighting adversaries supported by the other superpower or becoming involved in sponsoring the opponents of such forces.

Nor does my Nash-inspired concept mean that *change* in the major powers' relative positions is ruled out, nor even one or more powers' encouragement of other (nonmilitary) dynamics calling into question the very existence of another power's government. If such "existential" challenges arise by means *not* involving the direct application of another power's military force, I would still be willing to say that the environment remains strategically stable. This concept of strategic stability does not envision freezing a global status quo in place forever, but merely ruling out certain *modes* of competition and conflict—specifically, general war. Struggle may and in a sense must continue withal, and great powers may rise or fall by other means and for other reasons.

The persistence of *some* warring, even on a small scale, clearly makes it impossible, as an analytical matter, to rule out the escalation of minor conflicts into larger ones. The point is not that general war between major states is *impossible*, however, but that certain configurations seem to make it less likely than others. As demonstrated by the U.S.-Soviet rivalry of the Cold War, it is apparently quite possible for low-level proxy conflicts to occur without such combatants dragging their sponsors into the fray. The Korean War of 1950-53, however, illustrates the potential for problems, having brought Chinese and American forces into direct conflict—albeit one contained to a particular theater which did not escalate into a broader or more "existential" clash between these powers. One may deem a system strategically stable to the degree that relationships between the great powers are merely *resistant* to such escalatory pressure. Without recourse to a crude determinism, one can do no more than identify tendencies and likelihoods.

Nor, of course, is it inevitable that a strategically stable configuration will always remain so, for it may be that economic or other trends generate instabilities over time, such as by dramatically changing the balance of military power between states and thus making seem feasible direct military actions that might previously have been "unthinkable." This does not make present-day strategic stability meaningless, however, for what it *takes* to create such a turnaround will presumably vary, with a *more* stable status quo ante requiring more to change before it will degenerate into instability than would be necessary to degrade a *less* stable initial situation. Here again, stable systems will tend to be resistant to change, but this does not mean that none can occur.

It should also be recalled that the definition of strategic stability offered here only focuses upon the principal players in the international system: the states one might call the great powers. Through this lens, *small* players may perhaps face existential military crises from time to time without the stability of the system as a whole being affected. Their particular trajectories might be unhappy indeed, but it does not necessarily follow that international politics as a whole is thereby *strategically* unstable. It would surely set the bar too high to define system stability as the complete absence of *all* violent conflict. A Nash-inspired notion of strategic stability might usefully apply *as between* smaller powers in their local context, of course, but that is not our task here. For present purposes, we shall be discussing the global strategic *aggregate*, and confining our analysis to major states because major states are those that can materially affect that aggregate in the most direct and important ways.

As it is used herein, the concept of strategic stability is value-neutral. This is not to suggest that there is necessarily anything inherently "good" about its achievement, though of course this may frequently be the case. Especially where nuclear weapons are widely possessed among the great powers, for instance, the argument seems compelling. In most circumstances, ruling out general war is presumably a very good idea. But I would stop before saying that strategic stability is a per se good.

Indeed, strategic stability might sometimes impose tremendous costs, for it tends to privilege the status quo between the powers in question. How one evaluates the merits of such stability will depend upon who one is in the constellation of players, what status quo that stability enshrines, and what it serves to *permit*.

- For a power that seeks fundamental *change* in the strategic environment, strategic stability is probably unwelcome, for it imposes sharp limits on how change may be sought.

- Nevertheless, in some circumstances, strategic stability could serve to protect an aggressive rising power while it prepares itself for a *future* military challenge to the global order. (War by France and Britain against Adolf Hitler's Germany over the Austrian *Anschluss* or the invasion of Czechoslovakia in 1938 would technically have been an affront to strategic stability in Europe, but might have prevented greater stability challenges still to come.)
- Even where one might think strategic stability to be a salutary objective, moreover — as, for instance, in a balance between very powerful states whose clash could be catastrophic — it may have significant justice costs, such as by essentially "immunizing" a tyrannical regime against well-deserved foreign efforts to replace it by direct military means. (Strategic stability between the Axis and Allied powers on the eve of World War II, for instance, would have consigned much of Asia permanently to the Japanese yoke, and much of Europe to the jackboots of the Gestapo and the Nazi death camps.)
- Arrangements to ensure strategic stability might *facilitate* aggression against smaller powers, as occurred in 1939 when the Molotov-Ribbentrop Pact opened the door for aggression in erasing Poland from the map and dividing it between Nazi Germany and the Soviet Union. Even if not thus pre-arranged, furthermore, the immunity strategic stability tends to offer a power against direct military challenge from other important states could encourage unilateral external aggression against systemic "small fry" — or at least those *lacking* strong

military alliance relationships with other major states, at any rate—by leading an aggressor to believe that the victims of such predation will not be saved or avenged by outsiders. This may to some extent have been the case with the Soviet invasion of Afghanistan in 1979, or with the North Korean invasion of South Korea in 1950 after U.S. officials created the impression—not just in Pyongyang but also in Moscow and Beijing—that the Republic of Korea was outside America's "defense perimeter." (As for those smaller states that *do* have strong alliance relationships with great powers, however, one might argue that strategic stability is a precondition for their security, for it may be that these relationships provide deterrents to aggression only to the extent that they enable a minor player to *participate* in the stability of a great-power balance. *Post*-1953 South Korea may be a case in point.)

Depending upon the circumstances, therefore, stability can have decidedly unpleasant results. Though stability is presumably indeed often "good," it can in other circumstances help empower the perpetrators of both internal and external aggression, coexist with *local* violence and instability, act as an enabler for aggression, protect the instigators of brutal internal repression, or serve to protect a power during its rise to a position from which it can *challenge* the existing great-power balance. A policy of seeking strategic stability is not, therefore, necessarily a sign of international benevolence and virtue. Details matter, and the point here is that it is not substantively or morally sustainable to argue that strategic stability is a per se good. It may be good, or it may be, on the whole, harmful. In order to assess its net value, one needs to know a good deal more than simply that things were "stable."

Strategic Stability and Nuclear Weapons.

Though the term comes up frequently in discussion of nuclear weapons and arms control policy, moreover, I do not envision strategic stability as being inherently about nuclear weaponry. That said, of course, nuclear weapons *are* of special salience in this arena, because they may seem to offer some states a real hope of achieving security—that is, of leading *other* powers to conclude that general war against them is inadvisable—to a great extent *independent* of the state's actual ordinary (i.e., conventional) military strength. Nuclear weapons may have an enormous impact upon strategic stability, in other words, but the stability question neither begins nor ends with them. (Indeed, particularly with regard to new possessors among the minor states, nuclear weapons might provide relative security to some individual countries at a *cost* to strategic stability as we have defined it here, if such proliferation helped increase the risk of conflict between major powers—e.g., through the escalation of regional conflicts made more ugly and/or more likely by a proliferator's emboldenment, or if major states were forced to undertake policies in response to proliferation that affect their capabilities vis-à-vis other great powers.)

Here lies a broader point. The impact of nuclear weapons is probably especially great in geopolitical terms precisely because they *aren't* useful *only* to deter other such weapons—though many in the disarmament community would have it otherwise. They are important because they also deter *conventional* weapons, and nuclear weapons' possessors often hope to use them as a sort of fast-track road to security without the expense and inconvenience of having to defend themselves by other means. The United States and its North Atlantic Treaty Organization (NATO) allies relied upon nuclear deterrence to make up for a perceived disadvantage vis-à-vis Warsaw Pact conventional forces in Central Europe during the Cold War, for instance, and nuclear weapons seem today to be prized — or sought — by planners in Moscow, Beijing, Pyongyang, and Tehran alike for their presumed ability to counterbalance others' advantages in sophisticated conventional arms. Nor should one forget that nuclear weapons were first *used* not against a nuclear power but in order to help win a bitter *conventional* war.

Accordingly, one would argue the need to decouple the concept of specifically *nuclear* stability from *strategic* stability more generally. They are to some extent analytically distinct concepts, and conflating them would tend to obscure important points — such as the reasons why many states have pursued nuclear weapons in the past, why some seek them today, and an important reason that a country might *use* "the Bomb" (i.e., to win or to stave off defeat in an otherwise conventional conflict). Theoretically, moreover, a nuclear balance characterized by "complete" stability in nuclear terms — that is, a case in which more than one power possessed nuclear weapons but *no* circumstances existed in which these devices would be considered "usable" — might well be *unstable* under the definition of strategic stability used here: if asymmetries of conventional force or other circumstances made war attractive, nuclear weapons in this case might not deter it. This is why hopes for strategic stability in a nuclear-armed world *presuppose* that participants' nuclear arsenals are not *entirely* "self-canceling." In a multi-nuclear world, to deter general war with nuclear weapons requires some real possibility of weapons use—which is another way of saying that the success of nuclear deterrence requires that it be, to some degree, *imperfect*. Strategic stability and the specifically nuclear aspects of power-balancing are clearly related, but should not be confused.

In any event, on the assumption that this Nash-inspired concept of strategic stability is both coherent and useful, the following discussion will offer some thoughts on its relationship to arms control.

ARMS CONTROL AND ITS RELATIONSHIP TO STRATEGIC STABILITY

Categorizing Arms Control.

One sometimes hears it suggested that "arms control" and "disarmament" represent fundamentally different things—with the latter relating to the abolition of weapons, while the former amounts merely to *managing* and perpetuating a balance between their possessors. (Disarmament, in such characterizations, is invariably the true and noble calling; mere arms control smacks of compromise, and of granting at least some such devices an ongoing, and immoral, legitimacy.) Many observers, moreover, are not sure how to categorize agreements that focus not upon limiting capabilities but upon regulating behavior or transparency and confidence-building measures (T/CBMs). Because such measures emphasize information-sharing or other aspects of arms-related relations between the parties rather than arms limits per se, they are sometimes not afforded the status of arms "control."

In real world practice, however, such distinctions are hard to maintain. What are usually styled "arms control" agreements, for example, can involve not just caps (e.g., the Strategic Arms Limitation Treaty of 1972[1]) but cuts (e.g., the Strategic Arms Reduction Treaty [START] of 1991[2]), or even the prohibition and dismantlement of certain types of capability (e.g., intermediate-range ballistic missiles with the Intermediate Range Nuclear Forces [INF] Treaty of 1987[3]). At the same time, reputedly "disarmament" agreements sometimes permit the retention of some capabilities (e.g., riot control agents under the Chemical Weapons Convention [CWC],[4] or biological weapons agents retained for "prophylactic, protective, or other peaceful purposes" under the Biological and Toxin Weapons Convention [BTWC][5]), while both arms control *and* disarmament agreements commonly contain important T/CBM provisions regarded as being integral to their function (e.g., the notification and "cooperative measures" provisions of START,[6] the notification provisions in the New Strategic Arms Reduction Treaty [New START] protocol of 2010,[7] or the declaration provisions of the CWC).

It has also become routine for U.S.-Russian strategic arms agreements to establish a forum for bilateral consultation in which compliance concerns and other implementation issues can be raised[8] — a function for which the Treaty on the Non-Proliferation of Nuclear Weapons (NPT) uses a forum of its entire membership, meeting as part of that treaty's ongoing "Review Conference" process.[9] Finally, the category of CBMs frequently shades into weapons-independent behavioral regulation, as with the U.S.-Soviet Incidents at Sea Agreement of 1972, which set forth basic "Rules of the Road" designed to reduce the danger that confrontational maritime interactions would lead to broader conflict, including the use of nuclear weaponry.[10]

Rather than reify stark theoretical categorizations that do not exist in practice, this paper will adopt a broad understanding of arms control that includes: (a) bilateral and multilateral agreements and arrangements related to limiting, reducing, proscribing, and/or dismantling some sort of weaponry or other military-related technology (i.e., *capability-regulatory* measures); (b) efforts to develop and promote "best practices" or codes of conduct pertaining to the *use* of certain types of technology or capability (i.e., *behaviorally-regulatory* measures); and (c) steps related to transparency and confidence-building (i.e., *information-concessive* measures). (These are not mutually exclusive forms of arms control, of course, and they may be—and often are—employed in some combination.) One way or the other, these categories address themselves to the nature or scope of the threat states seem to pose to each other through their actual or potential possession of a particular type of military tool: capability-regulatory measures seek to restrict the availability of that tool, behavioral measures seek to constrain what is *done* with what tools one does possess, and information measures seek to make parties better informed about the situation they face.

Arms and Instability.

What, then, is the relationship between arms control—thus conceived—and strategic stability? Too often, discussions of arms control and strategic stability get bogged down by a quasi-theological assumption that (a) that strategic stability is per se good, and (b) arms control is *also* both per se good and inherently strategically stabilizing. It is useful, however, to explore these issues more carefully, for while strategic stability *can* be (and often is) a benefit to international peace and security — and while arms control *can* (and sometimes does) contribute thereto — neither of these things can be tenably asserted on an a priori basis. Having already exploded the first part of syllogism (i.e., the idea that strategic stability is inherently good), one can turn now to the second.

A serious discussion of the relationship between arms control and strategic stability requires understanding that the former does not *invariably* promote the latter. The most obvious example in this regard is perhaps the polar case, and in some ways the most ambitious one, of modern arms control: weapons elimination in the specific form of nuclear disarmament. (For present purposes, this discussion will leave aside the idea that it might be possible to devise "a Treaty on general and complete disarmament under strict and effective international control."[11] "Nuclear zero" is ambitious enough without waiting for the last steak knife to be beaten into a soup spoon, and nuclear abolition is at least still *talked about* in some quarters as a notional policy goal.[12]) Here the potential strategic stability argument *against* arms control is perhaps at its most stark, for if such stability is characterized by a balance of military power such that each major power finds general war with another such power to be less desirable than all other unilaterally-available alternatives, the successful abolition of a particular category of weaponry could in some circumstances *destabilize,* by removing one important reason for those war-dissuasive conclusions.

This is one of the things opponents of nuclear "zero" have said for some time: precisely to the degree that nuclear arsenals may *contribute* to strategic stability, their elimination would be destabilizing, by "mak[ing] the world safe again for large-scale conventional war" between the major states.[13] In fact, we have already encountered a similar problem above, where it was suggested that one power's use of nuclear weaponry to *perfectly* deter nuclear weapons use by a rival power could destabilize by removing a powerful disincentive for conventional conflict as the two arsenals' "self-cancel." Both circumstances—that is, "perfect" nuclear deterrence and complete nuclear disarmament—might actually end up being very similar situations, in that they would turn out to be highly *unstable* in strategic terms, notwithstanding their having precluded nuclear weapon use.

In reality, of course, no such deterrence could be perfect, since an attacker might have many reasons to worry that his maintenance of a nuclear arsenal might fail to *guarantee* immunity from a nuclear reprisal by the victim. Launch might occur accidentally or without authorization in time of crisis, for instance, or in a frenzy of emotional irrationality, or as a vengeful consequence of the perception that the victim had "nothing to lose" now anyway. Or perhaps the attacker might simply have miscalculated. As Thomas Schelling long ago made clear, risk manipulation and uncertainty play critical roles in deterrence.[14] Complete nuclear disarmament, however, is analytically very close to the hypothesized situation of perfect nuclear deterrence in which counterpoised arsenals cancel each other out *entirely*, for in both cases nuclear

215

weaponry would, in a functional sense, cease to exist. For this reason, arms control advocates who desire strategic stability might wish to steer clear of *both* polar cases.

Nor, though arms control is frequently touted as a way to increase strategic stability by preventing arms races, does it seem to be true, a priori, that arms competitions are inherently destabilizing. Racing behavior would presumably tend to be strategically destabilizing if it continued unconstrained in circumstances in which an uneven distribution of available financial or technical resources between the competing powers meant that such racing would over time give one of them a decisive advantage (e.g., one party could build weapons faster, better, and/or for longer). A race could be destabilizing if one party felt itself to have "won," if such a "victory" allowed it to make further favorable adjustments to its position — or fend off potential threats to that position — by means of general war. Alternatively, a race could be unstable if one side felt that the *other side's* progress was such that an acceptable status quo was likely to be upended if military action were not taken quickly to stop it.

Nevertheless, technically speaking, racing per se would not seem to be destabilizing in this conception as long as the competitors remain evenly matched enough that general war still seems inadvisable — or alternatively, where the parties' capabilities are so far *apart* that general war is felt to be unnecessary for the stronger and pointless (or even suicidal) for the weaker. There might be other reasons to desire capability-regulatory arms control in such a race situation — e.g., to save money, or to delimit the potential consequences of accidental or otherwise unplanned general hostilities (e.g., keeping arsenals small in order to limit the likely damage if deterrence fails) — but whether or not any particular "arms race" is strategically stable is an empirical question, not one to which the answer can be known a priori. Again, details matter.

POTENTIAL PITFALLS OF ARMS CONTROL

Destabilizing Capability "Lock-In."

It may also be useful here to introduce the idea — discussed, for instance, by Kenneth Lieberthal in a very different context[15] — of "static" versus "dynamic" stability. One may approach this challenge through the prism of Complexity Science and its offshoots in organizational theory, which suggest that in complex adaptive systems, something akin to stability is best achieved by frameworks inhabiting a sort of "sweet spot" between the flaccid incapacity of extreme flexibility and the dangerous brittleness of ossified rigidity, which some commentators describe as being "on the edge of Chaos" but carefully not *over* that edge. In terms of organizational behavior, such systems "live" longer where their elements link tightly enough to each other that the system can respond adaptively *as an organization* to unexpected perturbations from the environment, but not so rigidly that such perturbations cannot be *absorbed* without shattering it.[16]
Looking at arms control, nuclear weapons policy, and strategic stability through the lens of Complexity — as some commentators try to do, the author among them[17] — the question of strategic stability becomes one of whether arms control measures are likely to increase or decrease the strategic system's ability to absorb perturbations without dissolution. Here Complexity seems to underscore our point about the

difficulty of identifying an a priori rule, inasmuch as while it is to some extent the purpose of arms control to *prevent* perturbations (e.g., to prevent one party from "winning" an arms race and being tempted to try to revise the strategic map by means of general war), it might also be that the very restrictions some forms of arms control impose can *increase* the rigidity — and perhaps thus the brittleness — of the system. (Rather than trying to prevent perturbations, therefore, sensible approaches to capability-regulatory arms control should presumably aim to find the force postures that best position parties to *handle* strategic perturbations within the parameters of the control regime. Unfortunately, arms control does not always do this.)

The world is a dynamic place, after all, and the ambition of capability-focused arms control (in particular) to freeze in place some particular static snapshot of the parties' technological or numerical position may not always actually serve the interests of real stability over time. In some circumstances, then, arms control frameworks might actually be maladaptive incubators for instability. Even if shrewd statesmen can agree on a particular theory of precisely what is beneficially stabilizing, for instance, and can identify a particular mix of capabilities that it is desirable to try to fix in place, it is not a given that this theory will remain valid — or that a particular mix of capabilities remain conducive to strategic stability — over time as *other* parameters of the system change. Should circumstances change, arms control might destabilize the system by retarding one or more parties' ability to adapt safely to the new developments.

Using a hypothetical scenario as an illustration, imagine that future U.S. and Russian negotiators devised an ambitious arms reduction program pursuant to which both sides would cut their forces down to a strategic "monad" of the type of delivery system classical American nuclear theorizing regards as being most "survivable" and thus likely to guarantee the stability of a deterrence relationship: submarine-launched ballistic missiles (SLBMs) based on quiet, nuclear-powered submarines (SSBNs) on continuous long-range deterrence patrols far out at sea. Some might say that such forces are stabilizing because their immunity to pre-emptive attack allows their possessors to guarantee that any aggressor would face second-strike retaliation. Into this world, however — hard-wired as it would thus be for SLBM-dependent deterrence — imagine that there were introduced a "wild card" in the form of one party's sudden discovery of just the kind of miraculous new method for strategic anti-submarine warfare that eluded U.S. and Soviet scientists during their search for competitive advantage during the Cold War. In this context of technological surprise, arms control would have set the stage for a radical instability, tying the other party to a monadic deployment upon which it would now suddenly be entirely *unable* to rely in deterring potential aggression by its rival.

For analogous reasons, in fact, the seminal nuclear strategist Herman Kahn once warned against the perils of disarming "too much." He reasoned that a nuclear deterrent balance might actually be *more* stable with arsenals that were *not* extremely small, because such a posture might be able to absorb the impact of the sudden discovery of a hidden cache of illegal weaponry. "The ability to correct violations means that the military effect of the violations must be small in percentage terms of the current strategic balance," he wrote, and a larger arsenal base offers better chances of ensuring this.[18] His point about *numerical* absorptive capacity in the face of violations might also be made as strongly with regard to the ability of a more *diverse* arsenal to preserve deterrence in the face of technological change. "As a general rule . . . strategic 'hedging' is best served by diversity, such as in keeping a range of operationally deployed and stockpiled weapon types available in order to protect against single-mode failure or unwelcome technological surprise."[19] To the extent that it is the ambition of capability-focused arms control precisely to *constrain* parties' ability to respond to their strategic environment at discretion — e.g., by prohibiting the possession of certain numbers or types of systems — it seems inescapable that there is some potential for arms control to "lock in" maladaptive circumstances.

Such possibilities, indeed, are often implicitly recognized in arms control agreements themselves, which commonly contain withdrawal clauses. The NPT, for instance, provides that each party has "the right to withdraw from the Treaty if it decides that extraordinary events, related to the subject matter of this Treaty, have jeopardized the supreme interests of its country."[20] The recent New START agreement similarly provides that each party may withdraw "if it decides that extraordinary events related to the subject matter of this Treaty have jeopardized its supreme interests."[21] (Under the Vienna Convention on the Law of Treaties, a party's departure is permitted even where denunciation or withdrawal is *not* actually provided for in the instrument itself, as long as such a right "may be implied by the nature of the treaty."[22]) There would seem to be few, if any, arms control agreements from which their drafters imagined there to be *no* conceivable circumstances in which withdrawal was appropriate. Such mechanisms serve the function of trying to attenuate the dangers of "lock-in," by making escape from capability restrictions legally available.

The history of the Anti-Ballistic Missile (ABM) Treaty of 1972[23] may illustrate the problematic dynamics of "capability lock in" as well as any hypothetical. This agreement was, in effect, rooted in a particular theory of strategic stability—specifically, about the negative relationship between ballistic missile defense (BMD) and stability in the U.S.-Soviet context—pursuant to which defenses were thought to be destabilizing, in part because they would encourage a spiraling offense/defense arms competition and perhaps even prompt a pre-emptive strike if one superpower believed defenses would protect it against the other's retaliation. Under the ABM Treaty, each side was permitted to retain a minimalist, point-based defensive system at two sites, but nationwide defenses were banned. (The Soviets opted to build and keep active a BMD site protecting Moscow, and indeed have retained and somewhat updated it ever since, but the Americans shut down their only site in 1975 after only a few months in operation.[24])

What seemed like a good idea to the Americans at the time, however—on the basis of an anti-defense theory of strategic stability and under the conditions of highly competitive U.S.-Soviet nuclear rivalry during the Cold War—did not look so compelling in the post-Cold War era. Beginning to feel the pressure of changing circumstances, the administration of President Bill Clinton pursued negotiated re-interpretation of some treaty understandings with the Russians in order to accommodate the developing U.S. ABM testing agenda, and toyed with the idea of actually amending the instrument. Things came to a head under President George W. Bush, when American officials concluded, in effect, that the ABM Treaty had locked in a capability-regulatory status quo that under modern circumstances was potentially *destabilizing* — albeit not in the sense that it unsettled America's relationship with the other treaty party (Russia), but rather because of its impact vis-à-vis third parties.

What had been changing? After the collapse of the Soviet Union and the end of the Cold War, the competitive pressures of the Russo-American dyad looked much less menacing, and indeed both sides had been dramatically reducing their arsenals ever since the early 1990s. At the same time, however, the United States had come to perceive an ominous emerging threat from *third parties*: "rogue states" such as North Korea and Iran, which were rapidly developing and improving long-range missile capabilities even while working in various overt and covert ways to develop nuclear weapons that could be mounted upon such missiles.

In this new context, there now seemed to the Americans to be little danger of a spiraling offense/defense competition with the Russians — and indeed, despite post-Cold War reductions, Moscow's missile arsenal remained considerably larger than necessary to overwhelm any feasible U.S. defensive shield — and much to be gained from limited defenses capable of stopping attacks mounted by the kind of "entry-level" nuclear arsenals sought by the rogues. Thanks to the waning of the Russo-American nuclear competition and the rise of such small third-party threats, in other words, the anti-defense status quo of the ABM Treaty came to be seen in Washington as maladaptive, fixing in place a force mix that was no longer necessary for its original purpose but yet seemed likely to empower rogue states such as North Korea and Iran to use their emerging arsenals to bully their neighbors or even threaten the great powers, all of whom would be more or less defenseless against long-range ballistic missile attack. This was not "strategically destabilizing" in the sense that it necessarily increased the likelihood of general war between the existing great powers, but it seemed likely to make major regional conflict more probable and more costly — with some concomitant risk of great power involvement — to make major states more vulnerable vis-à-vis third-party proliferators, and even to help increase the *number* of major powers in the international system.

Accordingly, in December 2001 the United States announced its intention to withdraw from the ABM Treaty pursuant to its withdrawal clause. (These provided that a party could withdraw on 6 months' notice if it determined that "extraordinary events related to the subject matter of this Treaty have jeopardized its supreme interests."[25]) As White House officials explained:

> The circumstances affecting U.S. national security have changed fundamentally since the signing of the ABM Treaty in 1972. . . . Today, our security environment is profoundly different. The Cold War is over. The Soviet Union no longer exists. Russia is not an enemy, but in fact is increasingly allied with us on a growing number of critically important issues. . . . Today, the United States and Russia face new threats to their security. Principal among these threats are weapons of mass destruction and their delivery means wielded by terrorists and rogue states. A number of such states are acquiring increasingly longer-range ballistic missiles as instruments of blackmail [sic] and coercion against the United States and its friends and allies. The United States must defend its homeland, its forces and its friends and allies against these threats.

We must develop and deploy the means to deter and protect against them, including through limited missile defense of our territory.[26]

U.S. officials did not use the phrase, but they had clearly decided that it was necessary to escape the "capability lock-in" imposed by the Americans' own 1972 arms control agenda. Their withdrawal became effective in June 2002, and, despite ongoing Russian complaints about the alleged perils even of current scaled-back U.S. plans for missile defense,[27] the ABM Treaty remains today a dead letter.

The administration of President Barack Obama has been considerably more diffident about missile defense than its predecessor, but even present-day U.S. officials claim to remain committed to the goal of building a missile defense network capable of defending the entire United States — as well as key friends and allies overseas — from the new threats invoked by the Bush administration in the U.S. withdrawal from the ABM Treaty. Current policy, for instance, promises to "augment our current protection of the U.S. homeland against long-range ballistic missile threats, and to offer more effective defenses against more near-term ballistic missile threats."[28] Even Obama's scaled-back BMD plans involve capabilities beyond what the ABM Treaty would have permitted.[29] Flexibly coping with 21st century threats by avoiding the capability-regulatory "lock-in" imposed by a mid-Cold War anti-defense theoretical paradigm, has thus become a bipartisan priority in the United States.

Clearly, therefore, it is at least a *potential* problem for arms control that a particular capability-regulatory status quo, fixed in place today by an agreement, might not serve useful purposes tomorrow, and might actually destabilize. Implicit recognition that arms control regulations are capable of creating a problematic and potentially destabilizing ossification may perhaps also be found in the fact that the two most recent strategic agreements between the United States and Russia—the Moscow Treaty of 2002[30] and its successor, the New START agreement of 2010—permit each side considerable freedom to structure its specific mix of weapons systems as it sees fit within an overall set of treaty caps. This reflects the understanding that the two nuclear powers do not face identical situations, and that their needs may also evolve even during the duration of an agreement—and accordingly that it could be harmful to specify *too much* in an arms control agreement. Flexibility within the terms of a treaty—that is, a willingness *not* to provide for *complete* control of parties' future decisionmaking on weapons acquisition and deployment—seems to be valued in such negotiations, presumably at least in part because it reduces the danger that capability lock-in will imperil the interests of either side.

It is also not uncommon for arms control agreements to "sunset" after a specified period of time, thus automatically allowing an opportunity for whatever renegotiation the parties feel is appropriate under the prevailing circumstances at that point. (START expired on its own terms in December 2009, for instance, while New START specifies that it will terminate after 10 years.[31]) Along with the near-ubiquity of withdrawal clauses, such provisions suggest a clear understanding that changed circumstances can sometimes transform yesterday's wise arms limitation into tomorrow's dangerous straightjacket. Indeed, it was arguably one of the structural failings of the ABM Treaty that it had *no* "sunset" provision, even though it was negotiated simultaneously with the force caps of SALT I, which itself was merely styled an "interim" agreement with an intended duration of only 5 years.[32] Arms controllers thus need to be conscious of the challenges presented by "lock-in" dynamics, which in the right (i.e., wrong) circumstances can impede dynamic stability within the strategic system.

Displacement Effects.

To add to this litany of at least potential challenges, it is worth mentioning that just as conditions of strategic stability can serve to displace great power rivalry to alternative venues (e.g., proxy wars), arms control may sometimes have the effect of encouraging the *displacement* of arms competition to other areas — potentially in ways *more* detrimental to strategic stability than unregulated competition would have been in the capabilities that were actually subject to the agreement's regulation. The Washington naval treaties of the interwar years, for instance, went to some trouble to regulate great power competition in large battleships, but arguably at the cost of encouraging parties' more rapid transition to *less* (or non) regulated naval capabilities — specifically, submarines and naval aviation — that actually turned out to be genuinely "disruptive technologies" in the field, and the means by which later naval wars of the 20th century were won or lost. At the very least, the battleship-regulatory regime did not turn out to have quite the soothing strategic impact that its drafters presumably intended.[33]

More pointedly, many argue that the numerical limits imposed in the mid-1970s on U.S. and Soviet delivery systems[34] helped push the superpowers more quickly and thoroughly into the deployment of multiple, independently-targeted re-entry vehicles (MIRVs) aboard the ballistic missiles whose numbers were capped by SALT in 1972. Unable to aim at more targets by building more missiles than they had previously done—but still *wishing* to be able to hit more targets—Washington and Moscow invested in ways to do so with their *existing* missile force. MIRVing, a technology that emerged in the 1960s and had already begun to appear on the U.S. Minuteman missile in 1970, effectively became that answer, and it was ever more enthusiastically embraced by both sides thereafter.

This was, however, problematic, because nuclear analysts tend to believe that using MIRVs—at least in land-based silos the locations of which are known or knowable to an adversary—is less "stabilizing" than using single-warhead missiles, because the former make it more attractive for an adversary to strike pre-emptively, in order to maximize his counterforce "return on investment." In theory, for example—although this is a simplification of the complexities of nuclear targeting, which frequently involves assigning more than one weapon to each target, in order to ensure a high probability of destruction[35]—a single attacking weapon, hitting a MIRVed missile in its silo, can take several enemy warheads out of action with the expenditure of but a single attacking warhead. (Because firing a single MIRVed missile might allow this to occur several times, moreover, mutual possession of MIRVs makes preemption incentives especially high.) This gives each side the incentive to launch a first strike in time of crisis, for this highly-favorable exchange ratio advantage is lost if the other side fires first. These dynamics may also increase incentives to adopt launch-on-warning (LOW) postures pursuant to which one's own weapons fire upon learning of an incoming enemy attack, so that they depart before *his* missiles land. On account of the very short warning times involved, LOW is widely believed to be vulnerable to false alarms and other sorts of catastrophic accident.[36] The net effect may thus be greater strategic instability than before, especially in time of crisis.

This theory of MIRV instability was reflected in the START II agreement of 1993, which actually undertook to *prohibit* MIRVed land-based missiles,[37] though the treaty was never ratified by the Russian Duma. This notion is, moreover, still reflected in U.S. nuclear policy: the Obama Administration's 2010 *Nuclear Posture Review* pledged to reduce all U.S. intercontinental ballistic missiles (ICBMs) to a single warhead each, on the grounds that this step "will enhance the stability of the nuclear balance by reducing the incentives for either side to strike first."[38]

As noted, however, even though MIRV technology predated SALT, and would surely have been adopted to some degree whether or not there was a treaty, SALT restrictions gave the superpowers more incentives to move to pervasive MIRVing, including the eventual development of extremely large silo-based missiles carrying many warheads each: the U.S. Peacekeeper with 10, and the Russian SS-18 with potentially even more. Even today, most U.S. and Russian land-based intercontinental systems — and all submarine-based systems — are still MIRVed. If the common assumption about MIRV instability is correct, it may thus be that SALT-era *missile* limitations actually left the Cold War strategic arms race more "unstable" and pre-emption-evocative than they found it.

It would appear, therefore, that the possibility of such "displacement effects" is yet another factor that one must consider in evaluating the stability impact of arms control measures. Such dynamics presumably do not *always* occur, nor do arms control agreements by any means *necessarily* encourage alternative methods of competition that prove more unstable than the modalities of rivalry such agreements proscribe. Nevertheless, these are potential dynamics that cannot be taken lightly, and which deserve careful thought if arms control strategists are to maximize the odds of real success.

As an example of how displacement effects need to be taken into consideration in evaluating the likely impact of proposed future agreements, such issues might arise in connection with the Comprehensive Test Ban Treaty (CTBT)[39] — an agreement rejected by the U.S. Senate in 1999, but which the Obama administration has stated it wishes to re-introduce. In the improbable event that CTBT ever enters into force,[40] the treaty seems likely — by making it much harder for countries to engage in yield-producing nuclear tests — to tend to displace nuclear weapons competitions into areas that *don't* require testing (e.g., "gun-type" uranium weapons, or devices based upon "pre-tested" designs such as China's so-called CHIC-4 "export model," plans for which were reportedly supplied to Pakistan and then to Libya and perhaps also Iran, and which may also be the basis for a current North Korean weapon).[41] If this results in the proliferation of *secret* nuclear arsenals, without at least the "public accountability" of overt testing, it is an open question whether it would be an overall advantage for international peace and security over today's status quo of a world in which yield-producing tests are at least theoretically available. The CTBT's likely net impact upon strategic stability is far from clear, of course, and might yet be positive,

particularly if the present-day rarity and general stig-
matization of nuclear testing produces such displacement effects anyway, *irrespective* of the Treaty's entry
into force.[42] This is, however, the *kind* of question that
sophisticated arms control advocates need to address.
So far, though, few do.

When Arms Control Fails.

Before concluding this discussion of the potential strategic stability *costs* of arms control, it is worth
highlighting one more line of argument. There is extensive literature critiquing arms control agreements,
or at least particular ones, on the basis of how difficult
it is to evaluate the degree to which the other side is
actually *complying* with them—either because of some
potential for undetected violations, the difficulty of
detecting cheating in time to be able to do anything
in response to it, or a paucity of responsive options.
Other critiques have focused upon the peculiar challenges that may arise when open, liberal democracies
negotiate agreements with authoritarian states, political challenges to honesty in compliance assessment,
the perils of overestimating one's ability to verify an
agreement, the ways in which the negotiating *process*
can be a tool of potentially destabilizing manipulation,
and the potential impact of adversarial negotiation in
impeding improvements in one's relationship with the
other side.

Although these critiques raise important points—
ones that deserve careful attention from any serious
practitioner of the arms control art—they do not, for
the most part, bear directly on the questions of strategic stability that are the focus of this chapter. For
the most part, these challenges represent a different
category of problem than those hitherto discussed,

insofar as in such cases the damage is done more by the *incompleteness* of the arms control process (e.g., ineffective verifiability, one party's noncompliance, or simply an agreement's procedural stillbirth) than by its *success* in imposing the constraints it aims to create. Such circumstances of procedural defect represent instances in which arms control has *failed* on its own terms. As an analytical matter, the more interesting issues emerge where arms control measures may *succeed* on their own terms (e.g., successfully constraining both sides' development of a particular suite of capabilities) and yet may *still* have an ambivalent or even negative impact upon strategic stability. Bypassing such *failure* cases, therefore, the next section will discuss the problems arms control can create even in its "success."

Strategic Manipulation.

Into the category of arms control that can destabilize by succeeding, one must put measures that one side actually seeks for this reason — that is, steps that appear valuable to one state precisely *because* of their likely effect in *decreasing* another state's security through one or more of the dynamics discussed here. Indeed, it is for fear of such possibilities that some authors have urged that policymakers should maintain a cautious wariness, informed by awareness of how the *ideal* of arms control can sometimes be invoked for purposes of strategic manipulation.[43]

As an example of such a manipulative effort, one might cite Soviet support in the early 1980s for a "nuclear freeze,"[44] which seems clearly to have been an outgrowth of Moscow's desire to preclude NATO nuclear responses both to Soviet deployments of new ballistic missiles and to the Warsaw Pact's then-assumed conventional superiority in Europe.[45] Doubtless mindful of their numerical advantage, Soviet officials were also fond of declaring their support for the principle of not being the first to use nuclear weapons in a conflict[46] — something envisioned as a possibility by NATO nuclear planners precisely out of their fear that without such an option, weight of numbers might enable the Warsaw Pact to carry the day in a European war. Similarly, Russian and Chinese proposals for a convention aimed at "Prevention of an Arms Race in Outer Space" (PAROS)[47] have long been phrased in such a way as to shut down what these governments felt might be an area of (possible future) U.S. advantage in *space-based* weaponry, while leaving untouched their own (existing) ability to threaten critical *American* space assets through the use of *terrestrially-based* anti-satellite systems.[48] (Ground-based anti-satellite weapons would not be covered because they were not "in outer space.") Such arms control proposals were, in effect, *designed* to be strategically destabilizing as a result of capability-regulation lock-in effects that would affect the two sides in very different ways.

THE POSITIVE SIDE OF THE LEDGER

So far, the reader might be forgiven for concluding that arms control is at least valueless — and often downright dangerous — from the perspective of strategic stability. This, however, is not the case. Admittedly, this chapter has so far focused on the negative aspects with particular intensity, for they are not always well enough understood in the policy community. Yet, however useful it is to remember the potential negative side, this is *not* the whole story. In reality, arms control *can* play a valuable role in helping achieve or reinforce strategic stability. If there is a central point to this chapter, it is simply that this is not *always* the case. The analytical challenge for policymakers is to avoid the potential traps that arms control can create, while taking advantage of the benefits it can offer.

Capability-Regulatory Arms Control.

The Other Side of Strategic Manipulation.

Before addressing the question of when arms control-driven "lock-in" might actually *increase* strategic stability, let us briefly note — and then put aside — the possibility that one might actually *want* to create less stable circumstances. Strictly from the standpoint of strategic stability, maladaptively rigid "capability lock-in" is indeed undesirable. To conclude that an arms control agreement creating instability is per se a bad agreement, however, is to presume that strategic stability is a per se good. As discussed earlier, one should be cautious about such an assumption, for stability can have its costs.

Moreover, from the particular perspective of a *participant* in the world's geopolitical struggles, certain kinds of instability might be desirable. This is the flip side of the potential trap of strategic manipulation discussed above: sometimes a lopsidedly structured proposal would work to one's *own* advantage. Every historical instance of a destabilizingly manipulative arms control effort, after all — e.g., the "nuclear freeze" idea, or the various Sino-Russian PAROS proposals — presumably took that form precisely because, for its advocates, *that* kind of instability seemed advantageous. Accordingly, national leaders can be expected to look not disapprovingly upon arms control ideas that favor their side *irrespective* of these proposals' potentially negative impact on strategic stability. Where one stands on such questions, as the saying goes, depends upon where one sits, and what may be a trap for one person is simply a shrewd gambit for the other. That said, the focus here is on strategic stability, so the next section will cover the more interesting analytical question of when arms control can indeed serve that end.

Constraining Destabilizing Advantage.

To begin with, although arms races are not *intrinsically* destabilizing, a situation in which one side or the other "loses" such a race can be very much so. To the extent, therefore, that a capability-regulated arms control regime can keep a numerical arms race from developing to the point that the sheer pace of competition overwhelms one party's ability to keep up — e.g., if it lacks the financial resources or technical capacity to match its rival's build-rate — that regime would indeed conduce to strategic stability by preventing the more capable arms-builder from achieving a decisive advantage. From the advantage-possessing party's perspective, of course, such arms control might be "bad arms control," but a successful scheme of numerical restraint in such circumstances would leave the strategic environment more stable withal. Arms control promotes strategic stability not by constraining an arms race per se, but by preventing one side from *winning* it. This it is indeed capable of doing.

Capability-regulatory forms of arms control can also promote strategic stability where they prevent possession of or reliance upon a particular *type* of capability in ways, or to a degree, that would tend to destabilize the relationship. As noted earlier, for instance, it is widely believed that multiply-MIRVed silo-based ballistic missiles are intrinsically more "destabilizing" than single-warhead delivery systems, because they create especially acute incentives for an adversary to contemplate pre-emption in times of crisis.

If this theory of "MIRV instability" is correct, arms control between two nuclear powers could promote strategic stability by prohibiting multiple-warhead systems — precisely as the START II agreement *would* have done had it been ratified by Russia. Today, much work apparently remains to be done in constraining the presumed destabilizing effect of MIRVed missiles, for while the Americans are now planning to *de*-MIRV their silo-based force, the Russians announced in 2011 that they would be building a *new* heavy ICBM capable of carrying between 10 and 15 separate warheads.[49] This is a strange choice for a country that is supposedly concerned about the possibility of a U.S. first strike,[50] since by the warhead-for-warhead logic of MIRV instability theory, Russia's continuing attachment to MIRVs would seem to make American pre-emption *more attractive* in a crisis. At any rate, the example of MIRV technology and the crisis-instability it creates offers a concrete example of the type of situation in which capability-regulatory arms control could perhaps provide significant stability benefits.[51]

Arms control could also perhaps restrain parties to an agreement in a reciprocally asymmetrical way — *across* competitive domains — that conduces to strategic stability. If one country most fears the other's aircraft and that country most fears the first country's ships, for example, it might be fruitless to try to negotiate aerial or naval capability restrictions alone, and perhaps even destabilizing if they did. On the other hand, an arms control agreement that limited aircraft, while also constraining ships for both sides, would seem not just to offer something to each side, but actually to address the potential instability challenge presented by the specter of each side's unconstrained pursuit of some special comparative advantage. Otherwise, whoever moved fastest or managed to go furthest along their own particular road might be tempted to rewrite the strategic balance by force. Each side would have an incentive to abide by such an agreement, moreover, for fear that noncompliance would lead to the end of constraints upon the other side's asymmetric advantage. Such a scenario of imposing cross-domain restraints upon mutually-asymmetric comparative advantage is no doubt far from easy, but it offers another potential way to promote strategic stability.

Nonproliferation Regimes.

Multilateral capability-regulatory arms control of the sort that seeks to keep certain capabilities (e.g., weapons of mass destruction [WMD]) from proliferating beyond a pre-established group of possessors—as with the NPT, the most well known example of this type—presents an interesting analytical challenge. The principal aim of such instruments is, in effect, to promote a kind of strategic stability by preventing the spread of capabilities potent enough to permit new-acquirers to overawe or simply destroy their rivals, and to forestall the emergence of a world of ubiquitous WMD brinksmanship dangerously susceptible to unpredictable escalatory dynamics. To the extent that such regimes succeed in constraining such proliferation, therefore, one might conclude that stability is indeed well served.

Nevertheless, the stability calculus is more complicated than this simple description would suggest. In part, this is because strategic stability can potentially be threatened by a range of military tools beyond just the specific capabilities regulated by a WMD control regime. Where this is the case, the possessor of powerful nonregulated forces (i.e., conventional weaponry) might be able to threaten weaker states in ways to which the nonproliferation regime might actually serve to help *prevent* an effective response. In such cases, nonproliferation constraints could theoretically destabilize.

This, in fact, is the claim all but explicitly made by the Iranian theocracy vis-à-vis the United States as Tehran pushes forward with its development of a nuclear weapons capability in violation of its NPT obligations. One might even imagine such a proliferation-justification argument being made in the future against the People's Republic of China (PRC) by threatened governments in Australia, Japan, Mongolia, the Philippines, South Korea, Taiwan, or Vietnam — or perhaps against Russia by Georgia, one of the Baltic States, or others from among the endemically bullied ex-Soviet countries of the Kremlin's "near abroad." How plausible and legitimate such claims would be, of course, would depend greatly upon the circumstances. Nevertheless, they cannot be dismissed a priori as a matter of strategic logic.

Nonproliferation has been applied in different contexts. It has been used, for instance, as part of *prohibitory* capability-regulation systems, aiming to prevent the spread of dual-use materials or technologies that would make it easy for states to violate the abolition regime. This is, for instance, the approach taken with chemical weaponry under the CWC, and to some extent also with biological weaponry under the BTWC. By attempting to constrain parties' capability to achieve potentially militarily advantageous regime "breakout," such nonproliferation constraints aim to serve the interests of strategic stability.

Nonproliferation constraints have also been used in systems *not* built upon a foundation of complete prohibition. The NPT, for instance, has an explicitly two-tiered system in which a few states are in effect *permitted* nuclear weaponry, at least for the indefinite future.[52] (Their eventual disarmament is envisioned, but it is not actually required.[53]) For most parties, however, such tools are disallowed. The nonproliferation constraints built into the NPT system, therefore, are designed to prevent *others* from acquiring powerful tools that *some* are allowed to retain.

However understandable and unavoidable such a two-tiered structure may be as a matter of history and geopolitical reality, it can potentially create some tension within the regime from the perspective of strategic stability, insofar as the system offers no intrinsic barrier to *possessor* states' use of nuclear weaponry to intimidate or even attack nonpossessors. One could certainly debate whether it is *reasonable* for nonpossessors to fear the possibility of facing such nuclear threats in the modern world, but this is an empirical question that cannot be answered a priori. It might well be that such potential "nuclear threat" problems are in practice less troublesome — from a strategic stability perspective — than those that would be presented by having no NPT at all, and that there is no way to resolve the tensions within the treaty without either retreating to the magical thinking of immediate global abolition or permitting a *pro*-proliferation "cure" that would be worse than the disease. Nevertheless, analytical honesty compels one to acknowledge the existence of the problem: two-tiered systems do face potential internal tensions.

There is a further potential stability challenge inherent in any nonproliferation regime. If the managers of such a nonproliferation regime lack the good sense to couple their *weapons* nonproliferation rules with rules that also constrain the *facilitating technologies* used in developing such tools — or if they are simply *unable* to implement such rules — the net stability benefit of the regime would lessen over time. Already, for instance, the CWC's nonproliferation system is under considerable stress from the reconfigurable flexibility, global ubiquity, and increasing miniaturization of modern chemical production technology. The BTWC's effect in constraining the states' ability to develop biological and toxin weapons is under even more strain, given the worldwide spread and rapidly-evolving character of modern biotechnology, which made an effective verification protocol impossible.[54] Even "dual-use" nuclear weapons-related technology is harder to verify today than ever, thanks in part to the spread of potentially-plutonium-producing nuclear power reactors,[55] and in part to the development and spread of efficient and relatively concealable uranium-enrichment centrifuge technology that has replaced the huge and inefficient gaseous diffusion and other industrial-scale facilities of yesteryear.[56] In the NPT context, moreover, there seems to be considerable confusion about what the rules actually *are*, or should be, with respect to constraining technological diffusion.[57]

This is a potentially very serious problem, and is worth emphasizing. Especially, but hardly exclusively, in a world in which significant conventional military asymmetries persist, weapons nonpossessors have some incentive to "hedge" their strategic bets by preparing for the possibility of "breakout" from a nonproliferation regime. The motives for this, of course, might vary. Such hedging might be attractive, for example, in order to prepare for the possibility of *facing* aggression from a foreign power, but it might also be undertaken in order to make one's *own* anticipated future aggression more feasible. One country's hedging, moreover, might tend to elicit analogous behavior from others, giving its potential rivals more reason to prepare for the worst themselves. On account of the structural tensions described above, hedging might be all the more attractive for nonpossessors within the context of a tiered, "have/have not" regime such as the NPT system.

At any rate, if strategic hedging by technological acquisition is not *itself* to become the locus of considerable strategic instability, robust technology-diffusion controls are critical. To the extent that a nonproliferation regime ends up taking a *laissez-faire* approach to dual-use (i.e., potentially weapons-facilitative) technology, nonpossessors will have the *opportunity* to indulge any taste they develop for such hedging strategies by reserving a future nuclear weapons "option" for themselves.

There are some who have argued that the massive proliferation of nuclear weapons capabilities — or indeed nuclear weapons themselves[58] — would foster stability by creating a kind of universal deterrence. In fact, however, a system full of "virtual" weapons states, each merely a metaphorical stone's throw away from weaponization, would be quite problematic, for while a world of widespread nuclear "latency" is perhaps less immediately dangerous than a world of *actually* nuclear-armed powers, it could still, in crisis-stability terms, be perilous indeed. As noted at the beginning of this chapter, the Nash-inspired model of strategic stability tends to presume both that national decisionmaking is the rational product of cost-benefit calculations and that players are not radically mistaken in the beliefs they hold and assumptions they make about their counterparts. These assumptions are a useful heuristic, but they clearly abstract somewhat from reality. Significantly, the *degree* of their departure from that reality would probably nowhere be as great as in the case of a *fully* proliferated world, which — by forcing players simultaneously to try to calibrate security strategies along more axes than it is probably reasonable to expect fallible humans to be able to handle[59] — would give maximum scope for every mistake or miscalculation to spiral into catastrophic warfare.

Moreover, even through a prism of rational decisionmaking, a world of ubiquitous nuclear weapons "options" would compound long-understood problems of crisis stability arising out of what the seminal Cold War nuclear strategist Herman Kahn once described as a "mobilization war" — that is, a form of competition between two rival powers in which each positions itself to be most quickly able to activate an otherwise at least somewhat dormant military capability, and thereby to "achieve a militarily dominant position, enabling it to inhibit the diplomatic or military initiatives of its opponent."[60] As Thomas Schelling has pointed out in his powerful critique of the likely stability of a nuclear weapons abolition regime, such relationships can be very dangerous, for they not only give rise to dramatic escalatory possibilities in a crisis — as each side scrambles not to be caught napping by the *other's* mobilization — but could create incentives for the "winner" of such a race actually to *use* his weapons first, before the other side completes its own mobilization.[61] Kahn agreed, noting that mobilization racing from a position of disarmament could "create pressures toward preventative war,"[62] a dynamic which has elsewhere been compared to the partly mobilization-driven escalatory disaster that occurred in Europe in the summer of 1914.[63]

A world of ubiquitous nuclear "latency" among NPT non-nuclear-weapon states would be not unlike the world of mobilization-ready disarmed powers described by Kahn and Schelling, with all of its ugly potential to escalate uncontrollably even when facing only a relatively small crisis. In Schelling's description, such an environment sounds like a perilous one indeed:

> Every crisis would be a nuclear crisis, any war could become a nuclear war. The urge to preempt would dominate; whoever gets the first few weapons will coerce or preempt. It would be a nervous world.[64]

To be sure, Schelling's comments were aimed in particular at the stability challenges of a *wholly* nuclear-free world. A world of "mixed" capacities, in which some players already have nuclear weaponry while others merely hover on the *brink* of exercising a weapons "option," may be in some ways different. (If a weapons possessor were to provide credible "extended deterrence" to a nonpossessor ally, for example, this might help lessen the destabilizing pressures of crisis-stability logic by reducing the ally's incentives to rush to build and/or use its own weapons. U.S.-Japan and U.S.-South Korean relations already provide examples of this dynamic.) Nonetheless, in the relationships of "option"-possessing players *outside* such alliance frameworks — or wherever extended deterrence is insufficiently credible — Schelling's logic would seem to speak powerfully to a world of mixed capabilities as well.

A nonproliferation regime that neglects to give sufficient attention to stopping the spread of weapons-facilitative technologies, therefore, seems likely to undermine itself and sow the seeds for considerable strategic instability. This danger deserves more attention than it has hitherto received in the NPT context, where all too many otherwise sensible people seem astonishingly willing to join would-be proliferators in the regime-corrosive view that one should — or indeed "must" — actually *promote* the free flow of weapons-facilitating dual-use technology.[65] From the perspective of strategic stability, as an old mariners' map might have put it, there be dragons.

Transparency and Confidence-Building Measures.

So far, however, this chapter has focused almost entirely upon capability-regulatory arms control. As explained earlier this is only one of three approaches to arms control. What about behaviorally-focused and information-concessive arms control measures?

Information-focused approaches, for example — namely, transparency and confidence-building measures (T/CBMs) — "do" less than capability-restriction regimes, in the sense that they do not in themselves oblige any change in a party's force posture. Indeed, they do not usually, in themselves, change "facts on the ground" at all. Nevertheless, information-concessive arms control seems capable of providing some strategic stability benefit, and may be less vulnerable than a capability-focused regime to some of the rigidity problems we discussed earlier.

How can merely information-focused arms control affect stability? A key function of T/CBMs is to increase parties' understanding of the realities of the situation they face, though naturally the impact of such understanding will depend upon what this situation actually is. T/CBMs — e.g., data exchanges, the development of fora in which compliance or other concerns can be discussed, and other interactions designed to increase each side's understanding of the other's doctrines, capabilities, intentions, and strategic thinking — can make a relationship more stable where they help dispel distrust and suspicion rooted in *false* perceptions that otherwise might spur the sides to adopt policies or acquire capabilities that could destabilize the balance between them.

If one side believes the other is violating an existing agreement, for instance, the use of a discussion forum — a body such as the Joint Compliance and Inspection Commission set up under the START framework,[66] or the Bilateral Consultative Commission now established by New START[67] — might be able to resolve the issue to the extent that it results from a misunderstanding or difference in treaty interpretation. This could help avoid a situation in which one party feels the need to withdraw from the treaty, or to take some other measure that could destabilize the balance between them. Similarly, T/CBMs may be able to help ameliorate tensions and forestall destabilizing choices where one side wrongly believes the other is engaged in acquiring capabilities or is developing doctrines that present a new and dangerous threat. Even those with a reputation of being somewhat skeptical about arms control, after all, concede that "[n]egotiations can serve a straightforward purpose of communication between the parties," and that:

> [p]roblems that result from misunderstanding may become solvable if the parties come to understand more facts, better grasp each other's views, and appreciate a fuller range of possible solutions.[68]

T/CBMs may be useful, for example, in dispelling one party's uncertainty about the other side's approach to strategic issues, making it seem less important for the first party to adopt "hedging" strategies or other measures that might themselves tend to inflame tensions and elicit countervailing moves, with potentially destabilizing effect. This is, in fact, a claim frequently made about the potential utility of T/CBMs in the U.S.-China strategic relationship—that is, if only Beijing would accept them and move away from its traditional posture of deliberate opacity. According to a recent U.S. Government report on Chinese military power:

> many uncertainties remain regarding how China will use its expanding military capabilities. The limited transparency in China's military and security affairs enhances uncertainty and increases the potential for misunderstanding and miscalculation.[69]

As it is argued elsewhere—and as former U.S. Secretary of Defense Robert Gates himself indicated[70]—continuing American uncertainty about the nature and trajectory of China's ongoing buildup of nuclear forces is emerging as a "brake" on the willingness of U.S. leaders to consider deeper reductions in our nuclear arsenal.[71] At the same time, concerns about Beijing's intentions vis-à-vis its neighbors in the context of a considerable Chinese build-up of sophisticated *conventional* forces and regional power-projection capabilities[72] have led U.S. officials into a more ostentatious posture of countervailing moves in the Western Pacific, as part of a broad strategy of claiming to be "back" in Asia,[73] as well as a heightened interest among regional powers in capabilities that would provide means to resist Chinese encroachments.[74]

To the extent that transparency measures can help clear up such uncertainty by demonstrating that Beijing is *not* seeking or likely to become a formidable threat to the United States, or that Washington is not seeking to achieve military dominance over China, this would presumably do much to promote stability. Where mutual threats are misunderstood to be worse than they really are, in other words, T/CBMs can help make it less likely that each party will make destabilizing choices by making clear precisely how threatening the other side *isn't*. Partly for this reason, it is a high U.S. priority to promote military-to-military contacts and other interactions with the PRC that would reduce the opacity of Chinese strategic thinking and shed light on how officials there really view strategic policy, as well as demonstrate the benevolence of U.S. intentions and plans. The degree to which T/CBMs can ameliorate concerns about another party's intentions is limited, of course — since intentions are notoriously difficult to "know" with real assurance, and can in any event change — but such measures can provide at least *some* window upon intentions, and can offer considerable insight into another country's ability to *act* upon its intentions, even if they prove malign.

Of course, the degree to which genuine transparency reduces distrust and fear will depend upon what is revealed. It might be, for instance, that information-concessive measures serve not to *dispel* dark apprehensions but rather to *confirm* them. Sometimes there really *are* threats out there. Nevertheless, even where transparency *reveals* threats, dispelling uncertainty and misconceptions about the *lack* of a threat is hardly without value. Indeed, such transparency may serve the interests of strategic stability more directly even than in cases where it turns out to reveal the absence of a threat. Forewarned, as the saying goes, is forearmed — and a country that faces a threat *but does not know it* will probably do too little to protect itself, thereby increasing the odds that its challenger will be able to revise the strategic balance by force. An unwelcome encounter with strategic surprise, after all, is not conducive to strategic stability.

Some experts argue that the pursuit of arms control agreements can also have an important *symbolic* value, in that *seeking* arms control can *itself* function as a sort of confidence-building measure. Such a policy might, for instance, convey the message — accurately or otherwise — that the seeker wishes to live in peace, and seeks no strategic advantage over the other party. When this is the case, the mere pursuit of agreements in apparent good faith may serve as a form of confidence-building measure, helping soothe tensions and forestall destabilizing policy choices by the other party. It may be, furthermore, that negotiating is sometimes:

> useful as a way of making a point to *third parties*, whether or not agreement is achieved, or even expected. Talks can show the public in your own country or elsewhere, for example, that you are interested in a peaceful solution, even if the other side is not. Negotiations can [also] show that you have "gone the extra mile" before you resort to other action.[75]

Such ancillary effects, however, are probably not directly relevant from the perspective of strategic stability, for they do not clearly or directly bear upon the question of whether one power is able to adjust the strategic balance by force.

It may also be that reaching an arms control treaty may have value for one or more parties to some extent *irrespective* of the agreement's actual content. (Russia's insistence upon codifying already-agreed unilateral reductions into the Moscow Treaty of 2002, for example, may bespeak the Kremlin's desire to continue having legally-binding arms control arrangements with the United States less for their specific provisions than on account of a perception that such strategic arms deals represented the symbolic coinage of a diminished and insecure Russia's continued status as a genuine "superpower.") Sometimes the act of negotiating may *itself* amount to giving the other side a concession—as seems to be the case today with North Korea, which shows not the slightest sign of being willing to give up its nuclear weapons but nonetheless seeks nuclear talks with the United States in order to feed its own self-image as a nuclear weapons state and a world power that others must take seriously.[76] There does not seem to be a clear relationship, however, between such symbolic roles and the question of strategic stability that concerns the United States, so it is probably best to focus here upon information-concessive arrangements that more directly affect transparency, for this really can shape parties' reciprocal threat assessments.

Behavior Controls.

The reader will recall that "behavior-regulatory" arms controls are measures that seek to constrain not what parties actually *have* but instead what they *do* with it. Behavioral measures may seek to do this in a mandatory or legally-binding way, or as the sort of "best practices" guidance provided by a merely hortatory code of conduct. In effect, behavioral approaches seek to channel participants' policy choices away from forms of competition or interaction that are particularly destabilizing.

In general, behavioral measures are probably less susceptible to the potentially problematic "lock in" dynamics than is capability-focused arms control, because what is at issue here is only what one *does* with one's tools, rather than whether one can possess them at all. It is presumably easier just to employ something differently than it is to develop that thing in the first place, and if one needs to adjust to strategic surprise or to another party's perfidy, it is easier to revoke one's obligation to adhere to certain modes of behavior than it is to build a new weapons system or reactivate a demobilized military capability.

The flexibility and comparatively easy revocability of behavioral arms control commitments, however, are as much their weakness as their strength. Behavioral approaches may be somewhat less likely to ensure strategic stability than a well-crafted capability regime in part because all participants would understand how easy it *is* to change behavior for the worse. Through this lens, one might say that for this type of arms control, "verifiability" boils down only to ascertaining whether the rules have hitherto been followed. This may provide some window into a country's good faith and intentions to date, but such insight is inherently retrospective. In contrast to some capability-regulatory regimes — in which, for instance, violations may require time to execute (e.g., in building and deploying prohibited systems) — verifiers can here provide little assurance even about the very immediate future.

For this reason, the more dramatic sorts of behavioral pledges — whether or not they style themselves as being legally binding — often suffer from credibility problems. Perhaps the classic case in point here is the idea of a nuclear weapons "no first use" (NFU) rule. It has long been a high priority of the nuclear disarmament community to elicit NFU promises from the world's nuclear weapons possessors. In 2010, in fact, the Obama administration gestured to this movement by articulating a highly qualified negative security assurance (NSA) pledge whereby the United States promised not to use, or threaten to use, nuclear weapons against "non-nuclear weapons states that are party to the NPT and in compliance with their nuclear non-proliferation obligations."[77] The principal challenge with NFU promises, however, is not how cleverly or carefully they can be qualified, but rather the degree to which other parties feel they can really *rely* upon such pledges being followed in a grave crisis, when it matters most.

An NFU arms control agreement, such as Beijing promotes, would basically be a pledge — whether "legally binding" or otherwise — that no party would ever be the *first* to use nuclear weapons against another party. (If someone broke this pledge and *did* go first, all bets would presumably be off.) On a superficial level, this might sound pleasing, though it takes little reflection to recognize that precisely to the extent that such pledges *did* bind the parties, such an arrangement might present destabilizing "lock-in" problems where the signatory states were of greatly differing degrees of *conventional* military power. (If truly "immunized" against nuclear first use, the stronger state might feel free actually to *employ* its comparative advantage in conventional force.)

But the real problem of NFU is less such "lock-in" than the fact that such a pledge would probably not be believed in the first place. As I have pointed out elsewhere:

> it seems inherently unbelievable that an NFU pledge would be followed in all imaginable circumstances. Even if the promise had been sincerely offered and resolutely intended, one might wonder whether a country with nuclear weapons would be willing to place such stock in [its] NFU [pledge] that it would choose to lose a major war or countenance the emergence of a dramatic new threat without employing the one tool that might be able to turn things around.[78]

NFU promises might be credible coming from a country blessed with such conventional might that it would not *need* nuclear weapons in a confrontation with an adversary state, but in such circumstances NFU wouldn't really *add* anything either. The real value of an NFU pledge would come only where the nuclear weapons possessor might *need* to employ such tools — in which case the credibility of the promise would erode in direct proportion to the gravity of the situation facing that state. NFU would be most believable, in other words, only when it was most unnecessary.

Treating NFU as a sort of asymptotic case of behaviorally regulated arms control, therefore, one might suspect that agreements promising restraint in extreme circumstances are largely unbelievable. Indeed, as suggested by the example of NATO's long-standing "nuclear sharing" policy, it seems to be understood that whatever peacetime agreements may provide, parties will probably be willing to do, in extremis, whatever they think they need to do in order to survive. (Article I of the NPT provides that a nuclear weapon state may not transfer control of a nuclear explosive device to a non-nuclear-weapon state,[79] but NATO policy expressly anticipated that in the event of full-scale war with the Soviet Union, the United States would turn over pre-positioned stocks of nuclear gravity bombs for delivery by allied aircraft from nonweapon countries such as the Netherlands, Germany, and Turkey.[80] Even if it had been intended that the NPT would remain in force in time of war — and here one must remember that it has apparently always been NATO's legal position that in the event of general war the NPT "would not be controlling" in any event[81] — if a nuclear World War III were underway, issues of treaty noncompliance would surely seem trivial,[82] with few planners apparently willing to treat the law, as the saying goes, as a suicide pact.)

This is not to say, however, that behaviorally-focused measures are *always* incredible, for indeed it may be that behavior *can* be constructively modified in many instances. Such methods, in fact, may be especially valuable in *peacetime* contexts in which what is at issue is the proliferation of dangerous technologies such as ballistic missiles or nuclear weapons. Such circumstances do not raise the immediate and "existential" issues that bedevil NFU promises, and available historical examples suggest that even comparatively weak "code of conduct"-type approaches can often provide real benefits in this area. Since the spread of powerful military capabilities—if it *does* occur—can indeed have a significant impact upon strategic stability, it seems reasonable to impute to this sort of behavioral arms control a potentially valuable stabilizing effect.

The Missile Technology Control Regime (MTCR)[83]—and its associated Hague Code of Conduct (HCOC)[84]—provide a case in point. For the most part, there are few "hard" rules in the MTCR system, which is only "politically binding" anyway,[85] with members being left subject only to good-faith self-enforcement with regard to their collective pledge to exercise restraint in the transfer of ballistic missile technology to non-MTCR members.[86] Nevertheless, the normative force of the MTCR seems to have had some impact in constraining missile-related transfers.[87]

An analogous effort to establish standards for the transfer of sensitive nuclear technology, the Nuclear Suppliers Group (NSG), provides standards for restraint in exports of items listed on a "Trigger List" and a schedule of controlled dual-use goods.[88] Meanwhile, the Australia Group (AG) has similarly tried, since 1985, to address the proliferation of chemical- and biological-related technology.[89] (Today, efforts are also underway—involving the European Union and the United States—to develop an International Code of Conduct for Outer Space Activities, which it is said "will help maintain the long-term sustainability, safety, stability, and security of space by establishing guidelines for the responsible use of space."[90] Precisely what impact, if any, such a code would have in terms specifically of strategic stability is presently unclear, but the "code of conduct" model is clearly alive and well.) One need not believe that such constraints are foolproof, nor that they will necessarily be observed if the government in question thinks it is *really* important to do something a code discourages, in order to acknowledge that behavior-regulatory approaches can indeed have valuable effects in such things as slowing the spread of technologies that if unchecked could indeed affect strategic stability.

CONCLUSION

So what, then, is one to make of all this? If there is an overriding lesson to be learned from this long exploration of the relationship between arms control and strategic stability, it is that this relationship is exceedingly complicated. It is not merely that the value of strategic stability itself needs to be carefully examined rather than assumed uncritically, though this is certainly the case, but also that arms control does *not* always conduce to stability anyway. Details matter, complexity is pervasive, and it would be entirely unwarranted to posit a per se answer — either positive or negative — about the merits of arms control.

In designing arms control regimes, many traps await the unwary or the credulous. Subtle shadings of circumstance can turn a well-designed and stability-promoting arrangement into a destabilizing geopolitical canker, and indeed one's negotiating partner may be working very hard to skew stability dynamics in his favor. Capability-regulatory arms control can impose destabilizing rigidities as easily as it can restrain dangerous competitive dynamics, and the balance between such effects may also shift over time. At the same time, capability-focused regimes are certainly capable of providing real value, as can behavioral and information-centered approaches in their own distinctive ways.

For the policy community, then, the key lesson may simply be to avoid ideological complacency, remembering that arms control is neither inherently bad *nor* inherently good. It is simply a tool, and if one wishes to promote strategic stability — and to avoid engendering instability — there are many variables to take into consideration, and many dynamics of which one must be aware. Arms control *theory* needs to be de-theologized if arms control is to be *practiced* well, and the endeavor needs to be approached with an intellectual humility rooted in awareness that the strategic environment is difficult to shape, that effects are hard to predict, and that the world has a stubborn habit of changing over time in ways that sometimes make yesterday's certainties implausible or even counterproductive. One could do worse than to approach the task of arms control planning with a wary eye.

ENDNOTES - CHAPTER 6

1. Interim Agreement Between the United States of America and the Union of Soviet Socialist Republics on Certain Measures With Respect to the Limitation of Strategic Offensive Arms, May 26, 1972, entered into force October 3, 1972, (hereinafter SALT I), available from *cns.miis.edu/inventory/pdfs/aptsaltI.pdf*.

2. Treaty Between the United States of America and the Union of Soviet Socialist Republics on the Reduction and Limitation of Strategic Offensive Arms [START], July 31, 1991, entered into force December 5, 1994, available from *www.state.gov/www/global/arms/starthtm/start/start1.html*.

3. Treaty Between the United States of America and the Union of Soviet Socialist Republics on the Elimination of their Intermediate-Range and Shorter-Range Missiles, December 8, 1987, entered into force June 1, 1988, available from *www.state.gov/www/global/arms/treaties/inf1.html*.

4. Convention on the Prohibition of the Development, Production, Stockpiling and Use of Chemical Weapons and On Their Destruction, January 13, 1993, entered into force April 29, 1997, at Arts. I(5) & II(1) &, 7, banning chemicals that can cause harm used "for purposes not prohibited by this Treaty," but permitting the use of chemical agents for riot control purposes as opposed to "as a method of warfare," available from *www.opcw.org/index.php?eID=dam_frontend_push&docID=6357.*

5. Convention on the Prohibition of the Development, Production and Stockpiling of Bacteriological (Biological) and Toxin Weapons and on Their Destruction, April 10, 1972, entered into force March 26, 1975, at Art. I, banning "[m]icrobial or other biological agents, or toxins whatever their origin or method of production, of types and in quantities that have no justification for prophylactic, protective or other peaceful purposes," available from *www.opbw.org/convention/documents/btwctext.pdf.*

6. Protocol on Notifications Relating to the Treaty Between the United States of America and the Union of Soviet Socialist Republics on the Reduction and Limitation of Strategic Offensive Arms, July 31, 1991, entered into force December 5, 1994, available from *www.state.gov/www/global/arms/starthtm/start/notfypro.html#notfyproII.13.*

7. Protocol to the Treaty Between the United States of America and the Russian Federation on Measures for the Further Reduction and Limitation of Strategic Offensive Arms, April 28, 2010, entered into force February 25, 2011 (hereinafter New START Protocol) at Part Four, available from *www.state.gov/documents/organization/140047.pdf.*

8. See, e.g., START, *supra,* at Art. XV, establishing Joint Compliance and Inspection Commission; Treaty Between the United States of America and the Russian Federation on Measures for the Further Reduction of Strategic Offensive Arms, April 8, 2010, entered into force February 25, 2011 (hereinafter New START), at Part Six, discussing Bilateral Consultative Commission.

9. Treaty on the Non-Proliferation of Nuclear Weapons, July 1, 1968, entered into force March 5, 1970 (hereinafter NPT), at Art. VIII(3) providing for meetings every 5 years "to review the operation of this Treaty with a view to assuring that the pur-

poses of the Preamble and the provisions of the Treaty are being realised," available from*www.iaea.org/Publications/Documents/ Infcircs/Others/infcirc140.pdf.*

10. Agreement Between the Government of The United States of America and the Government of the Union of Soviet Socialist Republics on the Prevention of Incidents On and Over the High Seas, signed and entered into force May 25, 1972, available from *www.state.gov/t/isn/4791.htm.*

11. *NPT, supra,* from the Preamble.

12. See, e.g., President Barack Obama, remarks in Prague, April 5, 2009, available from *www.acronym.org.uk/docs/0904/ doc10.htm.*

13. Christopher A. Ford, "Why Not Nuclear Disarmament?" *The New Atlantis,* Spring 2010, quoting foreign diplomat, available from *www.thenewatlantis.com/publications/why-not-nuclear-disarmament.*

14. See, e.g., Thomas C. Schelling, *Arms and Influence,* New Haven, CT: Yale University Press, 1966, pp. 92-125, discussing risk manipulation in NATO nuclear strategy and other contexts.

15. See David Shambaugh, *China's Communist Party,* Washington, DC: Woodrow Wilson Center Press, 208, at 177-178, citing Lieberthal and using concepts in understanding the Chinese Communist Party's adaptation to changing circumstances.

16. See generally, e.g., Russ Marion, *The Edge of Organization: Chaos and Complexity Theories of Formal Social Systems,* Thousand Oaks, CA: Sage Publications, 1999, pp. 162, 167-169.

17. See Christopher A. Ford, "Playing for Time on the Edge of the Apocalypse: Maximizing Decision Time for Nuclear Leaders," George P. Shultz *et al.,* eds., *Deterrence: Its Past and Future,* Stanford, CA: Hoover Institution Press, 2011, pp. 217, 238-240. Scott Sagan's analysis of nuclear weapons accident risk reduction also owes much to such a framework, though he does not explicitly use the language of Complexity Science. See, e.g., Scott D. Sagan, *The Limits of Safety,* Princeton, NJ: Princeton University Press, 1991, pp. 264-278, discussing Charles Perrow's "normal

accident" theory, which partakes of a theory of maladaptively tight coupling.

18. Herman Kahn, *On Thermonuclear War*, Princeton, NJ: Princeton University Press, 1960, p. 248.

19. Christopher A. Ford, "Nuclear Weapons Reconstitution and its Discontents: Challenges of 'Weaponless Deterrence'," *in* Shultz *et al.*, *supra*, pp. 131, 188; see also, e.g., Patrice Stevens, "Strategic Weapons in the 21st Century: Hedging Against Uncertainty," *Nuclear Weapons Journal*, issue 2, 2009, pp. 3-4.

20. NPT, *supra*, at Art. X(1).

21. New START, *supra*, at Art. XIV(3).

22. Vienna Convention on the Law of Treaties, May 23, 1969, entered into force January 27, 1980, at Art. 56(1)(b, available from *www.ilsa.org/jessup/jessup11/basicmats/VCLT.pdf*. One imagines that arms control agreements — the purpose of which is generally thought to be to ensure the stability of a military balance between the parties — might have a plausible case to make that withdrawal rights are reasonable when the alternative is turning an agreement into an instrument of strategic instability.

23. Treaty Between the United States of America and the Union of Soviet Socialist Republics on the Limitation of Anti-Ballistic Missile Systems, May 26, 1972, entered into force October 3, 1972, terminated June 13, 2002 (hereinafter ABM Treaty), available from *cns.miis.edu/inventory/pdfs/aptabm.pdf*.

24. See, e.g., Arms Control Association, "The Anti-Ballistic Missile (ABM) Treaty at a Glance," undated fact sheet, available from *www.armscontrol.org/factsheets/abmtreaty*.

25. ABM Treaty, *supra*, at Art. XV(2).

26. Statement by the White House Press Secretary, December 13, 2001, available from *www.acq.osd.mil/tc/treaties/abm/ABMwithdrawal.htm*. It is commonplace in security studies to refer to the dangers of nuclear "blackmail" when in fact "extortion" is the more accurate term.

27. See, e.g., "Russia May Boost Nuclear Potential," *RIA Novosti*, February 26, 2012, quoting Russian Deputy Defense Minister Anatoly Antonov that the North Atlantic Treaty Organization (NATO) ballistic missile defense (BMD) is an outgrowth of "aspirations to shift the strategic balance of forces in Europe," available from *en.rian.ru/mlitary_news/20120206/171166824.html*.

28. See, e.g., White House Office of the Press Secretary, "Fact Sheet on U.S. Missile Defense Policy: A 'Phased, Adaptive Approach' for Missile Defense in Europe," September 17, 2009, available from *www.whitehouse.gov/the_press_office/FACT-SHEET-US-Missile-Defense-Policy-A-Phased-Adaptive-Approach-for-Missile-Defense-in-Europe*.

29. Compare, e.g., U.S. Missile Defense Agency, "The Ballistic Missile Defense System," fact sheet, July 19, 2011, available from *www.mda.mil/global/documents/pdf/bmds.pdf*, describing multi-layered approach to defending the United States against long-range missiles as well as shorter-range attacks, involving, inter alia: ground-based interceptors; sea-based BMD assets; networked ground- and sea-based radars; programs for boost-phase, mid-course, and terminal interception; and a national "command, control, battle management, and communications network," *with* ABM Treaty, *supra*, at Arts. I(2) and III, describing permissible BMD system as consisting of only two sites with a 150-kilometer radius centered on the national capital and a single intercontinental ballistic missile (ICBM) field limiting the number and location of ABM radars, and prohibiting "a defense of the territory of the country [as a whole]" and even "defense of an individual region".

30. Treaty Between the United States of America and the Russian Federation on Strategic Offensive Reductions, May 24, 2002, (hereinafter Moscow Treaty), available from *www.armscontrol.org/documents/sort*.

31. START, *supra*, at XVII(2), "This Treaty shall remain in force for 15 years unless superseded earlier by a subsequent agreement on the reduction and limitation of strategic offensive arms." New START, *supra*, at XIV(2), "This Treaty shall remain in force for 10 years unless it is superseded earlier by a subsequent agreement on the reduction and limitation of strategic offensive arms."

32. Compare SALT I, *supra*, at Art. XVII(2), "This Interim Agreement shall remain in force for a period of five years unless replaced earlier by an agreement on more complete measures limiting strategic offensive arms," *with* ABM Treaty, *supra*, at XV(1), "This Treaty will be of unlimited duration."

33. See, e.g., Conference on the Limitation of Armament Between the United States of America, the British Empire, France, Italy, and Japan, February 6, 1922, entered into force August 21, 1923, available from *www.ibiblio.org/pha/pre-war/1922/nav_lim. html*, from the Preamble, proclaiming parties' intention, with the treaty, to "maint[ain] . . . the general peace, and to reduce the burdens of competition in armament."

34. See SALT I, *supra*.

35. Even if one assumes that the attacker will allocate two weapons per target, the warhead-to-warhead exchange ratio against multiple independently-targeted re-entry vehicle (MIRVed) systems — or, alternatively, the ability of an attacking ballistic missile to destroy multiple enemy counterpart missiles, which is another way of looking at the same question — can still be sharply favorable. This effect was perhaps less dramatic with smaller systems such as the U.S. Minuteman, which carries three MIRVs, but it would become more salient over time with the "heavy" missiles that both sides came to develop in the 1980s, each capable of carrying 10 or more warheads.

36. See, e.g., Bruce Blair, *The Logic of Accidental Nuclear War*, Washington, DC: Brookings Institution Press, 1993.

37. Treaty Between the United States of America and the Russian Federation on Further Reduction and Limitation of Strategic Offensive Arms, January 3, 1993 (hereinafter START II), at Art. II(1), "each Party undertakes to have eliminated or to have converted to launchers of ICBMs to which one warhead is attributed all its deployed and nondeployed launchers of ICBMs to which more than one warhead is attributed . . . and not to have thereafter launchers of ICBMs to which more than one warhead is attributed," available from *www.acq.osd.mil/tc/treaties/start2/text.htm*.

38. U.S. Department of Defense, *Nuclear Posture Review Report*, April 2010, p. 23, available from *www.defense.gov/npr/docs/2010%20 Nuclear%20Posture%20Review%20Report.pdf*.

39. Comprehensive Nuclear-Test-Ban Treaty, September 10, 1996 (hereinafter CTBT), available from *www.ctbto.org/fileadmin/ content/treaty/treaty_text.pdf*.

40. For the CTBT to enter into force, it must be ratified by all countries listed in Annex 2 of the Treaty. See CTBT, *supra*, at Art. XIV(1). At present, even if the United States does ratify—an event that most observers think unlikely, at least in the near future—ratifications would remain to be had from the remaining Annex 2 countries of China, Egypt, India, Iran, Israel, North Korea, and Pakistan. Getting all of these is increasingly believed to be all but impossible, leading even fervent CTBT proponents such as United Nations (UN) Secretary-General Ban Ki-Moon to argue the need to "consider an alternate mechanism" to bring a comprehensive test ban into force. See UN Secretary-General Ban Ki-Moon, opening remarks to the Exhibition on "Putting an End to Nuclear Explosions," New York City, May 4, 2010, available from *www.un.org/sg/statements/index.asp?nid=4528*.

41. See Christopher A. Ford, "Test Ban Treaty, Take Two," *The New Atlantis*, Summer 2009, pp. 112-116, available from *www. thenewatlantis.com/publications/test-ban-treaty-take-two*. For more information about the CHIC-4, See Thomas C. Reed and Danny B. Stillman, *The Nuclear Express: A Political history of the Bomb and Its Proliferation*, Minneapolis, MN: Zenith Press, 2009, pp. 131, 250-252, 261-262, discussing CHIC-4; See *also* International Atomic Energy Agency, "Implementation of the NPT Safeguards Agreement and relevant provisions of Security Council resolutions in the Islamic Republic of Iran," GOV/2011/65, November 8, 2011, pp. 33-35, discussing evidence suggesting that Iran received information from [the A.Q. Khan] nuclear smuggling network similar to that provided to Libya, including a nuclear weapons design, available from *www.iaea.org/Publications/Documents/Board/2011/ gov2011-65.pdf*.

42. This is, however, a question to some extent analytically distinct from whether or not it is in the U.S. *interest* to ratify CTBT. That is a subject for another day.

43. See, e.g., Christopher Ford and Douglas Feith, "International Negotiations: A Tool to Serve our Interests," Hudson Institute papers on "Perspectives for the New Administration," January 2009, pp. 2-3, available from *www.hudson.org/files/publications/Ford%20and%20Feith%20-%20final%20lo-res.pdf.*

44. See, e.g., Leonid Brezhnev, "Prevention of Nuclear Catastrophe," *Pravda*, June 16, 1982, reprinted in *The USSR Proposes Disarmament, 1920s-1980s,* Moscow, Russia: Progress Publishers, 1986, pp. 245, 247; Yuri V. Andropov, "Excerpt from the Report by Yu. V. Andropov at a Jubilee Meeting in the Kremlin to Mark the Sixtieth Anniversary [sic] of the Formation of the Union of Soviet Socialist Republics," *Pravda*, December 21, 1982, reprinted in *Ibid.*, pp. 268, 269; "Statement by the Soviet Government," *Pravda*, May 28, 1983, reprinted in *Ibid.*, at 281, 283; Yuri V. Andropov and Tengiz N. Menteshashvili, "Excerpt from the Resolution of the USSR Supreme Soviet on the International Situation and the Soviet Union's Foreign Policy," *Pravda*, June 16, 1983, reprinted in *Ibid.*, pp. 285, 285-86.

45. See, e.g., Bill Winter, "Lawyers Join Hands Against Nuclear Arms," *ABA Journal*, Vol. 68, October 1982, p. 1202, recounting U.S. Defense Secretary Caspar Weinberger's complaint that a freeze would place the United States in "a position of permanent inferiority to the Soviets."

46. See, e.g., Yuri V. Andropov, "Excerpt from the Report by Yu. V. Andropov at a Jubilee Meeting in the Kremlin to Mark the Sixtieth Anniversary [sic] of the Formation of the Union of Soviet Socialist Republics," *Pravda*, December 21, 1982, reprinted in *The USSR Proposes Disarmament, supra*, p. 268; Brezhnev, *supra*, pp. 246-247.

47. See, e.g., "Draft Treaty on the Prohibition of the Stationing of Weapons of Any Kind in Outer Space," *Pravda*, August 12, 1981, reprinted in *The USSR Proposes Disarmament, supra*, pp. 240-242; "Possible Elements for a Future International Legal Agreement on the Prevention of the Deployment of Weapons in Outer Space, the Threat or Use of Force Against Outer Space Objects," working paper presented by the delegations of China, the Russian, Federation, Vietnam, Indonesia, Belarus, Zimbabwe, and Syria to the UN Conference on Disarmament, June 28, 2002, avail-

able from *www.cfr.org/china/possible-elements-future-international-legal-agreement-prevention-deployment-weapons-outer-space-threat-use-force-against-outer-space-objects/p12181.*

48. See, e.g., Christopher Ford, "Getting Ready to Get 'Space Weapons' Wrong," *New Paradigms Forum* website, August 27, 2009, available from *www.newparadigmsforum.com/ NPFtestsite/?m=20090827.*

49. See, e.g., Mark Schneider, "The Nuclear Forces and Doctrine of the Russian Federation and the People's Republic of China," prepared testimony before the U.S. House of Representatives Armed Services Subcommittee on Strategic Forces, October 14, 2011, p. 2.

50. See, e.g., André de Nesnera, "McFaul Takes Up Duties as US Ambassador to Russia," *VOA News*, January 12, 2012, available from *www.voanews.com/english/news/usa/McFaul-Takes-Up-Duties-as-US-Ambassador-to-Russia--137189763.html.*

51. See, e.g., James M. Acton, Michael S. Gerson *et al., Beyond New START: Advancing U.S. National Security Through Arms Control With Russia*, September 2011, p. 8, warning of stability implications of continuing Russian reliance on heavy MIRVed missiles and advocating a prohibition on new MIRVed ballistic missile systems, available from *csis.org/files/publication/110824_Acton_BeyondNewSTART_WEB.pdf.*

52. See NPT, *supra*, at Arts. I, describing nonproliferation obligations specific to nuclear weapon states (NWS); II, describing nonproliferation obligations specific to *non*-nuclear-weapon states (NNWS); III, describing safeguards obligations for NNWS; and IX (3), defining category of NWS.

53. See *id.*, at Art. VI, describing nuclear disarmament-related obligations); see also generally, e.g., Christopher Ford, "Debating Disarmament: Interpreting Article VI of the Treaty on the Non-Proliferation of Nuclear Weapons," *Nonproliferation Review*, Vol. 14, No. 3, November 2007, at 401-28, available from *cns.miis.edu/ npr/pdfs/143ford.pdf.*

54. See e.g., Ruth Whitehair and Seth Bruegger, "BWC Protocol Talks in Geneva Collapse Following U.S. Rejection," *Arms*

Control Today, September 2001, quoting Bush administration officials that proposed BTWC Protocol would have "almost no chance of discovering anything useful to the BWC" and "serve to misdirect world attention into non-productive channels," available from *www.armscontrol.org/print/900*; "U.S. rejects biological weapons checks," *Reuters*, December 9, 2009, quoting Obama administration officials reconfirming unfeasibility of protocol, available from *www.reuters.com/article/2009/12/09/us-arms-biological-idUSTRE5B82DG20091209*.

55. See e.g., Henry Sokolski, "Reactors and Bombs," *Weekly Standard*, January 23, 2012, available from *npolicy.org/article.php?aid=1138&rt=&key=reactors%20and%20 bombs&sec=article&author=*.

56. See e.g., Ford, "Nuclear Technology Rights and Wrongs," *supra*, pp. 50-53.

57. See *generally* e.g., *Ibid.*, pp. 8-27, describing existence of, and arguments made by, different interpretive camps.

58. See e.g., Kenneth N. Waltz *et al.*, *The Spread of Nuclear Weapons: More May Be Better*, Adelphi Papers, Vol. 21, No. 171, 1981.

59. Henry Sokolski has illustrated the challenges of such dynamics through charts comparing strategic relations in the present-day world of seven major nuclear-armed players — which produces 21 separate interactive dyads, each of which contains some potential for "strategic miscalculation" — and a more proliferated world of 17 players, in which the number of dyads spirals to 136. The emergence of still more players, of course, would make the contrast even sharper. See Henry Sokolski, "Nuclear 1914: The Worry Yet to Come," PowerPoint presentation at the Sandia National Laboratory, February 14-15, 2005, available from *www. npolicy.org/article_file/Slides021105SandiaNuclear19_020211_ 0809.pdf*.

60. Herman Kahn, *Thinking the Unthinkable in the 1980s*, New York: Simon & Schuster, 1984, p. 156.

61. See Thomas C. Schelling, "A World Without Nuclear Weapons?" *Daedalus*, Fall 2009, pp. 124, 127.

62. Herman Kahn, *On Thermonuclear War*, Princeton, NJ: Princeton University Press, 1960, p. 230.

63. Ford, "Nuclear Weapons Reconstitution and its Discontents," *supra*, pp. 149-50.

64. Schelling, *supra*, p. 127.

65. See generally Christopher Ford, "Misinterpreting the NPT," remarks at the Carnegie Endowment for International Peace, September 30, 2011, critiquing views advanced by Daniel Joyner in *Interpreting the Nuclear Non-Proliferation Treaty*, Oxford, UK: Oxford University Press, 2011, available from *www.newparadigmsforum.com/NPFtestsite/?p=1100*. For an alternative to the proliferation-facilitating interpretation of the NPT's technology-transfer provisions, see Ford, "Nuclear Technology Rights and Wrongs," *supra*.

66. START, *supra*, Art. XV.

67. New START, *supra*, Part Six.

68. Ford & Feith, *supra*, p. 2.

69. U.S. Department of Defense, *Annual Report to Congress on Military and Security Developments Involving the People's Republic of China*, Washington, DC: Office of the Secretary of Defense, 2010, p. 1, available from *www.defense.gov/pubs/pdfs/2010_CMPR_Final.pdf*.

70. See Amy Butler, John M. Doyle, and Michal Bruno, "Many Issues Still Unaddressed by Gates," *Aviation Week & Space Technology*, January 2, 2009, available from *www.aviationweek.com*, quoting Gates that "I'd begin to get pretty nervous if we begin to talk about below 1,500 [deployed U.S. warheads] just in view of the array of countries developing these systems and modernization programs in both Russia and China."

71. See, e.g., Christopher Ford, "The Treaty After Next?" remarks to the working group of the Project on Nuclear Issues at the Center for Strategic and International Studies, October 6, 2010,

available from *www.newparadigmsforum.com/NPFtestsite/?p=510*; Christopher Ford, "A Survey of the Nuclear Weapons Landscape," remarks to the Phoenix Committee on Foreign Relations, April 12, 2011, available from *www.newparadigmsforum.com/ NPFtestsite/?s=brake*.

72. See, e.g., Jim Fanell, "Marking China's 'Peaceful Rise,'" *Naval Intelligence Professionals Quarterly*, Winter 2011-12, p. 19, quoting *People's Daily* comment about China's sea trials of the ex-Soviet aircraft carrier *Varyag* that "China will use the aircraft carrier and other kinds of battleships to solve disputes."

73. See, e.g., "America in the Asia-Pacific: We're Back," *The Economist*, November 19, 2011, available from *www.economist. com/node/21538803*; Peter Alford, "US back in Asia to stay: Hillary Clinton," *The Australian*, January 14, 2010, available from *www. theaustralian.com.au/news/nation/us-back-in-asia-to-stay-hillary-clinton/story-e6frg6nf-1225819009663*.

74. See, e.g., Leithen Francis, "Turning Tide," *Defense Technology International*, February 2012, pp. 28-29, discussing Vietnamese, Filipino, Singaporean, and Malaysian military procurement strategies in light of Chinese claims and provocations in the South China Sea.

75. Ford & Feith, *supra*, p. 2, emphasis added.

76. See, e.g., Christopher Ford, "Challenges of North Korean Nuclear Negotiation," in Charles King Mallory IV, ed., *Aspen DPRK-USA Dialogue*, 2011, pp. 63, 69, available from *aspeninstitute.de/en/publication/download/29/Aspen+DPRK-USA+Dialogue+. pdf*; Christopher Ford, "Looking Ahead to the 2012 Nuclear Security Summit," remarks to the conference on "The Nuclear Security Summits: Impact and Assessment," Hudson Institute, September 13, 2011, available from *www.newparadigmsforum.com/ NPFtestsite/?p=1092*.

77. It was also noted, however, that the United States "reserves the right to make any adjustment in the assurance that may be warranted" by biological weapons threats. The report also indicated that there still exists a role for potential nuclear weapons first use in "deterring conventional or CBW attack" from nuclear

weapons possessors or states not in compliance with nuclear non-proliferation obligations. *Nuclear Posture Review Report*, *supra*, pp. viii, 15-16, 46.

78. Christopher Ford, "The Catch-22 of NFU," *New Paradigms Forum* website, January 4, 2011, available from *www.newparadigmsforum.com/NPFtestsite/?p=562.*

79. NPT, *supra*, at Art. I, "Each nuclear-weapon State Party to the Treaty undertakes not to transfer to any recipient whatsoever nuclear weapons or other nuclear explosive devices or control over such weapons or explosive devices directly, or indirectly; and not in any way to assist, encourage, or induce any non-nuclear-weapon State to manufacture or otherwise acquire nuclear weapons or other nuclear explosive devices, or control over such weapons or explosive devices."

80. See generally, e.g., Christopher Ford, "NATO, 'Nuclear Sharing,' and the 'INF Analogy,'" *New Paradigms Forum* website, March 30, 2011, available from *www.newparadigmsforum.com/NPFtestsite/?p=793.*

81. See generally, e.g., Brian Donnelly, "The Nuclear Weapons Non-Proliferation Articles I, II and VI of the Treaty on the Non-Proliferation of Nuclear Weapons," undated, arguments of British diplomat that the NPT "does not deal with arrangements for deployment of nuclear weapons within allied territory as this does not involve any transfer on nuclear weapons or control over them, unless and until a decision were made to go to war, at which time the Treaty would no longer be controlling," available from *www.opanal.org/Articles/cancun/can-Donnelly.htm.* U.S. officials made the same point to the U.S. Senate during the NPT's ratification debate in 1968. See, e.g., Martin Butcher *et al.*, "NATO Nuclear Sharing and the NPT—Questions to be Answered," PENN/BASIC-BITS-CESD-ASPR Research Note 97.3, June 1997, available from *www.bits.de/public/researchnote/rn97-3.htm.*

82. While NATO policy envisioned such transfer *in the event of full-scale war with the Soviet Union*, of course, such war thankfully never actually transpired. As a result, no such NPT Article I violation by the United States occurred. Those who maintain that the very existence of this NATO contingency plan amounts to an

NPT Article I violation—i.e., that anticipating the *possibility* of an Article I violation is *itself* a violation—are on embarrassingly weak analytical ground. *Cf.* Mayor Wolfgang Leidig [of the German municipality of Schwaebisch Gmuend], "NATO's Nuclear Sharing: A Threat to the NPT," remarks to the 2008 Preparatory Committee Meeting for the 2010 Review Conference of the Treaty on the Non-Proliferation of Nuclear Weapons, April 29, 2008, p. 2, "NATO nuclear sharing appears to breach these [NPT] obligations," available from *www.reachingcriticalwill.org/legal/npt/ prepcom08/ngostatements/NuclearSharing.pdf*.

83. Agreement on Guidelines for the Transfer of Equipment and Technology Related to Missiles, April 16, 1987, 26 I.L.M. 599 (hereinafter MTCR).

84. Hague Code of Conduct, November 25, 2002, available from *www.hcoc.at/#*.

85. See, e.g., Austrian Federal Ministry for European and International Affairs, "Hague Code of Conduct against Ballistic Missile Proliferation, HCOC," information sheet, undated, available from *www.bmeia.gv.at/index.php?id=64664&L=1*.

86. See generally Christopher Ford, "The Nonproliferation Bestiary: A Typology and Analysis of Nonproliferation Regimes," *NYU Journal of International Law and Politics*, Vol. 39, No. 4, Summer 2007, pp. 937, 970-971.

87. To give just one very recent example, it has been reported that even though Russia proved willing to transfer an entire nuclear-powered attack submarine to India—a sophisticated *Akula II*-class vessel recommissioned in Indian service as the *INS Chakra* on January 23, 2012—Moscow did *not* transfer the submarine's usual complement of long-range (3,000-kilometer) cruise missiles as well, because to do so would have constituted a breach of MTCR standards. See "India Acquires Nuclear Sub," *Defense Technology International*, February 2012, p. 10.

88. See International Atomic Energy Agency (IAEA), "Communication Received from the Permanent Mission of Brazil Regarding Certain Member States' Guidelines for the Export of Nuclear Material, Equipment, and Technology," IAEA Doc.

INFCIRC/254/Rev.9/Part 1, November 7, 2007, available from *www.ornl.gov/sci/risk/TriggerList11-2008.pdf*, transmitting guidelines and Trigger List.

89. See generally Australia Group, "The Origins of the Australia Group," undated, available from *www.australiagroup.net/en/origins.html*.

90. U.S. Secretary of State Hillary Clinton, remarks regarding plans for an International Code of Conduct for Outer Space Activities, January 17, 2012, available from *www.cfr.org/space/clintons-statement-international-code-conduct-outer-space-activities-january-2012/p27108*. The United States, however, has not proven willing to agree to a "space code" effort drafted earlier by the European Union.

CHAPTER 7

CONVENTIONAL WEAPONS, ARMS CONTROL, AND STRATEGIC STABILITY IN EUROPE

Jeffrey D. McCausland

INTRODUCTION

There is no question that Europe was the focal point for American strategy during the Cold War. From the end of World War II to the fall of the Berlin Wall, the European continent witnessed the largest buildup of military forces in human history. As a result, arms control became an invaluable diplomatic tool for ensuring stability between the superpower blocs and preserving Alliance solidarity. In this regard, "stability" is defined as the absence of war, and any nation wielding predominant power is considered stable. John Lewis Gaddis describes a "stable system" as generally being characterized by minimal direct violence, particularly between the superpowers. A stable system has methods to peacefully resolve disputes and ensure that low level disputes do not escalate to larger crises. In a larger sense, a system might be stable if it is self-regulating in the sense that the principal members establish the means, including agreed procedures, to counteract pressures that might jeopardize peace and further agreed procedures to resolve disputes.[1]

From the start, certain concepts were deemed key to the North Atlantic Treaty Organization's (NATO) agreed strategic approach as well as military and policy planning. Military sufficiency described the need to preserve sufficient forces and freedom of action to deter Warsaw Pact aggression and, should deterrence fail, defend Alliance territory. The physical presence of U.S. conventional forces in Europe was important not only from the standpoint of conventional deterrence, but also because of the linkage to the Alliance's nuclear capabilities and ultimately the American strategic arsenal. Any Soviet calculation about a conventional attack on Western Europe had to consider the possibility of escalation and nuclear war, especially since NATO policy retained the option to initiate the use of nuclear weapons due to its conventional inferiority vis-à-vis the Warsaw Pact.

With these concepts in mind, conventional arms control—in particular the Treaty on Conventional Armed Forces in Europe (often referred to as the CFE Treaty)—played an important role in the maintenance of stability. It supported conflict prevention and crisis management by providing transparency about the size and disposition of military forces. This reduced uncertainty and miscalculation between the two blocs. In many ways, the CFE Treaty and arms control in the European context in general sought to deal with the difficulties of extended deterrence and prevent war through the stabilization of deterrence.[2] Extended deterrence was seen to depend upon forward deployed American conventional forces as an explicit link between the direct defense of Europe and the U.S. central strategic deterrent. The CFE provided not only clear limits on these forces for both blocs, but also a system of verification/inspections that could be (and were) exercised during times of crisis to further maintain the stability of the system.

Periodic crises that could have resulted in war in Europe emphasized this requirement, which was especially important in the waning days of the Soviet Union. The transparency and predictability provided by the treaty gave reassurances to both sides which allowed Moscow to withdraw its forces from Eastern Europe without a dramatic increase in East-West tensions. During this time, the CFE Treaty assisted in the transition of the security environment and the development of a new relationship with the Russian Federation. It was also valuable following the wars in former Yugoslavia as arms control contributed to conflict resolution and the prevention of a recurrence of hostilities.

At the NATO Summit in Lisbon in November 2010, the Alliance agreed to three essential core tasks — collective defense, crisis management, and cooperative security.[3] All of these are essential to maintaining security on the European continent and ensuring continued stability. Clearly the CFE Treaty would seem to contribute positively to each of these tasks. In terms of "collective defense," the treaty provided not only predictability for NATO force planners but also the transparency over other forces on the continent. It also remained key to crisis management as it discouraged escalation. Finally, it continued an ongoing process of cooperation between NATO and the Russian Federation. Consequently, it is important to review the background of the agreement, examine its current status, and consider its role as part of contemporary European security architecture and stability.

CONVENTIONAL ARMS CONTROL AND THE CFE TREATY

In Paris, France, on November 19, 1990, the CFE Treaty was signed between members of NATO and the Warsaw Pact. At its signing, many analysts hailed it as "the cornerstone of European security," and it is clearly the most ambitious and far-ranging conventional arms control treaty in history. It underscored a transformation of European security that is still ongoing and whose end state many argue is unclear.[4]

The events that framed this transformation were both largely peaceful and remarkable. Only a year before, on November 9, 1989, the Berlin Wall, which had served as perhaps the primary symbol of the Cold War for nearly 40 years, came down. Six weeks prior to the Paris signing, Germany formally reunified into a single nation. The number of signatories has increased from 22 to 34. One of the Alliances, the Warsaw Pact, dissolved and the other, NATO, enlarged. A key signatory to the Treaty, the Soviet Union, disappeared and was replaced by a host of successor states. Finally, the nations that convened in Paris did so under the overall auspices of the Conference on Security Cooperation in Europe (CSCE). This organization has now grown to 56 members and become the Organization for Security Cooperation in Europe (OSCE), which reflects that it has now matured into an international organization. An adapted treaty that reflects many of these political changes was signed on November 19, 1999, at the OSCE Summit held in Istanbul, but it has not been ratified by the majority of the states involved.

The "Original" CFE Treaty and Adaptation.

The original treaty, signed in 1990, established limits on the aggregate total of conventional military hardware for the two blocs, required substantial reductions in each nation's conventional arsenal, and created an intrusive regime of inspections and verification. The talks had commenced in January 1988 and the following mandate was agreed upon to guide the negotiations:

The objectives of the negotiation shall be to strengthen stability and security in Europe through the establishment of a stable and secure balance of conventional armed forces, which include conventional armaments and equipment, at lower levels; the elimination of disparities prejudicial to stability and security; and the elimination, as a matter of priority, of the capability for launching surprise attack and for initiating large scale offensive action.[5]

This mandate is clearly consistent with our established definition of "stability." It further acknowledges that conventional arms control in many ways is technically a more complex undertaking than nuclear arms control. Conventional weaponry depends not only on a diversity of armaments and geography, but also other variables such as technology, doctrine, and organization. Consequently, arguments persisted throughout the Cold War over the relative strengths and weaknesses of NATO and Warsaw Pact conventional forces. This was in part due to the inherent imprecision of any supporting analysis. Still the principal sources of instability remained each side's ability to generate forces over time, a factor that the mandate clearly addresses. This includes time to prepare for attack, time for operational warning and political response, and time to mobilize defenses which are more important to ensure stability than static comparison of forces deployed in peacetime.[6]

The final agreement required Alliance or "group" limitations on tanks, artillery, armored combat vehicles, combat aircraft, and attack helicopters—known collectively as treaty-limited equipment (TLE)—in an area stretching from the Atlantic Ocean to the Ural Mountains. Subsequent national limits for each treaty signatory were determined during negotiations among the members of the two respective Alliances. Following the demise of the Soviet Union, the successor states (within the area of treaty application) determined their respective limits from the total allocated to the Soviet Union in May 1992. However, the three Balkan states (Lithuania, Latvia, and Estonia) did not participate in these discussions about "national limits" for the "successor" states of the Soviet Union. Rather, they argued that they had been "occupied territory" and therefore that their territory was no longer part of the Treaty's area of application. Following their entry into NATO, the Balkan states have indicated a willingness to accede to the adapted CFE Treaty if it enters into force.

Bloc limitations for NATO and the former Warsaw Pact were further restrained by a series of five geographic nested zones for land-based TLE with respective limits for each zone. This was done to achieve the goals established in the mandate to prevent the destabilizing concentration of conventional military armament. This construct had the effect of permitting free movement of equipment and units away from, but not towards, the central European region, which thus inhibited surprise attack in the area deemed — during the Cold War at least — to be the most vulnerable. This consequently contributed to stability on the continent.

The Soviet Union (and subsequently the Russian Federation) further accepted the so-called "flank zone." This portion of the agreement placed limits on ground-based systems in the Leningrad and North Caucasus Military Districts in the Russian Federation. Norway is part of the northern portion of the flank and the north Caucasus states, Turkey, Greece, Bulgaria, Romania, and Moldova are in the southern portion.

Limitations on helicopters and attack aircraft only apply to the entire area of application due to their ability to reposition rapidly.

Only 1 year after the signing of the initial agreement and as Treaty implementation was commencing, Russian leaders began arguing for adjustments to their equipment limits. They began raising concerns about Russia's equipment limitations, particularly in the flank region, and Moscow subsequently undertook a campaign to alter those limits. The CFE signatories reach a compromise at the first Review Conference in May 1996. The compromise permitted Russia to maintain higher force levels in the flank zone, established a May 1999 deadline for Moscow to meet these adjusted levels, and reduced the overall size of the flank zone. Still, the problem of Russian force levels in this area would continue to bedevil negotiators. It was exacerbated by Russian military operations in Chechnya (which is in the flank region) and the conflict between Russia and Georgia in 2008. Russian military experts expressed a concern that Moscow required higher force levels in the flank to deal with the insurgency in Chechnya. Some Western military experts believed that Russia had violated its force limits during the 2008 conflict.

At the same time, treaty signatories had already begun (as agreed at the 1996 CFE Review Conference) to embark on a "modernization" of the treaty, in order to adapt it more broadly to the changed European security architecture, one without a Soviet Union or a Warsaw Pact. These CFE Treaty adaptation negotiations continued from 1996-99, through a period in which the European landscape continued to evolve. Of direct relevance to the Treaty and conventional forces, NATO began its process of enlargement. The enlargement process, together with the dissolution of the Soviet Union, brought to the surface a number of Russian concerns. Moscow argued that changes needed to be made to the Treaty to ensure continued stability and that it remained consistent with its original objectives.

On November 19, 1999 (the ninth anniversary of the CFE Treaty), 30 leaders signed the Adapted Treaty. All 19 NATO members accepted lower cumulative national limits, and all signatories accepted the new structure of limitations based on national and territorial ceilings consistent with the principle of host nation consent for the presence of foreign forces on any country's territory. The agreement also provided enhanced transparency through increased quotas for mandatory on-site inspections, operational flexibilities to exceed ceilings temporarily, and an accession clause.

The states parties also adopted the "CFE Final Act." This document contains a number of political commitments related to the Adapted Treaty. They include: (1) reaffirmation of Russia's commitment to fulfill existing obligations under the treaty to include equipment levels in the flank region; (2) a Russian commitment to exercise restraint in deployments in its territory adjacent to the Baltic; (3) the commitment by a number of Central European countries not to increase (and in some cases to reduce) their CFE territorial ceilings; and (4) Moscow's agreement with Georgia and Moldova on the withdrawals of Russian forces from their territories. President Bill Clinton noted in his statement at the conclusion of the summit that he would not submit the agreement for review by the Senate until Russia had reduced to the flank levels set forth in the Adapted Treaty to include removing its forces from Georgia and Moldova.

The Adapted CFE Treaty included provisions to reflect the new security environment. Russia's concerns about the three Baltic republics achieving NATO membership were addressed by adding an accession clause to the Adapted Treaty. The 1997 NATO-Russia Founding Act also contained a key sentence to address Russia's concerns about stationed forces on the territory of new member states:

> NATO reiterates that in the current and foreseeable security environment, the Alliance will carry out its collective defense and other missions by ensuring the necessary interoperability, integration, and capability for reinforcement rather than by additional permanent stationing of substantial combat forces.[7]

The Russian "Suspension."

On December 12, 2007, the Russian Federation officially announced that it would no longer be bound by the restrictions of the 1990 CFE Treaty and suspended participation.[8] Moscow claimed that it took this action because the 22 NATO members bound by the 1990 agreement had not ratified the 1999 Adapted Treaty, and during a June 2007 extraordinary conference, it provided a further detailed list of "negative effects" of the conduct of NATO states.[9] These included overall NATO force levels, the flank limits, and other unspecified demands for additional transparency. In addition to these concerns, it was clear that Prime Minister Vladimir Putin and other Russian leaders were angry over a series of issues, including NATO enlargement, the independence of Kosovo, and plans to install essential components of a ballistic missile defense system on Polish territory. Nonetheless, Moscow reassured the other treaty signatories that it did not intend to dramatically increase its force levels in the territory adjacent to their borders.

In terms of ratification, NATO members have argued since the Istanbul Summit in 1999 that ratification remained contingent upon Russia complying with obligations it freely accepted when the Adapted CFE Treaty was signed. The most contentious issue was the NATO demand for the full removal of all Russian military forces from the territory of the former Soviet republics of Georgia and Moldova. Russia adamantly contested this linkage, and Russian Prime Minister Putin has publicly argued that "there is no legal link" between the Adapted CFE Treaty and these commitments.[10]

In response, NATO initially endorsed a "parallel actions package" in March 2008 in an attempt to avoid the Treaty's demise. The package represented a serious shift in the NATO position, as it called for NATO countries to begin the ratification process (which in some countries such as the United States might take several months) while Russia commenced its withdrawals. Once the forces left Georgia and Moldova, NATO countries would strive to complete ratification of the Adapted Treaty quickly. NATO members also pledged to address many Russian security concerns once the Adapted Treaty was in place.[11]

Unfortunately, the negotiations made little to no progress. This effort was largely undermined by the deteriorating relations between NATO countries and the Russian Federation in the aftermath of the conflict in Georgia in the late summer of 2008. The situation was further complicated by Moscow's subsequent decision to recognize South Ossetia and Abkhazia as independent nations.

Following the meeting of OSCE foreign ministers in June 2009, the so-called "Corfu Process" began to examine European security challenges. By early 2010, an effort was undertaken in the Joint Consultative Group (the body based in Vienna, Austria, designed to oversee treaty implementation and adjustments) to develop a framework document that would simply contain principles of conventional arms control that all nations could agree upon. It was hoped that this would serve as a basis for new negotiations, and in the interim offer each state the option of either complying with the existing CFE Treaty or the list of specific requirements described in the framework document.

At the NATO Lisbon Summit in November 2010, the Alliance reaffirmed its continued commitment to the CFE Treaty regime and all associated elements. While the ultimate goal remained to ensure the continued viability of conventional arms control in Europe by strengthening common security and stability, member states further recognized (as noted at the previous Summit) that "the current situation, where NATO CFE Allies implement the Treaty while Russia does not, cannot continue indefinitely."[12]

Despite these lofty goals, progress on achieving agreement on a framework document proved illusory. This was largely due to Russian insistence on disallowing any language in the framework document recognizing "host nation consent" for stationing foreign forces that included the phrase "within internationally recognized borders." Such insistence was obviously because of Russian recognition of the former Georgian provinces of Abkhazia and South Ossetia and the continued presence of Russian forces on their territory. By the summer of 2011, Russian Deputy Foreign Minister Aleksandr Grushko declared that the negotiations had "ended up in an impasse" and blamed the West for this development.[13]

The failure to achieve agreement on the framework document prior to the September 2011 Review Conference, with the fourth anniversary of the Russian suspension of participation in the agreement now rapidly receding, left Washington and its NATO allies with few choices. On November 22, 2011, the United States announced that "it would cease carrying out certain obligations" under the treaty with regard to the Russian Federation.[14] NATO allies quickly followed suit with similar announcements.[15] In addition, the United States and its allies argued that the sharing of sensitive data by treaty signatories with the Russian Federation should be considered a compliance violation, as the data should have been provided only to "active" participants in the agreement.

Despite these actions, it does seem clear that American and NATO policymakers do not wish to terminate the Treaty or argue that the Russian Federation is in "material breach." This is clear in a number of ways. First, November 2011 the announcement reaffirmed the U.S. willingness to implement the Treaty and carry out all obligations with the other signatories. Second, the announcement offered to resume full implementation with Moscow should it decide to return to compliance. Finally, the United States declared that, in the spirit of transparency, it will "voluntarily inform Russia of any significant change" in American forces in Europe.[16] Thus, the November 2011 announcement appears intended simply to acknowledge that, after 4 years, the United States and its NATO partners could not continue to fulfill Treaty obligations absent some reciprocity from Moscow.

What Have Been the Contributions of the CFE Treaty?

Some might argue that in terms of European stability, the demise of a Treaty negotiated during the Cold War has little significance on today's most pressing strategic challenges. Many policy experts, especially in Europe, however, still refer to the treaty as the "cornerstone of European security" and argue that it must either be revitalized or a new agreement negotiated. Still the agreement can only be truly evaluated against the backdrop of European security and stability since its creation.

Oddly, the treaty was signed to prevent, or at least reduce, the likelihood of conflict between NATO and the Warsaw Pact. Shortly after it was signed the Warsaw Pact and the Soviet Union both disappeared, so the true value of the Treaty must be considered in the context of the dramatic transition. In fact, some have argued that the "cornerstone" metaphor is misplaced. The CFE Treaty has not been a static agreement; Europe has weathered many changes, and the Treaty has been adapted to accommodate these new realities.

The Treaty also provided critical political reassurance, which has been a central key to maintaining stability in the system. For example, it proved important in assuaging concerns about German reunification and provided transparency during the withdrawal of massive numbers of Soviet forces from Eastern Europe. These withdrawals occurred following the signing of the Treaty on the German Reunification (September 12, 1990) by the Federal Republic, German Democratic Republic (East Germany), France, the United Kingdom, the Soviet Union, and the United States.[17] This agreement also contained significant additional restraints on military operations. Germany agreed to only deploy territorial units that were not integrated in the NATO command structure on the territory of the former East Germany. Bonn further agreed that no foreign troops would be stationed in its eastern states or "carry out any other military activity there" while the withdrawal of Soviet forces was ongoing. Finally, the reunification treaty also specified that "foreign armed forces and nuclear weapons or their carriers will not be stationed in that part of Germany or deployed there."[18]

In terms of the actual reductions of military equipment, the numbers are truly impressive. Treaty compliance resulted in the destruction of over 69,000 Cold War era battle tanks, combat aircraft, and other pieces of military equipment in the now 30 countries stretching from the Atlantic to the Ural Mountains (the area of application). In many ways, the treaty changed the face of European security by "establishing new, cooperative political-military relationships."[19] More than 5,500 on-site inspections have been conducted, which has created a new sense of political-military cooperation and openness. Obviously, the Russian suspension has placed this cooperation in jeopardy.

The true value of the Treaty and the associated transparency measures to European stability were demonstrated during the various conflicts in the Balkans. As the American troops prepared to depart for Bosnia in 1995, Russian inspectors conducted short notice inspections in accordance with the CFE Treaty. As a result, these military operations were conducted without a significant increase in tensions. The Dayton Accords that ended the initial conflict in the former Yugoslavia in 1996 also contain an annex that established a "CFE-like" agreement between the contending states. This treaty was nearly identical to the CFE Treaty in terms of limits, definitions, transparency measures, etc. Furthermore, all of the Balkan states participating in this agreement expressed a desire to accede to the full CFE Treaty at some point in the future. Finally, in 1999 Russia conducted an inspection at Aviano Airbase in Italy during the U.S.-led air campaign against Serbian forces in Kosovo. This helped allay to some degree Russian concerns about U.S. force deployments during this crisis.[20]

In fact, these transparency measures were critical to the maintenance of stability when the system was stressed by periodic crises. In fact, many experts believe the inspection regime may have contributed more to the reduction of tensions and crisis prevention during this dramatic transition in European security than the actual force reductions. Some argue that the Treaty's greatest value may be the entire CFE system, which encourages confidence through transparency. In the final analysis, the existing Treaty, as well as the Adapted Treaty, provides a forum for the major European states to debate, agree, and maintain a set of rules about conventional military power on the continent that is critical to overall stability.[21]

What Would Failure Mean?

So, what would the impact be if the CFE Treaty completely unravels and the flow of routinely provided information on conventional equipment, inspections to verify that information, and constraints on the levels of that equipment were to disappear? Sadly, it is not too far-fetched to imagine that this could cause a dramatic realignment of European security and have an adverse impact on stability. The loss of information and undermining of predictability could set the stage for historic animosities to resurface and lingering crises to potentially worsen.

For example, there have been suggestions that Azerbaijan is counting on the failure of the Treaty to provide it with an opportunity to increase its military forces. Such a development would clearly exacerbate tensions between Azerbaijan and Armenia, which remain embroiled in a long simmering conflict over Nagorno-Karabakh.[22] This struggle has resulted in over 15,000 casualties and over 800,000 Armenian and Azeri refugees since 1988. Second, Russia would also lose any transparency into the military forces of existing or future NATO members, as well as transparency into the deployment of NATO forces on the territory of new members. Finally, the Baltic republics would not be allowed to accede to the existing agreement and, consequently, there would be no mechanism to limit NATO forces or provide transparency about such forces on their territory.[23]

Many experts fear such developments might encourage an expansion in military forces or cause damage to other agreements to the detriment of stability on the continent. For example, some experts believe Russia might continue to place greater and greater reliance on nonstrategic nuclear weapons (NSNW) and reconsider its participation in the Intermediate-Range Nuclear Forces Treaty (INF) in an effort to improve its security posture. Senior Russian officials as well as President Putin have criticized this agreement as contrary to Russian national interests and threatened to abrogate Moscow's participation.[24]

Loss of CFE would also remove a valuable crisis management tool from European security architecture and damage arms control as an instrument to enhance overall stability on the continent. In this regard, some Balkan observers believe the demise of the CFE Treaty might mean an end to the arms control arrangements contained in the Dayton Accords. Obviously, such a development could contribute to renewed violence in that troubled region.

The collapse of the CFE Treaty could spill over into other aspects of the Russia-NATO relationship and undermine some of the cooperative European security structures that have been built over the last 15-plus years. Its demise could adversely affect the NATO-Russia Council, the OSCE, and prospects for building or enhancing future cooperation in other areas. Finally, if CFE is abandoned absent a new agreement, the benefits provided by conventional arms control would be difficult, if not impossible, to replace. Beyond that, if CFE is no longer a viable agreement, and the confidence-building aspects of the regime are destroyed completely, over time it is entirely possible that some states parties will likely seek alternative arrangements that will replace the security benefits they now derive from the treaty.

Finally, the dissolution of the CFE Treaty could also have a serious impact on relations between the United States and the Russian Federation. Moscow and Washington have had serious disagreements over the past decade and, at the onset of the Barack Obama administration, their bilateral relations were perhaps worse than any time since the end of the Cold War.[25] Early in the new administration, President Obama called for hitting the "reset button" in the relations between the two countries. Despite serious differences, the two sides successfully negotiated the New Strategic Arms Reduction Treaty (New START) by the spring of 2010, and it was subsequently ratified by both the United

States Senate as well as the Russian Duma. However, serious difficulties remain between the two countries. Washington has clearly stated its desire to negotiate limits on nonstrategic nuclear weapons in the near future, but the prospects for success in this effort would appear dim absent progress in conventional arms control.

The Way Ahead.

In seeking a way ahead, several cautions are in order. First, the historical record is clear that arms control can never be an "end" or objective of policy in itself. An arms control accord is neither good nor bad when examined in isolation. Each treaty or agreement has value only insofar as it provides a "way" to mitigate concerns over or threats to national security, enhance stability, and reduce the possibility of conflict or limit its consequences. Thus, a resurrection of the CFE Treaty or creation of a new agreement *de novo* must be consistent with both American and NATO security interests.

Second, at its very core any arms control agreement depends upon a harmony of interests among the signatories. This "harmony" is based on careful analysis by all potential parties that the benefits gained from entering the arms control regime outweigh the risks associated with the measures such a regime might require. These might include reducing military forces or accepting high levels of transparency that allow exchanges of sensitive data, verification, and inspections. One does not get something for nothing, particularly over the long term.

Third, it is often easy to dismiss the success of arms control since we lose sight of its focus. A successful agreement is one that contributes to the prevention of conflict and enhances stability. But measuring the efficacy of an arms control agreement is seeking to learn why things have not happened, an inherently more difficult endeavor. Arms control regimes, like deterrence, are difficult to correlate completely with causes and effects of policies, because their ultimate metrics are for events that we do not want to happen (wars, arms races, increased tensions, and so on).

If the Alliance is to use conventional arms control to achieve its stated goals, what are some of the elements that might be contained in a future arms control strategy? First, every effort should be made to maintain firm ceilings on conventional forces, particularly in volatile areas such as the North Caucasus and Balkans. This must occur even if the CFE Treaty is discarded, and new negotiations to limit conventional weapons commence. Second, any negotiation must include the Baltic and Balkan states as potential signatories to a future agreement. Third, the inspection regime associated with any future agreement must be simplified. This would seem logical based on today's reduced possibility of a major conflict. Still there will be particular concerns over Russian concentrations of forces on the part of those states that share borders with the Russian Federation.

Fourth and finally, every effort must be made to integrate efforts in conventional arms control with other arms control treaties and agreements in order to achieve the synergy of a comprehensive approach. This must include the Vienna Document (a politically binding agreement focused on confidence- and security-building measures) and the Open Skies Treaty. These agreements provide an existing level of reassurance concerning conventional forces that should not be discounted. This is particularly true in the current security environment where the prospects of a major conflict in Europe seem remote. Still both can be strengthened and improved. The Vienna Document has not been changed or even tweaked since 1999, despite Russia's indication of interest in new proposals.[26] But it is still critical to remember that ultimately these agreements, while important, may not be a full substitute for an agreement that includes legally binding limits, information exchanges, and a verification regime.[27]

CONCLUSIONS

A Western arms control expert once remarked that he felt like he was watching 300 years of European hostilities unfold during the course of CFE negotiations. Critics of this process are frequently captivated by the technical details of definitions, counting rules, stabilizing measures, inspection regimes, etc., and often overlook the connection between these points and larger security issues. While the "devil may be in the details," this accord is rooted in the collective attempt of over 30 sovereign states to improve their respective security and enhance stability on the continent. Historical antagonism has an impact, as well as contributing to the agreement's enduring value as Europe seeks a new architecture based on cooperative security.

With the rising threat of transnational issues such as nuclear proliferation and terrorism, the fate of conventional arms control in Europe may not top the priority agenda for NATO's leadership. But this may be precisely why a renewed effort in conventional arms control as a means of stability is appropriate for American and European leaders. European defense spending has been in steady decline for the past decade and may well continue on a downward trajectory in light of ongoing economic challenges.[28] At the NATO Summit in Prague in 2002, all NATO members endorsed a target for each country to spend at least 2 percent of its gross domestic product (GDP) on defense. By 2011, only three European members of the Alliance met this goal—Greece, the United Kingdom, and France—and the average expenditure was below 1.5 percent of GDP.[29] These developments, coupled with serious American economic challenges, caused Secretary of Defense Robert Gates to comment in his final speech at NATO headquarters:

> . . . if current trends in the decline of European defense capabilities are not halted and reversed, future U.S. political leaders—those for whom the Cold War was not the formative experience that it was for me— may not consider the return on America's investment in NATO worth the cost.[30]

While the original purpose of the treaty—to reduce the risk of conflict and short-warning attacks between two blocs—may be a thing of the past, the CFE Treaty continues to contribute to current and future European security and stability in crucial ways. Perhaps most importantly, the transparency and predictability that it provides serve as important stabilizing elements as European relationships continue to evolve, military forces modernize, and both sides of the Atlantic wrestle with the most serious economic crisis since the Great Depression. Policymakers on both sides of the Atlantic will ignore its contributions to European stability at their peril.

ENDNOTES - CHAPTER 7

1. John Spanier, *Games Nation Play*, New York: Holt, Rinehart, and Winston, 1984, pp. 95-96. See also John Lewis Gaddis, *The Long Peace: Inquiries into the History of the Cold War*, New York: Oxford University Press, 1987.

2. Philip Windsor, *Strategic Thinking – an Introduction and Farewell*, London, UK: Lynne Rienner Publishers, 2002, pp. 117-118.

3. North Atlantic Treaty Organization, "Lisbon Summit Declaration Issued by the Heads of State and Governments participating in the meeting of the North Atlantic Council in Lisbon," November 20, 2010, p. 1.

4. Dorn Crawford, *Conventional Armed Forces in Europe (CFE) – A Review and Update of Key Treaty Elements*, Washington: U.S. Department of State, March 2009, p. 2.

5. *Ibid.*, p. 5.

6. Schuler Foerster, William Barry, William Clontz, and Harold Lynch, *Defining Stability – Conventional Arms Control in a Changing Europe*, Boulder, CO: Westview Press, 1989, p. 5.

7. *Founding Act on Mutual Relations, Cooperation and Security between NATO and the Russian Federation*, signed in Paris, France, May 27, 1997, available from *www.nato.int/cps/en/natolive/official_texts_25468.htm*.

8. Zdzislaw Lachowski, "The CFE Treaty One Year After Its Suspension: A Forlorn Treaty?" *SIPRI Policy Brief*, January 2009, p. 1.

9. *Ibid.*, p. 4.

10. Wade Boese, "Russia Unflinching on CFE Treaty Suspension," *Arms Control Today*, May 2008.

11. *Ibid.*

12. NATO Public Diplomacy Division, "Press Release—Lisbon Summit Declaration," Brussels, Belgium: NATO Public Affairs, November 20, 2010, p. 9.

13. "Russia Says Consultation on Talks on Conventional Forces Treaty in Impasse," *Interfax*, July 4, 2011.

14. Victoria Nuland, "Implementation of the Treaty on Conventional Armed Forces in Europe," Washington, DC: Office of the Spokesperson, U.S. Department of State, November 22, 2011.

15. "UK Halts Military Data Sharing with Russia," *Ria Novosti*, November 25, 2011, available from *en.rian.ru/world/20111125/169036481.html*.

16. Nuland.

17. "Treaty on the Final Settlement with Respect to Germany," *NATO Review*, No. 5, October 1990, pp. 30-32.

18. *Ibid.*

19. U.S. Department of State, "Fact Sheet—Treaty on Conventional Armed Forces in Europe (CFE): Key Facts About the Current Treaty and Agreement on Adaptation," Washington, DC: U.S. Department of State, 2009.

20. Evgeny Morozov, "What do They Teach at the Kremlin School of Bloggers," *Foreign Policy* website, available from *neteffect.foreignpolicy.com/posts/2009/05/26/what_do_they_teach_at_kremlins_school_of_bloggers*.

21. Sherman Garnett, "The CFE Flank Agreement," Washington, DC: The Carnegie Endowment for International Peace, 1997, p. 1.

22. Lachowski, p. 6. This view was underscored by senior Georgian officials during discussions in Tbilisi, Georgia, in December 2010.

23. Some force planners might argue that this could provide the West with certain advantages. Still the absence of the Baltic re-

publics (as NATO members) from the current or any future agreement would not be consistent with efforts to maintain stability and reduce concerns in Moscow that could be inimical to overall stability.

24. Pavel Felgenhauer, "Russia Serious About INF Treaty Abrogation," *Eurasia Daily Monitor*, Washington, DC: The Jamestown Foundation, February 21, 2012.

25. Dmitri Trenin, "Thinking Strategically About Russia," Washington, DC: Carnegie Endowment for International Peace, December 2008, p. 1.

26. "Talking Points by Mr. Mikhail Uliyanov, Director of the Department for Security Affairs and Disarmament of the Ministry of Foreign Affairs of Russia, at the Annual Security Review Conference," Vienna, Austria: Organization for Security Cooperation in Europe, July 1, 2011.

27. Assistant Secretary of State Rose Gottemoeller, "Statement at the Annual Security Review Conference in Vienna, Austria," Washington, DC: U.S. Department of State, July 1, 2011.

28. Stephen Flanagan, *A Diminishing Transatlantic Partnership?* Washington, DC: Center for Strategic and International Studies, May 2011, p. viii.

29. Simona Kordosova, *NATO's Defense Budget in 2011,* Washington, DC: The Atlantic Council, November 2009, pp. 2-3.

30. Secretary of Defense Robert Gates, "The Future of the North Atlantic Treaty Organization," Speech at the headquarters of the North Atlantic Treaty Organization, Brussels, Belgium, June 10, 2011.

CHAPTER 8

RUSSIA AND STRATEGIC STABILITY

Matthew Rojansky

The author wishes to thank Harrison King for his excellent research assistance on this chapter; James Acton for his early and invaluable critique of the great power gambit; and Elbridge Colby, Mike Gerson, and other participants in the November 2, 2011, CNA workshop for their frank and thoughtful feedback.

According to data disclosed under the terms of the New Strategic Arms Reduction Treaty (New START) arms control agreement, the United States has 1,790 deployed strategic warheads, while the Russian Federation has 1,566.[1] Unofficial estimates of each side's forces in recent months have, however, placed the numbers as high as 1,950 for the United States and 2,600 for Russia.[2] In addition to treaty-accountable warheads deployed on long-range delivery systems, the two nuclear superpowers are estimated to possess well over 5,000 nonstrategic warheads and non-deployed warheads in reserve.[3] Taken together, the United States and Russia possess more than 95 percent of the world's existing nuclear weapons.

Although both sides' arsenals have decreased in size over the past 2 decades, both maintain a "triad" of delivery capabilities—with delivery vehicles based on air, land, and sea—and present roughly the same strategic counterweight to one another that they did during the Cold War. What has changed dramatically since the end of the Cold War is the nature of political and security relations between Washington and Moscow, which has in turn altered the context in which each side determines the appropriate role and potential use of its nuclear arsenal. The purpose of this chapter is to examine and seek to explain current attitudes on the Russian side toward the country's substantial nuclear arsenal, including how Russians understand strategic stability, and a set of issues closely linked to these, namely arms control, ballistic missile defense, and conventional precision weapons.

WHY STRATEGIC STABILITY IS SO IMPORTANT TO RUSSIA

A kind of cognitive dissonance prevails among Russian political leaders, defense planners and experts when it comes to fundamental questions about how Russia might use nuclear weapons and why they matter. On the one hand, Russians understand that the Cold War has ended and the world has changed. They recognize the present realities of geopolitics, technology, and the globalized economy, and accordingly understand that the role of nuclear weapons has also changed. As Academician and Director of the Academy of Sciences' Institute of World Economy and International Relations (IMEMO) Alexander Dynkin has stated:

> nuclear deterrence does not address the real threats of modern times, such as international terrorism, proliferation of weapons of mass destruction (WMD) and their delivery systems, ethnic and religious conflicts, clashes for energy supply and fresh water sources, to say nothing of the issues related to climate, environment, illegal migration, epidemics, cross-border crime, etc.[4]

On the other hand, Russia's still dominant share of the global nuclear weapons pie continues to endow Moscow with substantial geopolitical leverage and means that Russian attitudes can also shape realities to some degree. In fact, despite Russia's vast territory and mineral wealth, there is no other resource in which Moscow comes close to holding such an influential stake. With this dominance in mind, Russian thinkers are naturally inclined to accentuate both the likelihood and the negative consequences of behavior by other states that might degrade Russia's nuclear deterrent and thus compel Russia to take action. Doing so imbues Russia's positions on every issue that can be plausibly connected to nuclear weapons and strategic stability with greater significance for the rest of the world.

Emphasizing the stability or instability of the nuclear balance thus at least keeps Russia's hand on the scale of geopolitical power. During the Cold War, it was obvious that the Soviet Union's nuclear arsenal conferred substantial political power and influence upon Moscow. Today, the pathway from Russia's still substantial nuclear arsenal to global power and influence is much less clear. Indeed, other powers have risen and exceeded Russia in power and influence thanks to economic, demographic and conventional military strength—not nuclear weapons. This presents a significant problem for Russia, which finds all of its capabilities and options limited by the overall degradation of its global position that has accompanied the end of the Cold War and the corresponding decline of nuclear weapons as the defining attribute of great power status.

Emphasis on strategic stability is a way for Russia to maintain some leverage over the world's dominant power, the United States, and by extension over other great powers that are fast eclipsing Russia in every other sphere. Russia's reliance on strategic stability to preserve what remains of its great power status is certainly disturbing to some, including Dynkin, who writes:

> As to the dependence of Russia's security on nuclear weapons. . . . One has to have no faith at all in the Russian people to regard nuclear weapons (most of which are a Soviet legacy) as the sole attribute of Russia as a great power. One has to believe that Russia is non-competitive either in terms of conventional forces, research and development innovations, or in terms of improving the citizens' wellbeing and political life.[5]

Yet this is, unfortunately, precisely the case today. Consider not only Russia's obvious demographic decline since 1991,[6] but the rollback of its ability to project both hard and soft power throughout the post-Soviet space and the wider world.[7] In the very same conference publication in which Dynkin laments the cynicism of Moscow's nuclear dependence, his colleagues concede that, "nuclear weapons are perceived as the key security guarantee and an intrinsic attribute of a great power. Russia's vulnerable geostrategic position, weakness of its general purpose forces and inferiority in cutting edge military technology still more increase the attractiveness of nuclear arms."[8] It is possible that in the long term, Russia can address its deep structural problems, and begin to recover lost ground as a hub of culture and innovation, and even, perhaps, restore its demographic, economic and military might. Yet nuclear weapons are—thanks to the Soviet legacy—something Moscow has in relative abundance and can use today. In this context, Russian authorities would find it naïve and irresponsible not to extract maximum value from this resource.

Thus, despite the lamentations of some liberal-minded Russian experts, there is a general consensus among Russian security thinkers inside and out of government that Russia's nuclear arsenal is an important source of national power.[9] Beyond that, some in Moscow seek to leverage the nuclear arsenal to secure a relatively greater share of global political influence than would otherwise be available to them. Their position depends first on the premise that the post-Cold War world order is subject to the interaction of a handful of major global powers—what Russian Foreign Minister Sergei Lavrov has called an "objective trend toward a polycentric world"—and that Russia, a natural great power, should be one of several global power centers.[10] However, thanks to Russia's present weakness in most other measures of global power and influence, the country's relative strength and importance in the field of nuclear weapons must be treated as expansively as possible to support its great power aspirations more broadly.

THE GREAT POWER GAMBIT

To accentuate and justify its putative great power status, Moscow relies on a high-risk strategy of brinksmanship in its dealings with the United States and the West over nuclear weapons which can be thought of as a "great power gambit." To keep the stakes around Russia's nuclear arsenal high, Russia portrays as a major issue every move by the United States or its allies that might have even the most remote implications for strategic stability—a sine qua non of global security—so that the United States must either make concessions and allowances for Russia's objections or proceed against Russia's clear opposition. Of course, there is no guarantee that this risky strategy will yield the desired outcome. The upside if Russia wins via this gambit is that it is treated as an equal by the world's pre-eminent power, the United States, and thus it enjoys confirmation of its own great power status by extension. The downside if Russia loses — if Washington recognizes Russian objections for the exaggerations they are, and proceeds with its plans regardless — is that it demonstrates to the world just how little real power Russia actually has and makes it harder for Moscow to make credible threats to protect even vital interests. Whether the gambit is successful or not depends to a great degree on perceptions of Russia's capabilities and intentions by other powers, particularly the United States.[11]

Russian officials themselves miss no opportunity to underscore the centrality of stability in U.S.-Russia nuclear relations to the most serious questions of global peace and security. At the United Nations (UN) General Assembly, Foreign Minister Lavrov called for "solid legal guarantees" that missile defense would not jeopardize strategic stability. He argued that mere "statements to the effect that the build-up of global missile defense capabilities will not undermine the foundations of strategic stability are not enough. The issue is far too serious."[12] Former President Medvedev recently proposed a new European security treaty that would recognize the "principle of indivisibility of security," namely that no state can increase its security at the cost of other states' security.[13] In a speech in Washington, Lavrov interpreted "indivisible security" to demand equality between the two sides, and respect for one another's interests, and suggested that

U.S. missile defense plans would undermine such equality and respect, thus making the entire region less secure.[14]

Russian officials' views that the viability of Russia's nuclear deterrent is essential to strategic stability and to global security writ large commonly give rise to a thinly veiled threat to derail other U.S. priorities if they do not take Russian concerns seriously. Deputy Russian Foreign Minister Sergei Ryabkov has said that if the buildup of U.S. missile defenses "jeopardizes Russia's strategic nuclear capability [it] can be regarded as an exceptional event under Article 14 of the [New START] Treaty whereby Russia has the right to withdraw from this agreement."[15] Meanwhile, Deputy Prime Minister and former Russian Ambassador to the North Atlantic Treaty Organization (NATO) Dmitry Rogozin has threatened that failure to take Russian concerns about missile defense seriously might mean an end to Russia's cooperation on the Northern Distribution Network, a supply route for NATO forces that has become increasingly critical recently as U.S. relations with Pakistan have been strained.[16]

While Russian concerns about missile defense have been particularly acute, the broader message from the Russian establishment is that if the United States does not respect it as an equal, Russia will impose painful consequences. Former Chairman of the State Duma Foreign Relations Committee Konstantin Kosachev has told U.S. officials that unilateral actions by the United States that impact Russia's security may lead to suspension of Russia's cooperation on "Iran, Afghanistan, and especially [New] START."[17] Vladimir Putin's 2012 presidential campaign platform posed a similar ultimatum for the United States, stating that, "unilateral steps of our partners, without considering

Russia's opinion and interests, will be evaluated appropriately and receive action in response."[18]

Often, Russia's great power gambit has the feel of rhetorical bluster, particularly when Russians threaten consequences that would be equally, if not more, painful for Moscow as for Washington. Journalist Artem Gorbunov, for example, concludes from an interview with Defense Ministry counselor Igor Korotchenko that, "Obama must make a choice — either a reasonable compromise with Moscow, or a new arms race, in which there will be no winners."[19] Such an arms race, as the quotation implies, would cost Russia resources badly needed for economic modernization and social services. It is similarly costly for Russia to redeploy its forces and weapons in Europe, dispatch ships and troops to far flung hotspots, or impose energy or economic blockades on its neighbors, all of which have been seen by the Kremlin as leverage to improve its negotiating position. Most severe and costly of all is the threat that nuclear weapons may be used. Yet for Russians who are firmly committed to securing their great power status through a form of nuclear blackmail, proclaiming that Washington has a strategic choice to make and describing that choice in stark, all-or-nothing terms makes perfect sense.[20] Just as mutually assured destruction tried to prevent a nuclear exchange from starting in the first place, Russia's declamations of damage to strategic stability are meant to prevent the country's slide into irrelevance.

Russia's high-risk great power gambit is seldom acknowledged as such, but it nonetheless plays a key role in unifying a broad spectrum of Russian politicians and security thinkers around basically shared views when it comes to the impact of new developments on deterrence and strategic stability. From the most aggressive old Cold Warriors who still think of the United States as an adversary to worldly politicians concerned with the "new" security threats of the 21st century, nearly every serious Russian security thinker recognizes the value of preserving and enhancing Russia's power in the world. It is likewise widely acknowledged that nuclear weapons are one of Russia's few remaining "face cards." Thus, across many schools of thought and political camps, there is broad agreement that developments which might reduce the relative importance of Russia's nuclear arsenal should be resisted, whether this resistance is couched in terms of strategic stability or otherwise.

A SURVEY OF RUSSIAN VIEWPOINTS ON STRATEGIC STABILITY

The public positions of Russian experts and policymakers regarding strategic stability, not surprisingly, do not directly acknowledge the great power gambit described above. However, the spectrum of views on strategic stability held by the dominant majority in Russia is at least consistent with such an interpretation of Russia's interests. More importantly, thinking about the problem in these terms can help to explain some of the apparent inconsistencies within and between Russian views on the subject. Thus, before turning to the related issues of arms control, missile defense, and Conventional Prompt Global Strike capabilities, it is helpful to review the positions of various camps within the Russian security and political establishment on the core question of what strategic stability is, and why it matters.

THE "TRADITIONAL" VIEW

The traditional view of strategic stability, developed during the Cold War and largely shared by both U.S. and Russian strategic planners, is still best summarized by the 1990 joint U.S.-Soviet statement.[21] In this document, the sides agreed that they had the responsibility to ". . . enhance strategic stability. . . . For the first time ever, both sides will carry out significant reductions in strategic offensive arms . . . these reductions will be designed to make a first strike less plausible. The result will be greater stability and lower risk of war."[22] This has been and remains the most broadly shared nominal definition of strategic stability among Russian security thinkers and policymakers.

However, despite the joint statement's apparent endorsement of a common understanding of strategic stability between Moscow and Washington, the behavior of the two sides during much of the Cold War era reflected different understandings of strategic stability in practice.[23] This can be explained in part by the fact that the United States was the first country in the world to develop and deploy nuclear weapons — at least 3 years ahead of the Soviet Union — the first and only state to use them in an armed conflict, and for decades enjoyed a significant advantage in both the quality and the quantity of its nuclear forces relative to the Soviet Union. For Soviet leaders, the acquisition, deployment, and even the potential use of nuclear weapons therefore never required an abstract theoretical rationalization because the rationale was simply that the United States had them, and the Soviet Union had to match the power of the United States, if not its precise capabilities and deployments.

In addition, having had dramatically different experiences in World War II, the 20th century's defining conflict prior to the Cold War, as well as in previous eras of international relations, the United States and the Soviet Union naturally applied two different frameworks to their thinking about security and conflict generally, and about nuclear weapons and strategic stability specifically. Even though the communist ideological component of Moscow's approach to such questions is no longer a factor, Russian security thinkers are still influenced by some important principles of security thinking with deep historical origins predating the present period in international relations. These include the following:

- Burdened by the collective memory of multiple invasions of Russia and the Soviet Union from the Mongol Horde to Nazi Germany, Russians tend to believe that major wars happen and cannot be prevented but must be survived with minimal damage to the core political, military, and industrial capabilities of the state.[24] As the Russian proverb goes, eternal peace lasts only until the next war.

- Based on their own domestic experience as well as observation of other great powers, Russians can accept that decisions—including the decision to initiate conflict—are often made irrationally and against the obvious interests of the decisionmaker.[25]

- As the world's largest state and until only recently the last surviving great European empire, Russia believes in its uniqueness as a global great power—some think of Russia as the "third Rome"—and it accordingly needs both a unique global mission and unique capabilities.[26]

- From bitter experience at the hands of oppressive authorities, brutal criminals, and repeated foreign invasions and occupations, many Russians conclude that weakness of any kind will be exploited, and strength and power are necessary not only for prosperity, but simply for survival.[27]

In light of Russia's distinct historical experience of conflict and insecurity, it is no surprise that even those Russian thinkers who subscribe to the 1990 joint statement's definition of strategic stability evince a relatively low level of confidence that conflict can actually be prevented or minimized. This goes some way toward explaining the relatively greater focus among Russian experts on the broader strategic balance between nuclear powers, and on actions which might upset that balance, rather than the narrower balances of crisis stability and arms race stability that are integral to Western thinking about strategic stability.

The traditional definition of strategic stability on the Soviet/Russian side has been usefully paraphrased as, "such cumulative political, economic, military, and other measures implemented by [Cold War camps] that renders military aggression impossible for any of the sides."[28] In practice, this depended on a state of rough parity between the sides' military potential and strict limits on either side's efforts to alter that balance, a view which approximates the Western notion of arms race stability. But it is also evident on closer consideration of the available evidence that few Russian security thinkers actually believe that a state of true stability which prevents conflict could ever pertain.

Consider first of all the 2010 *Russian Military Doctrine*, which outlines three potential scenarios under which Russia might use nuclear weapons: "first, to retaliate against a nuclear strike on Russia or its allies; second, to retaliate against a chemical, biological, or radiological attack against Russia or its allies; and third, in case a conventional attack on Russia threatens the existence of the state."[29] While not yet explicitly deeming them as threats meriting a nuclear response, the doctrine "treats the policies, actions, and military programs of the United States and NATO as the biggest threats to Russia."[30] What is most worrisome for Russia about U.S. policies is in the 2010 U.S. *Nuclear Posture Review* (NPR). While the NPR explicitly rules out using nuclear weapons against non-nuclear weapons states in good standing with their nonproliferation obligations, it says nothing about the declared nuclear weapons states, like Russia, under the Non-Proliferation Treaty. From Moscow's perspective, the fact that the NPR does not rule *out* using nuclear weapons against the declared nuclear states means that the United States must be ruling it *in*. This interpretation, combined with the NPR's decision to "bolster" deterrence through missile defense, counterweapons of mass destruction (WMD) technologies, and other sophisticated conventional capabilities, drives much of Russia's recent concerns about U.S. nuclear policy.[31]

As a group of Russian nuclear experts recently concluded, "notwithstanding the improvement of relations between Russia and the West, the Russian military minds still proceed from the assumption that the United States and their allies are Russia's potential adversaries and have inherently aggressive strategic intentions."[32] For those Russians who hold to a traditional view of strategic stability as rough parity between two nuclear-armed camps which eliminates incentives to engage in military aggression or an arms buildup, current U.S. policy appears to call into question core assumptions about the post-Cold War balance of power and supports a cynical view of Western actions. It is therefore not surprising that some Russians conclude from the NPR "that the United States envisages the possibility of conducting a pre-emptive first strike in contradiction of the principles of strategic stability that is supposedly the basis of U.S. strategic arms reductions negotiations with Russia and strategic dialogue with China."[33]

Even if the realities of present-day security, political and economic relations — including extensive cooperation and even mutual dependence between Moscow and Washington — render deliberate nuclear attack highly improbable, these Russians still perceive a real possibility of conventional conflict between Russia and the West, which might escalate to a nuclear exchange. Indicators that the United States intends to substitute conventional for nuclear deterrence do not comfort them, and they see such momentum as a looming threat to their conception of strategic stability.

THE "ANTI-BULLYING" VIEW

A second prominent stream within the Russian security establishment approaches strategic stability as a tool for blocking aggressive encroachment by more powerful rivals, namely the United States and NATO. This view, in contrast to what I have described as the traditional definition of strategic stability, is less focused on maintaining a Cold War-style balance between nuclear forces to prevent actual conflict between nuclear powers escalating to nuclear exchange or to prevent an arms race. It instead focuses more on leveraging Russia's nuclear deterrent as a trump card to prevent what it perceives as bullying with respect to its core interests, especially in the post-Soviet space.

This "anti-bullying" view of nuclear deterrence is different from the traditional view in that it only makes sense in a post-Cold War context in which Russian power is obviously and substantially inferior to that of its erstwhile Cold War adversaries, the United States and NATO. Russia's ability to signal, threaten, or potentially use nuclear weapons in this context is about defending what Moscow understands to be vital national interests that might be threatened by the other side's expanding sphere of power and influence, including movements deep into formerly Soviet-dominated Eurasia. At the same time, this view is less dependent on precise parity between Russian and U.S. nuclear capabilities, because it sees the purpose of Russia's nuclear deterrent as not to prevent a nuclear attack per se, but to discourage conventional military, political, and economic "adventurism" by the West in what Russia considers its geopolitical backyard.

While it is true that political relations between Moscow and Washington are far warmer today than at any time in the past century, fears of U.S. power being used aggressively, recklessly, or irresponsibly in theaters close to Russia's homeland are still widespread, as is an abiding distrust of Washington's motives. As Dmitri Trenin has written, "the Russian establishment inherited a fear of an attack from the United States. Insecurity about the ends of U.S. power — especially since American power has grown so much since the end of the Cold War, even as Russia's has markedly declined — is a major problem in terms of Euro-Atlantic security, even though it may not even be recognized as such across the Atlantic."[34]

Moscow is constantly reminded of Washington's power by the presence of an expanded NATO alliance in the Baltic States and former satellites such as Poland, Romania, and Bulgaria, as well as in Afghanistan. Moreover, the NATO bombing of Yugoslavia in 1999 and Libya in 2011, as well as U.S. support over the past decade for the so-called color revolutions, Georgia's military buildup and Kosovo's independence, have all been taken as confirmation of Washington's tendency to use its power without due consideration of Russian interests. Even if the Barack Obama administration favors "reset" and equal partnership with Russia, the argument goes, Russians cannot know what the next election might bring, and there is more than enough virulently anti-Russian rhetoric to go around among U.S. politicians and experts on both sides of the aisle to justify this fear.[35]

Rather than prioritizing a steady and sustainable balance between U.S. and Russian nuclear forces on a strategic level to prevent armed conflict in general, the anti-bullying view seeks to apply nuclear deterrence to block actions that seem to be threatening to vital Russian interests, but that would likely not rise to such a level of importance for the United States and NATO. The latter would accordingly be unwilling to risk even a limited use of nuclear weapons to effectuate their goals and would reverse or adjust course. According to this view, Russia can and will rely upon its nuclear deterrent to up the ante for foreign powers that might consider meddling in what former President Medvedev has dubbed Russia's "sphere of privileged interests."[36] Thinkers of this school consider Russia's nuclear arsenal a valuable tool to remind headstrong and reckless Americans that there are limits to even Washington's power and influence, and that some foreign adventures are not worth the cost.

Some Russians criticize this approach for taking a hyper-sensitive, even paranoid, view of American power, which they argue is not anywhere near as threatening to Russia as analysts in this school believe. As former chief of staff to Russia's strategic forces General Viktor Yesin said, "There are many in Russian official circles who think only about what threatens Russia and what doesn't, and think Russia is the reason why NATO does things, even when it is not the real reason. It's a genetic problem."[37] Yet, recalling Russia's reaction to the 2010 NPR, it likely does not matter for the anti-bullying rationale whether actions perceived as hostile to Russia's vital interests are actually intended as such. Indeed, even if Washington and Brussels explicitly deny hostile intentions, this may simply be dismissed or taken as confirmation of duplicity. Russian Ambassador to Washington Sergei Kislyak's lukewarm reaction to the NPR sums up this skepticism: "We have to see how it's going to be implemented in real life . . . how it is going to be translated into cooperation. . . ."[38]

A possible silver lining for the West in the anti-bullying view is that its Russian adherents are less preoccupied with sustaining the size and structure of Russia's nuclear arsenal for the sake of strategic stability than those espousing the traditional view and may thus be more amenable to force reductions. Since they are concerned with persuading other powers not to overstep certain red lines around Russia's vital national interests, this camp's top priority is to preserve enough capability to send a clear deterrent message. Even a casual observer of the United States in the 2 decades since the end of the Cold War recognizes that the threshold for doing so falls far below any traditional Cold War notions of unacceptable damage, and a single nuclear strike on a single American city might even be sufficient to deter the United States from many actions inimical to Moscow's conception of its interests.[39] Even if some new U.S. capabilities such as ballistic missile defense (BMD) and Conventional Prompt Global Strike (CPGS) could potentially blunt a Russian strike, they surely could never block it entirely. In other words, because the anti-bullying view has relatively more modest aims for Russia's nuclear deterrent, the nation need not obsessively focus on preserving precise parity with the United States, though parity may still be desirable for other reasons described in this chapter. Moreover, advocates of the anti-bullying view may be wary of starting down a slippery slope to eventual nuclear irrelevance.

In at least one sense, the anti-bullying view of nuclear deterrence may not depend on nuclear weapons first and foremost. Although Moscow obviously wields far less power and influence than it did during the Cold War, Russian conventional capabilities have recovered somewhat since the chaotic 1990s when the government could not afford to pay officers or feed, clothe, and house soldiers, and when military stockpiles routinely went missing and sometimes ended up in the hands of foreign states and armed groups willing to pay cash.[40] Good order and discipline was restored under Vladimir Putin, who unabashedly proclaims that "the army saved Russia" from the chaos of the 1990s.[41] Looking at the recent past, Russians also see a difference of both capability and willpower between, on the one hand, Boris Yeltsin's botched and demoralizing first Chechen campaign in 1994-96 and his weak response to NATO's 1999 bombing of Belgrade, and on the other, Putin's iron-fisted suppression of North Caucasus separatists and Russia's fierce and effective conventional response to Georgia in 2008.

With this renewed confidence, Russians may actually aspire to do more than simply prevent and defend against Western bullying. Though memories of Russia's recent vulnerability and distrust of U.S. intentions remain acute, under Putin's leadership Moscow seeks a greater ability to project power both regionally and globally.[42] To this end, the great power gambit remains an important undercurrent to both the traditional and the anti-bullying views of deterrence and strategic stability. There is no inherent contradiction for Russians between seeking to preserve stability to protect their vital interests, while threatening to upset that very stability to win recognition of what they consider Russia's rightful great power status at the same time.

OTHER VIEWS

Two additional views of strategic stability bear mentioning, although they offer relatively less help in understanding the role of Russia's nuclear deterrent in theory and in practice. The first is what James Acton terms "diplomatic spackling paste" in Chapter 4 of this volume.[43] It refers to the approach taken by a few prominent Russians, including Foreign Minister Sergei Lavrov, that strategic stability, because it is generally desirable, is also a kind of shorthand for security more broadly. Thus, anything that appears to make Russia less secure, from NATO's encroachment into Eastern Europe, to provocations by former Soviet neighbors or disputes over energy supply routes, is "destabilizing."[44]

The other might be thought of as a domestic politics or "institutional interests" view. It lumps together various interest groups in Russia that place primacy on the country's nuclear deterrent, often citing concerns about strategic stability, but which are fundamentally motivated by their own institutional interests. Some are subject to a kind of path dependency: The Soviet Union's vast nuclear arsenal now belongs to Russia, and, they reason, since Russia has these weapons, it had better take them seriously.[45] Others, especially members of the strategic forces and broader military establishment, seek to persuade political leaders that Russia's nuclear deterrent is of paramount importance because this tends to insulate them from painful budget cuts that might affect other branches of the armed forces.[46] Most of all, Russia's still influential arms industry stands to gain from new investments to shore up the country's aging nuclear complex, as well as efforts to develop new technologies to match the West. Whether or not they genuinely believe their own rhetoric, these interest groups have every incentive to emphasize the grave dangers surrounding Russia in terms of strategic stability.

ARMS CONTROL

The history of U.S.-Soviet and U.S.-Russian arms control negotiations and agreements is a long and largely positive one. Since the Strategic Arms Limitation Treaty (SALT) of 1972, the two sides have signed eight agreements, ratified seven and implemented six, the latest of which is New START, signed and ratified by both sides in 2010.[47] As much or even more than their U.S. counterparts, Russians value these treaties and seek to keep in place some basic, legally-binding limitations on strategic nuclear forces, for the obvious reason that without binding limits, the much wealthier and more powerful U.S. side could provoke and win an arms race — unlikely and detrimental to Washington's interests though that may be.[48] But preserving existing agreements can be quite different from negotiating new ones. When it comes to new arms control negotiations with Washington in general, and a new round of post-New START arms control talks specifically, we can apply the spectrum of Russian views of strategic stability developed above to glean a few useful insights into Russia's interests and objectives.

Seen in terms of the great power gambit, U.S.-Russia arms control negotiations tend to hold great appeal. After all, there could hardly be a better confirmation of Russia's great power status than for that status to be implicitly acknowledged by the United States, when U.S. negotiators sit across a negotiating table from their Russian counterparts. Yet the benefits to Russia's great power preoccupation do not extend much beyond the mere fact of arms control negotiations taking place. Substantive advancement of such talks is much less appealing, since reciprocal concessions that might be offered by Washington are of limited practical value to Moscow, whose own concession is a one-way street leading to a dead end. Whereas the United States can move on from nuclear arms control talks to play a decisive role in negotiations on the global economy, climate change, conventional security, and practically any other issue, Russia's nuclear arsenal is a limited resource. The logic of the great power gambit dictates that Moscow's best hand to play is the one that keeps bilateral negotiations open the longest, with the least likelihood of real concessions being made by either side. Thus while multilateral talks engaging other Nuclear Non-Proliferation Treaty (NPT) nuclear weapons states might still satisfy Russia's great power ambitions, for the present bilateral negotiations are preferred.[49]

Under a more traditional Russian view of strategic stability, arms control negotiations are inherently neither good nor bad. Rather, it is the outcome of the negotiations that matters most. If negotiations must occur, the priority is to maintain absolute numerical parity between the two sides' capabilities. In today's context, this suggests an incentive on the Russian side to push for further reductions in deployed strategic forces (especially the more expensive delivery vehicles rather than deployed warheads), so that U.S. forces can be reduced to the relatively lower levels that Russia is now able to sustain. However, the countervailing pressure is that Russians continue to see U.S. tactical weapons in Europe, as well as the strategic arsenals of the United Kingdom (UK) and France, as effectively part of the overall nuclear potential against which Russia must maintain parity.[50] This thinking incentivizes Russians motivated by the traditional view of strategic stability to propose negotiations on a formula that includes the British and French strategic arsenals in the U.S. side's total, as well as to call for withdrawal of all tactical weapons to national territory, meaning evacuation of U.S. weapons from Europe.[51]

The Russian approach to strategic stability that prizes deterrence against U.S. "bullying" also places no particular value on new nuclear arms control negotiations. Certainly, it is essential to preserve legally binding arrangements that prevent the United States/NATO from developing and deploying overwhelming forces. However, new arms control negotiations are not especially desirable, because they are not in and of themselves able to prevent provocative or bullying actions by the United States and its allies, including in the particularly sensitive "near abroad" of the post-Soviet space. Russia's recent experience with the New START negotiations illustrates the danger, from Russia's perspective, that the U.S. side will simply "compartmentalize" nuclear arms control and all the other issues of concern to Russia.[52] Thus, unless the negotiations can expand to include other issues ranging from conventional forces to NATO's activities in the post-Soviet space, to BMD, they will hold little interest for Russians primarily concerned with blocking Western aggression writ large. Both sides recognize that such an infinitely expansive scope for negotiations is infeasible, and in any case, Russia has far fewer and less valuable bargaining chips outside the nuclear realm.

There are, of course, other interests and attitudes on the Russian side relevant to renewing nuclear arms control negotiations. Some senior officials view the continuation of any arms control dialogue—even if it could not be construed as formal treaty negotiations—as a forum for discussion of important issues with Washington. They also consider resumption or cessation of talks as an opportunity for signaling about the broader state of relations between Moscow and Washington: if things are going well, talks proceed; if poorly, they end. The "institutional" interests of Russia's nuclear weapons establishment are similar to the traditional view described above, except with greater skepticism towards any new negotiations that might threaten quantitative or qualitative reductions for both sides. Even if precise parity is maintained, reductions are to be resisted, since the bigger Russia's arsenal, the more resources it gets. Of course, this same establishment could support new negotiations that entailed a buildup of forces to current treaty limits to strengthen Russia's negotiating position, or a complete renewal of delivery systems to make them more effective despite a modest numerical reduction.[53]

BALLISTIC MISSILE DEFENSE

BMD is the single most contentious issue at present between the United States and Russia, and the ongoing controversy underscores basic differences in the two sides' understanding of strategic stability. Ever since the George W. Bush administration announced its plans to develop a missile shield based in Europe in 2007, Russian officials have vehemently opposed the idea, arguing that it is unnecessary and "destabilizing." The Obama administration's revised European missile defense strategy, the Phased Adaptive Approach (PAA), has not significantly eased tensions. In fact, as the administration has announced and formalized plans to place ground installations in Poland and Romania during the next decade, the urgency of Russian opposition has increased. In addition to the perception that NATO is doubling down on its expansion into the former Soviet sphere of influence, Russians see the placement of missile defense installations in Eastern Europe as inconsistent with Washington and Brussels' stated concern about a missile threat from the Middle East.[54]

In terms of the great power gambit, BMD is a problem primarily because Moscow has chosen to make it one. Setting aside Russia's claims that BMD may eventually be capable enough to upset strategic stability by negating Russia's deterrent, the real problem is that Washington is politically and strategically committed to BMD, irrespective of Russian objections. BMD re-

sponds to intensely felt U.S. insecurities about rogue
states, terrorists, proliferation, and other post-September 11, 2001 (9/11) threats, and no U.S. president, to say
nothing of the Congress, would be willing to weaken
U.S. defenses simply to mollify Moscow.[55] Unsuccessfully pressing against U.S. deployment of BMD could
represent the undoing of Russia's great power gambit, as the more Moscow pushes against it, the closer
it comes to exposing its inability to influence Washington — hardly the measure of a great power. From
this standpoint, the best possible solution for Moscow
would be for the United States to accept a "dual key"
or a truly "joint" system, which would make Russia
central to a core U.S. security interest going forward
and would allay Moscow's concerns about what was
being defended against.[56] If neither is possible, a face-saving compromise that fell short of real cooperation
but appeared to account for Russian concerns and preserved the image of Russian involvement might also
suffice.[57]

Those who adhere to a traditional view of strategic stability in terms of parity and mutual deterrence
are the least immediately alarmed over BMD. In fact,
many serious Russian experts acknowledge that BMD
only poses a potential problem in the longer term,
when the United States reaches the fourth phase of
the PAA, developing and deploying a new SM3 Block
II-B missile interceptor, and only then if it chooses to
vastly scale up the numbers of such interceptors.[58]
However, Russian experts take this potential threat to
strategic stability very seriously, and recognize that it
could become much more urgent if a new arms control agreement moves towards dramatic reductions
in Russia's arsenal, or if a future U.S. Administration
decides to pursue BMD capabilities on a larger scale,

as some have urged.[59] Thus, the traditionalists believe the best solution is to impose a legally binding limit on the numbers of U.S. interceptors they may deploy. While they are not opposed to variations on the co-operative missile defense proposal, they hold to the belief that offensive and defensive capabilities are closely related, and thus without binding limits on defensive capabilities, a new nuclear arms race will be inevitable.[60]

In contrast to the traditionalists, those who think of Russia's deterrent primarily as a shield against Western bullying are most concerned not by the prospect of BMD generally, but by its specific implementation in the European theater, and even more specifically in Central and Eastern Europe. While Moscow harbors no delusions that it can reassert its strategic dominance over former satellites that are now part of NATO and the European Union (EU), it is especially wary of enhanced U.S. and NATO activity in these states, as they are geographically closer to Russia.[61] Moreover, U.S. "boots on the ground" in Poland and Romania, even if only in the small numbers needed to man interceptor sites, symbolizes eastward momentum of the NATO Alliance. This causes Russians to question whether similar U.S.-manned installations might not soon appear in Ukraine or Georgia, former Soviet states which Russia sees as bulwarks of its "sphere of privileged influence," but which NATO has declared to be future candidates for membership.[62] From this standpoint, the preferred solution would be one proposed by President Medvedev before the November 2010 Russia-NATO summit at Lisbon: carve the region up into separate "zones of responsibility" for Russia and NATO missile defense, in effect recognizing separate spheres of influence.[63]

For Russians who think of strategic stability in terms of the broader state of relations with Washington, the biggest problem with BMD is that it is unilateral. As Washington presses ahead with this potentially game-changing new system, Moscow finds itself in the uncomfortable position of having to watch from the sidelines, receiving but never quite trusting U.S. assurances about the system's limited purposes. U.S. officials argue that BMD is designed solely to defend against attacks from rogue states, especially Iran. Besides Russia's strong disagreement with the United States about the extent and purpose of Iran's nuclear program, Russians simply do not accept that such a costly and elaborate new system could be for such limited purposes—like using "a sledgehammer to crack a nut," in the words of one expert.[64] Repeated U.S. assurances that BMD will not target Russia's deterrent missiles have actually increased Moscow's skepticism: ". . . [T]he harder the Americans try to convince the Russians that they mean no harm, the more the Kremlin becomes suspicious of US intentions."[65] Reassurance for those who simply distrust U.S. intentions could come in many forms, but would ideally include real cooperation on elements of the system ranging from early warning to the interceptors themselves. If this is not possible, a face-saving compromise must at least include a high degree of transparency today with credible, if not legally binding, assurances about the future.

Finally, the Russian nuclear establishment's institutional interests, while outwardly hostile toward BMD, may perceive in this development an opportunity. Moscow's growing rift with Washington over BMD has yielded threats from top Russian leaders that will require major new investments to carry out, such as the new heavy intercontinental ballistic missile (ICBM). Prime Minister Putin has said that if the United States rejects joint missile defense in favor of its own system, Russia will have to "put in place new strike forces . . . against the new threats which will have been created along our borders. New missile, nuclear technologies will be put in place."[66] In addition to threatening abrogation of the New START treaty, President Medvedev said that Russia may be forced into "retaliatory measures [including] developing the offensive potential of our nuclear capabilities," a scenario he calls reminiscent of the Cold War.[67] Thus, those who benefit from greater investment in Russia's strategic forces would have much to gain from a nuclear buildup over BMD. While unrealistic at present, Russia might also seek in the long term to augment deterrence by improving its own missile defense capabilities.[68]

CONVENTIONAL PROMPT GLOBAL STRIKE

Another emerging U.S. capability of concern to Moscow is the Conventional Prompt Global Strike (CPGS) system, designed to deliver a high precision conventional strike on a target anywhere around the world in a short period of time. The U.S. military envisions CPGS as an option that can enable quick and potentially pre-emptive action against terrorists and other rogue actors from long ranges when forward-deployed U.S. forces are not available or cannot be employed. However, because of the system's potential capability to target nuclear weapons and thus "disarm" a nuclear-armed adversary, it has also been recognized as a factor affecting deterrence and strategic stability.[69]

On the Russian side, the U.S. rationale for CPGS is met with hardy skepticism: "Although Russia has not been named as a potential foe, Moscow does not believe that such expensive conventional armed delivery vehicles are to be used solely against rogue nations."[70] From Moscow's perspective, the United States is simply citing terrorist threats and rogue states as a vague pretext to strengthen its military capabilities with an eye toward other nuclear powers, namely Russia.

Seen in terms of Russia's great power aspirations, CPGS presents a danger because of the potential revolution in military technology that it represents. If wars in the future can be fought at long range at the direction of senior leaders who need not worry about putting their troops in harm's way or risking retaliatory attacks on the homeland, then any state without such capabilities will be at a distinct disadvantage. To avoid slipping into the status of a "second class" military power, Russia will leverage the weight it still has as a nuclear great power to seek to outlaw CPGS by treaty, which the U.S. side is very unlikely to accept. More realistically, however, Moscow can seek to call Washington's bluff, by asking for binding limits or sufficient transparency on the numbers of CPGS systems so that CPGS remains effectively a "niche" capability which does not fundamentally impact Russia's nuclear deterrent, and thus does not jeopardize its great power status.

From the "traditional" standpoint, Russians find CPGS most threatening because it can potentially substitute for nuclear weapons in a disarming first strike:

> Russian officials and defense analysts are worried that such a capability, if expanded, would weaken Russia's deterrent by providing the United States with the abil-

ity to eliminate — or at least severely degrade — Russian nuclear forces and command and control systems in a pre-emptive strike without having to cross the nuclear threshold first.[71]

As with BMD, Russians acknowledge that this is not yet an urgent and immediate threat to strategic stability, but they believe it must be addressed in the context of any future arms control negotiations. Specifically, as U.S. CPGS capabilities advance, Russia will likely push to bring these systems within the scope of treaty limitations, either by simply counting them in the total number of deployed weapons on the U.S. side, or setting a separate cap for the numbers of such systems.[72] Moscow will not sit idly by for a future in which Washington has the capability to disarm or significantly degrade its nuclear deterrent without actually crossing the nuclear threshold itself.

Russians concerned about the prospect of reckless U.S. action within Moscow's "sphere" are discomforted as much by the capability that CPGS represents as by the prospect of misinterpretation. In conversations with former President George W. Bush, Russian officials highlighted the potential for grave misunderstanding in the event of a CPGS launch, arguing that it would be difficult to know whether conventional or nuclear weapons had been fired.[73] Indeed, as one scholar argues, Russia's early warning system may simply not detect a CPGS launch, correctly discern a missile's flight path, or differentiate between conventional and nuclear weapons during flight, all of which could lead to a nuclear crisis with catastrophic consequences.[74] Even if arrangements can ensure sufficient transparency around CPGS launches, perhaps along the lines of the proposed Joint Data Exchange

Center (JDEC), Russians see this capability as a potential magnifier of the U.S. tendency to project power irresponsibly. Considering Moscow's fury in response to the NATO bombing of Belgrade in 1999, and more recently to the NATO air operation in Libya, U.S. deployment and use of CPGS against targets in Eurasia or the Middle East is sure to provoke Russian unease.

If the two sides do not negotiate an arrangement to provide Russia sufficient assurances and transparency about CPGS, let alone to impose binding limits on the numbers of weapons deployed, Moscow has two options: The Kremlin can double down on threats that have already been made in response to BMD, namely by building up its strategic nuclear arsenal and adding more forward deployments in Kaliningrad and elsewhere close to NATO countries.[75] It can also seek to develop and deploy its own long-range conventional system as a counterweight to U.S. CPGS, and to signal that Russia remains a great power with fully modern military capabilities.[76] Both of these options are expensive and uncertain, and thus undesirable from the standpoint of most Russian experts, yet like any other military buildup, they would benefit a handful of powerful interests linked to the arms industry.

CONCLUSION

To date, evidence is mixed as to whether Russia's great power gambit pays real dividends for Russia's interests. On the one hand, the Obama administration remains firmly committed to plans for European missile defense under the rubric of PAA. In 2011, U.S. officials signed agreements with Romania and Poland to clear the path for ground-based interceptors to be deployed on the territory of these former Warsaw Pact states, despite strenuous Russian objections.[77] At the same time, U.S. negotiators continue to seek a way forward that accommodates Russia's concerns, seeking at least to avoid further deterioration of relations following a tense Russia-NATO summit in May 2012, heated rhetoric during both countries' 2012 presidential contests, and deepening distrust symbolized by the passage of reciprocal sanctions by Congress and the Russian Duma over human rights issues.[78]

One clear payoff for Russia's strategy has come with the announcement by U.S. officials that even though no immediate progress on arms control was expected, "strategic stability talks" would resume in 2012 to help define each side's interests and identify steps that could enhance stability.[79] While the Obama administration has much invested in the success of "reset" diplomacy with Russia, this continuation of the status quo is arguably much more favorable for Moscow than for Washington. By preserving its place across the negotiating table from the world's pre-eminent military and political power, and yet without offering significant concessions on any specific issues, Russia can have its great power cake and eat it too. In this sense, the present moment may represent a high water mark for the great power gambit.

Favorable as it is for Russia's high stakes strategy, the status quo cannot last forever. Once the most acute political infighting over the U.S. federal budget and the national debt have receded, Washington will turn once again to top national security and foreign policy priorities. The rogue missile threat from the likes of Iran, North Korea, and al-Qaeda will surely top the list, and they will underscore the importance of following through on planned BMD and CPGS development and deployment. As future milestones for these capabilities draw nearer, Russians will feel ever greater urgency to oppose them and ever more reluctance to move forward on a next round of post-START nuclear arms control.

In each case, looking ahead, arguments citing strategic stability will remain central to the conversation between Moscow and Washington. Naturally, it can benefit U.S. experts and policymakers to continue to pay close attention to the rationale cited by Russian officials for opposing both new U.S. capabilities and new arms control negotiations. It will also benefit both sides to recognize the wide range of attitudes toward strategic stability that inform Russian positions on nuclear and related issues, and yet often go unspoken. Among these, the great power gambit has been by far the most pervasive, and it is past time for both sides to pay better attention before either risks a dangerous outcome it does not intend.

ENDNOTES - CHAPTER 8

1. Steven Pifer, *Nuclear Arms Control in 2012*, Washington, DC: Brookings Institute, January 19, 2012, available from *www.brookings.edu/speeches/2012/0119_arms_control_pifer.aspx*.

2. Ian Kearns, *Beyond the United Kingdom: Trends in the Other Nuclear Armed States*, Washington, DC: British American Security Information Council (BASIC), November 2011, p. 8, available from *www.basicint.org/sites/default/files/commission-briefing1.pdf*.

3. *Ibid.*

4. Alexander Dynkin *et al.*, "Strategic Stability After the Cold War," paper presented at the Institute of World Economy and International Relations (IMEMO) conference, "Strategic Stability After the Cold War," Moscow, 2010, p. 6.

5. *Ibid.*, pp. 6-7.

6. As stated in a recent article in *Foreign Affairs*, "Since 1992, according to Rosstat, Russia's federal statistics agency . . . about 12.5 million more Russians have been buried than born-or nearly three funerals for every two live deliveries for the past 20 years," from Nicholas Eberstadt: "The Dying Bear: Russia's Demographic Disaster," *Foreign Affairs*, Vol. 90, No. 6, November-December 2011, p. 96.

7. As one Russian scholar has argued, "The imperial élan gone, Russian leaders define their country as a 'great power,' and this is broadly supported by the public, but what is the meaning of that term in the early 21st century? Russia's interests in the neighborhood are real, but a privileged zone of influence is a chimera. Moscow's current zone of influence extends only to Abkhazia and South Ossetia," from Dmitri Trenin, *Post-Imperium: A Eurasian Story*, Washington, DC: Carnegie Endowment for International Peace, 2011, p. 37.

8. Alexander Dynkin *et al.*, "Strategic Stability After the Cold War," paper presented at the Institute of World Economy and International Relations (IMEMO) conference, "Strategic Stability After the Cold War," Moscow, 2010, p. 10.

9. Dmitri Trenin, "Russian Perspectives on the Global Elimination of Nuclear Weapons," in Barry Blechman, ed., *Russia and the United States*, Washington, DC: The Stimson Center, July 2009, p. 1:

> As the self-perceived isolated great power in a highly competitive global environment, Russia regards nuclear weapons as the mainstay of both its security posture and status among the major powers of the 21st century . . . nuclear deterrence gives a measure of comfort to the Kremlin that Russia's vital interests will be respected under all circumstances by Washington and Beijing, whose military power and 'combined national might,' respectively, are now far greater than Russia's.

For a detailed look at the importance of nuclear weapons for Russia in the post-Cold War era, see Stephen J. Blank: "Russia and Nuclear Weapons," in Stephen J. Blank, ed., *Russian Nuclear Weapons: Past, Present, and Future*, Carlisle, PA: Strategic Studies Institute, 2011, pp. 293-364.

10. Sergei Lavrov, "Russia in a Multipolar World: Implications for Russia-EU-U.S. Relations," Speech at the Russian Embassy in Washington, DC, July 12, 2011, available from *europeaninstitute.org/~european/images/stories/programs/lavrov.remarks.pdf*.

11. Like Russian experts themselves, U.S. experts on Russia adopt a wide range of approaches to evaluating whether Russia is a friend or foe of the United States. Some concentrate on Russia's objective capabilities, citing the sheer size of Russia's arsenal, and its historical purpose to deter and intimidate Washington, as evidence that Russia must continue to occupy a top place in the U.S. national security outlook. As noted in a recent Center for the National Interest report, "Russia is the only nation that could destroy America as we know it in thirty minutes," from Graham Allison *et al., Russia and U.S. National Interests: Why Should Americans Care?* Washington, DC: Center for the National Interest, October 2011, p. 9. Similarly: "Russia's nukes are still an existential threat. Twenty years after the fall of the Berlin Wall, Russia has thousands of nuclear weapons in stockpile and hundreds still on hair-trigger alert aimed at U.S. cities," from James F. Collins and Matt Rojansky: "Why Russia Matters," *Foreign Policy*, August 18, 2010, available from *www.foreignpolicy.com/articles/2010/08/18/why_Russia_matters*. Others focus instead on the proliferation concerns related to Russia's nuclear arsenal, thinking of Russia's nuclear weapons not so much as weapons that might be used against the United States, but as dangers to global security more broadly. See, e.g., Charles K. Bartles: "Why Proliferate? Russia and the Non-Nuclear Weapon Regime," *Foreign Military Studies Office*, October 2007, p. 5, available from *fmso.leavenworth.army.mil/documents/Russia-Nukes.pdf*. Still others, including this author, combine Russia's nuclear potential with other important contributions to U.S. interests, such as the Russian-controlled Afghan Northern Distribution Network, to make the case that Russia maintains significant capabilities to either help or hurt U.S. security. Nikolas Gvosdev and Matthew A. Rojansky: "Keep the 'Reset' Moving," *The New York Times*, December 15, 2011, available from *www.nytimes.com/2011/12/16/opinion/keep-the-us-russia-reset-moving.html*.

12. Sergei Lavrov, "Statement," Speech at the 66th Session of the UN General Assembly, New York, September 27, 2011, available from *gadebate.un.org/66/russian-federation*.

13. Dmitry Medvedev, "Meeting with participants in the Munich conference on Security Policy," available from *eng.kremlin.ru/news/1173*.

14. Excerpt from Lavrov's speech:

> So [the] missile defense situation is the crux of the matter of indivisibility of security . . . this remains, I think, the single irritator of considerable importance in Russian-American relations. . . . We do hope that we can overcome it and will be, as Russia, doing anything we can to achieve a fairer view which would be based on equality, respect of the interest of each other and the respect for the security concerns of each other.

Sergei Lavrov, "Russia in a Multipolar World: Implications for Russia-EU-U.S. Relations," Speech at the Russian Embassy in Washington, DC, July 12, 2011, available from *www.europeaninstitute.org/images/stories/programs/lavrov.remarks.pdf*.

15. "Russia 'disappointed' by U.S. failure to provide missile guarantees," *RIA Novosti*, May 16, 2011, available from *en.rian.ru/russia/20110516/164052008.html*.

16. Cullison Alan: "Russia Considers Blocking NATO Supply Routes," *The Wall Street Journal*, November 28, 2011, available from *online.wsj.com/article/SB1000142405297020475340457706642110659245 2.html?mod=wsj_share_tweet*.

17. Excerpt from leaked cable sent from U.S. Embassy in Moscow. "Russian Duma Members Want US-Russia Relations Based On Trust And Dialogue," February 22, 2010, available from *www.cablegatesearch.net/cable.php?id=10MOSCOW391&q=defense%20missile*.

18. "Односторонние же шаги наших партнёров, не учитывающие мнения России и её интересы, получат соответствующую оценку и нашу ответную реакцию" ("Steps taken by our partners which are unilateral and fail to take into account Russia's opinions and interests will receive an appropriate evaluation and a reaction in kind"), from Vladimir Putin, "Сильная Россия в сложном мире" ("A Strong Russia in a Complex World"), available from *www.putin2012.ru/program/6*.

19. "Обаме предстоит сделать выбор - либо разумный компромисс с Москвой, либо новая гонка вооружений. Победителей в которой, как известно, не бывает," (Obama has a decision to make—either a reasonable compromise with Moscow, or a new arms race. As is known, there are no victors in such [an arms race].), from Artem Gorbunov: "Россия заткнет ПРО за пояс" ("Russia Will Tuck Missile Defense into Its Belt"), *News Info*, November 23, 2011, available from *www.newsinfo.ru/articles/2011-11-23/Medvedev_PRO/766304/*.

20. As Mikhail Delyagin, director of the Institute for Globalization Problems, has argued, "Это продолжение курса холодной войны на окружение России кольцом баз... Сейчас там размещаются не ракеты, а радар, но все равно это крайне неприятно. В содержательном плане нужно понимать, что американцы никогда не будут нашими партнерами, они всегда будут нашими стратегическими противниками, пока мы и они продолжаем существовать" ("This is a continuation of the Cold War path of encircling Russia with bases. . . . This time they are placing radars in them, not rockets, but it is nonetheless extremely unpleasant. Fundamentally, it is important to understand that the Americans will never be our partners; they will always be our strategic opponents, as long as we both exist"), from Viktor Savenkov: "Леонид Ивашов: Идет охват территории России и Китая" ("Leonid Ivashov: Russia and China Are Being Encircled"), *Svobodnaya Pressa*, September 2, 2011, available from *svpressa.ru/society/article/47455/*.

21. "Soviet-United States Joint Statement on the Treaty on Strategic Offensive Arms," June 1, 1990, available from *www.bits.de/NRANEU/START/documents/Washington90.htm*.

22. *Ibid.*

23. In Chapter 4 of this volume, James Acton cites David Yost's argument that Soviet behavior during the Cold War did not in fact conform to this conception of strategic stability. Rather, the Soviets pursued arms race competition that was not predicted or easily explained under the traditional conception of strategic stability. See David S. Yost: "Strategic Stability in the Cold War: Lessons for Continuing Challenges," *Proliferation Papers*, No. 36, Winter 2011, p. 22.

24. Indeed, repeated foreign invasions have had a profound effect on Russian society: "Centuries of a turbulent, violent history have left indelible marks on the Russian psyche, deeply coloring attitudes toward individual and national survival in a hostile, hierarchical environment," from Jerrold L. Schecter, *Russian Negotiating Behavior*, Washington, DC: United States Institute of Peace, 1998, p. 16. They have also reinforced the perceived need for greater security: "Naturally this painful experience of centuries of invasion has affected the Russian psyche, resulting in an obsession with security, which in turn induces an extreme habit of secrecy regarding defense matters and a belligerent attitude toward foreign countries," from Leon Sloss and M. Scott Davis, "The Soviet Union, the Pursuit of Power and Influence through Negotiation," in Hans Binnendijk, ed., *National Negotiating Styles*, Washington, DC: Foreign Service Institute, 1987, p. 18.

25. Georgian President Mikheil Saakashvili's decision to attack South Ossetia in August 2008, which quickly led to war with Russia, was seen as an irrational and costly decision. See, for example, President Medvedev's comments on Saakashvili's "dimwit gamble of 2008" in Dmitry Medvedev, Interview with Russian media officials, August 5, 2011, available from *eng.kremlin.ru/ news/2680*; for Georgians' opinions on the costs of war with Russia, see Dmitri Aleksandrov, "Главная ошибка Саакашвили" ("Saakashvili's Main Mistake"), *Vzglyad*, November 24, 2008, available from *vz.ru/politics/2008/11/24/231970.html*.

26. The idea of a "third Rome" still has currency in post-Soviet Russia: "Those Russians still fighting against the Western-oriented technological future cherish the images of a third Rome led by the Russian Orthodox Church, a communist utopia, or a Russian variation of a military-controlled market economy modeled on Pinochet's Chile," from Schecter, p. 16; "As long as Russia desires to be a great power it must remain a Eurasian power. Its geopolitical position and dimensions are the surest basis of its future great power status," from David Kerr: "The New Eurasianism: The Rise of Geopolitics in Russia's Foreign Policy," *Europe-Asia Studies*, Vol. 47, No. 6, 1995, p. 986.

27. A. V. Makarin and A. I. Strebkov, "Война и военная политика" ("War and Military Politics"), *Теория и история политических институтов* (*Theory and History of Political Institutions*), St. Petersburg, Russia: St. Petersburg University Press, 2008. Russian leaders have often stressed the necessity of national unity and strength throughout history:

> "... [T]he lesson that internecine conflict invites foreign incursion and that only unity, extending from princes to the people as a whole, ensures victory has become a constant of Russian military lore.... Today, the lesson holds firm, enshrined in such prominent venues as the 2003 three-volume military history of Russia, sponsored by the Ministry of Defense, or in the first volume of the massive thirty-volume project, The Military History of the Russian State. . .

See Gregory Carleton: "History Done Right: War and the Dynamics of Triumphalism in Contemporary Russian Culture," *Slavic Review*, Vol. 70, No. 3, Fall 2011, p. 618.

28. Alexander Dynkin *et al.*, "Strategic Stability After the Cold War," paper presented at the Institute of World Economy and International Relations (IMEMO) conference, "Strategic Stability After the Cold War," Moscow, 2010, p. 14.

29. Alexei Arbatov, *Gambit or Endgame? The New State of Arms Control*, Moscow, Russia: Carnegie Endowment for International Peace, March 2011, pp. 5; the actual text of the doctrine reads: "The Russian Federation reserves the right to utilize nuclear weapons in response to the utilization of nuclear and other types of weapons of mass destruction against it and (or) its allies, and also in the event of aggression against the Russian Federation involving the use of conventional weapons when the very existence of the state is under threat." See Carnegie Endowment, "Text of Newly-Approved Russian Military Doctrine," available from *www.carnegieendowment.org/2010/02/05/text-of-newly-approved-russian-military-doctrine/l8t*.

30. Arbatov 2011, p. 5.

31. *Nuclear Posture Review Report*, Washington, DC: Department of Defense, April 2010, pp. 15, 55.

32. Alexander Dynkin *et al.*, "Non-Nuclear Factors of Nuclear Disarmament: Ballistic Missile Defense, High-Precision Conventional Weapons, Space Arms," paper presented at the Institute of World Economy and International Relations (IMEMO) conference, "Missile Defense, Non-Proliferation and Deep Reduction of Nuclear Weapons," Moscow, 2010, p. 58.

33. Arbatov, 2011, p.10.

34. Dmitri Trenin, *Post-Imperium: A Eurasian Story*, Washington, DC: Carnegie Endowment for International Peace, 2011, p. 143.

35. Alexei Fenenko: "The cyclical nature of Russian-American relations," *RIA Novosti*, June 21, 2011, available from *en.rian.ru/valdai_op/20110621/164739508.html*.

36. President Dmitry Medvedev, Interview with Russian media officials, August 31, 2008, available from *archive.kremlin.ru/eng/speeches/2008/08/31/1850_type82912type82916_206003.shtml*.

37. General Viktor Yesin, Interview with author, June 2011.

38. James Acton, *Deterrence During Disarmament: Deep Nuclear Reductions and International Security*, New York: International Institute for Strategic Studies-Routledge, 2011, p. 64.

39. As one American scholar explained, "'Unacceptable damage' to the Soviet Union was variously defined by former Secretary of Defense Robert S. McNamara as requiring the ability to destroy a fifth to a fourth of its population and a half to two-thirds of its industrial capacity," from Kenneth N. Waltz, "Peace, Stability, and Nuclear Weapons," Washington, DC: Institute on Global Conflict and Cooperation, University of California, August 1995, p. 10.

40. As noted in a 1995 *Foreign Affairs* article, "Russia's economy has deteriorated to the point where officers have to work off-duty as farmhands to make ends meet. . . . Russian soldiers in and around Chechnya lack adequate clothing, rations, and shelter." Benjamin S. Lambeth: "Russia's Wounded Military," *Foreign Affairs*, Vol. 74, No. 2, March-April 1995, p. 91; for a closer look

at Russia's most notorious weapons trafficker, see Douglas Farah and Stephen Braun: "The Merchant of Death," *Foreign Policy*, November-December 2006, pp. 52-61; "Russia Missing Scores of Bombs-Lebed," *Reuters*, September 5, 1997, abstract available from *www.nti.org/analysis/articles/russia-missing-scores-bombs-lebed/*.

41. Vladimir V. Putin, "Being Strong: National Security Guarantees for Russia," *Rossiiskaya Gazeta*, February 20, 2012, available from *premier.gov.ru/eng/events/news/18185/*.

42. Tom Parfitt: "Russia plants flag on North Pole seabed," *The Guardian*, August 2, 2007, available from *www.guardian.co.uk/world/2007/aug/02/russia.arctic*; Dmitry Gorenburg, "Russian Naval Deployments: A Return to Global Power Projection or a Temporary Blip?" paper presented at the PONARS Eurasia conference, George Washington University, Washington, DC, 2009; "Syria and Russia: Wait and sea," *The Economist*, January 14, 2012, available from *www.economist.com/node/21542793*.

43. See Acton, Chap. 4, in this volume.

44. Sergei Lavrov, Speech to State Duma on New START Treaty, Moscow, January 2011, available from *www.mid.ru/brp_4. nsf/0/B4B970B7D9B7FAD9C3257818005CDBD2*.

45. The preservation of Russia's large nuclear arsenal requires constant maintenance and strategic planning:

As long as nuclear weapons and the research and industrial infrastructure supporting them continue to exist, political and military planning for their use must take place. Planning for nuclear use involves development of scenario-specific missions that pit nuclear assets against real or perceived threats. These missions provide formal rationales for continued maintenance of nuclear capabilities, for distribution of targets, for posture planning, as well as for research and development.

Nikolai Sokov, "Nuclear Weapons in Russian National Strategy," in Stephen J. Blank, ed., *Russian Nuclear Weapons: Past, Present, and Future*, Carlisle, PA: Strategic Studies Institute, U.S. Army War College, 2011, p. 197.

46. Indeed, Russia's military-industrial complex exerts significant influence over policymakers:

> . . . the political leadership already has given its defense industry and military a free hand in shaping Moscow's national security policy. Specifically, recent promises and commitments that Moscow has made regarding the future buildup of its strategic forces put Russia on a trajectory that's incompatible with substantial nuclear reductions. More directly, if all of the currently scheduled programs materialize, Russia will find itself in a situation where its strategic arsenal will start growing.

Pavel Podvig, "Russia's new arms development," *Bulletin of the Atomic Scientists*, January 16, 2009, available from *www.the-bulletin.org/web-edition/columnists/pavel-podvig/russias-new-arms-development*.

47. Arms Control Association, "U.S.-Russia Arms Control Agreements," available from *www.armscontrol.org/taxonomy/term/136*; for an arms control timeline, see Council on Foreign Relations, "U.S.-Russia Nuclear Arms Control," available from *www.cfr.org/world/us-russia-arms-control/p21620*.

48. For example, Dmitry Rogozin has called for legally-binding guarantees that missile defense will not threaten Russia's strategic nuclear arsenal. See Irina Kostiukova, "Чтобы мы понимали, что ни при каких условиях данная противоракетная оборона не будет развернута против российского стратегического ядерного потенциала, мы должны иметь надежные гарантии, в том числе юридические" ("For us to come to an understanding that this anti-missile defense system will never be turned against the Russian strategic nuclear capabilities, we must have reliable guarantees, including legal guarantees."), "Нам не хватает гарантий" ("We Do Not Have Enough Guarantees"), *Vzglyad*, May 16, 2011, available from *vz.ru/politics/2011/5/16/491681.html*; for more on U.S. nuclear superiority, see Keir A. Lieber and Daryl G. Press: "The Rise of U.S. Nuclear Primacy," *Foreign Affairs*, Vol. 85, No. 2, March-April 2006, pp. 42-54.

49. As Harvard professor Mark Kramer has argued, "Instead of bilateral arms control, the United States and Russia should be pushing for a regime of nuclear weapons transparency that would pertain to all the nuclear weapons states," in Mark Kramer, "End-

ing Bilateral U.S.-Russian Strategic Arms Control," paper presented at the PONARS Eurasia Policy Conference, Washington, DC, September 2011, p. 112; see importance of bilateral arms control to Russia in Stephen J. Blank: "Russia and Arms Control: Are There Opportunities for the Obama Administration?" Carlisle, PA: Strategic Studies Institute, U.S. Army War College, March 2009, available from *www.strategicstudiesinstitute.army.mil/pubs/summary.cfm?q=908*.

50. Alexei Fenenko: "Between MAD and Flexible Response," *Russia in Global Affairs*, June 22, 2011, available from *eng.globalaffairs.ru/number/Between-MAD-and-Flexible-Response-15242*.

51. Foreign Minister Lavrov has called for the withdrawal of tactical nuclear weapons to national territory: "При этом первым шагом в решении данной проблемы при всех обстоятельствах должен быть вывод ТЯО на территорию государства, которое им располагает, и уничтожение инфраструктуры его размещения за рубежом" ("In this case, the first step to solve this problem must in all circumstances be the withdrawal of tactical nuclear weapons from the territory of the state which possesses them and the destruction of the infrastructure it controls abroad"), in Sergei Lavrov, Speech at plenary session of Conference on Disarmament, March 1, 2011, available from *www.mid. ru/brp_4.nsf/sps/DC036EDF3687A901C325784600474F50*; Jacek Durkalec: "Reductions of Tactical Nuclear Weapons in Europe: Unbinding the Gordian Knot," Warsaw, Poland: Polish Institute of International Relations, Strategic File No. 16, May 2011.

52. Before New START was ratified in the Russian State Duma, Sergei Lavrov noted the impact of U.S.-Russia conventional imbalance on strategic stability: "Он заявил, что на стратегическую стабильность скорее оказывают влияние неядерные стратегические вооружения, над которыми работают в США, планы размещения оружия в космосе и дисбаланс в обычных вооружениях и вооруженных силах двух стран" ("He announced that strategic stability will be more influenced by the non-nuclear strategic weapons, which the USA is working on, plans for placing weapons in space and the imbalance in conventional weapons and armed forces between the two countries."), from Irina Kostiukova: "Ни одной ракеты резать не будем" (We Will Not Cut A Single Rocket), *Vzglyad*, January 14, 2011, available from *vz.ru/politics/2011/1/14/461002.html*.

53. Pavel Podvig: "Russia's Nuclear Forces: Between Disarmament and Modernization," *Proliferation Papers*, No. 37, Spring 2011, available from *www.ifri.org/?page=contribution-detail&id=6649&id_ provenance=97*.

54. Dmitry Rogozin has expressed skepticism about placing interceptors in Poland to defend against an Iranian missile attack. As *Der Spiegel* commented, "the defense system in Poland is too far away from Iran, according to [Dmitry] Rogozin. 'With missiles it is like with ducks,' he said. 'You are best off shooting them at the start, when they are flying lower and more slowly,'" from Matthias Schepp: "A New Arms Race Looms between Russia and US," *Der Spiegel*, December 6, 2011, available from *www.spiegel.de/ international/europe/0,1518,801961,00.html*.

55. White House, "Fact Sheet: Implementing Missile Defense in Europe," available from *www.whitehouse.gov/the-press-office/2011/09/15/fact-sheet-implementing-missile-defense-europe*; see letter reaffirming U.S. commitment to New START and missile defense in Senator Richard Lugar, "Lugar Responds to Proposed Missile Defense Amendment," available from *www.foreign.senate. gov/press/ranking/release/lugar-responds-to-proposed-missile-defense-amendment*.

56. Dmitry Medvedev, "Statement in connection with the situation concerning the NATO countries' missile defence system in Europe," available from *eng.news.kremlin.ru/transcripts/3115*; Dmitri Trenin: "The U.S.-Russia Reset in Recess," *The New York Times*, November 29, 2011, available from *www.nytimes.com/2011/11/30/ opinion/the-us-russian-reset-in-recess.html?pagewanted=2&_r=3*.

57. For example, the idea behind the recently-launched Euro-Atlantic Security Initiative (EASI) is to create "an inclusive Euro-Atlantic Security Community" where the United States, Russia, and European countries work together to address common security challenges. The authors of the EASI working group paper on missile defense call for the development of a joint defense system that features Russia as an equal partner. For more, see Stephen Hadley *et al.*, *Missile Defense: Toward a New Paradigm*, Washington, DC: Carnegie Endowment for International Peace, February 2012, available from *carnegieendowment.org/2012/02/03/missile-defense-toward-new-paradigm/9cvz*.

58. "The Russians realize that deployment of a truly capable U.S. BMD system is a matter of a relatively distant future . . .", in Mikhail Tsypkin: "Russian politics, policy-making and American missile defence," *International Affairs*, Vol. 85, No. 4, July 2009, p. 795; Sergei Lavrov describes Russia's fear of an expanded missile defense system: "А кроме того, мы прекрасно понимаем, что американская стратегическая ПРО будет развиваться, как технически, так и географически. Скорее всего, уже в обозримом будущем мы услышим разговор о сотнях и даже тысячах ракет-перехватчиков в самых различных частях планеты, включая и Европу" ("And in addition, we are well aware that the U.S. strategic missile defense will be developed, both technically and geographically. It is most likely that in the foreseeable future, we will hear of hundreds and even thousands of interceptor missiles in various parts of the world, including Europe."), in Russian Foreign Minister Sergei Lavrov, Interview with *Gazeta Wyborcza*, February 7, 2008, available from *www.mid. ru/brp_4.nsf/0/F7882ED08D806CD4C32573E90040BC50*.

59. Russian experts argue that the issue of missile defense and nuclear arms control are intertwined: "Дальнейшее сокращение ядерных вооружений России и США резко увеличит роль ПРО в стратегическом балансе…любые дальнейшие сокращения стратегических ядерных вооружений возможны только при сотрудничестве России и США в сфере ПРО" ("Further reduction of nuclear weapons in Russia and the U.S. will dramatically increase the role of missile defense in the strategic balance . . . any further reductions in strategic nuclear weapons will only be possible through cooperation between the U.S. and Russia in missile defense."), from Sergei Rogov *et al.*, "Судьба стратегических вооружений после Праги" ("The Fate of Strategic Weapons After Prague"), *Nezavisimaya Gazeta*, August 27, 2010, available from *www.ng.ru/printed/244375*; Senator DeMint comment on missile defense: "But, is it not desirable for us to have a missile defense system that renders their threat useless?" in U.S. Congress, "The New START Treaty (Treaty Doc. 111-5)," Hearings before the Committee on Foreign Relations, United States Senate, 111th Congress, 2nd sess., Washington, DC: U.S. Government Printing Office, 2010, p. 74.

60. "Medvedev sees arms race if missile shield not agreed," *BBC*, November 30, 2010, available from *www.bbc.co.uk/news/world-europe-11872801*.

61. Tsypkin, pp. 792-793.

62. *Ibid*, p. 796; as stated in the 2008 Bucharest summit declaration, "NATO welcomes Ukraine's and Georgia's Euro-Atlantic aspirations for membership in NATO. We agreed today that these countries will become members of NATO." "Bucharest Summit Declaration," April 3, 2008, available from *www.nato.int/cps/en/natolive/official_texts_8443.htm*.

63. Dmitry Zaks: "Medvedev warns West of new arms race," *AFP*, November 30, 2010, available from *www.google.com/hosted-news/afp/article/ALeqM5inQ7EshxwGdXDWtgBeblBdgHXFzg?docId=CNG.3133022946c01e9ed0150ebaf5299535.2c1*.

64. "Если они, как официально заявляется, ни за что не позволят Ирану создать ядерное оружие, то строить обширную и дорогостоящую систему ЕвроПРО для защиты от иранских ракет в обычном оснащении – значит стрелять из пушки по воробьям" ("If, as it is officially announced, they do not allow Iran to develop nuclear weapons, then building an extensive and expensive European missile defense system to protect against conventional Iranian missiles would be like using a sledgehammer to crack a nut."), in Alexei Arbatov: "Противоракетные перипетии" (Missile Defense Vicissitudes), *Nezavisimaya Gazeta*, November 7, 2011, available from *www.ng.ru/politics/2011-11-07/3_kartblansh.html*.

65. Tsypkin, p. 790.

66. Steve Gutterman: "Russia's Putin warns West over missile defense: report," *Reuters*, December 1, 2010, available from *www.reuters.com/article/2010/12/01/us-russia-putin-missiles-idUSTRE-6B01A620101201*.

67. Maria Antonova: "Medvedev warns of Cold War over missile defence," *AFP*, May 18, 2011, available from *www.google.com/hostednews/afp/article/ALeqM5g9u7mY_6A7uHvnGuL1n5KKAtjPTw?docId=CNG.721e4536dfb27a26cdf97735f3506862.2d1*.

68. "Russia to Bolster Missile Site Terrorism Defenses," *Global Security Newswire*, January 9, 2012, available from *www.nti.org/gsn/article/russia-bolster-missile-site-terrorism-defenses/*.

69. Craig Whitlock, "U.S. looks to nonnuclear weapons to use as deterrent," *The Washington Post*, April 8, 2010.

70. Alexei Arbatov, "Preventing an Arms Race in Space," in Alexei Arbatov and Vladimir Dvorkin, eds., *Outer Space: Weapons, Diplomacy, and Security*, Washington, DC: Carnegie Endowment for International Peace, 2010, p. 81.

71. James Acton *et al.*, *Beyond New START: Advancing U.S. National Security through Arms Control with Russia*, Washington, DC: Center for Strategic and International Studies, September 2011, p. 12.

72. As several Russian experts have argued, Russia will seek to impose limits on an enhanced Conventional Prompt Global Strike (CPGS) system: "Вряд ли Россия согласится не засчитывать такие ракеты в уровни СНВ. Это – угроза, которая может взорвать Пражский договор" ("Russia is unlikely to agree not to count these missiles within the START levels. This is a threat which could blow up the Prague agreement."), from Sergei Rogov *et al.*, "Судьба стратегических вооружений после Праги" ("The Fate of Strategic Weapons After Prague"), *Nezavisimaya Gazeta*, August 27, 2010, available from *www.ng.ru/printed/244375*; see also James Acton, *Low Numbers: A Practical Path to Deep Nuclear Reductions*, Washington, DC: Carnegie Endowment for International Peace, 2011, pp. 20-21.

73. David E. Sanger and Thom Shanker, "U.S. Faces Choice on New Weapons for Fast Strikes," *The New York Times*, April 22, 2010.

74. Pavel Podvig, "Russia and the Prompt Global Strike Plan," paper presented at the PONARS Policy Conference, Washington, DC, Center for Strategic and International Studies, December 2006, pp. 1-3.

75. Dmitry Medvedev, "Statement in connection with the situation concerning the NATO countries' missile defence system in Europe," available from *eng.kremlin.ru/transcripts/3115.*

76. As one Russian scholar has argued, "Even as Russian politicians, military, and non-governmental experts continue to criticize American plans for Global Strike, they simultaneously advocate acquisition of similar capability by Russia," from Sokov, p. 241. Putin has also announced the goal of developing "high precision weapons" that will be "capable of meeting combat goals that are comparable with the current role of the nuclear deterrence forces," while at the same time hedging by maintaining a robust nuclear deterrent. See Vladimir V. Putin, "Being Strong: National Security Guarantees for Russia," *Rossiiskaya Gazeta,* February 20, 2012, available from *premier.gov.ru/eng/events/news/18185/.*

77. "Ballistic Missile Defense Agreement Between the United States of America and Romania," September 13, 2011, available from *www.state.gov/r/pa/prs/ps/2011/09/172258.htm*; "Joint Statement on the U.S.-Poland Ballistic Missile Defense Agreement," September 15, 2011, available from *www.state.gov/r/pa/prs/ps/2011/09/172439.htm.*

78. Russia has threatened retaliation if the 2012 Chicago summit bears no fruit on missile defense: "President Dmitry Medvedev in November threatened to deploy new missiles against the shield if no deal is reached. NATO leaders have said they hope to arrive at a solution at a Russia-NATO summit in Chicago in May 2012." Nickolaus von Twickel, "Lavrov Warns U.S. on Missile Defense," *The Moscow Times,* January 19, 2012, available from *www.themoscowtimes.com/news/article/lavrov-warns-us-on-missile-deal/451270.html*; "U.S. wishes more progress in missile shield talks with Russia," *RIA Novosti,* January 10, 2012, available from *en.rian.ru/russia/20120110/170687726.html.*

79. David Alexander, "U.S., Russia arms negotiators plan stability talks," *Reuters,* January 12, 2012, available from *www.reuters.com/article/2012/01/12/us-usa-russia-armscontrol-idUSTRE80B29220120112.*

CHAPTER 9

PLACING A RENMINBI SIGN ON STRATEGIC STABILITY AND NUCLEAR REDUCTIONS

Lora Saalman

INTRODUCTION

In China, everything from its "peaceful rise" (*heping jueqi*) to "harmonious society" (*hexie shehui*) has been predicated on the necessity of maintaining stability to ensure continued economic growth. Yet in the nuclear realm, this has led to a paradox. While China's rapid development would enable it to greatly expand its nuclear arsenal, this same priority of economic progress has compelled it to forgo deleterious arms racing.[1] As part of this construct, interdependence is key.

Recent focus on interdependence in Washington circles[2] has begun to filter into the work of a small but growing number of Chinese analysts working on nuclear and related strategic issues.[3] In their view, instead of "numbers" under arms race or "transparency" under crisis stability,[4] it is interdependence driving bilateral nuclear relations. This web of economic and strategic ties is increasingly seen as providing a protective layer that ballistic missile defense cannot.

Interdependence has taken on increased importance, in part, because it fits neatly into the conceptual construct that drives China's relations with the rest of the world, one based on intertwined interests and economic incentives. Yet, along with "interdependence" (*huxiang yilai*), there exists a parallel and in many ways more pervasive discourse on comprehensive national power (CNP) (*zonghe guoli*) within China.[5] Within the nuclear realm, China's lack of comparative political, economic, and military power has been cited as constraining its ability to effectively participate in strategic stability talks or nuclear reduction negotiations.[6]

Despite this fact, Chinese claims of inadequate CNP are growing difficult to justify. China exerts a palpable and growing economic presence in the international community, which is increasingly bolstered by political and military prowess. This growing leverage may bring Beijing to the strategic stability discussion table, as it feels its interests and concerns are more likely to be heard. However, China's presence does not necessarily guarantee meaningful engagement, much less nuclear reductions.

So while much ink has been spilled in exploring whether China will race to parity in the face of U.S. and Russian nuclear reductions, not enough has been devoted to whether it has adequate incentives to move towards zero. Applying interdependence as a foundation for strategic stability suggests that Chinese experts may find the opportunity costs of disarmament too great. Moreover, it suggests that "strategic stability" in the U.S.-China context is ultimately the wrong term, at the wrong time, for the wrong set of strategic relations.

CHINA AND STRATEGIC STABILITY

While U.S.-China strategic stability came to the fore in the U.S. *Nuclear Posture Review* (NPR) released in 2010, bilateral strategic stability talks at the Track-II level have existed for years. Nonetheless, the concept's application vis-à-vis China in an official U.S. document has made it the term of choice in pursuing expanded and enhanced U.S.-China strategic dialogues since 2010.[7]

Strategic stability is generally understood to be divided into two forms: crisis stability and arms race stability.[8] These concepts were extensively analyzed in the U.S.-Soviet context and many believe they contributed to stabilizing the arms race between Washington and Moscow. In the U.S.-China strategic context, however, this heavily baggage-laden Cold War term and its conceptual implications have the potential to exacerbate some of the very issues the concept is supposed to help redress.

In an attempt to foster greater transparency and mutual trust, U.S. and other analysts have consistently pressed China to become more transparent in the nuclear realm. Yet, a long-standing mantra in China maintains that it is already transparent enough when it comes to nuclear posture and intent. Analysts assert that, were China to be more open about nuclear force structure and components, its ability to maintain a posture of limited, much less minimum, credible deterrence would be damaged.[9]

This is not merely a claim to frustrate U.S. interlocutors, but a reality. Overabundance of details about an arsenal predicated on a restrained nuclear posture and size enhances the ability to decapitate it, in largest part because it can help the stronger nation to narrow the scope of the targeting problem. Nuclear transparency is thus seen as leaving China more vulnerable, and is often seen as tantamount to the United States seeking primacy, whether nuclear or otherwise. Ultimately, the concept of transparency in China is predicated upon the idea that such openness is possible for the powerful, not the weak.

China's reticence to engage also stems from how the term "transparency" *(toumingdu)* has long been applied in the U.S.-China context. For decades, U.S. experts have applied the word as a means to pry greater engagement out of China on myriad subjects, leaving it overused, vague, and ultimately pejorative. Simply using the word "transparency," without specifics or targeted proposals for increased engagement will not lead to greater interaction. In fact, the term has become so negatively charged within China, that it is best not used at all.

Another issue is that the term "strategic stability" is ambiguous, providing ample room for unofficial interpretations to gain currency. The 2010 U.S. NPR applied this term repeatedly to characterize U.S. relations with both China and Russia, but ultimately did not define what it means in the U.S.-China context. Instead, Chinese experts fill in the blanks—and not necessarily in positive ways.

When both Chinese and U.S. official circles maintain such a lack of clarity, whether in terms of posture or rhetoric, unofficial evaluations and conclusions are more likely to gain a wider audience than they might otherwise achieve.[10] While this may be the price that both sides pay for strategic ambiguity, filtration of these analyses into official policy remains an ever-present possibility.

Strategic stability's ambiguity in U.S. pronouncements is also seen by many in China as part and parcel of U.S. efforts to maintain and augment its strategic advantage. In fact, Chinese experts who play a role in shaping China's political and military policies have already begun to assert that China must compensate for the primacy afforded the United States by such systems as ballistic missile defense (BMD) and conventional prompt global strike (CPGS).[11]

Whether via countermeasures, possessing the same systems, altering nuclear posture, or even increasing nuclear weapons numbers, Chinese strategic and technical experts are debating how best to respond to shifts in U.S. military planning that in their view appear aimed at them.[12]

Nuclear programs are just one part of a larger military restructuring on the part of the United States, much of which seem to be targeting China.[13] This has been amplified in the wake of the U.S. Department of Defense (DoD) January 2012 report delineating a shift in defense priorities, or "pivot," toward Asia and the Pacific.[14]

When combined with the U.S. transition from a focus on a quantity-based to a capabilities-based nuclear posture shored up by advanced conventional capabilities, China increasingly sees itself as the long-term U.S. target. In this light, calls for strategic stability talks are read within China as just another tactic in U.S. attempts to maintain the upper hand by forcing China into greater transparency.[15]

Faced with U.S. defense adjustments seen as directed at China, the greater transparency requested by the United States could actually exacerbate tensions rather than allay them if they seem to be part of an overall effort to augment American superiority. In the wake of increased U.S. emphasis on low nuclear numbers and advanced capabilities, however, what is most likely to result is not quantitative competition, but rather qualitative.

This stems from the fact that China's concept of credible minimum deterrence is not simply about nuclear warhead numbers, but also the planning, infrastructure, posture, and policies surrounding the arsenal. China is just as preoccupied with U.S. conventional force modernization as nuclear, if not more so.

Chinese analysts see Washington's gradual relinquishment of its nuclear arsenal as a way to liberate funds needed to expand U.S. expenditures on conventional forces, especially in the Asia-Pacific. Given China's self-proclaimed posture of being passive or responsive (*beidong*) to U.S. military shifts and threats, it would be likely to respond in turn.

Experts within China are still committed to retaliation or "striking back" (*fanji*) in the face of provocation, and this will be likely to drive China's conventional and strategic warhead numbers, force structure, and deployment.[16] As such, U.S. strategic planners need to be aware of the potential deleterious consequences of using a rigid and outdated strategic stability model, when those in China view such relations holistically and as being linked to comprehensive national power.

This balance, or rather imbalance, in power is especially sensitive to the development of U.S. BMD, CPGS, and other advanced conventional systems.[17] While these programs are real enough, even their specter has a real impact on Chinese perceptions. Long-defunct U.S. programs continue to emerge in Chinese experts' discussions as evidence of U.S. intent, such as the robust nuclear earth penetrator and the reliable replacement warhead.[18] The shelf life of these programs in Chinese discourse suggests that old assumptions about U.S. intent and the potential for nuclear coercion continue to play a profound role in the Chinese strategic psyche.[19]

As such, U.S. programs such as Phased Adaptive Approach (PAA), which is read by any number of analysts in China as missile defense "without end," has left Chinese planners in a spiraling debate over how best to respond.[20] An increased U.S. conventional military presence in Asia will do the same. When it comes to BMD, the Chinese response has been to undertake a transformation from observation of U.S. missile defense capabilities to pursuit of countermeasures and acquisition of these capabilities.[21] This response pattern promises to occur in any number of other weapons systems.

Thus, rather than quantitative race to parity, what China seeks is a qualitative race to parity. A qualitative race to parity implies that China would be compelled to pursue similar capabilities to keep apace of the United States, contrasted with a quantitative race to parity, under which China would be compelled to attain or exceed U.S. nuclear weapons numbers.

China learned from the Soviet Union's experience not to seek costly numerical parity with the United States. Doing so is seen as having a deleterious effect on even the most robust economy. Chinese experts also came away with the idea that the United States is only willing to meaningfully engage with an adversary that possesses the same systems. China's anti-satellite and ground-based missile interception tests reflect this logic. It is not uncommon to hear in China that such tests were meant to draw the United States back to the negotiating table.[22]

With the decline of Russia as a conventional weapons power, Chinese analysts have also noted that its reliance on nuclear weapons has only risen.[23] In the face of conventional inferiority vis-à-vis the United States, nuclear weapons still have a central role to play.[24] Security comes from having just enough capabilities to keep the United States at bay and avoiding an unfavorable quantitative race. Systems like BMD and CPGS are often viewed within China as U.S. attempts to draw it into just such an arms race.

In short, the U.S. expressed desire for enhanced strategic stability talks with China and Russia, in the very same document that argues BMD and CPGS pave the way to nuclear reductions, is contradictory. These systems are seen within China as undermining stability and harming the potential for nuclear disarmament. In some arenas, development and deployment of such systems may compel China to respond in ways that the United States wishes to avoid, such as the aforementioned qualitative race to parity.

A sole focus on nuclear forces absent broader considerations thus has the potential to exacerbate rather than ameliorate U.S.-Chinese tensions. This suggests that traditional Cold War concepts and definitions — such as "transparency," "arms race stability," or "crisis stability" — might not be the best rubrics to use in China's case. It also leads to the inevitable question as to whether there are other forms of strategic stability that might be more applicable in the Chinese context. If so, could interdependence serve as this new foundation?

"INTERDEPENDENT" STRATEGIC STABILITY

When it comes to U.S.-China strategic relations, the use of a strategic stability framework based on traditional constructs and assumptions of crisis stability and arms race stability is contrary — and potentially even counterproductive — to achieving stable strategic relations. As new permutations and definitions of strategic stability come under discussion, however, one of the most likely to receive acceptance in China is based on interdependence.[25]

In its current form, this oft-cited term in China underlies efforts to shape international perceptions regarding China's peaceful emergence in the international system. It is rooted in maintaining the prerequisite domestic, regional, and global stability needed to sustain China's economic growth.

Interdependence in the nuclear context posits that increasingly intertwined interests, in this case between the United States and China, would stay the hand of a country contemplating a nuclear attack. While of particular relevance in the economic realm, this term has increasingly been applied to the environmental and other consequences of nuclear exchange between two countries. In an interdependent world, collateral damage is difficult to control and would likely cause just as much harm to the initiator of the attack as to the recipient.

As a concept, interdependence corresponds with an ideational architecture that reaches back into Chinese annals to emphasize harmony, balance, and peace. These terms have been applied by China in recent years in an attempt to both shape and assuage domestic and international concerns over and fallout from its growth trajectory.[26] As such, they are applied to what might otherwise be seen as destabilizing trends, forming such combinations as "harmonious development" (*hexie fazhan*), "strategic balance" (*zhanlue pingheng*), and "peaceful rise" (*heping jueqi*).

This rhetorical constructivism operates on the premise of reducing the chance of China's rapid and uneven development triggering internal instability and external perceptions of hegemonic intent. China seeks to shape the world view. Much in the same way, China's nuclear strategy could also be considered constructivist in that it uses a cultural lens to attempt to justify and explain China's responsive nuclear posture and policy.[27] In doing so, Chinese interlocutors have ended up clouding the actual conditions on the ground with often vague and empty terminology that, just as with U.S. experts' use of the term "transparency," elicits questions of intent from the other side.

As part of this trend, enhanced stability, economic and other nonmilitary issues have increasingly begun to permeate U.S.-China strategic relations. The most recent evidence came with the establishment of the U.S.-China Strategic and Economic Dialogue (S&ED) in 2009. This was followed the next year by the Fifth U.S.-China Strategic Dialogue on Strategic Nuclear Dynamics,[28] during which senior Chinese participants voiced support for an economic and strategic mix when it comes to nuclear talks and negotiations.

This is not simply a coincidence. Strategic and economic convergence amplifies the strongest element of China's much sought-after comprehensive national power triad, namely economic power.[29] A number of Chinese experts have historically cited insufficient CNP as hindering China's ability to be more transparent and engage in high-level strategic stability or nuclear reduction talks.[30] Economics is the priority, in other words, and strategic issues are subservient to this overriding concern.

Yet, China's growing economic might and likely continuing growth erodes the argument that China has insufficient CNP to participate in serious discussions of its power. In fact, China's economic ascent places it in a much more advantageous negotiating position, particularly in forums where economic issues predominate or impinge upon strategic ones, such as at the U.S.-China S&ED. China appears to be leveraging its economic advantages to acquire bargaining power on strategic issues.

Pairing these concerns, in fact, mitigates a significant degree of the imbalance pointed to by such experts as Colonel (Ret.) Teng Jianqun as hindering U.S.-China strategic talks.[31] China's economic strength provides it with a stronger foundation and leverage when sitting at the table across from countries like the United States. Placing economic affairs at the forefront of such talks hits upon an arena in which China can and will exert the most influence, as visible in the following quotation:

> Peaceful rise and the peaceful transfer of global power under the nuclear balance is an incontrovertible law. Within Sino-U.S. strategic competition under the nuclear balance and the minimum level of mutually assured destruction-based strategic stability, economic power plays a decisive role. China's continuous economic growth will inevitably prompt a balance of power between China and the United States in the midst of China's peaceful rise. . . . Economic power is the most fundamental and deepest foundation of comprehensive national power, but the economic power of the United States is shrinking. [32]

Given U.S. economic difficulties and China's burgeoning growth in the past decade, political power and economic power have become increasingly connected within discussions in China. This shows that behind the constructivist prism through which China seeks to portray its "peaceful development," there are more realist calculations of relative power.

While these two pillars of CNP, namely economic and political, may not obviate all of China's concerns over a military gap, they place China on more equal footing. Most importantly, this status reduces China's opportunity costs of participating in higher-level strategic stability talks. However, there should be doubts as to whether they will lead to more substantive and productive Chinese engagement on strategic issues.

Interdependence is not only a recipe for stability, but also a potential cause of friction. China's tensions with the United States over fiscal policy, with Japan over rare earths exports, with India over resource exploration, with Vietnam over fossil fuel-rich deposits, and with Indonesia over shipping lanes are just a few of the tensions interwoven with increasing interdependence.

While not likely to lead to nuclear tension or conflict, such incidents should give pause in evaluating whether or not interdependence is a reliable foundation for strategic stability writ large. Even if isolated at the nuclear level, strategic stability predicated on interdependence is not necessarily more stable or predictable than that based on arms race stability or crisis stability.

For example, if the ultimate test of U.S.-China strategic stability were to occur, namely a conflict over Taiwan, interdependence would not necessarily prevent nuclear coercion or worse from occurring. In fact, for conflict to even erupt, the People's Republic of China (PRC) would have had to already make a conscious decision not to rely on its increasing economic and cultural interdependence with Taiwan.

In such a scenario, expecting interdependence to do for the United States and China what it could not do for the PRC and Taiwan represents a leap in logic and faith. While assuming that such a conflict would be conventional in nature, it would be a mistake to ignore the role of nuclear weapons in the background, shoring up capabilities and hopefully constraining conventional escalation.

Moreover, insertion of economic interdependence as a key variable in strategic stability talks also changes the dynamics of U.S.-China interaction. If getting Chinese officials to attend higher-level strategic stability talks is the aim, then this approach makes sense. However, if greater transparency and mutual compromise is the goal, then this methodology needs to be carefully evaluated in terms of effectiveness.

At the Track-I.V and Track-II level, there exists an array of events on strategic relations that are already quite broad in scope.[33] Even when focusing exclusively on nuclear relations, the range of issues raised at such meetings is so expansive that the discourse is often redundant, with the same list of complaints and concerns reemerging from year to year.[34]

There is no guarantee that placing nuclear discussions at the official level and in a framework that pairs economic and strategic concerns would allow for greater focus. Official engagement is beneficial to building a veneer of strategic trust, but expanding this discourse to cover all matter of strategic and economic issues is tantamount to taking what is already a diffuse field of strategic issues and setting the goal posts even farther apart.

On issues that constitute strategic stability talks, setting these posts far apart on such issues as disarmament and transparency may be exactly what China is seeking to do. Interdependent strategic stability could serve in providing Beijing with a low-cost means of participation, but not necessarily with a rationale for engaging in high-cost nuclear transparency or reductions. This is the reason that China's "costs" and "benefits" must be better understood.

CHINA'S DISARMAMENT CALCULUS

How serious is China about disarmament? In Chinese writings, the United States maintains leadership in the strategic arena,[35] while others are observing, waiting, and reacting. Even embedded in overall positive reactions to U.S. President Barack Obama's Prague speech in 2009 and the U.S. *Nuclear Posture Review* in 2010 remain Chinese caveats and wariness of U.S. intent.[36]

This internal discourse is not indicative of a country that is actively pushing towards nuclear disarmament. While Chinese experts and leaders have often voiced their support for nuclear disarmament, there is little to indicate that this commitment is more than rhetorical and passive.[37]

Thus, while international experts remain fixated on whether or not China's nuclear arsenal will "race to parity," there should be just as much if not more analysis on whether or not it will shrink or follow the path towards zero. In making this determination, it is critical to evaluate whether or not China believes it is in its best interest to do so. The reality is that there is little for China to gain and much for it to lose in a world free of nuclear weapons.

While Chinese arms control experts frequently assail the U.S. unwillingness to relinquish nuclear deterrence, China itself has not shown real willingness to do so. This is not simply a function of the U.S. nuclear arsenal. Even in a post-Obama Prague speech and the New Strategic Arms Limitation Treaty (New START) world, the role of China's nuclear deterrent remains paramount. Recent reports on China's test launching of DF-41, JL-2, and DF-5A missiles all point towards this fact.

Nuclear weapons have served and will likely continue to serve as China's cost-efficient equalizer with the United States.[38] In point of fact, they could be said to be a corrective measure for bolstering the military leg of the CNP triad, which despite its rapid growth continues to lag behind the political and economic sphere. For decades within China, nuclear weapons have lain in the background and served as the ultimate guarantors against political, economic, and military coercion. If conventional weapons become the primary form of deterrence in a nuclear free world, China's costs are only likely to rise.

Despite this fact, most studies on disarmament tend to divorce conventional military concerns from strategic. They tend to ignore that for not only the United States, nuclear disarmament is tantamount to significant conventional force restructuring. For China, conventional build-up is not necessarily lower in overall political and economic expenditure than maintenance of a minimum, or even limited, credible deterrent.

No matter whether in a nuclear or nuclear-free world, it is conventional weapons pursuits and advances, not nuclear ones, which ultimately threaten China's security and the interdependent equilibrium it seeks. In a nuclear world, systems like BMD and CPGS threaten to reduce or even decapitate the Chinese nuclear deterrent. In a nuclear-free world, these systems have the potential to force China to increase its expenditures on new conventional weaponry in air, land, sea, and space.

Unsurprisingly, facing these constraints, it would be difficult to make the case for genuine disarmament in China. Its analysts continue to argue that nuclear reductions remain largely a matter for the United States and Russia.[39] Statements from China's officials and experts continue to assert that China will participate in discussions when the time is "appropriate." Yet China is being deliberately vague in its rhetoric—the truth is that there is no truly appropriate time. As stated within China's 2010 *Defense White Paper*:

> China has always stood for the complete prohibition and thorough destruction of nuclear weapons. China maintains that countries possessing the largest nuclear arsenals bear special and primary responsibility for nuclear disarmament. They should further drastically reduce their nuclear arsenals in a verifiable, irreversible and legally-binding manner, so as to create the necessary conditions for the complete elimination of nuclear weapons. When conditions are appropriate, other nuclear-weapon states should also join in multilateral negotiations on nuclear disarmament. To attain the ultimate goal of complete and thorough nuclear disarmament, the international community should develop, at an appropriate time, a viable, long-term plan with different phases, including the conclusion of a convention on the complete prohibition of nuclear weapons.[40]

The above quotation, in spite of the certitude of its opening sentence, reflects this temporal uncertainty and hedging on the part of China. Chinese experts continue to cite President Obama's 2009 Prague speech declaring nuclear disarmament to be a goal that "will not be reached quickly—perhaps not in my lifetime" as a rationale for delay.[41] Similarly, the 2010 U.S. NPR declared that the United States will maintain its nuclear deterrence capabilities "as long as nuclear weapons exist."[42]

Both countries in their attempts to mitigate security concerns at home are left in a long-term sequencing standstill abroad. China may wish to have the United States and Russia go first, but implicit in their grand bargain is that they — much like the United States — want to go last. Since China's nuclear deterrent is a response to U.S. military power, as long as the United States retains such capability, in particular its formidable nuclear arsenal, China has a powerful incentive not to disarm.

Thus, when Chinese analysts argue for U.S. and Russian reductions of the role of nuclear weapons in their arsenal,[43] they overlook the fact that China would be hard pressed to do the same, even in response to a drastic or complete reduction on the part of the United States and Russia. Overall, there is no compelling argument for China to change the nuclear status quo.

China's smaller nuclear arsenal has served as an adequate means of deterrence, whether in the face of a massive Soviet and U.S. build-up or more comprehensive U.S. military capabilities and new nuclear entrants following the Cold War. Thus, while Chinese articles have frequently decried ongoing U.S. "Cold War thinking" (lengzhan siwei), devotion to "nuclear deterrence" (he weishe),[44] and "double standards" (shuangzhong biaozhun),[45] China also retains a conflicted, if not outright skeptical, stance towards disarmament at its core. This is despite its staunch rhetoric to the contrary.

China's reluctance to embark on disarmament is made easier by its position as the weaker — in nuclear terms — state that can point to the sluggishness of U.S. and Russian efforts at disarmament as justification for its own unwillingness to join in the discussion. Chinese experts can always raise U.S. efforts or initiatives that are lacking, thereby justifying China's own inaction.[46] As just one example:

It seems that although Obama issued the concept
of a 'nuclear-free world,' the pace of U.S. nuclear
weapon modernization will not stop. . . . the United
States intends to strengthen its capacity in construction of advanced conventional weaponry, including
prompt global strike capabilities, etc., while at the
same time not intending to engage in any form of
restraint on its development and deployment of missile defenses. These two aspects have the potential to
threaten strategic stability between great powers and
possibly have a significant impact on the U.S. nuclear
disarmament agenda.[47]

Even if the United States were to eliminate every
last warhead, the extant discourse within China about
U.S. ability to reconstitute its arsenal should give
pause as to how many — or in this case few — weapons would ever be "enough." There will always be the
chance for new advanced strategic and conventional
systems provoking adequate concern for China to
justify maintaining or even reconfiguring its nuclear
arsenal in response, such as conventional prompt
global strike.

When compared with the costs of conventional
arms races and the lowered threshold on conflict,
China's nuclear arsenal has not only kept U.S. nuclear,
but also conventional military, leverage at bay. Overwhelming conventional dominance, not just nuclear,
can be used for coercion. Thus, as much as coercion is
frequently couched in nuclear terms within China, it
impinges upon the whole concept of CNP within China. In a world free of nuclear weapons, conventional
coercion would only grow, as would the need to find
a deterrent replacement for nuclear weapons.[48]

So while it may seem that eliminating the U.S. nuclear threat is the key to China's ability to relinquish its own nuclear arsenal, this is not necessarily the case. In fact, in the absence of the nuclear equalizer, the demands of trying to maintain technological pace with U.S. conventional weapons developments could be even greater than simply maintaining a small nuclear deterrent. Learning from the Soviet experience, competing with the United States in a nuclear numbers game is a lose-lose, not "win-win" (*shuang ying*) scenario.

China appears to be pursuing strategic modernization aimed at maintaining this relationship vis-à-vis the United States. China is increasing its investments in conventional defense, options they select to counter U.S. capabilities in more cost-effective ways. China's pursuits in decoys and chaff to counter BMD, DF-21D missiles to deny naval access, and hit-to-kill technology featured in their anti-satellite and anti-ballistic missile test are just a few examples.[49]

As visible in Figure 9-1, these systems are much less costly than those required to counter a dominant U.S. conventional military in a nuclear free world, or engaging in a strategic arms race in a nuclear one.[50] Compared with its overall defense budget, estimated to be annually increasing by double digits, the cost chasm between China's strategic and conventional military modernization gapes even wider. Absent its nuclear force, China would face even greater pressure to expand its conventional capabilities to make up for the lost nuclear deterrent that forestalls U.S. coercion.

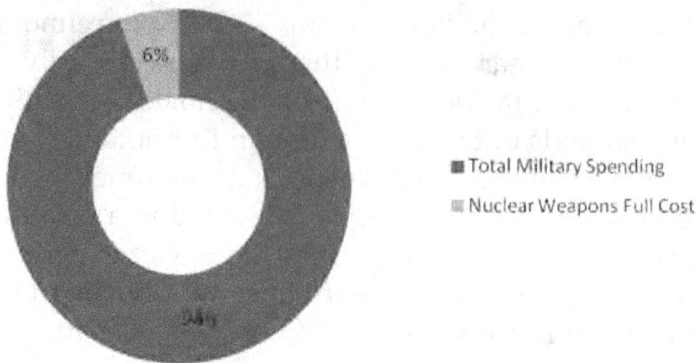

6%

■ Total Military Spending

▒ Nuclear Weapons Full Cost

Source: Bruce G. Blair and Matthew A. Brown, "World Spending on Nuclear Weapons Surpasses $1 Trillion per Decade," Global Zero Technical Report, *Nuclear Weapons Cost Study, Global Zero*, June 2011, available from *www.globalzero.org/de/page/cost-of-nukes*.

Figure 9-1. China's Total Military and Nuclear Weapons Spending 2011.

Factoring in U.S. conventional force improvements in the absence of a nuclear force, China would be required to possess more than the basic capabilities to keep pace with the United States and prevent a "science surprise" from occurring.[51] One test of anti-satellite or BMD capabilities would likely no longer be enough. Instead, China would be compelled to expand the quality, diversity, and number of its conventional weapons systems.

The budget for such aims would be likely to far exceed China's current conventional military expenditures. The nuclear option diminishes U.S. ability to use nuclear weapons or conventional military might to coerce China. As such, even while China's strategic culture may be evolving in response to U.S. military planning, one theme remains consistent.

China is looking to forestall coercion, whether nuclear or conventional.

Therefore, no matter the rhetoric within China supporting nuclear disarmament as its ultimate goal, it is not in China's interest from a political, economic, or military perspective. China is looking to redress a power gap, not a nuclear one. In an environment in which China feels that certain legs of its CNP remains lacking, nuclear weapons shore up this chasm.

CHINA'S SKEPTICISM ABOUT U.S. MOTIVES

Fueling concerns over the opportunity costs of engagement, Chinese experts remain unconvinced that the United States is genuinely interested either in disarmament or in strategic stability based on mutual vulnerability. While some Chinese experts seem to have embraced the concept, most notably Major General Yao Yunzhu,[52] any number of writings and exchanges on the subject suggest otherwise.

Instead of pursuing strategic stability that allows China to retain its retaliatory capability, the United States is pursuing the very nuclear posture and systems that Chinese experts repeatedly cite as shattering strategic stability.[53] According to an article in *Guoji Luntan*:

> Strategic advantage as pursued by the United States does not indicate that it would undertake a nuclear attack against China, would not be concerned about China's counter attack, or that it seeks to make China's nuclear counter attack ineffective. Rather it means that the United States is using its nuclear capabilities to constrain a rising China from challenging its hegemony. In the view of the United States, only by pursuing strategic advantage can it uphold Sino-U.S. strategic

stability and balance. But in China's view, U.S. maintenance of strategic advantage equates with a loss of balance in strategic stability between the United States and China and a loss of Sino-U.S. strategic stability. It is necessary for China to improve its strategic nuclear survivability and retaliatory capabilities, in order to safeguard Sino-U.S. strategic stability and balance.[54]

In part, this oft-echoed rationale points to why U.S. inclusion of BMD and CPGS in a document detailing nuclear reductions has not been well received within China.[55] If anything, mention of such systems completely contradicts the idea that the United States seeks strategic stability with China. BMD and CPGS are symbols of U.S. intent to eliminate mutual vulnerability in both a nuclear and non-nuclear world.

However, lest it be assumed that simply assuaging Chinese concerns over ballistic missile defense will be enough to mitigate overall misgivings about the path of nuclear disarmament, the majority of writings on the subject continue to place their focus squarely on U.S. conventional weapons advances and strategic advantage (*zhanlue youshi*).[56] As one Chinese expert put it:

> In September 2009, as China's national chairman Hu Jintao at the United Nations Security Council's Association for Disarmament and Nonproliferation has already expressed, other nuclear weapon states will enter into international nuclear reductions at an appropriate time. Because this is not based on amount, under the condition that the United States continues to maintain conventional advantage and is building global ballistic missile defense, the two countries will not have much in common.[57]

While BMD and CPGS are part of the discourse, they remain just two manifestations of a perceived overall U.S. intent to maintain its "absolute advantage" (*juedui youshi*), "absolute security" (*juedui anquan*), and "absolute hegemony" (*juedui baquan*).[58] Even U.S. attempts at nonproliferation and counterproliferation meet with frequent assertions that the United States seeks to "protect its hegemonic position" (*weihu qi baquan diwei*).[59] So while Obama's championing of disarmament has received some positive acknowledgement by Chinese scholars, criticisms of U.S. hegemony continue.[60]

Because of Chinese skepticism about nuclear disarmament and the perception of relative stasis at the nuclear level, conventional systems and future U.S. advances writ large are at the core of Chinese concerns. (See Figure 9-2.) Consequently, the United States has misplaced its focus on China's potential "race to parity."

Rather, conventional arms racing should be the paramount concern. Chinese experts remain intent on how the United States intends to maintain its dominance, and possibly even increase it with the removal of the nuclear option. Despite Chinese experts' arguments to the contrary, to prevent this from occurring, China's dependence on nuclear deterrence has become even greater than that of the United States.

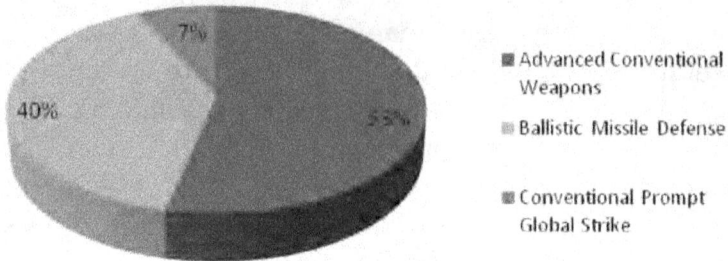

Source: Percentages derived from 139 Chinese articles covering strategic stability from periodicals including, but not limited to *Zhongguo guofang bao, Dangdai shijie, Nanjing zhengzhi xueyuan xuebao, Shijie jingji yu zhengzhi, Heping yu fazhan, Zhongguo zhanlue guancha, Gaige yu kaifang, Jiefangjun bao, Dongfang ribao, Beifang lunzhong, Guangming ribao, Guoji zhengzhi yanjiu, Guoji wenti yanjiu, Zhongguo shehui kexue yuan yuanbao, Guofang keji gongye, Liaowang xinwen zhoukan, Renmin ribao, Zhongguo gongcheng wuli yanjiuyuan keji nianbao, Xiandai guoji guanxi, Guoji zhanwang, Shijie zongheng, Shijie bao, Dangdai yatai, Xinhua meiri dianxun, Shijie jingji yu zhengzhi, Jianzai wuqi, Xiandai bingqi, Shijie bao, Taipingyang xuebao, Guoji guancha, Zhongguo hangtian, Dimian fankong wuqi, Guoji ziliao xinxi, Guoji luntan, Meiguo yanjiu, Guoji zhengzhi kexue, Guoji wenti yanjiu, Jiefangjun ribao, Guofang keji, Guoji jingji pinglun, Zhongguo jingji shibao, Jiefangjun bao, Dangdai yatai, Guoji zhengzhi, Waijiao xueyuan bao, Renmin luntan, Waijiao pinglun,* etc., downloaded from the Tsinghua University library electronic database and set to search parameters from January 1, 1915 - November 30, 2011.

Figure 9-2. Mentions of Conventional Systems in Chinese Articles on Strategic Stability.

If the United States were to relinquish its nuclear arsenal, its conventional military would serve to bolster U.S. security and by some Chinese experts' admissions place it in an even stronger position vis-à-vis the international community in a nuclear-free world. For China, eliminating its nuclear arsenal without an adequate conventional military to shore up its security and prevent coercion from occurring would place it at a severe disadvantage. Thus, an evaluation of China's opportunity costs suggests that global disarmament may not be in its best interest, no matter how interdependent U.S.-China interests become.

STABILIZING U.S.-CHINA STRATEGIC RELATIONS

Ultimately, whether arms race stability, crisis stability, or interdependent stability, the concept of "strategic stability" on the whole is misplaced when it comes to U.S.-China relations. Not only is the term too invested with the U.S.-Soviet power dynamic, it is also obsolete when it comes to current U.S.-China nuclear relations.

However, this is not so much a function of the United States' inability to effectively define the term "strategic stability" in the U.S.-China relationship. Rather, the problem is that the United States remains unable to define its relationship with China. The countless terms, from "co-stakeholders" to "strategic competitors," used to categorize and describe China and U.S. strategic relations over the years point to this very fact.[61]

By contrast, while experts in the United States have debated the U.S.-China relationship prior to and after the NPR, the response within China demonstrates that the essence of Chinese threat perceptions toward the United States has not greatly changed.[62] Whether claiming that the United States wishes to pursue "absolute advantage" or that China was "forced down" the nuclear path, Chinese experts remain unflinching in their rhetorical portrayal of U.S.-China nuclear relations.[63]

However, these arguments also remain contradictory and superficial. As long as the United States is undertaking structural changes to its nuclear posture, China by its own admission is acting in response. China's nuclear-related rhetoric may remain largely unchanged, but its nuclear posture and practice cannot be static if China is reacting to U.S. strategic posture adjustments.

This suggests that there is room for change in China's participation in such higher-level strategic talks, whether through the S&ED or another forum. China's stronger economic leverage vis-à-vis the United States places it in a stronger vantage point for engagement. Yet, while gains may be made in getting China to the table to discuss strategic issues, it is difficult to argue that these will lead to greater comity when it comes to such issues as strategic stability or disarmament.

Moreover, placing an emphasis on economic-based realities to forestall crises may not be tenable in periods of economic stress or downturns. An interdependence-based assessment that factors in both strategic and economic concerns shows that disarmament would be costly and would potentially erode China's ability to redress the gap its experts see in comprehensive national power.

If this is the case, then it is not so much the integration of strategic and economic issues that is the key to increasing U.S.-China strategic understanding, but rather integrating discussions of nuclear and strategic forces with those of conventional weapons developments. Nuclear and conventional forces ultimately interlink in Chinese analyses, so divorcing one from another is tantamount to missing the real race for parity occurring, in both qualitative and conventional terms.

Furthermore, the term "strategic stability" lends itself too easily to Chinese constructivism and abstract debates on nuclear war fighting posture and no first use (NFU) that continue to both dominate and obscure nuclear discourse and interactions.[64] These discussions must also be brought down from the theoretical to the practical level to focus on specific weapons systems and scenarios.

This can only occur through smaller scale, more targeted, and regularized meetings on specific security issues or weapons systems, such as NFU, BMD, CPGS, etc. Such meetings would also allow for the greater "transparency" and "mutual trust" that U.S. and Chinese interlocutors seek, without using these hollow terms or muddying the process with vague proposals.

Whatever the forum for interaction, the "strategic" component must not become sidelined to "economic" concerns or devolve into abstraction at such events as the U.S.-China S&ED. To prevent this, there needs to be increased research into and a case made for what exactly are the concrete benefits for China to engage on such issues as strategic stability and nuclear disarmament. Without this opportunity cost-oriented foundation, China's commitment to strategic stability talks and disarmament will remain rhetorical.

Despite Chinese experts' arguments to the contrary, it is not apparent that it is in China's interest to substantively engage on any of these issues. China sees itself as increasingly targeted by U.S. defense reorientation towards the Asia-Pacific and will likely make further qualitative nuclear and conventional adjustments to make up for any perceived or real lacunae in its security posture. Behind these shifts, nuclear deterrence promises to remain a key factor in filling any gaps between China and U.S. comprehensive national power.

In sum, no matter whether referring to strategic competition or strategic stability, labels applied to the U.S.-China power dynamic have proven to be transient. Instead, what linger are Chinese concerns over perceived U.S. attempts to negate China's ability to deter coercion, whether in a nuclear world or nuclear free world. In the final cost-benefit equation, a nuclear-free world is likely to be more economically and strategically costly for China than a nuclear one.

ENDNOTES - CHAPTER 9

1. Dr. Teng Jianqun, "Zhongmei he lingyu duihua de huigu yu zhanwang" ("Retrospect and Prospects for Sino-U.S. Dialogue in the Nuclear Arena"), *Guoji wenti yanjiu*, No. 3, March 2011, p. 28.

2. While much effort has been spent analyzing 36 references to China in the U.S. *Nuclear Posture Review* (NPR), experts in China and the United States would be well served by investing more time into just one: "The United States and China are increasingly interdependent and their shared responsibilities for addressing global security threats, such as weapons of mass destruction (WMD) proliferation and terrorism, are growing." *Nuclear Posture Review Report*, Washington, DC: U.S. Department of Defense, April 2010, available from *www.defense.gov/npr/docs/2010%20 Nuclear%20Posture%20Review%20Report.pdf*. Please see other references to interdependence in *NNSA Releases Final Request for Proposal for Consolidated Contract Competition for Nuclear Production Operations*, Washington, DC: National Nuclear Security Administration, December 14, 2011, available from *nnsa.energy.gov/ mediaroom/pressreleases/y12pantexrfp121411*.

3. These experts include Wang Honggang, Assistant Director of the Institute of American Studies at the China Institutes of Contemporary International Relations; Li Deshun, Ph.D. Candidate at the Department of International Relations of Tsinghua Universi-

ty; Fan Jishe, Deputy Director of the Center for Arms Control and Nonproliferation Studies at the Institute of American Studies of the Chinese Academy of Social Sciences; and Mei Ran, Assistant Professor at the Department of International Politics at Peking University among others. These findings are also based on interviews conducted by the author with China's arms control establishment of scientists and military and academic experts between April 2010 and September 2010, such as the China Arms Control and Disarmament Association (CACDA), Chinese Academy of Social Sciences (CASS), China Institute for Contemporary International Relations (CICIR), Academy of Military Sciences (AMS), China Institute of International Studies (CIIS), National Defense University (NDU), Shanghai Institute of Law and Politics, China Peace and Disarmament Association (CPAPD), Tsinghua University, and Fudan University. Li Deshun, Chapter VI. Recalibrating Deterrence Theory and Practice, in Lora Saalman, ed., *The China-India Nuclear Crossroads*, Carnegie-Tsinghua Center for Global Policy, Washington, DC: Carnegie Endowment for International Peace, 2012; Wang Honggang, "Meiguo de yatai zhanlue yu zhongmei guanxi de weilai fabu" ("America's Asia-Pacific Strategy and the Future of Sino-U.S. Relations"), *Xiandai guoji guanxi*, No. 1, January 20, 2011; Fan Jishe, "Meiguo he zhengce tiaozheng yu zhongguo de zhengce yingdui" ("U.S. Nuclear Policy Adjustments and China's Response"), *Guoji zhengzhi yanjiu*, No. 2, February 2010; Mei Ran, "Haijun kuozhan yu zhanlue wending: Cong yingde jingzheng dao zhongmei guanxi" ("Naval Expansion and Strategic Stability: China-U.S. Relations: From English-German Competition to China-U.S. Relations"), *Guoji zhengzhi yanjiu*, No. 4, April 2007; Wang Kaifeng, "Lengzhan hou meiguo sanwei yiti de he zhanlue yu dangdai guoji zhengzhi de liebian" ("U.S. Strategic Triad's Fission of Nuclear Strategy and Contemporary International Politics"), *Guoji zhengzhi*, No. 4, April 2001.

4. Xia Liping, "Lun goujian xin shiji daguo zhanlue wending kuangjia" ("On Building a Strategic Stability Framework for the New Century"), *Dangdai yatai*, No. 2, 2003, p. 48.

5. Yan Xuetong has exhaustively explored this issue of comprehensive national power, along with a host of other Chinese experts. Yan Xuetong, "Zhongguo jueqi de shili diwei" ("China's Rise and Power Ranking"), *Guoji zhengzhi kexue*, No. 2, February 2005, pp. 12-16; Zhao Baomin, "Jingji liliang de kaixuan-Zhong-

guo heping jueqi" ("Triumph of Economic Power-China's Peaceful Rise"), *Xi'an jiaotong daxue xuebao shehui kexueban*, No. 5, May 2010; Zhang Yeliang, "Aobama zhengfu de he zhengce" ("The Obama Administration's Nuclear Policy"), *Meiguo Yanjiu*, No. 2, February 2010, p. 13. Comprehensive National Power consists of political, military, and economic strength. Due to an error in the author's editing, the original report should have read "comprehensive national power." Lora Saalman, "China and the U.S. Nuclear Posture Review," The Carnegie Papers, Washington, DC: Carnegie-Tsinghua Center for Global Policy, Carnegie Endowment for International Peace Press, No. 2, Spring 2011, p. 6, available from *carnegieendowment.org/2011/02/28/china-and-u.s.-nuclear-posture-review/1ci*.

6. Interview conducted by the author with China's arms control establishment of scientists and military and academic experts between April 2010 and September 2010, in particular with one senior expert at the China Reform Forum.

7. Yao Yunzhu, "A Chinese Perspective on the Nuclear Posture Review," Proliferation Analysis, Washington, DC: Carnegie Endowment for International Peace, May 6, 2010; Saalman, "China and the U.S. Nuclear Posture Review," pp. 1-55.

8. This definition follows the conceptual logic of James Acton and Michael Gerson, in subsuming first-strike stability under the broader concept of crisis stability. "Beyond New START: Advancing U.S. National Security through Arms Control with Russia," Washington, DC: Center for Strategic and International Studies, September 2011.

9. Teng Jianqun, "Meiguo zheifan 'he touming' we na ban?" ("What Kind of 'Nuclear Transparency' is that of the United States?"), *Jiefangjun bao*, May 19, 2010, p. 004; Gu Yue, "Jiedu meiguo 2010 nian 'he taishi pinggu'" ("Interpreting the U.S. 2010 Nuclear Posture Review"), *Guofang keji gongye*, No. 5, May 2010, p. 66; Teng Jianqun, "Zhongmei he lingyu duihua de huigu yu zhanwang" ("Retrospect and Prospects for Sino-U.S. Dialogue in the Nuclear Arena"), *Guoji wenti yanjiu*, No. 3, 2011, p. 28.

10. Two examples of this trend are a Keir Lieber and Daryl Press article and the Dr. Phillip A. Karber project at Georgetown University on China's alleged underground arsenal. Each, in its own way, has impacted strategic calculations by Chinese and U.S. analysts. Keir Lieber and Daryl Press, "The Rise of U.S. Nuclear Primacy," *Foreign Affairs*, March/April 2006, pp. 42-55; William Wan, "Georgetown Students Shed Light on China's Tunnel System for Nuclear Weapons," *The Washington Post*, November 30, 2011, available from *www.washingtonpost.com/world/national-security/georgetown-students-shed-light-on-chinas-tunnel-system-for-nuclear-weapons/2011/11/16/gIQA6AmKAO_story.html*.

11. Interview and informal discussions held by the author with a ranking expert at the National Defense University and naval officer in the People's Liberation Army (PLA) Navy in China. Name withheld by author, in Lora Saalman, ed., *The China-India's Nuclear Crossroads*.

12. Jiang Yu, "Taikong jinglei: Fan dao ying shasheng wuqi de fa zhan ji zhongguo fan dao shiyan" ("Development of Hard-Kill Antimissile Weapon and China's Anti-Ballistic Missile Testing"), *Jianzai wuqi*, February 2, 2010, p. 14; Xiong Shicai, "Mei fandao wang nan fang zhongguo 'hangmu shashou'" ("U.S. Anti-Missile Network will Have a Hard Time Defending Against China's 'Aircraft Carrier Killer'"), *Guofang shibao*, October 4, 2010; Wang Meina, "Zhongguo hangmu shashou 'bu chu' meiguo fandao wang" ("China's Aircraft Killer 'Does Not Fear' the U.S. Missile Defense Network"), *Shijie bao*, September 15, 2010; Wang Yuting, "Mei hangmu fandao xitong fangbuzhu zhongguo daodan" ("U.S. Aircraft Carriers' Missile Defense Systems Cannot Fend Off China's Missiles"), *Guofang shibao*, September 1, 2010, p. 006.

13. Jackie Calmes, "A U.S. Marine Base for Australia Irritates China," *The New York Times*, November 16, 2011, available from *www.nytimes.com/2011/11/17/world/asia/obama-and-gillard-expand-us-australia-military-ties.html?pagewanted=all*.

14. Department of Defense, "Sustaining U.S. Global Leadership: Priorities for 21st Century Defense," January 2012, available from *www.defense.gov/news/Defense_Strategic_Guidance.pdf*.

15. For more information on "absolute security" and "absolute advantage," see Lora Saalman, "China and the U.S. Nuclear Posture Review," The Carnegie Papers, Washington, DC: Carnegie-Tsinghua Center for Global Policy, Carnegie Endowment for International Peace Press, No. 2, Spring 2011, p. 6, available from *carnegieendowment.org/2011/02/28/china-and-u.s.-nuclear-posture-review/1ci.*

16. Interview conducted by the author with China's arms control establishment of scientists and military and academic experts between April 2010 and September 2010, in particular with experts at National Defense University.

17. Tang Zhicheng, "Daguo boyi zhong, mei, e fazhan diji zhongduan fan dao xitong de xianshi kaoliang" ("Great Power Game: Practical Considerations on China, the United States, Russia and Their Development of Ground-based Missile Defense Systems"), *Xiandai bingqi,* June 2, 2010; "Zhongguo fandao jinzhui meiguo" ("China's Missile Defense in Hot Pursuit of the U.S."), *Shijie bao,* May 11, 2011; "Yi xiaoshi quanqiu daji: Meiguo rang shijie geng weixian?" ("Global Strike in One Hour: Is the U.S. Making the World More Dangerous?"), *Jinri guanzhu,* April 26, 2010, *CCTV.com,* available from *news.cntv.cn/program/jinriguan-zhu/20100426/105094.shtml;* Li Fang, "2009 nian meiguo daodan fangyu xitong zhongda shijian pandian" ("2009 Inventory of U.S. Missile Defense System Major Events"), *Zhongguo hangtian,* No. 4, April 19, 2010; Xu Xingju, "Meiguo fandao de xin fazhan ji qi dui zhonge de yingxiang" ("New U.S. Missile Defense Developments and Their Impact on China and Russia"), *Dimian fangkong wuqi,* No. 4, April 2001, pp. 26, 30.

18. See event summary: "NNSA Complex Modernization and Strategic Stability," Washington, DC, Carnegie-Tsinghua Center for Global Policy, December 9, 2011, available from *carnegietsin-ghua.org/issues/?fa=list&issue=971&lang=en;* Lora Saalman, "How Chinese Analysts View Arms Control, Disarmament, and Nuclear Deterrence after the Cold War," in Cristina Hansell and William C. Potter, eds., *Engaging China and Russia on Nuclear Disarmament,* Washington, DC: Center for Nonproliferation Studies, March 2009, available from *cns.miis.edu/opapers/op15/index.htm.*

19. See Wu Riqiang, "Certainty of Uncertainty: Nuclear Strategy with Chinese Characteristics," Stanford, CA: Stanford University, forthcoming.

20. Despite the fact that the Phased Adaptive Approach (PAA) is limited to four phases, it is still regarded in China as potentially limitless. In part, this is due to the following factors cited within China: 1) PAA planning is still thought to be worded ambiguously leaving room for future growth; 2) it was not initially expected that the Barack Obama administration would continue U.S. pursuit of missile defense, much less solidify or expand it; 3) PAA "blurs the distinction" between U.S. tactical and strategic missile defenses; and 4) PAA has contributed to making missile defense an unassailable and unquestioned piece of U.S. strategic architecture, which is destined to expand its reach into the Asia-Pacific. For just one example, see Paul Haenle, Dai Ying, Wang Haibin, Lora Saalman, Li Deshun, and Wu Riqiang, "Nuclear Taboo, Ballistic Missile Defense, and Nuclear Security," Event at the Carnegie-Tsinghua Center for Global Policy, available from *www. carnegieendowment.org/2010/05/11/nuclear-taboo-ballistic-missile-defense-and-nuclear-security/1tf6*; The White House, "Fact Sheet on U.S. Missile Defense Policy: A 'Phased, Adaptive Approach' for Missile Defense in Europe," Washington, DC: Office of the Press Secretary, United States, September 17, 2009, available from *www. whitehouse.gov/the_press_office/FACT-SHEET-US-Missile-Defense-Policy-A-Phased-Adaptive-Approach-for-Missile-Defense-in-Europe*.

21. See Lora Saalman, "China and Missile Defense: Creating Comity from Countermeasures" in Alexei Arbatov, ed., *Missile Defense: Confrontation and Cooperation*, Moscow, Russia: Carnegie Moscow Center Press, 2012.

22. Expert name withheld by author, "The Positive Factors of China's ASAT Test and Non-Weaponization in the Outer Space," Paper from conference on China's 2007 ASAT test attended by the author, Renmin University, February 2007.

23. Li Xuejiang, Zhang Guangzheng, Teng Jianqun, "Mei e he caijun geyou pansuan" ("U.S. and Russian Disarmament, Each Has Its Own"), *Renmin ribao*, May 2009, p. 6; Wang Haibin, "E mei guanyu fandao wenti de douzheng ji qi dui shijie junshi anquan de yingxiang" ("Struggle between Russia and the United States

over Missile Defense and its Impact on Global Military Security"), *Eluosi zhongya dongou yanjiu*, No. 11, November 2010; "Hewuqi de 'weishe'" ("Nuclear Weapons 'Deterrence'"), *Shijie zhishi*, No. 22, 2003, p. 22; Tang Shiqiang, "Bianhua zhong de e lianbang he zhanlue" ("Changing Nuclear Strategy of the Russian Federation"), *Guoji luntan*, No. 1, January 2002.

24. Cheng Qun, "Hou lengzhan shidai de zhongmei he guanxi fenxi" ("Analysis of China-U.S. Nuclear Relations in the Post-Cold War Era"), *Guoji luntan*, No. 6, November 2011, p. 40; Han Zhuangzhuang, "Lengzhan hou guoji hekuosan tezheng jiexi" ("Analysis Nuclear Proliferation Characteristics after the Cold War"), *Guofang keji*, No. 4, April 2010, pp. 81-99.

25. For more information on this new framework, please see the forthcoming doctoral dissertation of Li Deshun, Ph.D. Candidate at the Department of International Relations at Tsinghua University, "Xianghu yilai de zhanlue wendingxing" ("Interdependent Strategic Stability"), Tsinghua University, available from *www.tsinghua.edu.cn/publish/ir/4968/2011/201101120934353083136 55/20110112093435308313655_.html*.

26. It is important to remember that in China "propaganda" (*xuanchuan*) lacks the negative connotation it has in other countries. Alexander Wendt at the University of Chicago has had a significant influence on the international relations discourse in Chinese universities. This observation is based on the 4 years spent by the author in pursuing a Ph.D. within the International Relations Department of Tsinghua University.

27. In fact, one of the most common retorts by Chinese experts as to why China is not more transparent regarding its nuclear arsenal relates to its different "culture" (*wenhua*). These same Chinese experts often pair this argument with the observation that China's nuclear posture remains consistent and unchanging, whether in terms of no first use, negative security assurances, etc. Inherent within these two lines of reasoning is a contradiction. If China is responding to other countries, and their nuclear posture is changing, then so is that of China. So is China's nuclear culture. Li Yongcheng, "Aobama wuhe shijie changyi de zhanlue wenhua jieshi" ("A Strategic Culture Explanation of Obama's Nuclear-Free World Initiative"), *Dangdai shijie*, No. 5, May 2009, pp. 25-27.

28. This event was hosted by the Pacific Forum Center for Strategic and International Studies (CSIS) and the China Foundation for International and Strategic Studies (CFISS).

29. Yan Xuetong, "Zhongguo ying dui lingguo tigong junshi baohu xiaochu mei shili" ("China Should Provide Military Protection to Neighboring Countries to Remove U.S. Power"), *Xinhua wang – guoji xianqu daobao*, No. 6, June 1, 2011, available from *www.hysslz.com/dangjian/lilun/201106/20799.html*.

30. Interview conducted by the author with China's arms control establishment of scientists and military and academic experts between April 2010 and September 2010, in particular with one senior expert at the China Reform Forum.

31. Teng Jianqun, "Zhongmei he lingyu duihua de huigu yu zhanwang" ("Retrospect and Prospects for Sino-U.S. Dialogue in the Nuclear Arena"), *Guoji wenti yanjiu*, No. 3, 2011, p. 29.

32. Zhao Baomin.

33. These include at both the bilateral and multilateral level, U.S.-China Strategic Dialogue on Strategic Nuclear Dynamics, PIIC Beijing Seminar on International Security, The International Commission on Nuclear Non-proliferation and Disarmament (ICNND) Northeast Asia Regional Meeting, etc.

34. As just one example, at the International Commission on Nuclear Non-proliferation and Disarmament, ICNND Northeast Asia Regional Meeting in Beijing from May 21-23, 2009, a Chinese nuclear expert with decades of experience attending nuclear conferences commented that questions being raised were akin to those addressed at similar conferences in the 1980s.

35. Zhang Yeliang, p. 15.

36. Saalman, "China and the U.S. Nuclear Posture Review," pp. 1-55.

37. Hu Yumin, "Xin xingshi xia de he caijun wenti" ("Nuclear Disarmament Under a New Pattern"), *Guoji zhengzhi yanjiu*, No. 3, 2009, p. 17.

38. For the disparity in spending on strategic versus conventional military programs of various countries, including China, see Bruce G. Blair and Matthew A. Brown, "World Spending on Nuclear Weapons Surpasses $1 Trillion per Decade," Global Zero Technical Report, *Nuclear Weapons Cost Study, Global Zero*, June 2011, available from *www.globalzero.org/de/page/cost-of-nukes*.

39. Zhang Yang and Liu Jian, "Meiguo he zhanzheng jihua zai xin shiji de jiedu yu zai dingwei" ("Explaining and Redefining U.S. Nuclear War Fighting Plans in the New Century"), *Shijie jingji yu zhengzhi*, No. 3, March 2011, pp. 172-177.

40. The author adhered to the officially released translation for consistency. Chinese version available from "2010 nian zhongguo de guofang" ("China's National Defense 2010"), *Renmin ribao wang*, March 31, 2011, available from *politics.people.com.cn/GB/1026/14285970.html*; English version available from "Full text: China's National Defense in 2010," *English.news.cn*, March 31, 2011, available from *news.xinhuanet.com/english2010/china/2011-03/31/c_13806851.htm*

41. Embassy of the United States, Prague, Czech Republic, "Remarks of President Barack Obama," Hradčany Square, Prague, Czech Republic, April 5, 2009, available from *prague.usembassy.gov/obama.html*.

42. *Nuclear Posture Review Report*, Washington, DC: Department of Defense (DoD), April 2010, p. iii, available from *www.defense.gov/npr*.

43. Xu Jia, "Aobama zhengfu he zhengce shenxi" ("Analysis of the Obama Administration's Nuclear Policies"), *Guoji zhengzhi*, No. 10, 2009, p. 70; Wu Yujun, "E mei zhanlue wuqi tanpan qianjing ji dui zhongguo de yingxiang" ("Russia-U.S. Strategic Weapons Negotiations Prospects and their Impact on China"), *Zhongguo zhanlue guancha*, No. 6, 2009, p. 25; Cheng Qun, p. 40; Zhang Yeliang, p. 18.

44. Li Bin, "Zhongguo he zhanlue bianxi" ("Analysis of China's Nuclear Strategy"), *Shijie jingji yu zhengzhi*, No. 9, September 2006, p. 16.

45. Li Hong, "Fuza duoyuanhua de quanqiu he anquan huan-jing" ("Complex and Diversified Global Nuclear Security Envi-ronment"), *Heping yu fazhan*, No. 3, March 2010, p. 20.

46. Qian Wenrong, "Aobama 'wuhe shijie' changyi de zhen-shi yitu" ("Obama's 'Nuclear-Weapons-Free World"), *Heping yu fazhan*, No. 3, March 2010, p. 3; Li Hong, p. 19; Han Zhuang-zhuang, pp. 81-99.

47. Fan Jishe, "Renmin ribao guoji luntan: meiguo he zhengce de 'di san tiao daolu'" ("People's Daily International Forum: U.S. Nuclear Policy's 'Third Way'"), *Renmin wang*, April 20, 2010, available from *opinion.people.com.cn/GB/11407995.html*.

48. Zhang Chongfang, Wang Xiaojun, and Liu Jiang, "Mei e he caijun: Liangjian zhizeng" ("U.S.-Russia Nuclear Disarmament: Decreasing Numbers, Increasing Quality"), *Xinhua meiri bao*, April 12, 2010, p. 5; Wu Ting, "Meiguo shouti bu dui wuhe guojia dongyong hewuqi, yilang chaoxian chuwai" ("The United States for the First Time Mentions that it Will Not Use Nuclear Weapons Against NNWS, With the Exception of Iran and DPRK"), *Donfang zaobao*, April 7, 2010, p. A14.

49. Shi Yinhong, "Meiguo guojia daodan fangyu jihua yu zhongguo de duice" ("U.S. National Missile Defense and China's Countermeasures"), *Taipingyang xuebao*, No. 4, 2000, pp. 39-44.

50. Even factoring opacity into Chinese military budgeting for its conventional versus strategic force, this cost may be gauged. Taking into consideration the Stockholm International Peace Re-search Institute's estimate that China spent $114 billion on de-fense in 2010 and Global Zero's determination of $129 billion in Chinese expenditures on its military forces in 2011, what immedi-ately stands out in such studies is the relatively small portion of the total amount thought to be devoted to "researching, develop-ing, procuring, testing, operating, maintaining, and upgrading" China's nuclear arsenal of weapons and delivery systems. Even factoring in "environmental and health costs, missile defenses as-signed to defend against nuclear weapons, nuclear threat reduc-tion, and incident management," the number does not rise sub-stantially. If China's nuclear expenditures have hovered between

379

5 and 6 percent of its overall defense expenditures, particularly in light of other nuclear powers spending close to 10 percent, this further strengthens the argument that China's nuclear forces have cost it relatively little within its overall military modernization. Bruce G. Blair and Matthew A. Brown, "World Spending on Nuclear Weapons Surpasses $1 Trillion per Decade," Global Zero Technical Report, *Nuclear Weapons Cost Study, Global Zero,* June 2011, available from *www.globalzero.org/de/page/cost-of-nukes.*

51. Saalman, "China and the U.S. Nuclear Posture Review," p. 25.

52. Based on interactions since the release of the U.S. *Nuclear Posture Review* in April 2010 and referred to explicitly in an essay released in May of the same year. Yao Yunzhu, "A Chinese Perspective on the Nuclear Posture Review," *Proliferation Analysis,* Washington, DC: Carnegie Endowment for International Peace, May 6, 2010.

53. Sun Xiangli, "Zhongguo junkong de xin tiaozhan yu xin yicheng" ("Chinese Arms Control's New Challenges and New Agenda"), *Waijiao Pinglun,* No. 3, 2010, p. 14; Zhang Yeliang, p. 23; Liu Ziqin, "Shixi aobama zhengfu fangkuosan zhengce de tiaozheng" ("Analysis of Adjustments to the Obama Administration's Nonproliferation Policy"), *Xiandai guoji guanxi,* No. 4, 2011, p. 19; Wu Yujun, "E mei zhanlue wuqi tanpan qianjing ji dui zhongguo de yingxiang" ("Russia-U.S. Strategic Weapons Negotiations Prospects and their Impact on China"), *Zhongguo zhanlue guancha,* No. 6, 2009, p. 23.

54. Cheng Qun, p. 38.

55. Teng Jianqun, "He weishe xin lun" ("New Nuclear Deterrence Theory"), *Guoji wenti yanjiu,* No. 6, 2009, p. 14.

56. Chen Xinneng, "Jizao dui di jingdao wuqi weilai fazhan qushi" ("The Future Development Trajectory of Airborne Precision Guided Land-Targeting Weapons"), *Guoji zhanlue yanjiu,* No. 3, 2009; Wu Yujun, p. 23.

57. Teng Jianqun, "He weishe xin lun," p. 15.

58. "Aobama 'wuhewu shijie' changyi de zhenshi yitu" ("Obama's 'Nuclear-Weapons-Free World"), *Heping yu fazhan*, No. 3, 2010, p. 3; Wang Xiaowei and Wang Tian, "Lun aobama zhengfu 'qiao shili' waijiao de shizhi" ("On the Essence of the Obama Administration's 'Smart Power' Diplomacy"), *Heping yu fazhan*, No. 6, December 2009, pp. 1-4; Wang Zhijun, "Cong meiguo 'juedui anquan' linian kan aobama 'wuhe shijie' sixiang" ("A Look at Obama's 'Nuclear Free World' from the U.S. Philosophy of 'Absolute Security'"), *Heping yu fazhan*, No. 6, December 2009, pp. 12-16.

59. Wang Haibin.

60. Yin Chengde, pp. 55-59.

61. U.S. pursuit of conventional prompt global strike has just begun to appear in articles on strategic stability, deterrence, and military modernization in China. Due to its relative novelty, it appears more in interviews and discussions than in print.

62. Liu Ziqin, p. 15.

63. Teng Jianqun, pp. 27, 28; Zhang Yeliang, p. 13; Sun Xiangli, pp. 19-20.

64. Targeted interaction could include information exchange on ballistic missile defense (BMD) systems capabilities, and deployments. If BMD is not about China, then this should be feasible as a first step to exchange on future systems, such as CPGS.

CHAPTER 10

PROLIFERATION AND STRATEGIC STABILITY IN THE MIDDLE EAST

Austin Long

The author wishes to thank Richard Betts, El-bridge Colby, and Michael Gerson who provided very helpful comments on an early draft of this chapter. I have also benefited from discussions of these issues with Robert Jervis, Colin Kahl, Alan Kuperman, and Joshua Rovner.

The consequences of proliferation for strategic stability are critically important, with some experts being optimistic that nuclear weapons will lead to greater stability and others fearing that "more will be worse."[1] The consequences of proliferation for strategic stability, unfortunately for those seeking parsimony in assessment, depend highly on context. In some cases, proliferation will improve strategic stability, or at least not negatively affect it. In others, however, proliferation is likely to have profoundly destabilizing consequences.

If context is important, then the effect of proliferation on strategic stability cannot be evaluated in a purely theoretical vacuum. Instead, analysts of strategic stability must evaluate the form of proliferation, which can vary from a robust deployed arsenal to a "virtual bomb," along with the specific actors involved. For policymakers, the most critical arena for proliferation in the near future is the Middle East, so developing a contextual framework for considering its impact on strategic stability is the key goal of this chapter.

The chapter will proceed in three parts. The first briefly reviews the literature on proliferation and strategic stability. The second briefly describes the most relevant case of the effect of proliferation on strategic stability: the interaction of the United States, the Soviet Union, and China in the 1960s as the Chinese developed nuclear weapons. The third section explores the impact of Iranian proliferation on strategic stability in the Middle East.

THEORY ON PROLIFERATION AND STRATEGIC STABILITY

Strategic stability, defined here as a lack of incentive for either side of a crisis to use nuclear weapons first, has long been considered critical to evaluation of nuclear forces.[2] Adding new nuclear players could have profound impact on strategic stability, so the effect of nuclear proliferation on strategic stability has been widely debated in the theoretical literature for decades. As Peter Lavoy has noted, there are three basic theoretical camps: optimists, pessimists, and relativists.[3]

The optimist camp, exemplified by but not unique to Kenneth Waltz, is composed of those who are relatively sanguine about proliferation. While there is a spectrum of optimism, from absolute to qualified, these analysts and scholars generally argue that the deterrent value of nuclear weapons is so high that states will avoid crises and, even when they occur, crises will be more rather than less stable. Further, once the nuclear threshold is crossed and a state has a nuclear arsenal, nuclear weapons are relatively inexpensive and the marginal utility of large arsenals is small (in contrast to conventional weapons where, *ceteris pa-*

ribus, bigger and better is better). This reduces incentives for arms races between rivals. Thus, according to optimists, nuclear weapons help on both of the major foci of strategic stability- crisis stability and arms race stability.

While the optimists' argument makes proliferation sound positive, it rests on a few assumptions. A critical one is the survivability of nuclear weapons and their associated command and control on both sides in a crisis. If one side or both sides believe that either side is or both sides are vulnerable then there may be incentives to pre-empt in a crisis.[4] Of course, if one side believes itself vulnerable, it may seek to remedy this by expanding and improving its arsenal. This may trigger an expansion and improvement by the other side and a resulting spiraling arms race.[5] Pessimists about proliferation, such as Scott Sagan, point out that assumptions about survivable second strike capability on both sides of a crisis are at least sometimes belied by the facts.

In addition, the pessimist camp, which also ranges across a spectrum of pessimism, highlights other shortcomings of proliferation. Proliferation could increase the possibility of nuclear accidents.[6] It can increase the chance of unauthorized use of nuclear weapons.[7] It also might increase the probability of conventional war, as nuclear arsenals can in effect cancel one another out or lead to miscalculation about an opponent's response to conventional provocation, or both.[8] This latter point illustrates that strategic stability is not always an unalloyed good — it can produce the so-called stability-instability paradox, that while the "the military balance is stable at the level of all-out nuclear war, it will become less stable at lower levels of violence."[9]

Finally, there are the relativists, who argue essentially that the effects of proliferation on strategic stability are context dependent, varying based on the domestic characteristics of states. Lavoy highlights James Schlesinger and Robert Jervis as exemplars of this type.[10] In this chapter, I adopt the relativist perspective in examining the impact of proliferation on strategic stability. This is consistent with the view of most U.S. policymakers since John Kennedy, who have been relativists (common particularly during the Cold War) or pessimists (more common after the Cold War).

However, it is not just the domestic characteristics of states that matter for determining the context of proliferation. The relationships between states condition the impact of proliferation at least as much. The acquisition of nuclear weapons by a strong ally is substantially less likely to be destabilizing for a state than acquisition by a strong foe. Yet relationships between states, while shaped by history, are dynamic and malleable. Today's ally may be tomorrow's foe, or vice versa.

For example, consider U.S. views of Chinese proliferation. Initially, Chinese acquisition of nuclear weapons was so greatly feared in the United States that the John Kennedy administration seriously considered a preventive attack against the Chinese nuclear program in the early 1960s.[11] Yet scarcely 2 decades later, the Ronald Reagan administration in 1985 submitted a proposal to Congress for Sino-American civilian nuclear cooperation, a tacit endorsement of China's nuclear status.[12] It was not primarily radical development in the domestic characteristics of China that produced this change (though there was some as China moved from the leadership of the radical Mao Zedong to the pragmatic Deng Xiaoping).[13] China remained an authoritarian Marxist regime with revisionist claims on the status quo, including against Taiwan, a U.S. partner. Instead, what changed was the U.S. relationship with China, based largely on shared opposition to the Soviet Union.

Similarly, technical aspects of proliferation, such as force posture and doctrine, matter. The issues of arsenal survivability that optimist and pessimist alike have deemed crucial to stability since the pioneering work of Albert Wohlstetter (among others) are, in fact, part of the context of proliferation rather than simple exogenous variables. An arsenal that may seem flimsy and vulnerable in one context may be more than stable and sufficient in another.

The U.S.-China nuclear balance is again illustrative in this respect. The Chinese arsenal was woefully vulnerable to U.S. pre-emptive attack for many years due to the counterforce targeting capabilities of the U.S. arsenal.[14] Yet rather than take steps that might lead to serious crisis or arms race instability, Chinese leaders have only slowly (albeit appreciably) enhanced their intercontinental nuclear forces along with command and control in large part because in their view it takes very little to deter potential U.S. nuclear use.[15]

Moreover, proliferation itself is part of context, as it is not a binary variable with states either having a fully fledged arsenal or nothing at all. It spans a continuum with at least three additional values: hedged, recessed, and opaque. These additional values have implications for strategic stability different from either a major deployed arsenal or no capability at all.

A hedged (or latent) nuclear capability exists when a state has all of the technologies needed for an arsenal but has not combined them to produce weapons.[16] Japan is generally regarded as the paramount example of a hedged nuclear capability, though some argue this a byproduct of civilian energy programs rather than a coherent national strategy.[17] It has all of the assets needed for a weapon, from fissile material to potential delivery systems, yet has not pursued assembled weapons. This hedged capability, whether an intentional strategy or mere byproduct, has been noted by other states in its neighborhood yet has not substantially affected strategic stability (yet).

A recessed nuclear capability is one in which the state has some demonstrated nuclear capability and possibly rudimentary deliverable weapons but they are not acknowledged as having a major capability by the international system, the state, or both.[18] From its initial test in 1974 until at least the 1980s, India was in this category. Arguably Pakistan and India were both in this category though the mid-1990s.[19] North Korea appears to be in this category as well.

Finally, an opaque nuclear capability is one in which a state likely has a functional arsenal that is not publicly acknowledged and has not been demonstrated but is widely appreciated.[20] Israel is the only current example of this policy.[21] It is widely suspected to have an arsenal of dozens of weapons, with at least one design that was secretly tested with South African cooperation.[22] Yet Israel remains ambiguous in its discussions of nuclear weapons, simply pledging not to be the first to introduce nuclear weapons into the Middle East without discussing its force structure or doctrine.

These different values for the context of proliferation have important effects on strategic stability as these different values provide more or less time and clarity in a crisis. Two sides with hedged capabilities, for example, have little first strike pressure in a brief crisis as neither has weapons to use. In a longer crisis, the two might race to assemble weapons, but this is still a relatively stable environment. Likewise, two sides with recessed arsenals face little first strike pressure, at least at a strategic level, as weapons are not kept in deliverable form and neither is likely to be able to successfully target the others' arsenal. Conversely, two sides with opaque arsenals may actually be unstable as neither has a clear policy for use of weapons.

CHINESE PROLIFERATION AND STRATEGIC STABILITY

As noted, in the 1960s, the Chinese nuclear program was viewed with concern by both the Soviet Union and the United States. However, the level of concern of each varied over the course of the decade. In the early 1960s, as noted, U.S. policymakers considered a strike on Chinese nuclear facilities and reached out to the Soviets about the possibility of joint action. The Soviets, who had ended nuclear cooperation with the Chinese, were less concerned and did not agree. By the late 1960s, the tables had turned, and it was the Soviets who reached out to the United States about the possibility of striking Chinese nuclear facilities, only to be rebuffed. Ultimately, neither would take action against the Chinese program and strategic stability was not adversely affected as the Chinese arsenal matured in the 1970s and beyond, though not without a severe crisis in 1969.

This section briefly describes these events in an attempt to draw out salient points for considering future proliferation and strategic stability. This case is particularly relevant in the context of the current

Middle East, where preventive military action for counterproliferation has been taken in the past and is being contemplated again.[23]

The Chinese nuclear program began with decisions taken in the winter of 1954-55. Initially aided by the Soviets, the Chinese made slow but steady progress towards the production of fissile material.[24] The U.S. intelligence community was cognizant of this progress but had limited collection against many of the facilities located deep inside China. Nevertheless a National Intelligence Estimate (NIE) produced in December 1960, just before the Kennedy administration took office, described the program in some detail and gave the probable date for a first Chinese test as 1963.[25] The Chinese motivation appears to have been primarily to ensure retaliation against nuclear use by others, which would in turn limit nuclear coercion by the superpowers.[26]

The Kennedy administration was seriously concerned about Chinese proliferation for two reasons. The first, as William Burr and Jeffrey Richelson note, was that "a nuclear China could only weaken Washington's influence in the region and its capabilities to intervene on behalf of allies there." The Dwight Eisenhower administration had made use of the U.S. nuclear monopoly in Asia to coerce China, both in Korea and over the Taiwan Straits crises of 1954-55 and 1958. The second was that Chinese proliferation would spur regional and possibly global proliferation, which would in turn create instability.[27]

Note that there was not substantial concern in the U.S. intelligence community about Chinese irrationality with regard to nuclear weapons. Perhaps the most strident worry surfaced in a 1960 NIE warning that China's "arrogant self-confidence, revolutionary fervor, and distorted view of the world may lead Peiping to miscalculate risks. This danger would be heightened if Communist China achieved a nuclear weapons capability."[28] Even this remark was in an overall context of Chinese caution, especially outside the Taiwan Strait.

The Soviet attitude toward the Chinese program was beginning to change at the same time. Enthusiastic support for a Chinese nuclear capability apparently peaked around 1958, after which the Soviet leaders began to believe China might use nuclear weapons as a means to undertake adventurous action in Asia or even confront the Soviets. In the early 1960s, the Soviets began to wind down military assistance of all sorts, including nuclear.[29]

This emerging split was seen as a potential opportunity by the Kennedy administration. At the same time, a Special National Intelligence Estimate (SNIE) in 1963 using new collection sources produced a more detailed view of the Chinese program giving the administration additional impetus to action. The military and intelligence community began exploring plans for various overt and covert actions against the Chinese program.[30]

Soviet support or at least acquiescence seemed to be an important prerequisite for action, particularly military strikes. Several times over the course of 1963 members of the administration broached the possibility of joint U.S-Soviet action to prevent Chinese proliferation. However, Soviet Premier Nikita Khrushchev, despite growing Soviet trepidation about a nuclear China, was unwilling to further antagonize an erstwhile ally.[31]

In the fall of 1963, President Kennedy was assassinated and succeeded by Lyndon Johnson. Johnson's view of a Chinese nuclear capability was more relaxed than Kennedy's, and his impending election campaign in 1964 counseled caution on the military front. At the same time, new classified assessments presented a more sanguine view of a nuclear China, indicating that the U.S. position in the region would not be severely undermined if China went nuclear.[32] The summary of one major assessment produced in early 1964 noted:

> The ChiComs have demonstrated prudence in the use of military force. Their capability will be more important for its political-psychological than for its direct military effects — primarily because of the great disparity between U.S. and Chinese nuclear capabilities and vulnerabilities. . . . The ChiComs will hope that their nuclear capability will weaken the will of countries resisting insurgency; inhibit requests for U.S. assistance; put political pressure on the U.S. military presence in Asia; and muster support for Chinese claims to great power status. They may hope that it will deter us in situations where our interests seem only marginally threatened.[33]

However, National Security Adviser McGeorge Bundy and other National Security Council staff disagreed with this assessment, believing it too sanguine.[34] Though seldom mentioned directly in these discussions, the specter of Vietnam no doubt hung over Johnson's decisionmaking throughout the summer, particularly after the Tonkin Gulf incident in August.[35]

At the same time the intelligence community began to signal clear preparations for a Chinese nuclear test. The Johnson administration made one last approach to the Soviet Union in September 1964, which was again rebuffed. A Chinese nuclear test took place the next month, unhampered by U.S. action.[36] While not insignificant, the impact of the test for both the U.S. role in the region and for strategic stability was much less than some had feared at least for the next half-decade.

This limited impact was at least in part due to China's failure to move beyond a recessed arsenal. A U.S. NIE from February 1969 notes that, while they had tested thermonuclear bomb designs, the Chinese had not deployed even medium range ballistic missiles (MRBMs) equipped with nuclear warheads and was only beginning to deploy medium range jet bombers (based on the Soviet Tu-16). This was described as ". . . a regional strike capability in the sense that it could now have a few thermonuclear weapons for its two operational medium jet bombers."[37] Thus nearly 5 years after the test, China was still barely a nuclear power.

Yet if China's nuclear posture had not changed by 1969, other aspects of the context had, and the Sino-Soviet split had moved from rhetorical to violent. In March 1969, Soviet and Chinese forces clashed along the border between the two. These clashes, centered on a disputed island in the Ussuri River, lasted 2 weeks and included the use of tanks and artillery. They concluded with a tense stand-off rather than any resolution.[38]

There is some debate about the cause of this clash. Initial interpretations centered on Soviet aggressiveness after the 1968 Prague Spring and subsequent enunciation of the Brezhnev Doctrine. Revisionist accounts indicate that it was clearly the Chinese who initiated hostilities, to teach the Soviets "a bitter lesson" and to increase domestic unity during the difficult period of the Cultural Revolution. The latter explanation seems more valid, since it fits with Chinese patterns of manipulating external threats to produce domestic mobilization, with implications for strategic stability discussed below.[39]

The Soviets were shocked by this Chinese ambush and began considering responses. After some debate, with some who apparently argued for a pre-emptive strike on Chinese nuclear facilities while others counseled caution and diplomacy, the Soviets settled on a policy of conventional retaliation. Soviet forces shifted to the border over the summer of 1969 even as attempts at negotiation foundered.[40]

In August 1969 the Soviets launched their own ambush against Chinese border forces in Xinjiang province. The Chinese leadership was apparently as shocked by the act as the Soviets had been 5 months earlier. Moreover, the conventional military situation in sparsely populated Xinjiang was much more favorable to the Soviets.[41]

Even as this conventional action took place, Soviet diplomats and intelligence officers began to canvass international opinions about a pre-emptive strike against Chinese nuclear facilities. Inquiries were made with both the United States and the Warsaw Pact countries.[42] China's nuclear capability remained recessed and vulnerable at the time, consisting of perhaps a handful of liquid-fuelled medium range missiles and older medium range bombers, which would be vulnerable to Soviet air defenses. Command and control of the force was primitive as well. Both the Soviets and Chinese were cognizant of this vulnerability.[43] The Chinese also received intelligence about the Soviet inquiries in Eastern Europe, so they were also cognizant of the possibility of a Soviet strike coming at any time.[44]

The U.S. response to Soviet inquiries about preemptive action now mirrored Soviet responses to U.S. inquiries earlier in the decade. In approaching the United States, the Soviets argued that a strike would ensure that "the Chinese nuclear threat would be eliminated for decades." In addition, the strike would empower moderate leaders in China who were unhappy with Mao and the Cultural Revolution. The response was that the United States would view such a strike with "considerable concern."[45]

The crisis remained grave until, on his way back to Moscow from the funeral of North Vietnamese leader Ho Chi Minh in early September, Soviet Premier Alexei Kosygin stopped at the Beijing airport for a meeting with Chinese Premier Zhou Enlai. The meeting was blunt and to the point. Zhou immediately asked for clarification of the Soviet intentions regarding a preemptive nuclear strike and stated that this would lead to all-out war. At the same time, Zhou was also conciliatory, declaring the Chinese willing to make concessions along the border and noting China's "very many domestic problems."[46]

This meeting resulted in a relaxing of tensions, and the crisis seemed to have passed. At the same time, though, China remained deeply suspicious that this was all a ruse providing cover for a Soviet surprise attack. All major Chinese Communist Party leaders evacuated the capital in October 1969 for an extended period. Premier Zhou, for example, left his office in Zhongnanhai (the Chinese equivalent of the Kremlin) for a command bunker outside the capital and does not seem to have returned until February 1970.[47]

Five observations can be made about proliferation and strategic stability from the case of China in the 1960s. First, the impact of proliferation on strategic stability seems to have been less than either the Americans in the early 1960s or the Soviets in the late 1960s feared. No cascade of proliferation and arms racing took place, with the next nuclear power, India, only testing a decade after the Chinese (as discussed below). While this was in part due to actions by the United States, including reassuring allies and working to build a nonproliferation regime, it does indicate that proliferation chain reactions are at least sometimes controllable.[48] Likewise, the prospects for a major war between the United States and China appear to have peaked in the 1950s, before Chinese proliferation.

Indeed, rather than leading to declining influence in Asia, the U.S. decision not to launch a preventive attack on China actually paid long-term dividends. The previously described strategic rapprochement and nuclear accord between the United States and China in the 1980s would have likely been unthinkable after such an attack. The impact on strategic stability of proliferation and actions to prevent it must thus be measured in both likely near term and long term consequences.

Second, domestic concerns were central to the decisionmaking in all three countries, indicating that purely strategic concerns are not the only determinants of strategic stability both before and after proliferation. In the United States, Johnson's upcoming election campaign in 1964, where he ran as a "peace" candidate, moderated his concern about China's impending nuclear tests. In the Soviet Union, internal divisions between those favoring reliance on nuclear forces to deter China versus those who sought to conventionally balance Chinese forces along the border apparently had some effect on how the Soviets responded to the growing Chinese nuclear capability.[49]

Soviet perceptions of the impact on Chinese domestic politics of a nuclear pre-emptive strike were also at least articulated when the Soviets noted that such a strike would empower the anti-Mao clique. While it is unclear if the Soviets actually believed this or were merely looking for additional rationales for the strike that might garner U.S. support, it is clear that the Soviets at least believed the United States might believe this. The U.S. intelligence assessments of the impact of Chinese proliferation on Asia also drew on perceptions of the domestic characteristics of the region's regimes to argue that a nuclear China would not totally undermine U.S. influence.

The importance of domestic policy to Chinese actions related to proliferation and strategic stability is clearest. The chaos of the Cultural Revolution he had unleashed drove Mao to manipulate the Soviet threat to repair social cohesion in 1969. This was a major factor in precipitating the crisis, which would in all likelihood not have happened had Mao not needed the Soviet threat to mobilize the Chinese populace. As one Chinese scholar remarks:

> The Chairman's motives were mainly connected to his desire to change the tension created by an international conflict into a new source of continuous domestic mobilization. Indeed, coming at a time when Mao had attached overwhelming priority to bringing the Cultural Revolution to a successful conclusion, his most important foreign policy decisions have to be understood in that unique domestic context.[50]

As a corollary to the above, some would argue Mao was emboldened by Chinese acquisition of nuclear weapons to run risks he would not otherwise have in the name of domestic mobilization. However, Mao had run similar risks in the Korean War along with the 1954-55 and 1958 Taiwan crises with the United States for similar reasons. Yet in 1958, China was nowhere near a nuclear weapons capability of any sort and did not have a clear guarantee of Soviet extended deterrence.

If anything, Mao seems to have believed he was running a smaller risk in 1969 than in 1958. Mao and the Chinese leadership appear to have been shocked by the Soviet conventional response and threats of nuclear pre-emption in August 1969, indicating that they had not believed such a vehement response likely. Indeed, once the Soviet nuclear threat emerged, it seems clear that Chinese leaders realized quickly how vulnerable both they and their arsenal were, which made them amenable to a resolution (though still suspicious). This suggests that the corollary of nuclear acquisition fueling Chinese aggression is false.

The third observation emerges from this false corollary. Instead of Chinese proliferation producing overly bold Chinese action, misperception appears to have been at work as the Chinese surprise in August mirrored the Soviet surprise in March.[51] The interaction of the misperception of the two surprises produced the nuclear crisis. What the Chinese viewed as a minor skirmish to bolster the home front was viewed as a grave affront and possible taste of future actions by the Soviets. This produced what the Soviets viewed as a tit-for-tat conventional response and limited nuclear threat that the Chinese viewed as a possible prelude to all-out war.

This misperception even extended to the ostensible end to the crisis. The Soviets appear to have believed they offered the Chinese a face-saving way out of the crisis in September. Yet the Chinese do not appear to have believed the crisis was actually over for months, seeing the negotiation as a mask for a Soviet surprise attack. If such misperception and apprehension color a crisis between erstwhile allies, it is certainly likely to color almost any crisis as states proliferate. Stability, in other words, can be a delicate thing because of the likelihood of misperception in crisis.[52]

This misperception could have produced a much less stable crisis, except for the fourth observation, that the form of Chinese proliferation reduced rather than exacerbated time-sensitive first strike incentives on both sides. The Chinese arsenal was recessed in 1969, with few weapons and modest delivery systems. It was not survivable, nor was its command and control. In contrast, the Soviet arsenal was robust and fully developed, though it had command and control weaknesses. This disparity meant that the Soviets felt they could hold Chinese nuclear assets at risk even if the Chinese were alerted to an impending attack. This reduced the imperative to strike quickly and by surprise for the Soviets enabling them to wait and evaluate the course of diplomacy.

Conversely, the Chinese knew that if they launched a first strike, it would not prevent massive Soviet retaliation nor would it be capable of inflicting unacceptable damage to Soviet society, so they too had little incentive to strike first. A paradox emerges here, as a larger and more survivable Chinese arsenal might have made the crisis more rather than less acute. The Soviets would have had more incentive to strike early and without warning, while the Chinese might have adopted a more robust policy to launch a counterattack on warning of Soviet attack or even to pre-empt themselves, particularly after September 1969 when the Chinese were acutely concerned about Soviet duplicity. Thus not yet thoroughly survivable and capable arsenals may pose the most significant challenges to strategic stability.

While the possibility of pre-emptive nuclear attack is not in keeping with Chinese thinking on nuclear weapons, other countries in similar situations might believe differently. This further underscores the importance of domestic factors, such as leadership and organizational concerns. In China, the response to the threatened Soviet strike was to begin a relatively modest increase in the size and survivability of the arsenal, which did not decrease strategic stability. [53]

The fifth observation is the role of nuclear "third-parties" in producing bilateral strategic stability. Both the Soviet rejection of U.S. overtures for preventive action in the early 1960s and the U.S. rejection of Soviet overtures in the late 1960s exerted some restraining and stabilizing effect. While it is difficult at present to quantify how much these rejections affected decision-making, they nonetheless seem to have played some role. Lyle Goldstein, who views the U.S. role in dissuading Soviet pre-emption in 1969 as generally overstated, concedes it "likely that the United States did play a role in Soviet calculations."[54] Similarly, Richelson and Burr note that, given President Johnson's domestic constraints and more relaxed viewpoint on China, the Soviet "negative response effectively settled the argument over direct action."[55]

STRATEGIC STABILITY AND PROLIFERATION IN THE MIDDLE EAST

At present, concerns about strategic stability and proliferation center on the possibility of Iranian acquisition of nuclear capability.[56] Current Iranian efforts are centered on a centrifuge program for enriching uranium that has an ostensible commercial and research focus but has caused concern that the Iranians are, at a minimum, seeking a hedged nuclear capability.[57] The impact of Iranian proliferation would be most immediately and acutely felt by Israel, which currently is reported to possess the pre-eminent example of an opaque nuclear capability. The Arab states of the region, most especially Saudi Arabia, would also be affected by an Iranian bomb. This section explores the possible impact of Iranian nuclear capability on strategic stability and is divided into two parts. The first focuses specifically on the bilateral Israeli-Iranian relationship while the second examines the broader regional impact.

A nuclear Iran is considered by many Israelis as the prelude to a second Holocaust. Even Israelis that are more sanguine about deterring Iran from using nuclear weapons are extraordinarily anxious about the prospect of an Iranian bomb because of its implications for Israel's strategic position and freedom of action, the potential for an unstable balance between the two nations, and the possibilities of an emboldened Iran. If Iranian acquisition occurs despite the best efforts of the international community, Israel will be forced to make hard choices about its strategic posture.[58]

Any discussion of the impact on strategic stability by Israeli responses to a nuclear-armed Iran should acknowledge that it is probable that Israel will have exercised every possible option to halt or delay the Iranian nuclear program. This could include, in the last resort, the use of force via air strikes.[59] The failure of these efforts (implicit in the assumption that Iran has acquired nuclear weapons) and specifically the military option will have an enduring effect on the region, including Israel's responses to an Iran that has despite its best efforts acquired nuclear weapons.

The political ramifications of failure, both domestic and international, for Israel would be profound. It will have been unable to prevent a regional rival from obtaining nuclear weapons, a goal that has been a cornerstone of Israeli security policy since its enunciation by Menachem Begin more than 30 years ago.[60] This will, in turn, affect how Israel responds to the challenge of a nuclear Iran, interacting with Israeli domestic politics. Israelis will have a much harder time simply shrugging off the anti-Semitic and Holocaust-denying rhetoric of some Iranian leaders. While this rhetoric may target a domestic audience inside Iran, it is simply too close to other patterns of behavior that resulted in the killing of many Jews. This will push all Israelis towards a more hawkish response.

It is also possible that any action by a nuclear Iran, whether it remains hedged or deploys, will be interpreted by Israel as a result of Iran being "emboldened" by its nuclear capability. Israel may thus feel it must react more strongly to Iranian action to prove that Iran's nuclear capability is not a shield for bad behavior. This could be destabilizing as it could lead to Israeli overreaction to Iranian action—a version of the stability-instability paradox. Michael Gerson indicates this may have been at work in the 1969 crisis between the Soviets and Chinese, with the Soviets incorrectly believing the Chinese were emboldened by nuclear weapons and responding harshly as a result.[61]

In the short run, the major impact on strategic stability would occur after a failed Israeli military effort to destroy Iranian nuclear facilities. This would prompt an Iranian response, potentially using both its own military assets and its proxies/allies Hezbollah and Hamas. Iran's ability to effectively attack Israel directly is not robust, with what is likely to be a relatively limited supply of conventional armed Shahab 3 ballistic missiles (perhaps as many as 100 but possibly fewer).[62]

However, unlike 1991, the United States would not in all likelihood be conducting an extensive air campaign against Iran and its launchers (though this is not impossible to imagine depending on the exact dimensions of the Iranian response). Israel would thus have an incentive to launch retaliatory strikes. It is unclear what the political limit of this escalation spiral would be, but its outcome would affect subsequent Israeli and Iranian actions.

Hezbollah's capability is substantially greater due to proximity, but Israel's ability to counter these attacks with offensive operations is also greater. The conflict would therefore probably look much like the 2006 Israel-Hezbollah conflict, though Israeli forces would be better prepared. However, Hezbollah is also likely to be better prepared.[63] The same is true to a lesser extent of Hamas, which has probably learned lessons from the 2009 war. It has certainly expanded both its rocket arsenal and allegedly its anti-aircraft capability.[64] While none of the three threats are existential, they may combine to inflict nontrivial damage on Israel, potentially including hundreds of civilian casualties. This will further empower hawkish responses to an Iranian nuclear capability.

Central to any Israeli response to a nuclear Iran would be the future of its reported nuclear arsenal and its deterrent value. As noted, Israel's nuclear posture has, from the beginning, been one of opacity as embodied in the 1967 phrasing of Prime Minister Levi

Eshkol: "Israel will not be the first to introduce nuclear weapons into the neighborhood."[65] This phrasing used "introduce" in the sense of an overt arsenal, not "a bomb in the basement." This long-standing Israeli policy of nuclear opacity was intended to provide deterrence against conventional threats from Israel's neighbors while minimizing potential responses from the United States, the international community, and its neighbors.[66] While useful for decades, this opacity may no longer seem appropriate for deterring a regional rival that is, rhetorically at least, dedicated to the end of the Israeli state. Some Israeli strategists outside of the government have already begun to call for an end to nuclear opacity if Israel is forced to confront a nuclear armed Iran.[67]

One factor likely to weigh heavily on the Israeli response is the form an Iranian nuclear arsenal takes. If the Iranian arsenal is purely hedged, with no testing and weaponization, then Israelis might see no need to revise the policy of opacity. It would be costly to do so with minimal benefit in terms of deterrence, as Iran would have no readily available weapons to deter.

If Iran tests and deploys even a small number of weapons, moving from a hedged to a recessed posture, Israel will likely be under extraordinary pressure to respond likewise. Moreover, an Iran that tests a nuclear weapon will give Israeli leaders political cover to end the policy of nuclear opacity, which has been wearing thin in the past decade.[68] Eshkol's formulation indicated Israel would not be the first, but said nothing about being the second regional proliferator. Israel could thus be said to have upheld its implicit promise to the United States and the international community. An Iranian nuclear test would also be such a strong potential driver (though as noted below perhaps not an insurmountable one) of regional proliferation that an Israeli declaration and test would only provide marginal additional impetus.

Thus the form of Iranian proliferation will likely have major impact on Israeli response. If Iran's nuclear capability remains hedged, the two countries could both exist in a strategically stable balance of mutual opacity.[69] Israel would not feel first strike pressure in a crisis, and Iran would still have a capability that could be called on in extremis (such as threats of regime change) while also enhancing Iranian prestige. Yet if confronted by a much larger hostile power that has tested a nuclear device, both domestic politics and strategic considerations would push Israeli leaders towards testing and the unambiguous deployment of a nuclear arsenal.

Domestic politics will weigh heavily here and, as noted, are part of the context of strategic stability. Most or all of the largest parties in the current Knesset will be implicated in failing to prevent Iran from going nuclear. There will therefore be pressure to ameliorate that failure and the unambiguous deployment of a nuclear arsenal would do much towards that end. If Israel has attempted to use military force to destroy Iran's nuclear program, the likely subsequent conflict with Iran and its proxies will only reinforce the incentive to end nuclear opacity in favor of clear nuclear deterrence.

Israel could likely test a weapon quite quickly, particularly if preparations were made in advance of an anticipated Iranian nuclear test. A deployed nuclear arsenal would take longer, as it would require the formulation of doctrine, command and control, and basing for the deployed weapons. Israel appears to have taken certain steps in this regard but would need to do more particularly in terms of nuclear declaratory policy.[70]

In terms of nuclear doctrine, Israel would most critically have to make decisions about targeting of weapons and timing of nuclear use. In terms of targeting for deterrence, Israel would have to decide what to hold at risk—countervalue targets (Iranian cities, oil fields, and other economic targets), counterforce targets (Iranian nuclear weapons and other military targets), or some combination.[71] It seems likely that Israel would, like the United States, plan for at least the option of holding both sets of targets at risk, as only counterforce targeting offers the possibility of limiting damage to the Israeli population while countervalue targeting raises the costs of Iranian action.[72]

In terms of timing, Israel would have to decide two key aspects. First, what will be the role of pre-emption in Israeli nuclear doctrine? Would Israel seek a posture that would try to disarm an Iranian nuclear force in the event of conflict? A combination of nuclear counterforce targeting and pre-emption would have the possibility of, in extremis, greatly limiting the Iranian nuclear threat by destroying or degrading the effectiveness of Iranian nuclear weapons before they could be used. However, a pre-emptive doctrine would undermine strategic stability, making war a more likely outcome in a crisis, increasing Iran's incentives to strike early and on even fractional warning, and provoking an arms race as Iran seeks to build a survivable second strike capability as Israel builds up to forestall such survivability.[73] Indeed, Israel might one day be tempted to use its "wasting asset" of nuclear superiority in a *preventive* war. The United States considered similar action against the Soviets at the beginning of the Cold War.[74]

Second, if Israel used its arsenal, either pre-emptively or in response to an Iranian strike, would it expend its entire available arsenal in one fell swoop or would it withhold some portion of the arsenal? The former simplifies planning as well as command and control considerations yet leaves Israel little bargaining leverage for war termination. The latter requires substantially greater effort in command and control, which will likely be damaged by any Iranian nuclear strike.[75]

Given Israel's small size and concern about Iranian rhetoric regarding the end of the Israeli state, it seems likely Israel would adopt a pre-emptive posture with minimal regard for withholding. This was the U.S. posture in the 1950s for similar reasons—though the United States is much greater in size, it was deeply concerned about limiting damage to its population and also felt that command and control made withholding impractical. Also, the United States believed it was practical to be able to aim at disarming the still small and immature Soviet force of the time.[76] Israel has historically been pre-emptive in the use of conventional force, which will probably color thinking on nuclear force.

A deployed rather than opaque Israeli nuclear arsenal would not be substantially different from the overall force structure Israel currently is reported to have. It would likely be based around a triad of mobile land-based ballistic missiles, submarine launched cruise missiles, and strike aircraft. The difference would be in procedures for handling routinely deployed weapons as well as changes in force posture to ensure a survivable second strike. This might include hardening or dispersing ballistic missiles, keeping multiple submarines with nuclear weapons at sea

407

at all times, and maintaining on alert some portion of its long-range strike aircraft dedicated to the nuclear strike role.[77]

Israel will need to make clear decisions about command and control of the forces, and continue to develop early warning capability. Warning of attack will be important not just for Israeli nuclear forces but also for its missile defenses, which will need prompt and accurate warning to intercept Iranian missiles. Israel has devoted substantial resources to missile defense, much of it in cooperation with the United States. U.S. cooperation is particularly important to provide warning as well as tracking of incoming missiles, via the U.S. Defense Support Satellite (DSS) architecture and also an X-band radar deployed in Israel. It is worth noting that the radar is operated by U.S. personnel, creating an ongoing operational U.S. military presence in Israel for the first time (not counting peacekeepers).[78]

The foregoing has focused on Israeli responses, but strategic stability in this case is bilateral. Iranian decisions about whether to retain a hedged nuclear capability (the ability to quickly deploy a weapon but no existing weapons) or to press forward towards some form of deployed arsenal will be influenced by the actions of others. An Iran that has experienced an Israeli counterproliferation strike will be more likely to seek a deployed rather than hedged nuclear capability because it will likely calculate that there are no advantages to restraint, and a deployed capability would make the consequences of future strikes higher for Israel.

If the Iranians decide a hedged capability is insufficient, this will in turn require the Iranians to make many of the decisions noted above for the Israelis. They likely will initially have a vulnerable arsenal based around a handful of warheads on fixed or land-mobile ballistic missiles.[79] These weapons will not have a robust command and control in this early period nor will Iran have highly capable early warning.

This arsenal will be similar to that of the Chinese in 1969. However, the overall context for Iran will be different. On the positive side, Israel and Iran do not share a border, preventing the sort of clash that took place between Chinese and Soviet forces in 1969. Yet this may not forestall crises, given the history of conflict between the two states.

Other differences are even more worrisome. Israel, a much smaller country than the Soviet Union, is vastly more vulnerable to an attack on its cities by a small arsenal, meaning Iran might believe (correctly or not) that pre-emption is viable even without a large arsenal. Unlike China in 1969 and after, Iran will potentially have experienced a military attack directed at its nuclear capabilities from Israel and so be acutely concerned about another, though this time with nuclear weapons. Combined with the vulnerability of both the arsenal and its command and control, these factors will push Iran towards pre-delegating nuclear use authority to military commanders in the Iranian Revolutionary Guard Corps to avoid possible disarming and/or decapitation by an Israeli strike, a classic instance of a destabilizing measure.[80] Further, the Iranians, with weak early warning and aware that Israeli missile defenses will be more effective following a pre-emptive strike that reduces the number of missiles to intercept, will be pushed towards early first use of nuclear weapons to forestall Israeli pre-emption. This would be a very delicate balance of terror indeed, with both Israel and Iran on a hair trigger.[81]

Note, however, that very little is publicly known about the Iranian leadership's views of nuclear weapons or strategy. A 2009 RAND study remarks, "[s]ince we do not have access to a debate about nuclear weapons within the leadership itself, we can only conjecture the role of the Guards in such a debate."[82] It is possible that Iranian elites, including the Revolutionary Guards, simply will not view nuclear weapons or strategy in the same way current nuclear powers do.

Further, while Iranian elites do not face the same degree of electoral pressure as Israeli elites, they are nonetheless divided into factions.[83] An Israeli preventive military strike will also likely empower more hawkish elements in Iran, such as the Revolutionary Guards. Contrary to the Soviet arguments about empowering moderates in China via preventive military action, the available evidence from Israel's own preventive counterproliferation strikes in Iraq and Syria suggests otherwise. In Iraq after the strike at Osirak, Saddam Hussein remained in power and, in fact, continued to pursue nuclear weapons with at least as much vigor.[84] In Syria, the strike at Dayr az Zawr does not seem to have reduced the power of the Assad regime.[85]

An Israeli military strike against Iranian nuclear facilities may enable the Iranian regime to mobilize flagging domestic support. The Iranian regime certainly used the Iraqi invasion in 1980 as an opportunity to do so. As Ray Takeyh has noted ". . . the Islamic Republic welcomed the conflict as a means of consolidating its power, displacing its rivals, and transforming Iran's political culture."[86]

The parallel to the Chinese in 1958 and 1969 is clear in this case. As with the Chinese, the Iranian regime, after successfully rallying the population in the wake of an Israeli strike, might decide in the future that provoking a crisis with Israel (or some other state such as Saudi Arabia or the United States) is once again necessary to bolster its domestic cohesion. But, like China in 1969, it might then find itself in what has become a nuclear confrontation it had not anticipated due to misperception.

Indeed, the problem of misperception would almost certainly be worse than the Chinese in 1969. While the issue was acute in the Soviet-Chinese example, the two were previously allied with broadly similar regimes and leaders who were at least somewhat familiar with one another. This helped enable the resolution in September 1969 (though as noted the Chinese remained on alert). In cases where there is a wide gulf in regime type compounded by previous military conflict misperception is likely to be endemic and dangerous, as was the case between the United States and Iraq in the period 1990-2003.[87]

While the Iran-Israel relationship is already marked by covert confrontation, an overt military strike would likely trigger further misperception.[88] This was again the case with Iran and Iraq, with Iranian leaders choosing to pursue the war onto Iraqi soil after ejecting Iraqi troops from Iran in 1982 in part because of misperceptions about Iraq. This decision lead to years of bloody stalemate and is reviled inside Iran now, yet there is little reason to believe a similar misperception is unlikely in the future.[89]

If the foregoing is correct, then for both strategic and domestic reasons the optimal course to promote strategic stability between Iran and Israel in the short run is for Israel to take preventive action against the Iranian program. This will almost surely delay the timeline for the Iranian program to produce fissile material by roughly 1 to 3 years, preserving the Israeli regional nuclear monopoly and postponing the day when the two countries become nuclear adversaries.[90] However, this is also the worst course for promoting strategic stability in the long run, as the result will be that when Iran does achieve nuclear capability both sides will have strong domestic and strategic incentives to deploy arsenals that will provide them with substantial incentive to act first in a crisis as well as promoting arms races between the two. This could well have been the result of strikes against China by either the United States in 1964 or the Soviets in 1969.

Conversely, if Israel does not act, then in the short run strategic stability will suffer as the Israeli regional nuclear monopoly ends. Yet the strategic and domestic imperatives to deploy fully developed arsenals as well as the possibility of misperception will be more manageable in the absence of an Israeli strike. Thus in the long term, Israel and Iran may live with opaque and hedged capabilities respectively, which will enhance strategic stability as neither will have first strike incentives in crisis or face arms race pressures. The Iranians will have to live with a hedged capability and the Israelis will have to live with the Iranians having that capability.

The role of the United States as a nuclear third-party will be critical to maintaining strategic stability between the two. Just as the United States played a role in limiting the Soviet-Chinese crisis in 1969, it will have to do likewise with Iran and Israel. It should take all measures possible to prevent an Israeli preventive strike and to ensure that Iranian capabilities remain hedged.

Central to this will be assurances to the Israelis that the United States will take military action if the Iranians attempt to move from a hedged capability to deployed weapons by producing fissile material. This is the currently articulated "red line" for the Barack Obama administration, as Secretary of Defense Leon Panetta noted in an interview in January 2012:

> Are they trying to develop a nuclear weapon? No. But we know that they're trying to develop a nuclear capability. And that's what concerns us. . . . And our red line to Iran is to not develop a nuclear weapon. That's a red line for us.[91]

This position, to use force if an Iranian attempt to produce fissile material is detected (or possibly if the Iranians take other actions that indicate it may be seeking to do so, such as refusing access to inspectors), is distinct from the position that the United States should use force to prevent Iran from even having a hedged capability.[92] Indeed, in order to be effective, such a threat to use force if Iran seeks to move beyond a hedged capability must be matched by reassurance that if it does not seek to do so military force will not be used.

The central purpose of this guarantee to use force backed up by reassurance to the Iranians would be to enable both Iran and Israel to live with a hedged Iranian capability by preventing an Israeli military action. This may seem paradoxical, threatening to use force to preserve strategic stability. Yet by carefully bounding the threat, the United States will be able to reassure both sides.

However, such assurances will have inherent limits to their credibility for both technical and political reasons. On the technical side, at present the combination of intelligence collection and international inspections have proved highly capable of monitoring the Iranian nuclear program and detecting Iranian attempts to build covert facilities (such as the Fordow facility Western intelligence revealed in 2009). However, no intelligence agency can promise 100 percent probability of success in detecting clandestine efforts or that such a detection would be sufficiently timely and reliable to enable military action. Moreover, maintaining this collection and analysis effort is costly and difficult.[93] Thus there are inherent limits to the ability to credibly guarantee that an Iranian attempt to move from a hedged to a deployed capability will be detected and stopped by military action. While at present the capability to do so is judged to be high, this is subject to change (e.g., if the Iranians are able to build more advanced centrifuges that would enable them to more rapidly produce fissile material).

Apart from the technical limits to the credibility of assurances to prevent Iranian breakout from a hedged capability there are political limits to credibility. Even if the current U.S administration were able to make ironclad guarantees to the current Israeli administration, such guarantees could be revoked by a future administration. Nor is any administration likely to provide a truly ironclad guarantee as this would greatly limit its political flexibility.[94] The same is true of reassurances to the Iranians, who distrust the United States regardless.

Therefore for both technical and political reasons, the United States is not likely to be able to credibly assure Israel that it will prevent Iran from moving beyond a hedged capability. This means that the Israelis may take military action, which as noted is likely to lead both sides to unambiguously deploy weapons. In this case, the United States must actively reassure Israel that it need not act first in crisis. This may mean a formal security guarantee, though even this may have limited efficacy, particularly given that in this case the United States would not have been able to credibly guarantee it would take military action to forestall Iranian nuclearization. Iranian proliferation has implications beyond the Iran-Israel relationship. Turkey, Egypt, Saudi Arabia, and the United Arab Emirates (UAE) are all potential candidates for acquiring a nuclear capability in the wake of Iranian proliferation. Of these, Turkey is already firmly under the North Atlantic Treaty Organization (NATO) nuclear umbrella and is steadfast in its nonproliferation commitments.[95] Egypt is in turmoil and economically weak, following the so-called Arab Spring.[96] As Egypt has already abandoned nuclear ambitions, it is an unlikely candidate for a near-term renaissance.[97] The UAE has signed a nuclear sharing agreement with the United States that is being trumpeted as the "gold standard" for nonproliferation.[98]

At present Saudi Arabia is the most likely candidate in the region for proliferation in anything like the near term. It is relatively stable and has enormous wealth, the latter which it is alleged to have used to help bankroll the Pakistani nuclear program.[99] Saudi Arabia has also publicly indicated it may pursue nuclear weapons in the event of Iranian proliferation.[100]

Balanced against this capability and expressed interest in proliferation is the Saudi reliance on the United States for much of its security needs.[101] This reliance gives the United States leverage against Saudi proliferation, as it could threaten to reduce or eliminate its current support for the regime if it pursues nuclear weapons. The United States has in the past persuaded both Taiwan and South Korea to halt efforts to proliferate, so there is clear precedent for successful use of security and other forms of assistance as a lever against proliferation.[102] This leverage will likely be sufficient to prevent Saudi proliferation, but the remainder of this chapter will proceed from the assumption that efforts to dissuade the Saudis fail.

A Saudi nuclear capability could range in the short term from hedged to recessed; in other words, the Saudis might be content with the capacity to build a weapon if necessary, or they may need to deploy a small arsenal. As with Israel, much will depend on the form of Iranian proliferation. If Iran is content with a hedged capability, it seems likely the Saudis would be as well. This would be the most strategically stable environment, as Iran and Saudi Arabia remain hedged and Israel opaque in terms of nuclear capability.

However, a recessed Iranian capability would pressure the Saudis to have a similar capability. Yet the Saudi arsenal would likely be much like the Iranian arsenal—small, relatively vulnerable, with poor command, control, and early warning. Both sides would thus be vulnerable to pre-emption in a crisis, which could arise over either state's actions in the region. For example, tensions rose when Saudi forces aided the repression of Shi'a uprisings in Bahrain.[103] As with Iran and Israel, the possibility of misperception between the Sunni monarchy and Shi'a Islamic regime is high.

A Saudi recessed nuclear capability also has implications for the Israelis. While the Saudi-Israeli relationship is not nearly as contentious as the Iran-Israel relationship or even the Saudi-Iran relationship, neither is it wholly pacific. The two do not have formal diplomatic relations, and Israel is wary of increasing

416

Saudi conventional capability, much less a nuclear capability. Israel would thus have to posture its arsenal towards both Saudi Arabia and Iran, who would have to do likewise.

This three-cornered relationship looks to some extent like the United States, Soviet Union, and China in the 1960s (and after), though the bipolar relationship between the first two dominated that triangular dynamic. As noted, the Chinese attitude towards nuclear weapons and lack of resources limited the potential for arms racing and time pressures during crisis. In short, the triangular relationship was unequal, with the Soviet Union and United States much more capable than China and China willing to live with that state of affairs.

It is unclear that Saudi Arabia or Iran would be as content to be the weak point in an unbalanced triangle as was China. Israel certainly would not and Iran as noted is highly unlikely to be following an Israeli preventive strike. U.S. reassurances to Saudi Arabia in this case might help but, given that Saudi acquisition of nuclear weapons would be a vote of no-confidence in existing U.S. commitments, this seems a weak reed.

A nuclear Middle East characterized by recessed arsenals is therefore likely to be less stable than the Cold War and potentially less stable than the current balance in South Asia (itself no picture of stability). Recessed arsenals will be vulnerable but capable of inflicting unacceptable damage to the region's most developed nuclear power, Israel. This is different from the Soviet-China case, where the Chinese recessed arsenal was vulnerable to pre-emption but not able to inflict unacceptable damage on the Soviets.

Conversely, a Middle East characterized by hedged and opaque capabilities is likely to be much more stable. Yet a Middle East with survivable arsenals is also likely to be stable, particularly if some sort of arms limitation can be agreed to that would limit the size of arsenals. Unfortunately, to reach the stable equilibrium of survivable arsenals requires leaving the stable equilibrium of hedged capabilities (in other words, states will have to actually deploy weapons) and thus passing through an unstable period of vulnerable arsenals.

Finally, the three-cornered Iran-Israel-Saudi relationship will have implications for further proliferation in the region. A 2008 report by a Senate Foreign Relations Committee staff member argues that while Egypt is unlikely to seek nuclear weapons directly in response to Iranian acquisition, subsequent acquisition of a recessed arsenal by the Saudis and the end of Israeli opacity would amplify the pressure for Egyptian proliferation.[104] While this report predates the end of the Mubarak regime and the future of the Egyptian government is very much in flux, the pressures described in this report may still push Egypt to proliferate. This in turn might put more pressure on other countries in the region. While such concerns about nuclear tipping points and chain reactions have been overstated in the past, they cannot be discounted.[105]

The current policy focus on preventing any proliferation, hedged or not, in the Middle East makes it less rather than more likely that proliferation will remain hedged. This is particularly true of Israeli military action, which will incentivize Iran to deploy a recessed arsenal that will in turn incentivize Saudi deployment and possibly further proliferation. Thus another paradox emerges as the most direct and vigorous efforts to maintain the strategically stable status quo may end up producing the least strategically stable future.

The United States should therefore adjust its goal in the region to focus on ensuring that proliferation remains hedged rather than attempting to prevent any type of proliferation. This appears to be the direction in which U.S. policy is tacitly heading, based on the articulation of red lines, but a clearer articulation of this goal would help align all U.S. actions and policies in the region. Unfortunately, a clear public articulation of this purpose would both invite domestic criticism of the administration as well as potentially weaken the bargaining ability of the administration. Ideally, the administration could internally articulate such a position, but it would almost invariably leak.

CONCLUSION

The implication of proliferation for strategic stability is thus highly contingent on a variety of contextual factors. This is unfortunate for lovers of parsimonious prediction, as neither uniform optimism nor pessimism is warranted. Instead, analysts must examine the domestic, international, and technical aspects of proliferation to estimate its effects on stability.

Most notably, the foregoing demonstrates that the dictum, attributed to Otto von Bismarck, that preventive war is like "committing suicide for fear of death"[106] is likely very true in the context of proliferation and strategic stability. The Cold War stability between China, the United States, and the Soviet Union was enabled by a variety of factors, but this stability could easily have been undermined had preventive military action by either the United States, Soviet Union, or both, been undertaken. A counterfactual history of that triangular relationship where China had experienced preventive attacks on its nuclear program would likely result in much lower strategic stability for all three corners of the relationship. The same seems to be true of Iran and the Middle East in the future, with the paradoxical complication that a carefully calibrated threat of preventive action may be one of the best ways to forestall actual preventive action.

ENDNOTES - CHAPTER 10

1. Summarized well in Scott Sagan and Kenneth Waltz, *The Spread of Nuclear Weapons: A Debate Renewed*, New York: W.W. Norton, 2002; and Peter Lavoy, "Review Essay: The Strategic Consequences of Nuclear Proliferation," *Security Studies*, Vol. 4, No. 4, Summer 1995.

2. See Glenn Kent and David Thaler, *First-Strike Stability: A Methodology for Evaluating Strategic Forces*, Santa Monica, CA: RAND, 1989, pp. 2-6.

3. Lavoy, "The Strategic Consequences of Nuclear Proliferation."

4. On survivability of arsenals and stability, see, inter alia, Albert Wohlstetter, "The Delicate Balance of Terror," *Foreign Affairs*, Vol. 37, No. 2, January 1959; and Kent and Thaler. For discussion of the importance of survivable command and control for stability, see, inter alia, John Steinbruner, "National Security and Strategic Stability," *Journal of Conflict Resolution*, Vol. 22, No. 3, September 1978; Leonard Wainstein *et al.*, *The Evolution of U.S. Strategic Command and Control and Warning, 1945-1972*, Alexandria, VA: Institute for Defense Analyses, 1975 (declassified 1992, originally classified TOP SECRET); and Ashton Carter, "Communications Technologies and Vulnerabilities," in Ashton Carter, John Steinbruner, and Charles Zraket, eds., *Managing Nuclear Operations*, Washington, DC: Brookings Institution, 1987.

5. On spirals, see, *inter alia*, Robert Jervis, "Cooperation Under the Security Dilemma," *World Politics*, Vol. 30, No. 2, January 1978.

6. See, *inter alia*, Scott Sagan, *The Limits of Safety: Organizations, Accidents, and Nuclear Weapons*, Princeton, NJ: Princeton University Press, 1993.

7. See, inter alia, Peter Feaver, "Command and Control in Emerging Nuclear Nations," *International Security*, Vol. 17, No. 3, Winter 1992/1993.

8. See, inter alia, Glenn H. Snyder, "The Balance of Power and the Balance of Terror," in Paul Seabury ed., *The Balance of Power*, San Francisco, CA: Chandler, 1965; Richard Betts, "Nuclear Peace and Conventional War," *Journal of Strategic Studies*, Vol. 11, No. 1, March 1988; and Barry Posen, "U.S. Security Policy in a Nuclear-Armed World or: What if Iraq Had Had Nuclear Weapons?" *Security Studies*, Vol. 6, No. 3, Spring 1997.

9. Robert Jervis, *The Illogic of American Nuclear Strategy*, Ithaca, NY: Cornell University Press, 1984, p. 31.

10. James Schlesinger, "The Strategic Consequences of Nuclear Proliferation," in James Dougherty and John Lehman, *Arms Control for the Late Sixties*, Princeton, NJ: Van Nostrand, 1967; and Robert Jervis, "The Political Implications of Nuclear Weapons: A Comment," *International Security*, Vol. 13, No. 2, Fall 1988.

11. William Burr and Jeffrey Richelson, "Whether to 'Strangle the Baby in the Cradle': The United States and the Chinese Nuclear Program, 1960-64," *International Security*, Vol. 25, No. 3, Winter 2000/2001.

12. Shirley Kan and Mark Holt, "U.S.-China Nuclear Cooperation Agreement," Washington, DC: Congressional Research Service, 2007. It took 13 years to fully implement the agreement, however.

13. This is not to downplay the changes in China between 1964 and 1985, but it does argue that the basic character of the Chinese government had not changed.

14. See Keir Lieber and Daryl Press, "The End of MAD? The Nuclear Dimension of U.S. Primacy," *International Security*, Vol. 30, No. 4, Spring 2006; Keir Liber and Daryl Press, "The Nukes We Need: Preserving the American Deterrent," *Foreign Affairs*, November/December 2009; Glenn Buchan, *et. al., Future Roles of U.S. Nuclear Forces: Implications for U.S. Strategy*, Santa Monica, CA:

RAND, 2004, esp. p. 92; and Hans Kristensen *et al.*, *Chinese Nuclear Forces and U.S. Nuclear War Planning*, Washington, DC: Federation of American Scientists/Natural Resources Defense Council, 2006.

15. Jeffrey G. Lewis, "Chinese Nuclear Posture and Force Modernization," *The Nonproliferation Review*, Vol. 16, No. 2, July 2009; and M. Taylor Fravel and Evan S. Medeiros, "China's Search for Assured Retaliation: The Evolution of Chinese Nuclear Strategy and Force Structure," *International Security*, Vol. 35, No. 2, Fall 2010.

16. See Avner Cohen and Benjamin Frankel, "Opaque Nuclear Proliferation," *Journal of Strategic Studies*, Vol. 13, No. 3, p. 20.

17. For the strategic viewpoint, see, inter alia, Ariel Levite, "Never Say Never Again: Nuclear Reversal Revisited," *International Security*, Vol. 27, No. 3, Winter 2002/2003. For the view that there is no coherent hedge, see Llewelyn Hughes, "Why Japan Will Not Go Nuclear (Yet): International and Domestic Constraints on the Nuclearization of Japan," *International Security*, Vol. 31, No. 4, Spring 2007.

18. The term recessed as used here is similar to but slightly different from the term as introduced in Jasjit Singh, "Prospects for Nuclear Proliferation," in Serge Sur, ed., *Nuclear Deterrence: Problems and Perspectives in the 1990s,* New York: United Nations Institute for Disarmament, 1993. See also Devin Hagerty, "Nuclear Deterrence in South Asia: The 1990 Indo–Pakistani Crisis," *International Security*, Vol. 20, No. 3, Winter 1995–96. Hagerty defines a similar concept as "existential deterrence." However, Hagerty's categorization has overlap between opaque and recessed nuclear capability while I regard them as analytically distinct.

19. Neil Joeck, *Maintaining Nuclear Stability in South Asia*, London, UK: International Institute for Strategic Studies, 1997; and Vipin Narang, "Posturing for Peace? Pakistan's Nuclear Postures and South Asian Stability," *International Security*, Vol. 34, No. 3, Winter 2009/10.

20. See Avner Cohen and Benjamin Frankel, "Opaque Nuclear Proliferation," *Journal of Strategic Studies*, Vol. 13, No. 3, September 1990.

21. Avner Cohen, *Israel and the Bomb*, New York: Columbia University Press, 1998.

22. Israeli testing, particularly the so-called Vela Incident of 1979, still remains debated in the U.S. intelligence and national security community. See Thomas Reed and Danny Stillman, *The Nuclear Express: A Political History of the Bomb and Its Proliferation*, Minneapolis, MN: Zenith Press, 2009, pp. 176-180.

23. It is also a case where more primary source material is available than the other relevant case, that of Indian and Pakistani proliferation. Space constraints prevent detailed discussion of this case but in addition to the sources in footnote 19, see Peter Lavoy, ed., *Asymmetric Warfare in South Asia: The Causes and Consequences of the Kargil Conflict*, Cambridge, UK: Cambridge University Press, 2009; Sumit Ganguly and S. Paul Kapur, eds., *Nuclear Proliferation In South Asia: Crisis Behaviour and the Bomb*, New York: Routledge, 2009; and Scott Sagan, ed., *Inside Nuclear South Asia*, Stanford, CA: Stanford University Press, 2009.

24. John Wilson Lewis and Xue Litai, *China Builds the Bomb*, Stanford, CA: Stanford University Press, 1988.

25. See discussion in Burr and Richelson, pp. 59-60. See also National Intelligence Estimate 13-12-60 "The Chinese Communist Atomic Energy Program," December 13, 1960 (originally classified TOP SECRET Code Word, declassified May 2004), available from the Central Intelligence Agency (CIA) Freedom of Information Act (FOIA) Reading Room.

26. See Jeffrey Lewis, *The Minimum Means of Reprisal: China's Search for Security in the Nuclear Age*, Cambridge, MA: MIT Press, 2007; and Fravel and Medeiros.

27. Burr and Richelson, pp. 61-62, quotation on p. 61. For details on nuclear threats against China in 1954-55 and 1958, see Richard Betts, *Nuclear Blackmail and Nuclear Balance*, Washington, DC: Brookings, 1987, pp. 59-62, 71-79. For details on planning for strike against China in the early 1950s, see Matthew Jones, "Targeting China-U.S. Nuclear Planning and 'Massive Retaliation' in East Asia, 1953–1955," *Journal of Cold War Studies*, Vol. 10, No. 4, Fall 2008.

28. National Intelligence Estimate 13-60, "Communist China," December 6, 1960 (originally classified SECRET, declassified May 2004), p. 4, available from the CIA, FOIA Reading Room.

29. See Sergei Goncharenko, "Sino-Soviet Military Coopera-tion," in Odd Arne Westad, ed. *Brothers in Arms: The Rise and Fall of the Sino-Soviet Alliance, 1945-1963*, Washington, DC: Woodrow Wilson Institute, 1998; and Viktor Gobarev, "Soviet Policy To-wards China: Developing Nuclear Weapons, 1949-1969," *Journal of Slavic Military Studies*, Vol. 12, No. 4, December 1999.

30. Burr and Richelson, pp. 64-69. See also Special National Intelligence Estimate 13-2-63, "Communist China's Advanced Weapons Program," July 24, 1963 (originally classified SECRET, declassified May 2004), available at CIA's FOIA Reading Room.

31. Burr and Richelson, pp. 70-71, 75-76.

32. *Ibid.*, pp. 76-82.

33. "The Implications of a Chinese Communist Nuclear Capa-bility," paper prepared in the State Department Policy Planning Council, n.d. *Foreign Relations of the United States 1964-1968*, Vol. XXX, document 30.

34. See Memorandum for the Record, April 20, 1964, *Foreign Relations of the United States 1964-1968*, Vol. XXX, document 29.

35. See the discussion in Memorandum from Robert W. Komer to the President's Special Assistant for National Security Affairs, September 18, 1964, *Foreign Relations of the United States 1964-1968*, Vol. XXX, document 51. This memorandum reports a White House planning lunch, with references to Southeast Asia, but not Vietnam specifically.

36. Burr and Richelson, pp. 84-91.

37. National Intelligence Estimate 13-8-69, "Communist Chi-na's Strategic Weapons Program," February 27, 1969 (originally classified TOP SECRET, declassified June 2004), p. 1; available in CIA FOIA Reading Room.

38. Yang Kuisong, "The Sino-Soviet Border Clash of 1969: From Zhenbao Island to Sino-American Rapprochement," *Cold War Studies*, Vol. 1, No. 1, August 2000; Lyle Goldstein, "Return to Zhenbao Island: Who Started Shooting and Why It Matters," *The China Quarterly*, Vol. 168, 2001; and Michael Gerson, "The Sino-Soviet Border Conflict: Deterrence, Escalation, and the Threat of Nuclear War in 1969," Alexandria, VA: Center for Naval Analyses, 2010.

39. See discussion in Yang and Goldstein, "Return to Zhenbao Island." On the theory of foreign policy and domestic mobilization as well as early Chinese Communist use, see Thomas Christensen, *Useful Adversaries: Grand Strategy, Domestic Mobilization, and Sino-American Conflict, 1947-1958*, Princeton, NJ: Princeton University Press, 1996. Taylor Fravel argues that the domestic explanation is not compelling given the timing of military action but this hinges on Mao's ability to rapidly and accurately perceive domestic requirements and then translate that into external action. See Taylor Fravel, *Strong Borders, Secure Nation: Cooperation and Conflict in China's Territorial Disputes*, Princeton, NJ: Princeton University Press, 2008, pp. 214-215. Gerson accepts a halfway point, where domestic explanation is not primary but is important. See Gerson, pp. 30-31.

40. Yang, pp. 32-33. Note that Soviet action in this case might be considered preventive, as a Chinese nuclear attack was not imminent. On the other hand, such an attack would have been following a Chinese conventional attack so it would not have been preventive as the term is typically used.

41. Yang, p. 34-35.

42. Yang, p. 34 and Gobarev, pp. 46-47. On the outreach to the United States, see also William Stearman, "Memorandum of Conversation," August 18, 1969 (originally classified SECRET/Sensitive, declassified January 17, 1997), available at the George Washington University National Security Archive. This records the broaching of the question of the U.S. reaction to an attack on People's Republic of China (PRC) nuclear capability by a Soviet Embassy official in Washington.

43. See Lyle Goldstein, "Do Nascent WMD Arsenals Deter? The Sino-Soviet Crisis of 1969," *Political Science Quarterly*, Vol. 118, No. 1, Spring 2003, pp. 67-71. There is dispute about the nuclear capability of the DF-2 missile, deployed in 1966, as Goldstein notes. National Intelligence Estimate 13-8-69 indicates that the U.S. intelligence community did not believe it was nuclear armed. Even if it were, its range was less than 1000 miles, limiting its ability to hold much of the Union of Soviet Socialist Republics (USSR) at risk.

44. Yang, p. 36.

45. See Stearman's Memorandum of Conversation, pp. 1-2.

46. Yang, p. 38.

47. Yang, pp. 40-41, 47.

48. For an overview of U.S. efforts in this period to control proliferation and relevance to contemporary cases, see Francis Gavin, "Blasts from the Past: Proliferation Lessons from the 1960s," *International Security*, Vol. 29, No. 3, Winter 2004/2005; and Francis Gavin, "Same As It Ever Was: Nuclear Alarmism, Proliferation, and the Cold War," *International Security*, Vol. 34, No. 3, Winter 2009/2010.

49. Gobarev, pp. 40-41.

50. Yang, p. 48.

51. The foundational work is Robert Jervis, *Perception and Misperception in International Politics*, Princeton, NJ: Princeton University Press, 1976. A useful summary is Charles Duelfer and Stephen Dyson, "Chronic Misperception and International Conflict: The U.S.-Iraq Experience," *International Security*, Vol. 36, No. 1, Summer 2011, pp. 75-78.

52. See Gerson, pp. 57-59, for similar conclusions.

53. On Chinese force development and domestic factors, see Lewis, *The Minimum Means of Reprisal*; and Fravel and Medeiros.

54. Goldstein, "Do Nascent WMD Arsenals Deter?" p. 75.

55. Burr and Richelson, p. 88. Some might argue the converse, that third parties produce instability. Yet the best examples of this, such as the alliances of World War I, precede the nuclear revolution and therefore may be of less relevance in situations involving nuclear proliferation. See Thomas Christensen and Jack Snyder, "Chain Gangs and Passed Bucks: Predicting Alliance Patterns in Multipolarity," *International Organization*, Vol. 44, No. 2, Spring 1990.

56. This section, following the official assessments of the U.S. intelligence community, assumes Iran does seek at a minimum a hedged nuclear capability. See James Clapper, "Unclassified Statement for the Record on the Worldwide Threat Assessment of the U.S. Intelligence Community for the Senate Select Committee on Intelligence," January 31, 2012, pp. 4-5.

57. For a current overview of the program and concerns about it, see International Atomic Energy Agency, "Implementation of the NPT Safeguards Agreement and Relevant Provisions of Security Council Resolutions in the Islamic Republic of Iran," February 24, 2012.

58. On the overall context of the Iran-Israel relationship, see Dalia Dassa Kaye, Alireza Nader, Parisa Roshan, *Israel and Iran: A Dangerous Rivalry*, Santa Monica, CA: RAND, 2011.

59. See Jeffrey Goldberg, "The Point of No Return," *The Atlantic*, September 2010; and Ronen Bergman, "Will Israel Attack Iran?" *New York Times Magazine*, January 25, 2012, for discussion of the politics of such a strike. On the technical aspects of such a strike, see Whitney Raas and Austin Long, "Osirak Redux? Assessing Israeli Capabilities to Destroy Iranian Nuclear Facilities," *International Security*, Vol. 31, No. 4, Spring 2007.

60. See discussion in Shlomo Brom, "Is the Begin Doctrine Still a Viable Option for Israel?" in Henry Sokolski and Patrick Clawson, eds., *Getting Ready for a Nuclear-Ready Iran*, Carlisle, PA: Strategic Studies Institute, U.S. Army War College, 2005.

61. Gerson, p. 55.

62. See *Iran's Ballistic Missile Capabilities: A Net Assessment*, London, UK: International Institute for Strategic Studies, 2010; and Shahab-3/4 entry, *Jane's Strategic Weapons Systems*, February 12, 2012.

63. For brief discussion of some lessons and responses by both sides, see Jonathan Levinson, "A Third Lebanon War," *Small Wars and Insurgencies*, Vol. 23, No. 2, May 1, 2012.

64. Uzi Rubin, *The Missile Threat from Gaza: From Nuisance to Strategic Threat*, Tel Aviv, Israel: Bar-Ilan University, 2011; and "Egypt Seizes Gaza-bound Anti-Aircraft Missiles," *Jerusalem Post*, February 11, 2012.

65. See Cohen, *Israel and the Bomb*; and Shai Feldman *Israeli Nuclear Deterrence: A Strategy for the 1980s*, New York: Columbia University Press, 1982.

66. See Cohen, *Israel and the Bomb*; and Shai Feldman *Israeli Nuclear Deterrence: A Strategy for the 1980s*.

67. Louis Rene Beres, "Israel Should Selectively Reveal Its Nuclear Arsenal to the World," *U.S. News and World* Report, June 14, 2010; and Dima Adamsky,"The Morning After in Israel," *Foreign Affairs*, Vol. 90, No. 2, March/April 2011.

68. Indeed, even some U.S. officials have publicly, if tacitly, noted Israel's arsenal. See Rose Gottemoeller, "Opening Statement at the Third Session of the Preparatory Committee for the 2010 Nuclear Non-Proliferation Treaty Review Conference," May 5, 2009, available from *www.state.gov/t/avc/rls/122672.htm*.

69. For a similar argument, see Avner Cohen, "Israel Ponders a Nuclear Iran," *Bulletin of the Atomic Scientists*, August 17, 2010.

70. See Louis Rene Beres, "Israel's Uncertain Strategic Future," *Parameters*, Spring 2007. This summarizes the report of a longer project that argues for an end to nuclear opacity and the articulation of doctrine if a regional power proliferates.

71. While I group them under the term counterforce, some distinguish between "counterforce," specifically targeting enemy nuclear forces, and "countermilitary," targeting other military forces.

72. See Lawrence Freedman, *The Evolution of Nuclear Strategy*, 3rd Ed., London, UK: Palgrave MacMillan, 2003.

73. See Kent and Thaler on survivability.

74. Marc Trachtenberg, "A 'Wasting Asset': American Strategy and the Shifting Nuclear Balance, 1949-54," *International Security*, Vol. 13, No. 3, Winter 1988-89.

75. See Wainstein, *The Evolution of U.S. Strategic Command and Control and Warning*; and Carter, "Communications Technologies and Vulnerabilities." These highlight how difficult and costly survivable nuclear command and control and effective early warning is, even in large countries like the United States. While Israel would no doubt try to improve its nuclear command and control, it would not be easy or guaranteed to succeed.

76. David Alan Rosenberg, "A Smoking Radiating Ruin at the End of Two Hours," *International Security*, Vol. 6, No. 3, Winter 1981/82.

77. This may all seem trivially easy to those steeped in the nuclear balance of the late Cold War. Yet making those adjustments is costly and takes time.

78. See discussion in Jeremy Sharp, "U.S. Foreign Aid to Israel," Congressional Research Service Report RL 33222, Washington, DC: Congressional Research Service, December 4, 2009, pp. 7-9.

79. The limiting factor on the Iranian arsenal size in the near term will be fissile material. The entire set of Iranian centrifuges available as of 2012, even if unconstrained by inspections or military action, are unlikely to produce more than 2-3 bombs worth of fissile material per year. See Austin Long, "Stall Speed: Assessing Delay of the Iranian Nuclear Program via Israeli Military Strike," forthcoming.

80. On the International Risk Governance Council (IRGC) see Frederic Wehrey *et al.*, *The Rise of the Pasdaran: Assessing the Domestic Roles of Iran's Islamic Revolutionary Guards Corps,* Santa Monica, CA: RAND, 2009; and Afshon Ostovar, *Guardians of the Islamic Revolution: Ideology, Politics, and the Development of Military Power in Iran, 1979–2009,* Ph.D. dissertation, University of Michigan History, 2009. For a more general overview of the Iranian military, see Stephen Ward, *Immortal: A Military History of Iran and Its Armed Forces,* Washington, DC: Georgetown University Press, 2009.

81. A similar argument is advanced in Louis Rene Beres, "Israel's Bomb in the Basement: A Second Look," *Israel Affairs,* Vol. 2, No. 1, Autumn 1995.

82. Jerrold D. Green, Frederic Wehrey, and Charles Wolf, Jr., *Understanding Iran,* Santa Monica, CA: RAND, 2009, p. 31.

83. David Thaler *et al.*, *Mullahs, Guards, and Bonyads: An Exploration of Iranian Leadership Dynamics,* Santa Monica, CA: RAND, 2010.

84. Malfrid Braut-Hegghammer, "Revisiting Osirak: Preventive Attacks and Nuclear Proliferation Risks," *International Security*, Vol. 36, No. 1, Summer 2011. Note that while correct about Iraqi activity after the Osirak strike, I believe Braut-Hegghammer vastly understates the degree of Iraqi pursuit of nuclear capability before the Osirak strike. See in this regard Hal Brands and David Palkki, "Saddam, Israel, and the Bomb: Nuclear Alarmism Justified?" *International Security*, Vol. 36, No. 1, Summer 2011.

85. Syrian leader Bashar al-Assad did not even acknowledge the strike for 6 months, hardly indicative of something causing major regime instability. See "Assad Says Facility Israel Bombed Not Nuclear," *Reuters*, April 27, 2008.

86. Ray Takeyh, "The Iran-Iraq War: A Reassessment," *Middle East Journal*, Vol. 64, No. 3, Summer 2010, p. 367.

87. See Duelfer and Dyson.

88. For an admittedly partisan discussion of this covert conflict, see Ronen Bergman, *The Secret War with Iran: The 30-Year*

Clandestine Struggle Against the World's Most Dangerous Terrorist Power, New York: Free Press, 2011.

89. Takeyh, pp. 370-372, 383.

90. On length of delay, see Long, "Stall Speed."

91. Interview on *Face the Nation*, January 8, 2012, available from *www.cbsnews.com/8301-3460_162-57354645/panetta-iran-cannot-develop-nukes-block-strait/*.

92. See Matthew Kroenig, "Time to Attack Iran," *Foreign Affairs*, January/February 2012, for an articulation of this position.

93. See discussion in Michael Crawford, "Exploring the Maze: Counter-proliferation Intelligence," *Survival*, Vol. 53, No. 2, April/May 2011.

94. Such a guarantee might be thought of a "chain-gang" as described by Snyder and Christensen.

95. Mustafa Kibaroglu, "Turkey, NATO and Nuclear Sharing: Prospects After NATO's Lisbon Summit," in Paul Ingram and Olivier Meier, eds., *Reducing the Role of Tactical Nuclear Weapons in Europe: Perspectives and Proposals on the NATO Policy Debate*, Washington, DC: Arms Control Association, 2011.

96. See, inter alia, Liam Stack, "Pressed by Unrest and Money Woes, Egypt Accepts I.M.F. Loan," *New York Times*, February 19, 2012.

97. On Egypt's abandoned nuclear efforts, see James Walsh, "Bombs Unbuilt: Power, Ideas, and Institutions in International Politics," Ph.D. dissertation, Massachusetts Institute of Technology Political Science, 2001, chapters 6 and 7.

98. See Richard Lugar, "Obama's Nuclear Misstep," *The National Interest*, February 21, 2012.

99. Gawdat Bahgat, "Nuclear Proliferation: The Case of Saudi Arabia," *Middle East Journal*, Vol. 60, No. 3, Summer 2006.

100. "Prince Hints Saudi Arabia May Join Nuclear Arms Race," *Associated Press*, December 6, 2011.

101. See Bahgat.

102. For an overview of U.S. efforts to discourage proliferation in Taiwan and South Korea, see Jonathan Pollack and Mitchell Reiss, "South Korea: The Tyranny of Geography and the Vexations of History," and Derek Mitchell, "Taiwan's Hsin Chu Program: Deterrence, Abandonment, and Honor," both in Kurt Campbell *et al.*, *The Nuclear A Tipping Point: Why States Reconsider Their Nuclear Choices*, Washington, DC: The Brookings Institute, 2004.

103. Thomas Erdbrink and Joby Warrick, "Bahrain Crackdown Fueling Tensions between Iran, Saudi Arabia," *Washington Post*, April 22, 2011.

104. Bradley Bowman, "Chain Reaction: Avoiding a Nuclear Arms Race in the Middle East," Report to the Committee on Foreign Relations, U.S. Senate, February 2008.

105. See Gavin, "Same as It Ever Was."

106. See *www.goodreads.com/quotes/219546-preventive-war-is-like-committing-suicide-out-of-fear-of-death*.

ABOUT THE CONTRIBUTORS

JAMES M. ACTON is a senior associate in the Nuclear Policy Program at the Carnegie Endowment for International Peace. His latest book, *Deterrence During Disarmament: Deep Nuclear Reductions and International Security*, was published in the Adelphi series in 2011. He is the co-author of a second Adelphi book, *Abolishing Nuclear Weapons*, and co-editor of the follow-up volume, *Abolishing Nuclear Weapons: A Debate*. He is a member of the International Panel on Fissile Materials, and during 2010–11 co-chaired the Next Generation Working Group on U.S.-Russia Arms Control. Dr. Acton holds a Ph.D. in theoretical physics from Cambridge University.

ELBRIDGE COLBY is a principal analyst and division lead for global strategic affairs at the Center for Naval Analysis. Previously, he served as policy advisor to the Secretary of Defense's Representative for the New Strategic Arms Reduction Treaty (New START), as an expert advisor to the Congressional Strategic Posture Commission, as a staff member on the President's Commission on the Intelligence Capabilities of the U.S. regarding weapons of mass destruction (WMD), with the Coalition Provisional Authority in Baghdad, Iraq, and with the State Department. Mr. Colby has also been an adjunct staff member with the RAND Corporation and has served as a consultant to a number of U.S. Government bodies. Mr. Colby is a graduate of Harvard College and Yale Law School.

CHRISTOPHER A. FORD is a Senior Fellow at Hudson Institute in Washington, DC. Previously, he served as U.S. Special Representative for Nuclear Nonproliferation, as Principal Deputy Assistant Secretary of State, and as General Counsel to the Senate Select Committee on Intelligence. The author of *The Mind of Empire: China's History and Modern Foreign Relations* (2010) and *The Admirals' Advantage: U.S. Naval Operational Intelligence in World War II and the Cold War* (2005), and co-editor of *Rethinking the Law of Armed Conflict in an Age of Terrorism* (2012), Dr. Ford also writes for and manages the *New Paradigms Forum* website (available from *www.NewParadigmsForum.com*).

MICHAEL S. GERSON is a principal analyst and project director at the Center for Naval Analysis, where his work focuses on nuclear and conventional deterrence, nuclear strategy, arms control, and WMD proliferation. From September 2011 to September 2012, he was on loan from CNA to the Office of the Secretary of Defense, where he worked on a range of strategic issues associated with the Middle East and homeland defense. In 2009, he was a staff member on the *Nuclear Posture Review,* where he was a lead author of a report on international perspectives on U.S. nuclear policy and posture. Mr. Gerson has presented his work on strategic issues at numerous universities and think tanks, and has published several articles and chapters in academic journals and books. He recently served as co-chair of the Next Generation Working Group on U.S.-Russian Arms Control, sponsored by the Center for Strategic and International Studies (CSIS), and co-authored the working group's final report, *Beyond New START: Enhancing US National Security Through Arms Control with Russia.* Mr. Gerson holds a B.A. with Special Honors in history from the University of Texas, and an M.A. in international relations from the University of Chicago.

COLIN S. GRAY is Professor of International Politics and Strategic Studies at the University of Reading, England. He worked at the International Institute for Strategic Studies (London), and at Hudson Institute (Croton-on-Hudson, NY) before founding the National Institute for Public Policy, a defense-oriented think tank in the Washington, DC, area. Dr. Gray served for 5 years in the Ronald Reagan administration on the President's General Advisory Committee on Arms Control and Disarmament. He has served as an adviser to both the U.S. and British Governments (he has dual citizenship). His government work has included studies of nuclear strategy, arms control, maritime strategy, space strategy and the use of special forces. Dr. Gray has written 25 books, including *The Sheriff: America's Defense of the New World Order* (University Press of Kentucky, 2004); *Another Bloody Century: Future Warfare* (Weidenfeld and Nicolson, 2005); *Strategy and History: Essays on Theory and Practice* (Routledge, 2006); *Fighting Talk: Forty Maxims on War, Peace, and Strategy* (Potomac Books, 2009); *National Security Dilemmas: Challenges and Opportunities* (Potomac Books, 2009); *The Strategy Bridge: Theory for Practice* (Oxford University Press, 2010); *War, Peace, and International Relations: An Introduction to Strategic History*, 2nd Ed. (Routledge 2011); and *Airpower for Strategic Effect* (Air University Press, 2012). His next book will be on strategy and defense planning. Dr. Gray is a graduate of the Universities of Manchester and Oxford.

RONALD F. LEHMAN II is the Director of the Center for Global Security Research at Lawrence Livermore National Laboratory.* Dr. Lehman is also the Chairman of the Governing Board of the International Science and Technology Center and Vice Chair of the

U.S. Department of Defense Threat Reduction Advisory Committee. Dr. Lehman was Director of the U.S. Arms Control and Disarmament Agency, Assistant Secretary of Defense for International Security Policy, Ambassador/U.S. Chief Negotiator on Strategic Offensive Arms (START I), and Deputy Assistant to the President for National Security Affairs. He served with the United States Army in Vietnam.

AUSTIN LONG is an Assistant Professor at the School of International and Public Affairs and a Member of the Arnold A. Saltzman Institute of War and Peace

Studies at Columbia University. He was previously an Associate Political Scientist at the RAND Corporation and has consulted extensively on security issues. Dr. Long holds a B.S. from the Sam Nunn School of International Affairs at the Georgia Institute of Technology and a Ph.D. in political science from the Massachusetts Institute of Technology.

JEFFREY D. MCCAUSLAND is a Distinguished Visiting Professor of Research and the Minerva Chairholder at the U.S. Army War College in Carlisle, PA. He serves as a Visiting Professor of International Security at Dickinson College and a senior fellow at the Clarke Forum. He is a Senior Associate Fellow at the Abshire-Inamori Leadership Academy at the Center for Strategic and International Studies in Washington, DC. He is also a Senior Fellow at the Stockdale Center for Ethical Leadership at the U.S. Naval Academy and the Carnegie Council for Ethics in International Affairs in New York. Dr. McCausland serves as a national security consultant for CBS Radio and Television.

MATTHEW ROJANSKY is the deputy director of the Russia and Eurasia Program at the Carnegie Endowment, where he works on Euro-Atlantic and U.S.-Russia security relations, and on security in former Soviet Eastern Europe. He is a participant in the Dartmouth Dialogues, a 50-year-old U.S.-Russia Track Two process, and organizes a track 2 task force on the Transnistria conflict. Previously, Mr. Rojansky was executive director of the Partnership for a Secure America (PSA), an organization founded by Lee Hamilton and Warren Rudman with a group of two dozen former senior leaders from both political parties to seek to restore productive bipartisan dialogue on U.S. national security and foreign policy challenges. He has clerked for Judge Charles E. Erdmann at the United States Court of Appeals for the Armed Forces, the highest court for the U.S. military, and served as a consultant on legal issues related to the Middle East peace process. He holds a B.A. from Harvard College and a J.D. from Stanford Law School.

LORA SAALMAN is an associate in the Nuclear Policy Program at the Carnegie Endowment for International Peace based at the Carnegie-Tsinghua Center for Global Policy in Beijing. Dr. Saalman's research focuses on Chinese nuclear weapon and nonproliferation policies and Sino–Indian strategic relations. Prior to joining the Endowment in April 2010, Dr. Saalman served as a research associate at the Wisconsin Project on Nuclear Arms Control, as a visiting fellow at the Observer Research Foundation in New Delhi, and at the James Martin Center for Nonproliferation Studies. Dr. Saalman earned her undergraduate degree with honors at the University of Chicago, and holds a Ph.D. from Tsinghua University in Beijing, where she was the first American to earn a doctorate from its Department of International Relations and earned an award for outstanding Chinese-language dissertation and graduate work upon graduation.

THOMAS C. SCHELLING is a Distinguished Professor of Economics at the University of Maryland. In 2005, he was awarded the Nobel Prize in Economics for enhancing the "understanding of conflict and cooperation through game-theory analysis." He has been elected to the National Academy of Sciences, the Institute of Medicine, and the American Academy of Arts and Sciences. In 1991, he was President of the American Economic Association, of which he is now a Distinguished Fellow. He was the recipient of the Frank E. Seidman Distinguished Award in Political Economy and the National Academy of Sciences award for Behavioral Research Relevant to the Prevention of Nuclear War. In 1990, he left the John F. Kennedy School of Government, where he was the Lucius N. Littauer Professor of Political Economy. He has also served in the Economic Cooperation Administration in Europe, and has held positions in the White House and Executive Office of the President, Yale University, the RAND Corporation, and the Department of Economics and Center for International Affairs at Harvard University. Most recently, he has published on military strategy and arms control, energy and environmental policy, climate change, nuclear proliferation, and terrorism. Other interests include organized crime, foreign aid and international trade, conflict and bargaining theory, racial segregation and integration, the military draft, the health policy, the tobacco and drugs policy, and ethical issues in public policy and in business. Schelling is best known for his books, *The Strategy of Conflict* and *Micromotives and Macrobehavior*.

C. DALE WALTON is an Associate Professor of International Relations at Lindenwood University in St. Charles, Missouri. His previous career experience includes teaching at the University of Reading (UK) from 2007 to 2012, serving on the faculty of the Defense and Strategic Studies Department at Missouri State University from 2001 to 2007, and working as a Senior Analyst with the National Institute for Public Policy. He was an H. B. Earhart Fellow while a Ph.D. student at the University of Hull (UK). Dr.

Walton's research interests include strategic relationships and security problems in Asia, geopolitics and the changing geostrategic environment, U.S. military and strategic history, and the influence of religious and ideological beliefs on strategic behavior. Dr. Walton is the author of *Grand Strategy and the Presidency: Foreign Policy, War, and the American Role in the World* (Routledge, 2012), *Geopolitics and the Great Powers in the Twenty-first Century: Multipolarity and Revolution in Strategic Perspective* (Routledge, 2007), and *The Myth of Inevitable U.S. Defeat in Vietnam* (Frank Cass/Routledge, 2002). He is co-author of *Understanding Modern Warfare* (Cambridge University Press, 2008), and has published more than 70 chapters, scholarly articles, and book reviews. Dr. Walton holds a Ph.D. from the University of Hull (UK).

U.S. ARMY WAR COLLEGE

Major General Anthony A. Cucolo III
Commandant

*****

STRATEGIC STUDIES INSTITUTE
and
U.S. ARMY WAR COLLEGE PRESS

Director
Professor Douglas C. Lovelace, Jr.

Director of Research
Dr. Steven K. Metz

Editors
Mr. Elbridge A. Colby
Mr. Michael S. Gerson

Director of Publications
Dr. James G. Pierce

Publications Assistant
Ms. Rita A. Rummel

*****

Composition
Mrs. Jennifer E. Nevil

www.ingramcontent.com/pod-product-compliance
Lightning Source LLC
Chambersburg PA
CBHW060957280326
41935CB00009B/746